2000

LLEWELLYN'S

SUN SIGN BOOK

Forecasts by
Gloria Star

Book Editing and Design: Andrea Neff
Cover Art and Design: William Merlin Cannon

Copyright 1999

Llewellyn Publications
A Division of Llewellyn Worldwide, Ltd.
P.O. Box 64383 Dept. K954-7 St. Paul, MN 55164-0383
ISBN 1-56718-954-7

1999

JANUARY	FEBRUARY	MARCH	APRIL

JANUARY
S M T W T F S
            1 2
 3 4 5 6 7 8 9
10 11 12 13 14 15 16
17 18 19 20 21 22 23
24 25 26 27 28 29 30
31

FEBRUARY
S M T W T F S
    1 2 3 4 5 6
 7 8 9 10 11 12 13
14 15 16 17 18 19 20
21 22 23 24 25 26 27
28

MARCH
S M T W T F S
    1 2 3 4 5 6
 7 8 9 10 11 12 13
14 15 16 17 18 19 20
21 22 23 24 25 26 27
28 29 30 31

APRIL
S M T W T F S
             1 2 3
 4 5 6 7 8 9 10
11 12 13 14 15 16 17
18 19 20 21 22 23 24
25 26 27 28 29 30

MAY
S M T W T F S
                   1
 2 3 4 5 6 7 8
 9 10 11 12 13 14 15
16 17 18 19 20 21 22
23 24 25 26 27 28 29
30 31

JUNE
S M T W T F S
       1 2 3 4 5
 6 7 8 9 10 11 12
13 14 15 16 17 18 19
20 21 22 23 24 25 26
27 28 29 30

JULY
S M T W T F S
             1 2 3
 4 5 6 7 8 9 10
11 12 13 14 15 16 17
18 19 20 21 22 23 24
25 26 27 28 29 30 31

AUGUST
S M T W T F S
 1 2 3 4 5 6 7
 8 9 10 11 12 13 14
15 16 17 18 19 20 21
22 23 24 25 26 27 28
29 30 31

SEPTEMBER
S M T W T F S
          1 2 3 4
 5 6 7 8 9 10 11
12 13 14 15 16 17 18
19 20 21 22 23 24 25
26 27 28 29 30

OCTOBER
S M T W T F S
                1 2
 3 4 5 6 7 8 9
10 11 12 13 14 15 16
17 18 19 20 21 22 23
24 25 26 27 28 29 30
31

NOVEMBER
S M T W T F S
    1 2 3 4 5 6
 7 8 9 10 11 12 13
14 15 16 17 18 19 20
21 22 23 24 25 26 27
28 29 30

DECEMBER
S M T W T F S
          1 2 3 4
 5 6 7 8 9 10 11
12 13 14 15 16 17 18
19 20 21 22 23 24 25
26 27 28 29 30 31

2000

JANUARY
S M T W T F S
                   1
 2 3 4 5 6 7 8
 9 10 11 12 13 14 15
16 17 18 19 20 21 22
23 24 25 26 27 28 29
30 31

FEBRUARY
S M T W T F S
       1 2 3 4 5
 6 7 8 9 10 11 12
13 14 15 16 17 18 19
20 21 22 23 24 25 26
27 28 29

MARCH
S M T W T F S
          1 2 3 4
 5 6 7 8 9 10 11
12 13 14 15 16 17 18
19 20 21 22 23 24 25
26 27 28 29 30 31

APRIL
S M T W T F S
                   1
 2 3 4 5 6 7 8
 9 10 11 12 13 14 15
16 17 18 19 20 21 22
23 24 25 26 27 28 29
30

MAY
S M T W T F S
    1 2 3 4 5 6
 7 8 9 10 11 12 13
14 15 16 17 18 19 20
21 22 23 24 25 26 27
28 29 30 31

JUNE
S M T W T F S
             1 2 3
 4 5 6 7 8 9 10
11 12 13 14 15 16 17
18 19 20 21 22 23 24
25 26 27 28 29 30

JULY
S M T W T F S
                   1
 2 3 4 5 6 7 8
 9 10 11 12 13 14 15
16 17 18 19 20 21 22
23 24 25 26 27 28 29
30 31

AUGUST
S M T W T F S
       1 2 3 4 5
 6 7 8 9 10 11 12
13 14 15 16 17 18 19
20 21 22 23 24 25 26
27 28 29 30 31

SEPTEMBER
S M T W T F S
                1 2
 3 4 5 6 7 8 9
10 11 12 13 14 15 16
17 18 19 20 21 22 23
24 25 26 27 28 29 30

OCTOBER
S M T W T F S
 1 2 3 4 5 6 7
 8 9 10 11 12 13 14
15 16 17 18 19 20 21
22 23 24 25 26 27 28
29 30 31

NOVEMBER
S M T W T F S
          1 2 3 4
 5 6 7 8 9 10 11
12 13 14 15 16 17 18
19 20 21 22 23 24 25
26 27 28 29 30

DECEMBER
S M T W T F S
                1 2
 3 4 5 6 7 8 9
10 11 12 13 14 15 16
17 18 19 20 21 22 23
24 25 26 27 28 29 30
31

2001

JANUARY
S M T W T F S
    1 2 3 4 5 6
 7 8 9 10 11 12 13
14 15 16 17 18 19 20
21 22 23 24 25 26 27
28 29 30 31

FEBRUARY
S M T W T F S
             1 2 3
 4 5 6 7 8 9 10
11 12 13 14 15 16 17
18 19 20 21 22 23 24
25 26 27 28

MARCH
S M T W T F S
             1 2 3
 4 5 6 7 8 9 10
11 12 13 14 15 16 17
18 19 20 21 22 23 24
25 26 27 28 29 30 31

APRIL
S M T W T F S
 1 2 3 4 5 6 7
 8 9 10 11 12 13 14
15 16 17 18 19 20 21
22 23 24 25 26 27 28
29 30

MAY
S M T W T F S
       1 2 3 4 5
 6 7 8 9 10 11 12
13 14 15 16 17 18 19
20 21 22 23 24 25 26
27 28 29 30 31

JUNE
S M T W T F S
                1 2
 3 4 5 6 7 8 9
10 11 12 13 14 15 16
17 18 19 20 21 22 23
24 25 26 27 28 29 30

JULY
S M T W T F S
 1 2 3 4 5 6 7
 8 9 10 11 12 13 14
15 16 17 18 19 20 21
22 23 24 25 26 27 28
29 30 31

AUGUST
S M T W T F S
          1 2 3 4
 5 6 7 8 9 10 11
12 13 14 15 16 17 18
19 20 21 22 23 24 25
26 27 28 29 30 31

SEPTEMBER
S M T W T F S
                   1
 2 3 4 5 6 7 8
 9 10 11 12 13 14 15
16 17 18 19 20 21 22
23 24 25 26 27 28 29
30

OCTOBER
S M T W T F S
    1 2 3 4 5 6
 7 8 9 10 11 12 13
14 15 16 17 18 19 20
21 22 23 24 25 26 27
28 29 30 31

NOVEMBER
S M T W T F S
             1 2 3
 4 5 6 7 8 9 10
11 12 13 14 15 16 17
18 19 20 21 22 23 24
25 26 27 28 29 30

DECEMBER
S M T W T F S
                   1
 2 3 4 5 6 7 8
 9 10 11 12 13 14 15
16 17 18 19 20 21 22
23 24 25 26 27 28 29
30 31

Table of Contents

2000 Sun Sign Forecasts

2000 Sun Sign Articles

Meet Gloria Star

All of the horoscopes and sign descriptions for this book were written by Gloria Star. An internationally renowned astrologer, author, and teacher, Gloria has been a professional astrologer for over two decades. She has written the forecasts for the *Sun Sign Book* for Llewellyn since 1990, and has been a contributing author of the *Moon Sign Book* since 1995. Her most recent work,

Astrology: Woman to Woman, was released by Llewellyn in April 1999. She is the author of *Optimum Child: Developing Your Child's Fullest Potential through Astrology*, now translated into four languages. She also edited and co-authored the book *Astrology for Women: Roles and Relationships* (Llewellyn 1997). Her astrological computer software, *Woman to Woman*, was released by Matrix Software in 1997. Ms. Star has contributed to two anthologies—*Houses: Power Places in the Horoscope* (Llewellyn 1990), and *How to Manage the Astrology of Crisis* (Llewellyn 1993).

Listed in *Who's Who of American Women* and *Who's Who in the East*, Gloria is active within the astrological community, where she has been honored as a nominee for the prestigious Regulus Award. She has served on the faculty of the United Astrology Congress (UAC) since its inception in 1986, and has lectured for groups and conferences throughout the United States and abroad. A member of the advisory board for the National Council for Geocosmic Research (NCGR), she also served on the steering committee for the Association for Astrological Networking (AFAN), was editor of the *AFAN Newsletter* from 1992 to 1997, and is now on the advisory board. She currently resides in the shoreline township of Clinton, Connecticut.

New Concepts for Signs of the Zodiac

The signs of the zodiac represent characteristics and traits that indicate how energy operates within our lives. The signs tell the story of human evolution and development, and are all necessary to form the continuum of whole life experience. In fact, all twelve signs are represented within your astrological chart!

Although the traditional metaphors for the twelve signs (such as Aries, the Ram) are always functional, these alternative concepts for each of the twelve signs describe the gradual unfolding of the human spirit.

Aries: The Initiator is the first sign of the zodiac and encompasses the primary concept of getting things started. This fiery ignition and bright beginning can prove to be the thrust necessary for new life, but the Initiator also can appear before a situation is ready for change and create disruption.

Taurus: The Maintainer sustains what Aries has begun and brings stability and focus into the picture, yet there also can be a tendency to try to maintain something in its current state without allowing for new growth.

Gemini: The Questioner seeks to determine if alternatives are possible and offers diversity to the processes Taurus has brought into stability. Yet questioning can also lead to distraction, subsequently scattering energy and diffusing focus.

Cancer: The Nurturer provides the qualities necessary for growth and security and encourages a deepening awareness of the emotional needs. Yet this same nurturance can stifle individuation if it becomes smothering.

Leo: The Loyalist directs and centralizes the experiences Cancer feeds. This quality is powerfully targeted toward self-awareness, but can be short-sighted. Hence, the Loyalist can hold steadfastly to viewpoints or feelings that inhibit new experiences.

Virgo: The Modifier analyzes the situations Leo brings to light and determines possibilities for change. Even though this change may be in the name of improvement, it can lead to dissatisfaction with the self if not directed in harmony with higher needs.

Libra: The Judge is constantly comparing everything to be sure that a certain level of rightness and perfection is presented. However, the Judge can present possibilities that are harsh and seem to be cold or without feeling.

Scorpio: The Catalyst steps into the play of life to provide the quality of alchemical transformation. The Catalyst can stir the brew just enough to create a healing potion, or may get things going to such a powerful extent that they boil out of control.

Sagittarius: The Adventurer moves away from Scorpio's dimension to seek what lies beyond the horizon. The Adventurer continually looks for possibilities that answer the ultimate questions, but may forget the pathway back home.

Capricorn: The Pragmatist attempts to put everything into its rightful place and find ways to make life work out right. The Pragmatist can teach lessons of practicality and determination, but can become highly self-righteous when short-sighted.

Aquarius: The Reformer looks for ways to take what Capricorn has built and bring it up to date. Yet there is also a tendency to scrap the original in favor of a new plan that may not have the stable foundation necessary to operate effectively.

Pisces: The Visionary brings mysticism and imagination, and challenges the soul to move beyond the physical plane, into the realm of what might be. The Visionary can pierce the veil, returning enlightened to the physical world. The challenge is to avoid getting lost within the illusion of an alternate reality.

Understanding the Basics of Astrology

Astrology is an ancient and continually evolving system used to clarify your identity and your needs. An astrological chart—which is calculated using the date, time and place of birth—contains many factors which symbolically represent the needs, expressions, and experiences that make up the whole person. A professional astrologer interprets this symbolic picture, offering you an accurate portrait of your personality.

The chart itself—the horoscope—is a portrait of an individual. Generally, a natal (or birth) horoscope is drawn on a circular wheel. The wheel is divided into twelve segments, called houses. Each of the twelve houses represents a different aspect of the individual, much like the facets of a brilliantly cut stone. The houses depict different environments, such as home, school, and work. The houses also represent roles and relationships: parents, friends, lovers, children, partners. In each environment, individuals show a different side of their personality. At home, you may represent yourself quite differently than you do on the job. Additionally, in each relationship you will project a different image of yourself. Your parents rarely see the side you show to intimate friends.

Symbols for the planets, the Sun, and the Moon are drawn inside the houses. Each planet represents a separate kind of energy. You experience and express that energy in specific ways. (For a complete list, refer to the table on the next page.) The way you use each of these energies is up to you. The planets in your chart do not make you do anything!

The twelve signs of the zodiac indicate characteristics and traits that further define your personality. Each sign can be expressed in positive and negative ways. (The basic meaning of each of the signs is explained in the corresponding sections ahead.) What's more, you have all twelve signs somewhere in your chart. Signs that are strongly emphasized by the planets have greater force. The Sun, Moon, and planets are placed on the chart according to their position at the time of birth. The qualities of a sign, combined with the

Signs of the Zodiac

Aries	♈	The Initiator
Taurus	♉	The Maintainer
Gemini	♊	The Questioner
Cancer	♋	The Nurturer
Leo	♌	The Loyalist
Virgo	♍	The Modifier
Libra	♎	The Judge
Scorpio	♏	The Catalyst
Sagittarius	♐	The Adventurer
Capricorn	♑	The Pragmatist
Aquarius	♒	The Reformer
Pisces	♓	The Visionary

energy of a planet, indicate how you might be most likely to use that energy and the best ways to develop that energy. The signs add color, emphasis, and dimension to the personality.

Signs are also placed at the cusps, or dividing lines, of each of the houses. The influence of the signs on the houses is much the same as their influence on the Sun, Moon, and planets. Each house is shaped by the sign on its cusp.

When you view a horoscope, you will notice that there appear to be four distinctive angles dividing the wheel of the chart. The line that divides the chart into a top and bottom half represents the horizon. In most cases, the left side of the horizon is called the Ascendant. The zodiac sign on the Ascendant is your rising sign. The Ascendant indicates the way others are likely to view you.

The Sun, Moon, or planet can be compared to an actor in a play. The sign shows how the energy works, like the role the actor plays in a drama. The house indicates where the energy operates, like the setting of a play. On a psychological level, the Sun represents who

The Planets

Sun	☉	The ego, self, willpower
Moon	☽	The subconscious self, habits
Mercury	☿	Communication, the intellect
Venus	♀	Emotional expression, love, appreciation, artistry
Mars	♂	Physical drive, assertiveness, anger
Jupiter	♃	Philosophy, ethics, generosity
Saturn	♄	Discipline, focus, responsibility
Uranus	♅	Individuality, rebelliousness
Neptune	♆	Imagination, sensitivity, compassion
Pluto	♇	Transformation, healing, regeneration

you think you are. The Ascendant describes who others think you are, and the Moon reflects your inner self.

Astrologers also study the geometric relationships between the Sun, Moon, and planets. These geometric angles are called aspects. Aspects further define the strengths, weaknesses, and challenges within your physical, mental, emotional, and spiritual self. Sometimes, patterns also appear in an astrological chart. These patterns have meaning.

To understand cycles for any given point in time, astrologers study several factors. Many use transits, which refer to the movement and positions of the planets. When astrologers compare those positions to the birth horoscope, the transits indicate activity in particular areas of the chart. The *Sun Sign Book* uses transits.

As you can see, your Sun sign is just one of many factors that describes who you are—but it is a powerful one! As the symbol of the ego, the Sun in your chart reflects your drive to be noticed. Most people can easily relate to the concepts associated with their Sun sign, since it is tied to their sense of personal identity.

Using this Book

The horoscopes in the following section are based on the sign the Sun was in at the time of your birth. Although we can examine a number of your needs and life situations from this information, a professional astrologer would explore many other factors to help guide you. If you would like more information, you might appreciate the personalized insights you'll receive from a competent, professional astrologer.

I've described the year's major challenges and opportunities for every Sun sign in the "Year Ahead" section. The first part of each section applies to all individuals born under the sign. I've also included information for specific birth dates that will help you understand the inner changes you'll experience during 2000. The section illustrates your fundamental themes for the year ahead. They will be the underlying principles present throughout the year. These cycles comprise your major challenges and opportunities relating to your personal identity. Blend these ideas with the information you find in the monthly forecast section for your Sun sign and Ascendant.

To best use the information in the monthly forecasts, you'll want to determine your Ascendant or rising sign. If you don't know your Ascendant, the tables following this description will help you determine your rising sign. They are most accurate for those born in the continental United States. They're only an approximation, but they can be used as a good rule of thumb. Your exact Ascendant may vary from the tables according to your time and place of birth. Once you've approximated your ascending sign using the tables or determined your Ascendant by having your chart calculated, you'll know two significant factors in your chart. Read the monthly forecast sections for both your Sun and Ascendant to gain the most useful information.

Your "Rewarding and Challenging Days" sections indicate times when you'll feel more centered or out of balance. The rewarding days are not the only times you can perform well, but you're likely to feel better integrated! These days support your expression of individual identity. During challenging days, take extra time to center yourself by meditating or using other techniques that help you feel more objective.

These guidelines, although highly useful, cannot incorporate all the factors influencing your current life situation. However, you can use this information for an objective awareness about the way the current cycles are affecting you. Realize that the power of astrology is even more useful when you have a complete chart and professional guidance.

2000 at a Glance

This final year of the century definitely has its ups and downs. Although everyone may feel drawn toward the future, staying in the present moment is always a crucial factor in attaining success and manifesting accomplishments. But everything is pointing toward the excitement of a new millennium. With Neptune and Uranus both transiting in Aquarius, technology and scientific developments will capture the imagination of the public—and movies and television will continue to drive trends. Renewed interest in space exploration is also likely, and discoveries in astronomy may look like science fiction coming to life.

Even though innovations may be exciting, there will be resistance to anything that appears to be against nature. This argument will probably surface more than once during 2000, and if attempts are made to legislate development, those who are steadfast in their convictions may defy authority in surprising ways. On the political front, human rights issues may also gain momentum, and government controls from nations ignoring these fundamental rights can be more readily exposed. That does not mean changes will occur overnight, but with increased awareness, action is more likely. These high-friction scenarios are a reflection of the ongoing battle between Saturn and Uranus, transiting in square to one another throughout the year. The most volatile period of this cycle arises during the late summer, when revolutionary action is most intense.

Religion and politics continue to intermingle, and there may be confusion between higher truth and false, greedy ideologies. Since the collective consciousness is subject to manipulation (all advertisers know this, of course), the spin doctors we so frequently associate with politics may be hard at work in other arenas, too.

In the personal domain, individuals are challenged to determine how attitude and self-worth affect motivation. Even though quality of life may sound good, accomplishing the task of determining what that means is another story. Extracting personal values from the propagandized version of what's important will be one of the crucial issues for individuals during 2000. Demanding that the media tell the truth may be another part of the picture, too—because the impact of manipulated information is becoming quite clear.

Additionally, personal relationships need careful exploration. Venus and Mars both spend time in retrograde cycles this year, indicating a year of defining drives, desires, and deeper needs. If you're unhappy with your relationship, your knee-jerk reaction is likely to be critical complaints about the other person. But it is an ego-driven need for satisfaction that sets the pace of this critical evaluation, and by first looking at yourself to determine how you might improve your personal attitudes you will accomplish the most positive changes.

Preparing for the future can be exceptionally rewarding, but remember to live in the present moment, too. This year promises ample opportunities to discover how you deal with multiple levels of power and how you can launch your life into a truly promising future. Set your sights on uplifting dreams and hopes, and start the countdown....

Have a marvelously satisfying year!

Ascendant Table

Your Time of Birth

Your Sun Sign	6–8 a.m.	8–10 a.m.	10 a.m.– Noon	Noon– 2 p.m.	2–4 p.m.	4–6 p.m.
Aries	Taurus	Gemini	Cancer	Leo	Virgo	Libra
Taurus	Gemini	Cancer	Leo	Virgo	Libra	Scorpio
Gemini	Cancer	Leo	Virgo	Libra	Scorpio	Sagittarius
Cancer	Leo	Virgo	Libra	Scorpio	Sagittarius	Capricorn
Leo	Virgo	Libra	Scorpio	Sagittarius	Capricorn	Aquarius
Virgo	Libra	Scorpio	Sagittarius	Capricorn	Aquarius	Pisces
Libra	Scorpio	Sagittarius	Capricorn	Aquarius	Pisces	Aries
Scorpio	Sagittarius	Capricorn	Aquarius	Pisces	Aries	Taurus
Sagittarius	Capricorn	Aquarius	Pisces	Aries	Taurus	Gemini
Capricorn	Aquarius	Pisces	Aries	Taurus	Gemini	Cancer
Aquarius	Pisces	Aries	Taurus	Gemini	Cancer	Leo
Pisces	Aries	Taurus	Gemini	Cancer	Leo	Virgo

Your Time of Birth

Your Sun Sign	6–8 p.m.	8–10 p.m.	10 p.m.–Midnight	Midnight–2 a.m.	2–4 a.m.	4–6 a.m.
Aries	Scorpio	Sagittarius	Capricorn	Aquarius	Pisces	Aries
Taurus	Sagittarius	Capricorn	Aquarius	Pisces	Aries	Taurus
Gemini	Capricorn	Aquarius	Pisces	Aries	Taurus	Gemini
Cancer	Aquarius	Pisces	Aries	Taurus	Gemini	Cancer
Leo	Pisces	Aries	Taurus	Gemini	Cancer	Leo
Virgo	Aries	Taurus	Gemini	Cancer	Leo	Virgo
Libra	Taurus	Gemini	Cancer	Leo	Virgo	Libra
Scorpio	Gemini	Cancer	Leo	Virgo	Libra	Scorpio
Sagittarius	Cancer	Leo	Virgo	Libra	Scorpio	Sagittarius
Capricorn	Leo	Virgo	Libra	Scorpio	Sagittarius	Capricorn
Aquarius	Virgo	Libra	Scorpio	Sagittarius	Capricorn	Aquarius
Pisces	Libra	Scorpio	Sagittarius	Capricorn	Aquarius	Pisces

How to use this table: 1. Find your Sun sign in the left column.
2. Find your approximate birth time in a vertical column.
3. Line up your Sun sign and birth time to find your Ascendant.

This table will give you an approximation of your Ascendant. If you feel that the sign listed as your Ascendant is incorrect, try the one either before or after the listed sign. It is difficult to determine your exact Ascendant without a complete natal chart.

Astrological Glossary

Air—One of the four elements. The air signs are Gemini, Libra, and Aquarius.

Angles—The four points of the chart that divide it into quadrants. The angles are sensitive areas that lend emphasis to planets located near them. These points are located on the cusps of the First, Fourth, Seventh, and Tenth Houses in a chart.

Ascendant—Rising sign. The degree of the zodiac on the eastern horizon at the time and place for which the horoscope is calculated. It can indicate the image or physical appearance you project to the world. The cusp of the First House.

Aspect—The angular relationship between planets, sensitive points, or house cusps in a horoscope. Lines drawn between the two points and the center of the chart, representing the Earth, form the angle of the aspect. Astrological aspects include conjunction (two points that are 0 degrees apart), opposition (two points, 180 degrees apart), square (two points, 90 degrees apart), sextile (two points, 60 degrees apart), and trine (two points, 120 degrees apart). Aspects can indicate harmony or challenge.

Cardinal Sign—One of the three qualities, or categories, that describe how a sign expresses itself. Aries, Cancer, Libra, and Capricorn are the cardinal signs, believed to initiate activity.

Chiron—Chiron is a comet traveling in orbit between Saturn and Uranus. Although research on its effect on natal charts is not yet complete, it is believed to represent a key or doorway, healing, ecology, and a bridge between traditional and modern methods.

Conjunction—An aspect or angle between two points in a chart where the two points are close enough so that the energies join. Can be considered either harmonious or challenging, depending on the planets involved and their placement.

Cusp—A dividing line between signs or houses in a chart.

Degree—Degree of Arc. One of 360 divisions of a circle. The circle of the zodiac is divided into twelve astrological signs of 30 degrees each. Each degree is made up of 60 minutes, and each minute is made up of 60 seconds of zodiacal longitude.

Earth—One of the four elements. The earth signs are Taurus, Virgo, and Capricorn.

Eclipse—A solar eclipse is the full or partial covering of the Sun by the Moon (as viewed from Earth), and a lunar eclipse is the full or partial covering of the Moon by the Sun.

Ecliptic—The Sun's apparent path around the Earth, which is actually the Earth's orbit extended out into space. The ecliptic forms the center of the zodiac.

Electional Astrology—A branch of astrology concerned with choosing the best time to initiate an activity.

Elements—The signs of the zodiac are divided into four groups of three zodiacal signs, each symbolized by one of the four elements of the ancients: fire, earth, air, and water. The element of a sign is said to express its essential nature.

Ephemeris—A listing of the Sun, Moon, and planets' positions and related information for astrological purposes.

Equinox—Equal night. The point in the Earth's orbit around the Sun at which the day and night are equal in length.

Feminine Signs—Each zodiac sign is either masculine or feminine. Earth signs (Taurus, Virgo, and Capricorn) and water signs (Cancer, Scorpio, and Pisces) are feminine.

Fire—One of the four elements. The fire signs are Aries, Leo, and Sagittarius.

Fixed Signs—Fixed is one of the three qualities, or categories, that describe how a sign expresses itself. The fixed signs are Taurus, Leo, Scorpio, and Aquarius. Fixed signs are said to be predisposed to existing patterns, and somewhat resistant to change.

Hard Aspects—Hard aspects are those aspects in a chart that astrologers believe to represent difficulty or challenges. Among the hard aspects are the square, the opposition, and the conjunction (depending on which planets are conjunct).

Horizon—The word horizon is used in astrology in a manner similar to its common usage, except that only the eastern and western horizons are considered useful. The eastern horizon at the point of birth is the Ascendant, or First House cusp of a natal chart, and the western horizon at the point of birth is the Descendant, or Seventh House cusp.

Houses—Division of the horoscope into twelve segments, beginning with the Ascendant. The dividing line between the houses are called house cusps. Each house corresponds to certain aspects of daily living, and is ruled by the astrological sign that governs the cusp, or dividing line between the house and the one previous.

Ingress—The point of entry of a planet into a sign.

Lagna—A term used in Hindu or Vedic astrology for Ascendant, the degree of the zodiac on the eastern horizon at the time of birth.

Masculine Signs—Each of the twelve signs of the zodiac is either "masculine" or "feminine." The fire signs (Aries, Leo, and Sagittarius) and the air signs (Gemini, Libra, and Aquarius) are masculine.

Midheaven—The highest point on the ecliptic, where it intersects the meridian that passes directly above the place for which the horoscope is cast; the southern point of the horoscope.

Midpoint—A point equally distant to two planets or house cusps. Midpoints are considered by some astrologers to be sensitive points in a person's chart.

Mundane Astrology—Mundane astrology is the branch of astrology generally concerned with political and economic events, and the nations involved in these events.

Mutable Signs—Mutable is one of the three qualities, or categories, that describe how a sign expresses itself. Mutable signs are Gemini, Virgo, Sagittarius, and Pisces. Mutable signs are said to be very adaptable, but sometimes changeable.

Natal Chart—A person's birth chart. A natal chart is essentially a "snapshot" showing the placement of each of the planets at the exact time of a person's birth.

Node—The point where the planets cross the ecliptic, or the Earth's apparent path around the Sun. The North Node is the point where a planet moves northward, from the Earth's perspective, as it crosses the ecliptic; the South Node is where it moves south.

Opposition—Two points in a chart that are 180 degrees apart.

Orb—A small degree margin used when calculating aspects in a chart. For example, although 180 degrees form an exact opposition, an astrologer might consider an aspect within 3 or 4 degrees on either side of 180 degrees to be an opposition, as the impact of the aspect can still be felt within this range. The less orb on an aspect, the stronger the aspect. Astrologers' opinions vary on how many degrees of orb to allow for each aspect.

Outer Planets—Uranus, Neptune, and Pluto are known as the outer planets. Because of their distance from the Sun, they take a long time to complete a single rotation. Everyone born within a few years on either side of a given date will have similar placements of these planets.

Planets—The planets used in astrology are Mercury, Venus, Mars, Jupiter, Saturn, Uranus, Neptune, and Pluto. For astrological purposes, the Sun and Moon are also considered planets. A natal or birth chart lists planetary placement at the moment of birth.

Planetary Rulership—The sign in which a planet is most harmoniously placed. Examples are the Sun in Leo, and the Moon in Cancer.

Precession of Equinoxes—The gradual movement of the point of the Vernal Spring Equinox, located at 0 degrees Aries. This point marks the beginning of the tropical zodiac. The point moves slowly backward through the constellations of the zodiac, so that about every 2,000 years the Equinox begins in an earlier constellation

Qualities—In addition to categorizing the signs by element, astrologers place the twelve signs of the zodiac into three additional categories, or qualities: cardinal, mutable, or fixed. Each sign is considered to be a combination of its element and quality. Where the element of a sign describes its basic nature, the quality describes its mode of expression.

Retrograde Motion—Apparent backward motion of a planet. This is an illusion caused by the relative motion of the Earth and other planets in their elliptical orbits.

Sextile—Two points in a chart that are 60 degrees apart.

Sidereal Zodiac—Used by Hindu or Vedic astrologers. The sidereal zodiac is located where the constellations are actually positioned in the sky.

Soft Aspects—Soft aspects indicate good fortune or an easy relationship in the chart. Among the soft aspects are the trine, the sextile, and the conjunction (depending on which planets are conjunct).

Square—Two points in a chart that are 90 degrees apart.

Sun Sign—The sign of the zodiac in which the Sun is located at any given time.

Synodic Cycle—The time between conjunctions of two planets.

Trine—An aspect where two points in a chart are 120 degrees.

Tropical Zodiac—The tropical zodiac begins at 0 degrees Aries, where the Sun is located during the Spring Equinox. This system is used by most Western astrologers and throughout this book.

Void-of-Course—A planet is void-of-course after it has made its last aspect within a sign, but before it has entered a new sign.

Water—One of the four elements. Water signs are Cancer, Scorpio, and Pisces.

Meanings of the Planets

The Sun

The Sun indicates the psychological bias that will dominate your actions. What you see, and why, is told in the reading for your Sun. The Sun also shows the basic energy patterns of your body and psyche. In many ways, the Sun is the dominant force in your horoscope and your life. Other influences, especially that of the Moon, may modify the Sun's influence, but nothing will cause you to depart very far from the basic solar pattern. Always keep in mind the basic influence of the Sun and remember all other influences must be interpreted in terms of it, especially insofar as they play a visible role in your life. You may think, dream, imagine, and hope a thousand things, according to your Moon and your other planets, but the Sun is what you are. To be your best self in terms of your Sun is to cause your energies to work along the path in which they will have maximum help from planetary vibrations.

The Moon

The Moon tells the desire of your life. When you know what you mean but can't verbalize it, it is your Moon that knows it and your Sun that can't say it. The wordless ecstasy, the mute sorrow, the secret dream, the esoteric picture of yourself that you can't get across to the world, or that the world doesn't comprehend or value—these are the products of the Moon. When you are misunderstood, it is your Moon nature, expressed imperfectly through the Sun sign, that feels betrayed. Things you know without thought—intuitions, hunches, instincts—are the products of the Moon. Modes of expression that you feel truly reflect your deepest self belong to the Moon: art, letters, creative work of any kind; sometimes love; sometimes business. Whatever you feel is most deeply yourself is the product of your Moon and of the sign your Moon occupies at birth.

Mercury

Mercury is the sensory antenna of your horoscope. Its position by sign indicates your reactions to sights, sounds, odors, tastes, and touch impressions, affording a key to the attitude you have toward the physical world around you. Mercury is the messenger through which your physical body and brain (ruled by the Sun) and your inner nature (ruled by the Moon) are kept in contact with the outer world, which will appear to you according to the index of Mercury's position by sign in the horoscope. Mercury rules your rational mind.

Venus

Venus is the emotional antenna of your horoscope. Through Venus, impressions come to you from the outer world, to which you react emotionally. The position of Venus by sign at the time of your birth determines your attitude toward these experiences. As Mercury is the messenger linking sense impressions (sight, smell, etc.) to the basic nature of your Sun and Moon, so Venus is the messenger linking emotional impressions. If Venus is found in the same sign as the Sun, emotions gain importance in your life, and have a direct bearing on your actions. If Venus is in the same sign as the Moon, emotions bear directly on your inner nature, add self-confidence, make you sensitive to emotional impressions, and frequently indicate that you have more love in your heart than you are able to express. If Venus is in the same sign as Mercury, emotional impressions and sense impressions work together; you tend to idealize the world of the senses and sensualize the world of the emotions to interpret emotionally what you see and hear.

Mars

Mars is the energy principle in the horoscope. Its position indicates the channels into which energy will most easily be directed. It is the planet through which the activities of the Sun and the desires of the Moon express themselves in action. In the same sign as the Sun, Mars gives abundant energy, sometimes misdirected in temper, temperament, and quarrels. In the same sign as the Moon, it gives a great capacity to make use of the innermost aims, and to make the inner desires articulate and practical. In the same sign as Venus, it quickens emotional reactions and causes you to act on them, makes for ardor and passion in love, and fosters an earthly awareness of emotional realities.

Jupiter

Jupiter is the feeler for opportunity that you have out in the world. It passes along chances of a lifetime for consideration according to the basic nature of your Sun and Moon. Jupiter's sign position indicates the places where you will look for opportunity, the uses to which you wish to put it, and the capacity you have to react and profit by it. Jupiter is ordinarily, and erroneously, called the planet of luck. It is "luck" insofar as it is the index of opportunity, but your luck depends less on what comes to you than on what you do with what comes to you. In the same sign as the Sun or Moon, Jupiter gives a direct, and generally effective, response to opportunity and is likely to show forth at its "luckiest." If Jupiter is in the same sign as Mercury, sense impressions are interpreted opportunistically. If Jupiter is in the same sign as Venus, you interpret emotions in such a way as to turn them to your advantage; your feelings work harmoniously with the chances for progress that the world has to offer. If Jupiter is in the same sign as Mars, you follow opportunity with energy, dash, enthusiasm, and courage, take long chances, and play your cards wide open.

Saturn

Saturn indicates the direction that will be taken in life by the self-preservative principle which, in its highest manifestation, ceases to be purely defensive and becomes ambitious and aspirational. Your defense or attack against the world is shown by the sign position of Saturn in the horoscope of birth. If Saturn is in the same sign as the Sun or Moon, defense predominates, and there is danger of introversion. The farther Saturn is from the Sun, Moon, and Ascendant, the better for objectivity and extroversion. If Saturn is in the same sign as Mercury, there is a profound and serious reaction to sense impressions; this position generally accompanies a deep and efficient mind. If Saturn is in the same sign as Venus, a defensive attitude toward emotional experience makes for apparent coolness in love and difficulty with the emotions and human relations. If Saturn is in the same sign as Mars, confusion between defensive and aggressive urges can make an indecisive person—or, if the Sun and Moon are strong and the total personality well-developed, a balanced, peaceful, and calm individual of sober judgment and moderate actions may be indicated. If Saturn is in the same sign as Jupiter, the reaction to opportunity is sober and balanced.

Uranus

Uranus in a general way relates to creativity, originality, or individuality, and its position by sign in the horoscope tells the direction in which you will seek to express yourself. In the same sign as Mercury or the Moon, Uranus suggests acute awareness, a quick reaction to sense impressions and experiences, or a hair-trigger mind. In the same sign as the Sun, it points to great nervous activity, a high-strung nature, and an original, creative, or eccentric personality. In the same sign as Mars, Uranus indicates high-speed activity, love of swift motion, and perhaps love of danger. In the same sign as Venus, it suggests an unusual reaction to emotional experience, idealism, sensuality, and original ideas about love and human relations. In the same sign as Saturn, Uranus points to good sense; this can be a practical, creative position, but, more often than not, it sets up a destructive conflict between practicality and originality that can result in a stalemate. In the same sign as Jupiter, Uranus makes opportunity, creates wealth and the means of getting it, and is conducive to the inventive, executive, and daring.

Neptune

Neptune relates to the deepest wells of the subconscious, inherited mentality, and spirituality, indicating what you take for granted in life. Neptune in the same sign as the Sun or Moon indicates that intuitions and hunches—or delusions—dominate; there is a need for rigidly holding to reality. In the same sign as Mercury, Neptune indicates sharp sensory perceptions, a sensitive and perhaps creative mind, and a quivering intensity of reaction to sensory experience. In the same sign as Venus, it reveals idealistic and romantic (or sentimental) reaction to emotional experience, as well as the danger of sensationalism and a love of strange pleasures. In the same sign as Mars, Neptune indicates energy and intuition that work together to make mastery of life—one of the signs of having angels (or devils) on your side. In the same sign as Jupiter, Neptune describes intuitive response to opportunity generally along practical and money-making lines; one of the signs of security if not indeed of wealth. In the same sign as Saturn, Neptune indicates intuitive defense and attack on the world, generally successful unless Saturn is polarized on the negative side; then there is danger of delusion and unhappiness.

Pluto

Pluto is a planet of extremes—from the lowest criminal and violent level of our society to the heights people can attain when they realize their significance in the collectivity of humanity. Pluto also rules three important mysteries of life—sex, death, and rebirth—and links them to each other. One level of death symbolized by Pluto is the physical death of an individual, which occurs so that a person can be reborn into another body to further his or her spiritual development. On another level, individuals can experience a "death" of their old self when they realize the deeper significance of life; thus they become one of the "second born." In a natal horoscope, Pluto signifies our perspective on the world, our conscious and subconscious. Since so many of Pluto's qualities are centered on the deeper mysteries of life, the house position of Pluto, and aspects to it, can show you how to attain a deeper understanding of the importance of the spiritual in your life.

2000
Sun Sign Book
Forecasts

By Gloria Star

Aries

The Ram
March 20 to April 18

♈

Element:	Fire
Quality:	Cardinal
Polarity:	Yang/Masculine
Planetary ruler:	Mars
Meditation:	"I actively pursue the fulfillment of my destiny."
Gemstone:	Diamond
Power stones:	Bloodstone, carnelian, sapphire, ruby
Key phrase:	"I am"
Glyph:	Ram's head ♈
Anatomy:	Head, face
Colors:	Red, white
Animal:	Ram
Myths/legends:	Artemis, Jason and the Golden Fleece
House:	First
Opposite sign:	Libra
Flower:	Geranium
Key word:	Initiative

Positive Expression:	Misuse of Energy:
Independent	Impatient
Courageous	Abrasive
Intrepid	Childish
Assertive	Rash
Innovative	Careless
Self-reliant	Reckless
Energetic	Blunt

Aries

Your Ego's Strengths and Shortcomings

Forging ahead with courage and enthusiasm, you're the pioneer eager to take on new challenges. In many respects you're a trailblazer, and fulfilling your role as "The Initiator" of the zodiac keeps you on the move. Waiting is definitely not your style.

Since your focus is on the path before you, you prefer to stay in the moment. You realize that mustering the best of your energy is much easier that way. You readily tap into the energy of Mars, your ruling planet, harnessing the power, assertiveness, and drive necessary to accomplish your goals. Your daring exuberance can seem abrasive to others if left unchecked, yet you shine forth in a world of apathetic observers who would wait for someone else to get the job done! When someone or something blocks your path, your first response may be to forge ahead, but you can be abrasive if you've forgotten to consider the effects of your actions and words.

In some ways, you may remain the naive child, always certain that if you want something, then you should be able to have it—now. It is that same quality and intensity that instill you with passion, helping to keep your creativity alive throughout your life. This is the source of joy radiating from your soul that inspires others to believe in possibility.

Shining Your Love Light

Falling in love may be at the top of your list of favorite things to accomplish in life! You adore the rush of energy, the flirtation and play of the chase, and the exhilaration of the conquest. The problem with love is sustaining passion, and you may wonder if it's really love when the flames calm to a slow, steady fire. Since you do enjoy the playful side of love, you'll be happier with a partner who can stand the heat, with the shy types sometimes overwhelmed by your spirited disposition. To hold your interest, a partner will need to allow you ample independence, since when you feel free, love flows much easier and has a chance of staying alive.

Since you are a fire sign, you'll feel most comfortable with the other fiery temperaments—Aries, Leo and Sagittarius—who also enjoy a more adventurous approach to love. Your powerful attraction to your zodiac opposite, Libra, stems from your fascination with his or her refined sensibilities, although you may feel pressured by his or her standards of perfection.

With another Aries, the flames of love can be immensely powerful, but if tempers flare or competition arises, those flames can burn out of control. Taurus' sensuality prompts you to slow down and enjoy the experience, but ultimately a slow pace gets on your nerves. With Gemini, a battle of wits can fan the flames of desire, and the mental challenges are the catalyst for your chemistry. Cancer's tender hugs soothe your soul, but you can feel put off if you're scolded for being late for dinner. Leo ignites the lover in your personality, prompting you to pour out your heartfelt desires, but she or he will expect your loyalty.

Virgo is strangely enticing and can be a lifelong friend, but you may not like the expectations. Scorpio provokes unbridled intensity, but if control games arise you'll feel like skipping out—quickly. You're invigorated by Sagittarius' humor and come-hither antics and feel right at home sharing your dreams. With Capricorn you're enticed by the promise of security, but too many rules and commitments can inhibit your passionate side. Aquarius puts you at ease, and since you both love your freedom, you can develop friendship and excitement in your relationship. Pisces provokes a powerful sense of the mystical and you can feel a strong bond, even though you may never know exactly where you stand.

Making Your Place in the World

You need a career that helps you develop your self-respect, and will appreciate physical and mental challenges associated with your work. You might prefer to work independently, and occupations in the travel industry, sales, auto design and mechanics, or beauty and hair design can provide the right scenario for success. The excitement of politics and the endless challenges of medicine may capture your interest.

The physical demands of a job in occupational or physical therapy, athletics, coaching, dancing, police work, fire fighting, or the military can be rewarding. To answer your creative drives, metalworking, welding, jewelry or fashion design may hold your interest.

Whatever your choice, your job must provide ample room to exercise your leadership and offer a chance for you to try new ideas.

Power Plays

Your competitive spirit is quite recognizable, and when you're facing a challenge head-on, your sense of power is readily engaged. Your desire to own your personal power stems from your need to develop your sense of autonomy, which is a primary drive. Growth-oriented goals provide the perfect backdrop for realizing your power and keep your vitality functioning at an optimum level. However, if your drive is fueled by guilt, shame, mistrust, or anger, your aims can lead to destructive paths. By taking full responsibility for your thoughts and actions, you're on the way to actualizing your power.

Taking the lead in situations that call for action enhances your feelings of power. Unlike some, you are invigorated by facing apparently insurmountable obstacles, although your motivations may require some scrutiny. Even though you like to be in the lead, when others hold you back, you can defer to feelings of resentment. Selfish or domineering behavior brings out the least attractive side of your personality, and when you're feeling a lack of respect, it is this behavior that can surface, subsequently undermining your personal power. Maintaining an illumined connection to your inner and higher self helps you meet your challenges in a manner that will, indeed, blaze your pathway, and one that others may eagerly follow.

Famous Aries

Maya Angelou, Jackie Chan, Charles Chaplin, Joan Crawford, Doris Day, Celine Dion, Linda Goodman, Billie Holiday, Thomas Jefferson, Elton John, Rodney King, Anne McCaffrey, Pat Robertson, Diana Ross, Dane Rudhyar, Tennessee Williams, Bob Woodward.

The Year Ahead for Aries

After a year of increasing confidence and optimism, you're ready to funnel your creativity into strengthening your resources while you refine your goals. Balancing expansion and restraint is not the easiest task, but you're seeing the value of holding back long enough to steady your foothold before you take the next leap.

The planet Jupiter completes its cycle in your sign in mid-February, and then, from February 14 through July 1, your confidence regarding finances is uplifted thanks to Jupiter's influence in your solar chart's Second House of material resources. From July through December, you're on the move while Jupiter travels in the sign of Gemini, stimulating fresh ideas and a desire to explore new territory. These cycles strengthen your faith in your ideas and enhance your self-worth. With your personal esteem on the rise, you may feel you're capable of accomplishing almost anything. To avoid excessive limitations in the future, it's crucial that you establish some boundaries to avoid overextending your finances, overobligating your time, or overindulging in the good things of life. All in all, Jupiter's influence this year helps build your self-confidence and leaves a residue of good humor!

Saturn's influence targets your Second House of material worth and personal values, continuing its cycle of last year. By paying careful attention to the manner in which you are utilizing your resources, you can build a sound financial base, but you're also continuing to repay the lapses in judgment or results of impulse spending from the past. Forge ahead and stay with your plan, since your attention to the details of your finances and desire to strengthen your personal worth may require you to maintain your course of frugality. You can also build significant resources this year, since Jupiter joins Saturn in this arena, increasing your opportunities to shape your personal financial empire! It is fortunate that Saturn and Jupiter's influence are operating together in this facet of your life, since the balance between expansion and consolidation can definitely benefit your personal resources when properly exercised.

While Uranus' disruptive force brings an unsettled quality to your plans and goals, you may also feel more inclined to consider options that involve significant change. The excitement that accompanies this transit helps you maintain an open mind, and you'll continue to feel inclined to associate with others who share your interests. The slow-moving cycles of Neptune and Pluto emphasize your need to feel better connected to a community, and whether you're becoming more involved in local politics or a spiritual group or simply strengthening your circle of friends, you're forging powerful associations.

There are four solar eclipses during the year 2000, a significant astronomical occurrence that happened only five times during the twentieth century (including the year 1935, when there were five solar eclipses). For you, the eclipses draw your attention to the questions of right livelihood, personal security, and the need to become more in touch with the flow of love. These periods will be more carefully defined in your monthly forecasts for February, July, and December. On an emotional level, getting in touch with your calling in life may feel more important, and you may need to spend extra time away from external influences reflecting upon the truly important things you're working to create.

If you were born between March 20 and 27, you're feeling the effects of Uranus transiting in semisquare to your Sun, prompting you to break away from unnecessary restraints and to express your individuality and independence. It's easy to overreact during this cycle, leaping too far or too quickly into things that you may not be fully prepared to handle. However, it's an excellent time to break free from situations that are counterproductive to your growth by stepping into new territory or experimenting with more open-ended relationships. Identifying goals that reflect your needs and help you gain recognition for your talents and abilities is easier, but maintaining the focus necessary to realize those goals can be difficult under this influence. However, Ariens born between March 20 and 22 are also experiencing the stabilizing force of Saturn transiting in sextile aspect to your Sun. This cycle's influence lasts throughout the summer of the year 2000, but if you're paying attention to timing, you can target the summer to make introductions, launch an important project, or finalize agreements.

For those born between March 23 and 28, Neptune is transiting in sextile to your Sun, strengthening your imagination and deepening your spirituality. During this year, you may feel that your accomplishments are more meaningful if they answer a higher purpose. Although this is an excellent time to become more involved in charitable outreach, it can also be a phenomenal period of enhanced awareness and increased artistic stimulus. By devoting a portion of your time and energy to your inner being, your intuitive insights can grow more powerful under this influence. The link between mind, body, and spirit strengthens during this time, and incorporating holistic and alternative therapies into your healing practice can also enhance your overall well-being.

If you were born between March 29 and April 5, you're feeling the impact of Pluto's transit in trine to your Sun. Although this can mark a period of increasing influence, the extent of your leverage depends upon what you do with the energy of this cycle. You can sit back and simply enjoy an easier period of growth, or, if you prefer a more active involvement, you can utilize this time to actively open doors that were previously closed and step into arenas that allow you to more fully utilize your talents and abilities. If you're still in the process of developing your skills, this can be an excellent time to align yourself with situations that enhance your abilities and opportunities, such as the appropriate teacher or a supportive company.

If you were born between April 5 and 12, your individuality and need for independence work to your benefit while Uranus travels in sextile aspect to your Sun. In many respects, your professional and personal associations are keys to your advancement, and your leadership and influence can be phenomenal assets. If you've been hesitant or uncertain about the best time to break away from old restraints and forge new pathways, this is the time. You may feel more ready, and the elements around you seem much more compatible to your growth. You're also benefiting from Neptune's transit in quintile aspect to your Sun, enhancing your ability to tap into your special creative sensibilities or to develop your talents, although you will need to put forth the effort to cultivate these talents to make the most of this cycle. Additionally, Chiron's cycle in trine aspect to your Sun helps to clarify your life purpose during this time of positive self-assertiveness. Uncovering your higher purpose brings healing and hope into your life, and this can be an extremely hopeful period. You're discovering that the stories about "right livelihood" are more than stories—they are essential elements of creating a life that allows you to be who you are, without reservation.

If you were born between April 1 and 20, you're feeling the challenge of embracing the stabilizing force of Saturn as it transits in semisextile to your Sun. To experience the positive benefits of this period, it is necessary that you establish a firm footing before taking the next steps in your growth. That means you may have to complete obligations and find ways to shoulder responsibilities that still allow you to move forward with confidence. Saturn's energy is about reality, focus, and discipline. By incorporating these qualities in a conscious manner, your choices will reflect maturity and awareness. If you ignore the need to take responsible action, you are likely to be blocked in your attempts to move forward, or may find that you're carrying burdens that slow your progress. If you've skipped steps in the past, you may have to satisfy them during this cycle. In the long run, you're forging a more stable base for progress, although the process can seem rather labored, especially if you're fighting it! Should you discover resistance, make an effort to determine its origin, since unfounded fears can be a problem you had not anticipated. For those born between April 17 and 20, the benefits of your intuitive awareness will be more marked, since Uranus is transiting in quintile aspect to your Sun. By listening to these flashes of insight, your choices and actions may seem to be more clearly on the mark, which can be extremely helpful when you're trying to get ahead of the game!

Tools to Make a Difference

The planetary cycles draw your attention to your security and financial issues. With so many changes in the world around you disrupting your stability, it's easy to become mistrustful or uncertain. Bring your focus to the parts of your life you can control. Become more conscious of the way you're using or wasting your resources—from energy, to time, to material things. You may discover that it's more comfortable to simplify. Also, the resource of friends becomes invaluable, and sharing concerns, talents, and efforts with a community of friends can be fulfilling for all involved.

Build your endurance and stamina this year, and promise yourself ample time for physical activity. Releasing stress and tension can be a challenge. If you're concentrating on getting stronger, you might forget to compliment your strength building with ample flex time. Stretching, whether through exercises like hatha yoga or basic body stretches, is necessary to avoid becoming too tense. If you want to employ aromatherapy as part of your overall healing and balancing, you'll respond nicely to inhalations of geranium and lavender. If you're plagued with headaches, the aromatic properties of basil and cajeput will be helpful, and for muscular pain try inhaling eucalyptus and clary sage, or add these essential oils to massage oils to enhance the effectiveness of your massage.

During your meditations, allow yourself to feel as though you are rising above the intensity and heaviness of everyday experiences. Imagine that you are floating above your body, watching yourself become more and more relaxed. Eventually, you rise far above your physical environment, flying over the landscape, looking down on the earth below. Everything seems so much more connected from this point of view, with the colors blending together in a magical patchwork. You can see the connections from one place to the other and realize that there is very little separating one neighborhood or town from the next. When you return from your meditation, remember this sense of interconnection, and in your everyday dealings with friends and coworkers, hold in your heart and mind the knowledge that we are all one family on planet earth.

Initiating the Millennium

Breaking away from old paradigms, you enter the millennium with the challenge to strike out on paths that help you fulfill your unique destiny. Evaluate your resources and the way you utilize them, and learn to think for yourself when it comes to understanding and managing your finances. Gain true autonomy by embracing those experiences that will bring real freedom while honoring your responsibilities. Dumping your responsibilities will only delay your progress!

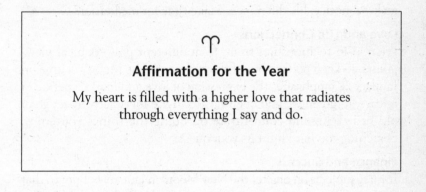

Affirmation for the Year

My heart is filled with a higher love that radiates
through everything I say and do.

Aries/January

In the Spotlight
Strengthen your reputation by aligning with others whose aims and ideals are in harmony with your own. Rely on your creative insights to elevate your status, and use your enthusiasm appropriately since you can overdo it.

Wellness and Keeping Fit
Combine fitness with fun. The social aspect of sports fires your interest and helps you maintain your commitment. Inner fitness makes a noticeable difference. Make time for meditation.

Love and Life Connections
Friction in relationships stems from different philosophical viewpoints, so keep politics out of the bedroom! The Moon's eclipse on January 20 emphasizes the expression of love and marks a period of release, forgiveness, and opening. To invite love, actively let go of old heartache and concentrate on doing the things you enjoy. Searching too hard inhibits your quest.

Finance and Success
Initiate projects on or after the New Moon on January 6. Prior to that time, examine contracts to expose weak links. Budgets may need to be redone, and you'll have more success obtaining the cooperation of others if you can illustrate your plans. Momentum builds from January 17-24, when meetings, travel, or publication can further your cause. Leave situations open for alteration on January 20.

Cosmic Insider Tip
You have big dreams, and they are manifesting in unusual ways. Practical considerations are important, even though your enthusiasm will get the ball rolling from January 8-22.

Rewarding Days
3, 4, 8, 9, 12, 13, 14, 17, 21, 22, 30, 31

Challenging Days
1, 5, 6, 19, 20, 23, 25, 26, 27

Affirmation for the Month
I am ready to experience unconditional love.

Aries/February

In the Spotlight

The solar eclipse gets the big press, and its influence can boost the impact of setting goals. Unexpected changes among your friends and associates can open the way for new directions in your own life.

Wellness and Keeping Fit

Your physical vitality gets a lift when Mars enters your sign on February 11. Although your energy is stronger, it's easy to overdo it. Pamper your body near the time of the Full Moon on January 19.

Love and Life Connections

You need some excitement, but will not have to go far to find it. While you might have hesitated in the past, your eagerness and passion emerge during the eclipse on February 5, setting the stage for an experience of love that sends your heart soaring. Knowing the appropriate time and place makes a difference in the outcome since you may feel some disapproval from superiors or a parent if you're pushing the boundaries of "acceptability."

Finance and Success

Technological and innovative options give your career a boost. Stepping into a new situation from February 5-19 can put you on the fast track to success. Get things rolling before Mercury turns retrograde on February 21, and use the remainder of the month to complete projects. Unfamiliar situations out of your area of expertise can create setbacks after the Full Moon on February 19.

Cosmic Insider Tip

Your competitive nature grows more intense after February 11, and knowing when to assert yourself or how far to go is a critical element in your bid for success. Be attentive to reactions.

Rewarding Days

4, 5, 9, 10, 13, 14, 17, 18, 26

Challenging Days

1, 2, 14, 15, 21, 22, 23, 29

Affirmation for the Month

I trust my intuitive sensibilities to guide me when logic may fail.

Aries/March

In the Spotlight
Although you're eager to make progress, some things are simply not yet ready. Complete old business now. Apply your energy to things you can control and let go of what you cannot direct.

Wellness and Keeping Fit
To release the excessive tension you're accumulating, stay active. Mars is in your sign through March 22, stimulating your need to strengthen your body. A fitness class might be the perfect solution.

Love and Life Connections
An interesting prospect appears, sparking your imagination and your passionate drive; but there's a restriction. It could be circumstances or time, but you might also hesitate because you're uncertain. Make overtures from March 1-7 and after the Full Moon on March 19. Connect with your old friends through March 13, and forge associations with talented and fascinating individuals who are new to your circle. Make time for romance on March 3, 6, 16, 17.

Finance and Success
While Mercury continues its retrograde through March 14, you may be stuck in limbo on important business deals. Patience is your best option, since fighting against the tide will only diminish your enthusiasm. Look into budgetary dilemmas and work on community projects after the New Moon on March 6. After March 21 you'll feel more unfettered and able to effectively influence change.

Cosmic Insider Tip
Overly idealistic opportunities can seize your interest after March 12, but there can be hidden traps and problems. Careful research can ultimately save time and money.

Rewarding Days
2, 7, 8, 11, 12, 16, 17, 25, 26, 30

Challenging Days
1, 13, 14, 20, 21, 27, 28

Affirmation for the Month
Letting go of the past opens the way for new beginnings.

Aries/April

In the Spotlight
Attracting more interesting circumstances in your relationships and better results from your career lifts your spirits. Target your goals and you'll see very specific results. It's one of those times to "be careful what you ask for, because you might get it." Intention is everything.

Wellness and Keeping Fit
Work toward increasing your endurance. It's easy to make excuses about not staying on target with your fitness goals, and you may need to try something different.

Love and Life Connections
Venus moves into Aries on April 6, stimulating your ability to show your assets to your best advantage. Although this is a period of powerful attraction, if you overexaggerate or take the route of poor taste, your efforts will quickly backfire. Initiate an amorous relationship during the Aries New Moon on April 4, and solidify commitments near the Full Moon on April 18.

Finance and Success
The influence of Mars, Jupiter, and Saturn through your sector of personal finance galvanizes your ability to make the most of your resources. There's a temptation to step over the line of good judgment and spend more than you can afford after April 16. At work, schedule meetings or build your network from April 14-29, when your influence can kindle the support that will advance your standing.

Cosmic Insider Tip
Enlist the assistance of others whose special talents compliment your own from April 12-21. Cooperative ventures during this time respond best to your leadership.

Rewarding Days
3, 4, 8, 12, 13, 21, 22, 26

Challenging Days
10, 11, 16, 17, 18, 23, 24

Affirmation for the Month
I endeavor to make the most of all my resources.

Aries/May

In the Spotlight
Everything focuses on resources: money, time, assets, and ownership. Although you are not what you own, it may be difficult to separate your possessions from your sense of self. Reshape your values to serve your truest sense of worth.

Wellness and Keeping Fit
Although your energy is strong, you may feel weighted down. Lift your spirits by keeping your commitment to staying fit. Vary your routine when you're feeling stuck, and be sure to stretch. Loosen up with a massage midmonth.

Love and Life Connections
When you have an opinion, people know about it, but keeping some of your ideas to yourself might maintain the peace when a difference of opinion could create a ruckus. You're feeling the need for excitement and may even have a change of heart near the Full Moon on May 18, but simply walking away may not be an option. Talking about your feelings is easiest after May 14.

Finance and Success
Create budgets and financial plans after the New Moon on May 3, when you have a clear idea about what you want and how to get it. You will not feel right giving over control of your finances, and will be happier even in contractual agreements and partnerships if you have the reins. Schedule presentations and business meetings from May 15-31, but save your pet projects for May 28-30.

Cosmic Insider Tip
Maintaining leadership can be thwarted if your attitudes are too selfish or controlling. You are free when all are free.

Rewarding Days
1, 2, 5, 6, 9, 10, 18, 19, 28, 29

Challenging Days
4, 7, 8, 13, 14, 17, 21, 22

Affirmation for the Month
True abundance is meant to be shared.

Aries/June

In the Spotlight
Progress on all fronts arises as your resources increase and valuable connections are formed. Travel can play an integral role, but you may also be quite successful utilizing other methods to stay in touch.

Wellness and Keeping Fit
Take advantage of outdoor activities and team sports when improving your fitness, and continue your quest for variety to maintain your interest. Your nervous system may need a nutritional boost, and altering your attitudes helps dissipate frustration.

Love and Life Connections
If it's been a while since you made an overture to a sibling or friend, cross those bridges on the New Moon on June 2. Keeping emotional boundaries intact is easier, but a meeting of the minds is also promising. A love relationship blossoms when you take it on the road. Consider sharing a short journey to a romantic hideaway. Interject more whimsy into your life. Laugh long and often.

Finance and Success
Your ideas capture interest where it will make a difference. Near and during the Full Moon on June 16, you're in an exceptional position to alter the opinions of others, and you may also be inspired by a mentor whose ideas open new vistas. Watch for competitive developments after June 15. The manner in which you handle your competitors has powerful implications.

Cosmic Insider Tip
Try something extraordinary to alter your course from June 2-16. You're in no mood to repeat the past and are ready to experiment with possibilities few have dared to explore.

Rewarding Days
2, 5, 14, 15, 16, 19, 25, 26, 29

Challenging Days
3, 4, 10, 11, 17, 18

Affirmation for the Month
My thoughts and words are inspired by divine truth.

Aries/July

In the Spotlight
Eclipses everywhere! Your attention to maintaining the balance between personal and professional needs requires diligent effort. Situations at home can reach crisis proportions, but that can be good if you're making growth-oriented change.

Wellness and Keeping Fit
Emotionally trying circumstances can take their toll on your health. Your mind and body can get out of balance, but reclaiming your life is easy when you recognize where there is a deficiency.

Love and Life Connections
The solar eclipse on July 1 and the lunar eclipse on July 16 emphasize family and security issues, and you may feel you have little choice but to pay attention. Your leadership and courage are strong, and by the time the solar eclipse on July 30 occurs, you'll see positive effects of creative solutions to most problems. The manner in which you handle turmoil will determine long-range effects.

Finance and Success
Your expenditures for needs at home can be well worth the outlay, although that may not diminish your anxiety! Plan carefully and you're not likely to spend unnecessarily. Investments fare best after July 13, since Mercury's retrograde, along with other celestial events, may bring complications. Observe reactions from superiors to avoid alienating the wrong people in your quest to get ahead.

Cosmic Insider Tip
If you feel that your life direction is temporarily out of your hands, surrender to the flow and make choices that help you maintain stability. Crisis is a chance to break destructive patterns.

Rewarding Days
3, 4, 12, 13, 17, 22, 23, 26, 30, 31

Challenging Days
1, 2, 6, 7, 8, 9, 14, 15, 16, 28

Affirmation for the Month
I am safe in the face of change.

Aries/August

In the Spotlight
Your momentum toward achieving success is stronger thanks to your faith in your talents. Confirmation of your efforts comes through endorsements from others whose influence boosts your reputation.

Wellness and Keeping Fit
Recreational activities enhance your wellness. An active vacation could be the solution to releasing stress and improving your health after August 11. Consult a health practitioner after August 23.

Love and Life Connections
A new love interest may enter the picture, and things move fast after August 8. Express what's in your heart, and by the time the Full Moon occurs on August 15, the object of your affection is likely to return your adoration. The value of your friendships may be more important than an affair, and if your attention is directed toward more platonic relationships, these, too, prosper. One thing is certain: asserting yourself is much easier now.

Finance and Success
Speculative ventures, artistic endeavors, and investments are productive. A special project reaches a peak midmonth, and the momentum can carry you for quite a while. Solidify your professional network through positive communication, meetings, or supportive endorsements. If you're eager to alter your work environment or schedule, institute changes with the New Moon on August 29.

Cosmic Insider Tip
You've regained your inspiration and may feel more free than you've felt for a long time. Assure your success by using your opportunities to your best advantage from August 1-19.

Rewarding Days
8, 9, 13, 14, 18, 19, 22, 23, 27, 28

Challenging Days
3, 4, 6, 10, 11, 25, 26, 31

Affirmation for the Month
My creative inspiration flows from love and true compassion.

Aries/September

In the Spotlight

Amorous relationships and partnerships draw your attention, and it's easier to express your intentions and feelings. If you prefer to open your heart through your creative endeavors, these, too, show high levels of inspiration.

Wellness and Keeping Fit

It's easy to push past your physical limits, but by September 17 you're paying the price for too much of a good thing! Take stock of the way you feel. Fine tuning now creates energy for later.

Love and Life Connections

Under the influence of Venus and Mercury, you're giving serious consideration to what you want from a partnership. If you're in a good situation, it's time to renew vows; but if you're feeling uncertain, take it one step at a time, and be attentive to your true feelings during the Full Moon on August 13. You'll feel more inclined to go to the next level after the New Moon on August 27.

Finance and Success

Showcase your talents or launch special projects that will benefit from increased exposure from September 1-17. Although unexpected changes can alter your plans from September 1-3, more reliable opportunities manifest, and your confidence is on the rise on September 4. Your work load may increase after September 18. Keep your priorities clearly identified in order to meet your obligations.

Cosmic Insider Tip

You're filled with creative ideas and gain favorable support from others through September 17. By initiating actions during this time, you'll encounter fewer obstacles. Show your gratitude.

Rewarding Days

4, 5, 9, 10, 14, 15, 20, 23, 24

Challenging Days

1, 2, 7, 8, 21, 22, 27, 28

Affirmation for the Month

My will is guided by truth and love.

Aries/October

In the Spotlight
When working out the details of agreements, Mercury's retrograde cycle gives you a chance to take a second look before making final decisions. Know your own hidden agenda!

Wellness and Keeping Fit
Physical complaints resulting from excess are troublesome until after October 7. You may uncover hidden problems.

Love and Life Connections
Misunderstandings in an intimate relationship can be the result of unresolved problems that seem to surface at the most inconvenient times. Breakthroughs are possible if you're both open to releasing your attachment to the way things used to be in favor of healing change. The Aries Full Moon on October 13 marks a powerful time of release and confrontation, when your patience wears thin. After October 20 you're pursuing a new vision.

Finance and Success
Ironing out legal and contractual agreements can seem like torture since satisfying all concerned may be a daunting task. Unless time is of the essence, use Mercury's retrograde from October 18 onward to research problems and work out details. Financial arrangements are likely to be at the core of the most sticky issues, and others may not deliver their part of the bargain. Technicalities surface with the New Moon on October 27.

Cosmic Insider Tip
To avoid getting caught holding a very heavy burden resulting from uncooperative attitudes, clarify details from October 6-12, or postpone final decisions until next month.

Rewarding Days
2, 3, 7, 11, 12, 13, 16, 20, 29, 30

Challenging Days
4, 5, 6, 18, 19, 24, 25, 31

Affirmation for the Month
Healing arises as I release resentment, guilt, and pain. I am free!

Aries/November

In the Spotlight
Your competitive spirit needs a healthy outlet. Identify your challenges and determine the best ways to meet them; otherwise, conflicts may arise on their own, putting you on the defensive.

Wellness and Keeping Fit
Emotional and physical problems are inextricably linked, and unless you're getting to the core of your emotional distress, body ailments may not be resolved. Seek support from a counselor near the Full Moon on November 11.

Love and Life Connections
Although you may yearn for a more spiritual bond with the one you love, there can be blocks to achieving your desire. Explore unconditional love toward yourself before you attempt to shine this light on others, since failing to accept your own strengths and limitations will make it virtually impossible to accept another's. An inspiration opens the way for love during the New Moon on November 25.

Finance and Success
Hidden problems lurk beneath the surface during Mercury's retrograde through November 7 and until November 16. Wait to sign contracts until after November 25. Special interest projects provide an excellent outlet for your leadership after November 12. Travel or a period of retreat brings renewed perspective after November 24, when presentations or advertising also boost success.

Cosmic Insider Tip
Although you like to count on logic, the facts alone may not relieve your uneasiness. Trust your intuitive sensibilities, and be wary of others who might attempt to manipulate your decisions.

Rewarding Days
4, 8, 9, 12, 13, 17, 25, 26, 30

Challenging Days
1, 2, 14, 15, 21, 22, 28, 29

Affirmation for the Month
I look beneath the surface for the hidden truths.

Aries/December

In the Spotlight
Optimistic about future endeavors, you're forging into new territory to manifest your vision. The changes you create can lead to a crisis if others are uncertain of your motivations or feel threatened by your success.

Wellness and Keeping Fit
Funneling your energy into a physical challenge improves your confidence, and you'll enjoy involvement in team sports, a fitness class, or working out with a friend. The outdoors beckons.

Love and Life Connections
Whether you're seeking a new love, inspiration, or a way to breathe life back into an existing relationship, taking an active role makes all the difference. Sharing cultural or academic pursuits can lead to a meeting of hearts and minds, or travel may open fresh horizons near the time of the Full Moon on December 11. Family matters need special attention later, with change in family hierarchy emphasized during the solar eclipse on December 25.

Finance and Success
Your plans may challenge the expectations others have of you, but if you're willing to illustrate or explain your ideas, you may actually gain support instead of engendering hostility. Publishing, advertising, or legal concerns fare best from December 4-23, and you can easily enlist endorsements from December 11-16, when you may also be influential in aiding another whose talents impress you.

Cosmic Insider Tip
Your ideals are highest from December 9-23, when your enthusiasm opens vistas previously unseen. Pursue something extraordinary.

Rewarding Days
1, 2, 5, 6, 10, 11, 14, 15, 23, 24, 28

Challenging Days
12, 13, 18, 19, 25, 26

Affirmation for the Month
I celebrate the changes in my life.

Aries Action Table

These dates reflect the best—but not the only—times for success and ease in these activities, according to your Sun sign.

	JAN	FEB	MAR	APR	MAY	JUN	JUL	AUG	SEPT	OCT	NOV	DEC
Move					14-31	1-22	18-31	1-6				
Start a class						2, 3					25, 26	
Join a club		5, 6										
Ask for a raise				4								
Look for work	1-17							6-31	1-6			
Get pro advice	25, 26	21-23	20, 21	16, 17	13-15	9-11	7, 8	3, 4, 31	1, 27, 28	24-26	21, 22	18, 19
Get a loan	27, 28	24, 25	22, 23	18-20	16, 17	12, 13	9-11	6, 7	2-3, 29-30	27, 28	23, 24	20, 21
See a doctor		5-29	1-31	1-13				22-31	1-6			
Start a diet	23, 24	19, 20	18, 19	14, 15	11, 12	7, 8	5, 6	1-2, 28-30	25, 26	22, 23	18-20	16, 17
End relationship				18								
Buy clothes								7-21				
Get a makeover				4, 5								
New romance								30, 31				
Vacation	2-4, 30-31	26, 27	24-26	21, 22	18, 19	14-16	12, 13	8, 9	4-6	1-3, 29-30	25, 26	22-24

Taurus
The Bull
April 19 to May 19

♉

Element:	Earth
Quality:	Fixed
Polarity:	Yin/Feminine
Planetary Ruler:	Venus
Meditation:	"I lovingly safeguard my environment."
Gemstone:	Emerald
Power Stones:	Diamond, blue lace agate, rose quartz
Key Phrase:	"I have"
Glyph:	Bull's head ♉
Anatomy:	Throat, neck
Color:	Green
Animal:	Cattle
Myths/Legends:	Cerridwen, Isis and Osiris, Bull of Minos
House:	Second
Opposite Sign:	Scorpio
Flower:	Violet
Key Word:	Conservation

Positive Expression:	**Misuse of Energy:**
Substantial	Obstinate
Persistent	Avaricious
Prosperous	Greedy
Enduring	Unyielding
Loving	Covetous
Calm	Lethargic
Steadfast	Possessive

Taurus

Your Ego's Strengths and Shortcomings

Driven to build a steadfast and reliable place for yourself in the world, your sensibilities allow you to embrace the true value of your experiences. In truth, you're hungry for abiding love, and once you've opened your heart and developed an attachment, your devotion to the people, ideals, and expressions you hold dear can be unfaltering. A dependable provider, you play the role of "The Maintainer" of the zodiac, radiating steadfast reliability that can comfort others weathering the storms of life.

Your effortless connection to the energy of Venus attracts beauty, and you may be especially fond of naturally occurring splendor. Artistic and musical expressions warm your heart, and you may have special talents in these areas. Your efforts to conserve resources range from maintaining the earth's precious commodities to the finest creations of humanity, and your eye for quality and endurability is consistently valid.

Change is rarely easy for you, since the threat of losing anything will be taken quite personally. In fact, your resistance and stubbornness are legendary, and if you feel threatened you can be downright uncooperative. By realizing that you are more than what you have, change becomes easier, especially when it's time to release something you've outgrown or that is no longer in your best interest. This process opens the way to experience the never-ending flow of pure love.

Shining Your Love Light

A sensual and expressive lover, you express a strong yet tender passion in the right circumstances. Your search for a relationship that can endure the test of time can prompt you to hold back, even when you know your heart is touched by another. The idea of losing someone you love can be crushing, and if you are in an uncertain relationship, feelings of jealousy can be a signal that your self-worth is threatened. All relationships go through evolutionary change, and love itself is a process that requires room for these transformations.

It's easiest for you to make a connection to the other earth signs—Taurus, Virgo, and Capricorn—who share your appreciation for practicality and stability. Attracted to Aries, you may never feel quite comfortable with his or her need to be on the move just when you're settling in. With another Taurus, commitment can be easy if it's the right match. Gemini's versatility challenges you to become more adaptable, but keeping up with his or her changeability can drive you nuts. Your shared desire for family and home can lead to easy contentment with Cancer. Leo's appeal is drama and loyalty, but ego conflicts can definitely arise.

Virgo can be your ultimate lover, engaging in deeply sensual and pleasurable experiences of love. Libra's refined grace entices, but his or her indecision stimulates too much uncertainty. Your zodiac opposite, Scorpio, can be highly attractive and passionate, but you've met your match when it comes to possessiveness. Sagittarius' generosity and playfulness are enjoyable, but you may not spend much time together. Capricorn compliments your philosophical values and can be helpful in your drive to accomplish financial and emotional stability. Aquarius simply does not give you sufficient personal attention. With Pisces, you can float into fanciful romance while creating a place to bring your hopes to life.

Making Your Place in the World

Even though you seek stability through your career, you're also looking for a place where your unique talents can shine. In the arts, you may enjoy sculpting, pottery, or handicrafts, or you may be an accomplished musician. You might also prefer to channel your creativity into the beauty industry or clothing design or sales.

Your sense of structure can find a place in architectural design, carpentry, or building. Your environmental sensibilities can be directed into landscape design, gardening, the floral industry, farming, ranching, or forestry. You have a natural business sense and know how to manage your resources. You might even enjoy managing the resources of others and may consider a career in retail merchandising, finance, banking, real estate, or investment. Museums and art galleries can also be lucrative and fulfilling options.

Power Plays

Building a strong foothold, you can cultivate the power of shaping a fortress that allows you to hold on, wait for the right time, and persevere through adversity. Although you crave a life of peace and comfort, your ability to fight to preserve what you have should never be underestimated.

Surrounded by a loyal family, friends, and ample resources, you feel secure. An internal struggle arises if you are forced to choose between having someone or something and letting go of your attachments. Forced to release something you see as yours, your vulnerability can stimulate the power of greed or possessiveness. Endings can leave you feeling empty and powerless if you've incorporated a sense that your things or relationships are an integral part of your being and feel that losing them is destructive to you. Learning when and how to say good-bye actually fortifies your power.

Acknowledging the value of others and sharing your resources with them is your ultimate compliment, but you also discover a kinship that leads to truly abundant living when you give of yourself and your wealth. Honoring Mother Earth through sound use of her resources strengthens your sense of power, since you are interested in assuring the supply of your needs. Your truest expression of eternal love can arise through taking steps that will secure a positive future for your children and those generations who are now only a whisper on the winds of time.

Famous Taurus

Mary Kay Ash, James Beard, Tony Blair, Scott Carpenter, Sheena Easton, G.H. Fahrenheit, Audrey Hepburn, Coretta Scott King, George Lucas, Dennis Rodman, David O. Selznick, Jerry Seinfeld, Rudolph Valentino, Orson Welles, Tammy Wynette.

The Year Ahead for Taurus

The year 2000 ushers in a period of expanded stability for you. The need to change is there, and in some instances changes you cannot control will require that you make prudent decisions before the dust settles! As a general rule, you have at least one foot on the ground and continue to move toward the fulfillment of your hopes and dreams. The manner in which you incorporate modifications will determine the pace of your success and the long-term impact, and welcoming instead of resisting a transformation in your life path makes room for more rewarding creativity. Of course, you prefer reliable and reasonably predictable options, but since the rules of the game are changing, promises may not always be fulfilled. Inconsistency can torment your desire to get things settled, but rolling with the punches softens the effects.

The transit of Jupiter highlights an increase in your confidence and expansion of your material worth. From February through July, Jupiter travels in Taurus, marking a cycle of exceptionally good fortune and opportunity. Jupiter transits through your sign every twelve years, and you can make the most of it by taking advantage of fortunate meetings, promoting your talents, and taking wide-ranging steps to develop your career or business. Your trust in the law of abundance is fortified, and showing your gratitude for your success will take you even further. If you become too self-indulgent during this period, you're likely to feel the resulting inertia rather quickly. From July through December, Jupiter transits through your solar Second House, marking a period of financial growth. It's tempting to spend more than you have, so keep one eye on your limitations to avoid digging a hole of debt.

Saturn completes its transit in Taurus this year, offering a stabilizing influence of self-discipline and clarity of vision. If you're willing to work hard during this cycle, you can accomplish more than you realize, since you're literally proving your ability and worth to yourself, and others will be likely to judge your progress. Sometimes it feels like you're being restrained while Saturn transits in your sign—and you are! The restraints are the limitations imposed by what is realistically possible and can also come from the social system itself. Cooperating with the rules makes your life easier—going against them will definitely provide setbacks. The problem is that the rules are changing, making it more difficult to determine an assured course of action. Look for situations that include growth potential, but watch out for your fears. They can be pure dead weight!

Uranus continues its transit in Aquarius, illuminating your need to allow your individuality to shine through your career and life path choices. The rebellious side of you needs some room to breathe. (Yes, you definitely have one!) The very slow-moving planets, Neptune and Pluto, draw your attention to the importance of making choices that favor healthy progress. Neptune highlights your solar Tenth House of career and reputation, and you may feel very strongly that it's time to surrender your life to a path that truly allows you to make a difference in the world. It's easy to be overly idealistic during this cycle, though, and you may also be tempted to make choices that would satisfy someone else more than satisfying your own needs. Pluto's influence targets the area of healing and emotional attachment, and you may become increasingly aware of the deeper motivations driving you in your choices and actions. This is an excellent cycle for the exploration of metaphysical studies and also marks a time when you become more aware of your understanding of the ultimate transformational experiences of life.

There are four solar eclipses during the year 2000, an unusual occurrence indicating the potential for critical changes. The impact of the eclipses is much like an intensified awareness of issues or needs. The year 2000 eclipses highlight your need to balance the changes that will allow you to open your horizons and give your creative ideas room to grow with your responsibilities to family and tradition. In some respects, you will develop new traditions as you release many of the drives and motivations that have held you back. It's time to fashion traditions of your own. Alterations in your family hierarchy can emerge, and the lines between factions are drawn around philosophical differences.

If you were born between April 20 and 24, you're experiencing an exciting cycle that can awaken your unique talents and abilities. Uranus is transiting in quintile aspect to your Sun, marking a period of powerful self-expression. This is an excellent time to study with a master teacher, or, if you're confident in your abilities, to explore options that will allow you to further develop your skills. If you teach, you may find that you're attracting prodigious students and that working with them inspires a renewed sense of hope.

If you were born between April 23 and 28, you're feeling the impact of Neptune transiting in square aspect to your Sun. This can be a confusing period, particularly if you are unclear about the best direction to pursue in regard to your career. You are also more apt to be led astray by others who have their own interests foremost in their minds; therefore it is crucial that you explore what is real for you before you make major changes. Your desire during this cycle centers around a need to incorporate greater compassion into your life and to let go of the trappings that inhibit your expression of love and creativity; but knowing what to release and when to let it go can create confusion. Consider this a period of unburdening—a time when you determine that you can let go of the attitudes, fears, and circumstances that are not in harmony with your higher needs. Develop your spirituality and make a deliberate connection to your inner self, but balance that with activities and experiences that ground your energy. The trap of this cycle is excessive idealism; the hope is surrendering to true peace.

If you were born between April 29 and May 5, you're making a series of major adjustments. Pluto's transit in quincunx aspect to your Sun stimulates the release of attachments and helps you get in touch with your inhibitions and self-defeating attitudes. Intimate relationships and joint financial matters can be the catalyst for alterations, and although you may not be able to just walk away from a nonproductive situation, you're certainly ready to change the way you deal with it. Taxes, inheritance, and shared resources can be frustrating, but accomplishing resolution is probable, though you may not like the arrangements! Watch for health issues, since weaknesses in the body are likely to surface, but in a manner that is a bit confounding. The complex interweaving of body, mind, and spirit is very apparent during this cycle, and when one element of your life is out of adjustment, symptoms can surface in another area. So, if it appears that money matters are the problem, it's quite conceivable that the issue underneath it all is a lack of trust or a fear of intimacy! These conundrums are common during this phase, and the solutions are as variable as an individual's needs. Just don't be content to settle for something that simply scratches the surface when you may really need a complete renovation!

If you were born between May 2 and 21, you're feeling the pressure and discipline of Saturn transiting in conjunction to your Sun. This is a testing cycle, and if you've been making choices and changes that reflect and support your true needs, the outcome of this period can be one of confirmation. Still, you'll be asking questions of yourself and your circumstances to ascertain whether or not you're in the right situation for your current requirements. Responsibilities can loom large, and if your burden seems too heavy, it may be time to drop part of it, particularly if you're carrying more than your share of the load. In the areas of your life where you've been making excuses and not taking responsibility for fulfilling your needs, it's time to determine what's in the way. This is a major maturation phase and marks a period that is akin to laying a foundation, and you want to make that foundation stable, strong, and capable of enduring through time. Therefore, eliminating situations that can undermine that strength is necessary. Saturn conjuncts your Sun once every twenty-eight to thirty years, a cycle that usually lasts for about a year. It's a critical year—a time to evaluate, test, and clarify who you are, what you need, and where you're going. Look in the mirror and ask yourself these questions, and trust that the reflection you see will be one of truth and honesty. If at any time in your life you're going to need honesty with yourself, this is it! Take advantage of this test, because it is a powerful gift.

If you were born between May 5 and 12, you're experiencing the disruptive influence of Uranus transiting in square aspect to your Sun. This cycle clearly contrasts with Saturn's push for stability described above, and when these two phases are happening at the same time, it's tempting to try to wipe the slate clean and start over. Fortunately, your previous learning experiences can be a valuable asset in helping you determine where you need to break away and free yourself and where you need to stand firm through what can be a stormy period. However, it is absolutely crucial that you determine where the inhibitions reside in your life, why they are there, and what you need to do to release them. Blind rebellion will only create setbacks, but serious evolutionary change will allow you to dig into your attitudes and determine how to unlock your wings so that you can learn to fly. Granted, those first attempts leaving terra firma can seem rather disconcerting to a Taurus because you like to feel the stability of earth beneath your feet. Think of this as a time when you learn to jump higher and trust that gravity will bring you where you need to land, but don't try jumping with too much weight in your backpack!

Tools to Make a Difference

Since the unsettling effects of changes around you can leave you feeling out of control, you need to find things that have a centering and grounding effect. Saturn's transit can seem rather heavy, and the unreliable alterations in twenty-first century life can leave you feeling uncertain. One thing, though, is always certain: your inner self and the connection you have to that serene voice is a tremendous asset. Cultivate your appreciation for your own resourcefulness. Begin to think about why you're working so hard, and incorporate time into your schedule to enjoy the fruits of your labors. Connect with nature more frequently. Let your sensual side operate to its fullest somewhere, whether it's through a trusting sexual relationship or channeled into a creatively expressive endeavor. This is the time to embrace the essence of your being and to appreciate all that you are.

You may also feel more physically tense, and staying active helps maintain your endurance, but you also need to concentrate on increasing your flexibility. Your body's definitely showing its weaknesses, but at least you know where to start on improvements! To help relax, try herbal tea containing hops, chamomile, and valerian in the evening when you're ready to wind down. Ask your massage therapist to use an oil scented with clary sage to help relieve tension. If you're feeling a bit depressed, try inhalations of patchouli, geranium, or frankincense. Since your throat tends to respond to stress rather easily, keep a throat-soothing tea on hand.

During your meditations, allow your consciousness to float to a space of inner calm. Once you're relaxed, imagine that you are walking just beyond your door, but as you open it, you feel cool, moist air scented with the freshness of spring. As you step outside, you enter a beautiful garden filled with the most amazing colorful flowers and lush greens of every shade. In the center of the garden is a tree, and hanging from the tree is a magnificent swing. You cannot resist the swing and gently begin to push yourself away from the earth, holding firmly to the ropes as you swing higher and higher. Your vantage point from the utmost arc of the swing allows you to see a world that is peaceful and perfect, and you can see the path that will take you there. When you return to your normal consciousness, remember that anytime you need to change your perspective, it might be as simple as swinging from your garden tree!

Initiating the Millennium

The challenge of creating a sturdy foundation for your long-range plans has never been so important as it is now. Entering the millennium knowing that you are on target increases your confidence in yourself and your goals, but you also know that you must do the work necessary to manifest them. This is the time to do the painstaking work of generating reliable support, building a framework that will withstand the tests of time.

♉

Affirmation for the Year

Everything I do in the name of love keeps
the flame of hope burning brightly in my life.

Taurus/January

In the Spotlight
Making your mark is easy if you have well-defined goals. You're concentrating on practical matters that allow you to advance your career.

Wellness and Keeping Fit
To effectively reduce the impact of stress, stay active. Fitness classes are good challenges. Get to the core of any chronic distress, tackling issues from multiple levels, including the psychological level.

Love and Life Connections
Deeply romantic desires can meet with practical frustrations, particularly if there's an obstacle in your path. To revitalize love, travel or share a time of retreat near the New Moon on January 6 to talk over your hopes and dreams and let your passions have free rein. Family issues can loom large during the lunar eclipse on January 20, when situations previously under wraps percolate to the surface. Release unrealistic expectations.

Finance and Success
Financial concerns center around tax or joint resources and can spoil your plans if you fail to address the best ways to handle them. You're the master of practical finance, but emotional influences may have warped your judgment. Now it's time to sort through those matters. Career pressures are on the rise after January 20, when you're vulnerable if you've not been paying attention to changes in command or revised expectations.

Cosmic Insider Tip
Worrying about your security can actually waste energy that is much better applied to the task. Fears forcing you to hold onto something may be unfounded. Look at the bigger picture.

Rewarding Days
5, 6, 10, 11, 15, 16, 19, 20, 23, 24

Challenging Days
1, 2, 8, 9, 21, 22, 27, 28, 30

Affirmation for the Month
I am willing to put the effort into making my dreams a reality.

Taurus/February

In the Spotlight
Career and situations that promote your advancement and strengthen your reputation are paramount. Part of your success is determined by the image you create for yourself. Much of what you do now will make a lasting impression.

Wellness and Keeping Fit
Enrolling in a tai chi or martial arts class can be quite stimulating since you are fascinated by physical disciplines that are intermingled with philosophical teachings.

Love and Life Connections
The Sun's eclipse on February 5 draws your attention to your life path and the reasons you've made specific choices, including relationship commitments. The influence from your parents cannot be understated, and a family crisis can bring that into focus. Breaking the pattern of family fate can be accomplished without total destruction. Seek support from others with open-minded attitudes.

Finance and Success
Changes in your career may be voluntary, but may also be due to circumstances beyond your control. It's time to break out of inhibiting ruts and move onto a path that allows you to grow and prosper on all levels. Network and commune with others in your field to build your reputation, and take advantage of the Full Moon on February 19 to make presentations or showcase your talents.

Cosmic Insider Tip
Mercury turns retrograde on February 21, and from that time through the end of the month you'll accomplish more by concentrating on situations already in motion.

Rewarding Days
1, 2, 6, 8, 11, 12, 15, 16, 19, 20, 29, 30

Challenging Days
4, 5, 17, 18, 24, 25

Affirmation for the Month
I am responsible for the fulfillment of my own destiny.

Taurus/March

In the Spotlight
Excessive idealism can set up future disappointments, so before you make promises, carefully consider potential outcomes. Think of this as a period of preparation, research, and networking. Concrete circumstances are more reliable later.

Wellness and Keeping Fit
The inner aspects of fitness are important. You're also in an excellent cycle for utilizing creative visualization. Extra rest from March 1-24 prepares you for a period of increased activity.

Love and Life Connections
Social situations near the New Moon on March 6 provide an opportunity to meet unique individuals. Your reticence to express feelings of love and tenderness gives way to an easier connection after March 13, and by the Full Moon on March 19, romance is blossoming. Love creates transformational changes and from March 22-26 brings you face to face with your fears of intimacy.

Finance and Success
Until Mercury completes its retrograde cycle on March 14, you may feel stymied by situations you cannot control. Vague promises leave you feeling uncertain about your career, and if changes are underway, you may not see where they're heading. Leave room for unexpected developments, and take advantage of openings created by another stepping aside. Finances improve, but you're reluctant to spend.

Cosmic Insider Tip
Although Jupiter is in your sign, there is conflict from Neptune's illusory energy. It's almost like being stuck in heavy fog. Travel with care and wait a while before you make commitments.

Rewarding Days
1, 5, 6, 9, 10, 13, 14, 18, 19, 27, 28

Challenging Days
2, 3, 16, 17, 22, 23, 24, 30, 31

Affirmation for the Month
I believe in myself and trust my intuitive insights.

Taurus/April

In the Spotlight
Mars and Jupiter bring their fiery stimuli into your life, prompting confidence and assertiveness. It's the perfect time to emphasize a pet project, take a stand on important issues, or blaze a trail toward advancement.

Wellness and Keeping Fit
Staying active gives you the energy you need to get everything done. You need a healthy outlet for your competitive edge. Training with an expert puts you right on target.

Love and Life Connections
You're now ready to take the risk of going after the one you adore. Your confident edge can be highly attractive, and you're not likely to take "no" for an answer if you sense that the object of your affection is interested. Travel can factor into romance, and a fresh outlook emerges during the New Moon on April 4. Romance fares best from April 1-6, and then after April 23.

Finance and Success
Promoting your ideas, creations, or yourself secures your position, although you may have strong competition in the process. Your endurance wins the day, and your practical sensibility can attract an excellent opportunity to advance or invest. Avoid rash actions near the Full Moon on April 18, when pushing tradition aside too quickly can get you into trouble.

Cosmic Insider Tip
It's been over eleven years since Mars and Jupiter have transited together in your sign. The doors you open now can set the stage for amazing growth, and the platform looks secure.

Rewarding Days
1, 2, 5, 6, 7, 10, 11, 14, 15, 23, 24, 25, 29, 30

Challenging Days
12, 13, 18, 19, 20, 26, 27

Affirmation for the Month
I am confident in my abilities to create a life of abundance.

Taurus/May

In the Spotlight
This is definitely your month, and if you've set your mind on something, the potential of getting it is quite strong. Clarity of intention in cooperation with your highest needs brings delightful and memorable results.

Wellness and Keeping Fit
On some levels, you simply feel that indulging your every whim is the least you deserve. Incorporating healthy options into your daily routine strengthens your vitality. Maintaining flexibility is paramount.

Love and Life Connections
Love flows through your heart; you're experiencing an exceptional period of attraction. Talk about your feelings from May 1-14, when expressing affection in myriad ways is easy. You may feel that you have a new lease on life with the Taurus New Moon on May 3. Partnerships are highlighted during the Full Moon on May 18, when the old guard drops away. Hello, true love!

Finance and Success
Investments grow rapidly, although what was once a stable asset may seem like a roller coaster for a while. Real property fares well, and you may be moving or renovating property. Purely speculative ventures require further research, especially in a changing climate. Artistic and creative ventures are especially rewarding this month, so use your special talents to help you get ahead.

Cosmic Insider Tip
Bridging the gap between the inner and outer worlds is easier, but you have to start with the connection to your inner self.

Rewarding Days
3, 4, 7, 8, 11, 12, 21, 22, 26, 30, 31

Challenging Days
9, 10, 16, 17, 23, 24, 25

Affirmation for the Month
My words and actions are guided by a higher love.

Taurus/June

In the Spotlight
Financial planning keeps you on firm footing, allowing you to make the most of your resources. Time management becomes a critical factor. Think of your time as money before you agree to obligate it!

Wellness and Keeping Fit
Diversify your fitness activities to avoid losing interest. Psychological dimensions of wellness are important, and you'll discover that ignoring emotional issues drains your energy. Talk about your concerns.

Love and Life Connections
Your commitment opens the way for deeper levels of understanding, but you're likely to run headlong into your own inhibitions during the Full Moon on June 16. Your partner's fears can also be awakened as you're challenged to leave the past behind. If you're single, embrace the experience of directing the course of your life on your own terms to increase your self-confidence. Newfound freedom emerges after June 20.

Finance and Success
Business deals hinge on budgetary details, and a power broker stepping into the picture during the New Moon on June 2 can threaten your plans unless you're armed with information. Meetings, presentations, or business travel can alter the course of your career, and your ideas attract an appreciative audience. Sign contracts from June 8-22. Reconsider unfinished plans after June 23.

Cosmic Insider Tip
Disruptions are less threatening since you're standing on fairly certain ground, but that does not mean you can close your mind. Remaining open to new ideas keeps you one step ahead.

Rewarding Days
3, 4, 7, 8, 9, 17, 18, 22, 23, 27, 28

Challenging Days
5, 6, 12, 13, 14, 19, 20, 21

Affirmation for the Month
I honor my needs to love fully and to be loved in return.

Taurus/July

In the Spotlight
With two solar eclipses and one lunar eclipse, this month is filled with intense changes. For you, this is a time to expand your horizons and articulate your plans and ideas with clarity and confidence. Know what you want!

Wellness and Keeping Fit
Take a break. Brief excursions offer healthy diversions, and giving your mind something to digest is important, too. Get in touch with the earth to ground and balance your energy.

Love and Life Connections
Healing your relationships with siblings encourages new directions during the solar eclipse on July 1. Love relationships prosper through a meeting of the minds, and sharing a journey near the time of the lunar eclipse on July 16 can open exceptional dimensions of understanding. By July 30, when the second solar eclipse arises, family issues can reach a critical point. The hierarchy is evolving.

Finance and Success
Networking and getting in touch with old contacts open a world of possibilities. Jupiter enters your solar Second House, marking several months of increased resources. Wait until Mercury is direct (after July 17) to sign long-term contracts or make major purchases, since obligations made during this time can have hidden problems. Thinking of buying a new car? Invest from July 18-22.

Cosmic Insider Tip
Emotionally bound issues alter the course of the economy, and your own resources may change along with those of the collective. Fortunately, you're on an upward spiral!

Rewarding Days
1, 2, 5, 6, 14, 15, 20, 21, 24, 25, 29

Challenging Days
3, 4, 9, 10, 11, 17, 18, 30, 31

Affirmation for the Month
My words reflect compassionate understanding.

Taurus/August

In the Spotlight

Your playful side needs room to operate, although integrating fun with family obligations can leave somebody out of the picture. Extending your budget can also be a problem unless you've planned ahead. Otherwise, simplifying may be your only option!

Wellness and Keeping Fit

Tension increases. Uncontrollable situations can drain your energy, but you can rebuild by working out regularly and altering your diet.

Love and Life Connections

Some elements of home life are pleasurable, and making changes that improve your environment can soften turmoil; but there is friction on the home front that builds to a peak during the Full Moon on August 15. Your feelings of love may be challenged if someone from the past surfaces. Romance blossoms during the New Moon on August 29 as fear begins to subside.

Finance and Success

Alterations in your career path can lead to competition, and you're ready to take a stand for yourself and your ideals. If you're dissatisfied, you may feel it's finally time to strike out on a new path. Money can be a key factor, particularly if you're not being paid what you're worth; but that's changing as you create a stable platform that allows room for your artistry—and pays you what you deserve. Make your move after August 23.

Cosmic Insider Tip

Your powers of attraction are operating at peak capacity, and putting your efforts and energy into something you hold dear adds to your momentum during the New Moon on August 29.

Rewarding Days

1, 2, 10, 11, 12, 16, 20, 21, 25, 29, 30

Challenging Days

6, 7, 8, 13, 14, 27, 28

Affirmation for the Month

Love and logic work together to create fulfillment of my needs.

Taurus/September

In the Spotlight
Keeping up with the details at work may leave you feeling like you're behind the eight ball, especially if finances are not improving rapidly enough. Money may not be the real problem.

Wellness and Keeping Fit
Consulting with a health care practitioner helps provide the insights that lead to improvements. Eliminate stress when possible. Otherwise, alter your routine and improve your nutrition to better support your changing needs.

Love and Life Connections
Unfulfilled expectations undermine the integrity of a close relationship. Express what's in your heart during the Full Moon on September 13, and if you still can't get past barriers, talk about your concerns with a close friend. Differences in values emerge as a primary problem and can be the final straw if you cannot reach resolutions. You are in no mood to change who you are and what you need.

Finance and Success
Artistic endeavors offer a chance for you to showcase your talents and build your reputation, even if you are operating in a competitive arena. Delays in receiving money owed to you can dampen your enthusiasm. You may be unwilling to sit on a nonproductive investment. Partnership options are promising after September 25, but what are you required to bring to the table?

Cosmic Insider Tip
Setting reasonable boundaries puts you at an advantage after September 17, although some are likely to accuse you of being too stubborn. Remind them that stability is one of your best assets!

Rewarding Days
7, 8, 12, 13, 16, 17, 18, 21, 22, 26

Challenging Days
2, 3, 9, 10, 11, 23, 24, 29, 30

Affirmation for the Month
My work is rewarding on many levels.

Taurus/October

In the Spotlight

Social situations provide opportunities to advance your reputation. Relationships take a high priority, but there are barriers that must first be addressed!

Wellness and Keeping Fit

Invigorating recreational activities fill fitness requirements. Resolving chronic problems requires action on your part. Question health professionals if you're uncertain about your treatment.

Love and Life Connections

Partnerships come into intense focus, and if you truly appreciate one another it's important to share your affections to stabilize your relationship. Resistance can arise if you're struggling with feelings of attraction to someone else, although the appropriate nature of a new relationship comes into question near the time of the Full Moon on October 13. Deception can create major problems during the New Moon on October 27.

Finance and Success

Contractual negotiations follow a rocky path, and you'll probably prefer to wait until you feel more confident about an agreement. Although Mercury retrogrades from October 18 to November 7, it will seem like it's in retrograde all month! Wavering commitments leave you wondering who you can trust, so keep your eye on obligations to make sure you can carry the load on your own if necessary.

Cosmic Insider Tip

Spending money before it's in your hand creates anxiety from October 1-10, although you may feel you have no choice in the matter. Try to find the best deal and go from there.

Rewarding Days

4, 5, 10, 14, 15, 18, 22, 23, 31

Challenging Days

1, 7, 8, 20, 21, 27, 28

Affirmation for the Month

I joyfully extend my appreciation to others for their support.

Taurus/November

In the Spotlight
Working cooperatively with others tests your patience, particularly if you're stuck with responsibilities that do not belong to you. To get everything done, you may have to let go of nonproductive elements.

Wellness and Keeping Fit
You may be tempted to try something extraordinary for which you are not fully prepared. Avoid high-risk situations and take care driving. You're accident-prone right now.

Love and Life Connections
Tension concerning partnerships builds to a peak during the Taurus Full Moon on November 11, when your patience may finally be spent. Before you assume that excessive controls come from your partner, examine other elements in your life. Perhaps your partner is only a convenient target for other frustrations; however, if you're in an unhealthy situation, it's definitely time to change it. Explore underlying issues near the New Moon on November 25.

Finance and Success
Communication in general is filled with misunderstandings and the potential for deception. Others who view you as competition can undermine your position, and attempting a peaceful option can actually leave you vulnerable. The facts work to your advantage, but you have to employ them! Contracts and legal matters fare best after November 18.

Cosmic Insider Tip
Convening with others who share your philosophies strengthens your position after November 14, but talking religion and politics with some people definitely gets you into hot water.

Rewarding Days
1, 2, 6, 7, 10, 11, 14, 15, 19, 20, 28, 29

Challenging Days
3, 4, 16, 17, 18, 23, 24, 30

Affirmation for the Month
My intuitive insights are a valuable asset.

Taurus/December

In the Spotlight
Academic pursuits, travel, advertising, and publishing are the outlets that help you expand your options at this time. Your ideas can capture the imagination of others, although your own ability to change can be called into question.

Wellness and Keeping Fit
Competitive sports can be a positive outlet for releasing tension and hostility, but you need to keep boundaries clearly defined to avoid injury. You may need more rest than usual midmonth.

Love and Life Connections
Your attraction to someone may be nothing more than infatuation, but that might not be enough to stop you from exploring it! The Full Moon on December 11 stirs your imagination, prompting you to seek romance and share your dreams. More realistic qualities emerge by the time of the solar eclipse on December 25, when spiritual ideals and hope for the future align your heart's desire with your highest needs.

Finance and Success
Business travel or conferences provide an excellent forum to share your ideas and talents from December 1-9, and again after December 23. Determining exactly where your company is heading can be confusing early in the month. Your money seems to be heavily obligated, but investments are growing—just not fast enough!

Cosmic Insider Tip
Channeling your imagination into creative ventures after December 9 is safer than banking on a vague situation. Enjoy the ecstasy of romance, even if you cannot control where it's taking you.

Rewarding Days
3, 4, 8, 9, 12, 13, 16, 17, 25, 26, 31

Challenging Days
1, 2, 14, 15, 20, 21, 28, 29

Affirmation for the Month
I trust my higher self to guide my words, steps, and actions.

Taurus Action Table

These dates reflect the best—but not the only—times for success and ease in these activities, according to your Sun sign.

	JAN	FEB	MAR	APR	MAY	JUN	JUL	AUG	SEPT	OCT	NOV	DEC
Move								7-21				
Start a class	6, 7						1, 2					
Join a club			6, 7									
Ask for a raise					4							
Look for work	1-17								8-28			
Get pro advice	1-2, 27-29	24, 25	22, 23	18-20	16, 17	12, 13	9, 10	6, 7	2-3, 29-30	27, 28	23, 24	20, 21
Get a loan	3-4, 30-31	26, 27	24-26	21, 22	18-20	14-16	12, 13	8, 9	4, 5	2-3, 29-30	25, 26	23, 24
See a doctor				13-29					8-27			
Start a diet	25, 26	21-23	20, 21	16, 17	13-15	10, 11	7, 8	3, 4, 31	1, 27, 28	24-26	21, 22	18, 19
End relationship					18							
Buy clothes								22-31	1-6			
Get a makeover					4, 5							
New romance								29, 30				
Vacation	5, 6	1-3, 29	1, 27, 28	23-25	21, 22	17, 18	14-16	10-12	7, 8	4-6, 31	1-2, 28-29	25-27

Gemini

The Twins
May 20 to June 19

♊

Element:	Air
Quality:	Mutable
Polarity:	Yang/Masculine
Planetary Ruler:	Mercury
Meditation:	"My mind is linked to the Source."
Gemstone:	Agate
Power Stones:	Emerald, aquamarine, alexandrite
Key Phrase:	"I think"
Glyph:	Pillars of Duality ♊
Anatomy:	Hands, arms, shoulders, lungs, nervous system
Colors:	Yellow, orange
Animal:	Monkeys, talking birds, flying insects
Myths/Legends:	Peter Pan, Castor and Pollux
House:	Third
Opposite Sign:	Sagittarius
Flower:	Lily of the Valley
Key Word:	Versatility

Positive Expression:	Misuse of Energy:
Articulate	Gossipy
Flexible	Unsettled
Perceptive	Unfocused
Clever	Prankish
Sophisticated	Erratic
Rational	Fickle
Perspicacious	

Gemini

Your Ego's Strengths and Shortcomings

You're blessed with the gift of youthful curiosity leading you through a lifetime of diversity and fascination with interesting ideas. Your intellectual focus brings you in contact with all kinds of people and situations, helping you fulfill your role in the zodiac as "The Questioner."

Your adaptability aids you when you're facing stubborn attitudes or unusual circumstances, and you're likely to be the one called upon to act as a negotiator since you can identify common ground. Making connections is natural for you and attracts people from all walks of life, helping to satisfy the development of your multifarious mind. A love of travel or literature may prompt your pursuit of academic goals and also colors your relationships. Because you're usually juggling several projects at once, others who are uncertain of your commitment may feel frustrated by your mercurial nature. It's fortunate that you can talk your way out of tight spots, since sometimes you can be accused of playing both sides against the middle!

Through your easy connection to the communicative energy of Mercury, you are likely to develop a multifaceted personality. Intuitive awareness and logical perception are a natural blend, and you understand that some things cannot be answered through rationale alone. Your ingenuity stems from this integration. The thirst for awareness driving you to continually explore ultimately leads you to surrender your mind to the universal mind, where you discover your true nature and find answers to your most insatiable questions.

Shining Your Love Light

Finding a single individual to fill your needs in a relationship may seem impossible since you're likely to have many friends who fulfill different levels of need. Before you decide to settle into a singular commitment, you'll play the field until you find a person who can offer the intellectual connection you crave while encouraging your sense of personal freedom. You can be an excellent partner, but may have difficulty expressing the complexities of deeper emotional issues.

However, once you experience a true meeting of the minds, it's easy to allow the love in your heart to pour forth.

As an air sign, you love to talk and socialize and may feel most comfortable around the other air signs—Gemini, Libra and Aquarius—whose social nature makes you feel right at home. You're powerfully attracted to your zodiac opposite, Sagittarius, whose adventurous capacities can be thrilling—until you run into his or her wanderlust.

Aries' independence is invigorating, and you'll adore the passion. With Taurus, earthiness is the key to pleasure, although you may get bored with his or her easygoing pace. Another Gemini can be fun and will understand your need for change, but you can drive one another to distraction if your personal boundaries are weak. Cancer's nurturing sensitivity is comforting, but financial squabbles can ensue if he or she is too protective. Uplifted by Leo's flair for the dramatic and heartwarming support, you may feel genuine love. With Virgo, you're fine in the realm of ideas, but can become restless if he or she gets stuck in all the details.

Drawn to Libra's alluring artistry and good taste, you'll always feel an easy comfort. Scorpio's emotional intensity is fascinating until you get caught in the web of possessiveness. With Capricorn you can develop a deep connection, but may never feel completely free to be yourself. Aquarius shares your philosophies while stimulating your need to reach beyond limitations. Fantasy-filled nights are the key to enjoying Pisces, but you can get confused about what he or she wants during normal waking hours!

Making Your Place in the World

You need a career path that offers independence and flexibility, and may actually alter it more than once over the course of your lifetime. By developing your communication skills and intellectual processes, your choices can reflect precisely what you need: variety.

You can be successful as an educator or counselor, and have a knack for public relations, politics, advertising, broadcasting, writing, or speaking. Highly technical careers, including computer science, may hold your interest, since they provide an opportunity to work with your hands and your mind. Exercising your manual dexterity in drafting, musical pursuits, design, dentistry, or secretarial areas can be satisfying. Even the performing arts can provide an excellent path in fields like acting, pantomime, storytelling, clowning, juggling, or comedy.

Power Plays

Since you are keenly aware of the power of the mind, your provocation to show your best qualities arises when knowledge and ideas hold the keys to influencing growth and change. Others may look to you for insight and understanding, and you feel powerful when you grasp an idea clearly and can illustrate it to others.

Although dazzling others with your brilliance may be one option, you will be most satisfied when you've gone beneath the surface into the realm of true wisdom. Otherwise, your contagious enthusiasm and wit can project an air of superficiality that can undermine your position. You're the bridge builder—creating the path that links what has gone before with what is yet to come. Your power may be most evident when divergent factions struggle for resolution to a crisis.

Understanding the importance of education is natural for you, and regardless of your work, you may find that you're continually supporting the needs of youth, whose nature will always be akin to your own. Your sense of power emerges when you connect to the strength of Divine Intelligence, and from that lofty plane you can lift the spirit of humanity to heights that empower us as a whole.

Famous Geminis

Paula Abdul, Josephine Baker, Sandra Bernhard, Bjorn Borg, George Bush, Ralph Edwards, Lukas Haas, Dan Jansen, Curtis Mayfield, Marilyn Monroe, Ally Sheedy, Brooke Shields, Johnny Weismuller, Venus Williams, Queen Victoria.

The Year Ahead
for Gemini

This is your year! If there are obstacles in your path, you can either see a way around them or use them as stepping stones to further your aims. Your attitude is one of confidence. Development of your career stems from the integration of your hard work and past experience, but your advancement is due more to your ability to pave the way with fresh ideas that are a testimony to your faith in the higher order.

The great news is that Jupiter—the planet of abundance, prosperity, and expansion—is in your sign from July through the end of the year. With good planning, you can use this cycle to open doors and make connections that will serve you for years to come. Since Jupiter transits in your sign only once every twelve years, this is, indeed, a remarkable time to take advantage of opportunities along your path. Prior to the summer, Jupiter will be transiting through your solar Twelfth House, marking a period of spiritual confirmation and expanding inner awareness. By utilizing the first half of the year as a period of surrender to your inner self, you can build a connection to your spiritual essence that, once you're ready to take flight, functions as your wings. It is the cycle of Jupiter in your sign that provides the stimulus to soar! The potential downfalls during these Jupiter transits revolve around a tendency to overdo it. Be particularly attentive to your promises, since in your time of confidence, you may commit to things that are difficult to deliver. Realize that more may be required than you initially expect, and you may need room for adjustments. It's also crucial that you find the best possible way to show your gratitude, and that you accept the accolades and rewards coming your way with grace and humility.

Saturn's transit works like a preview for the following two years. During most of the year, Saturn's energy of restraint and clarification will be stimulating your need to release the vestiges of your past that you've outgrown; but during August and September, Saturn slips into Gemini for a brief period, allowing you to glimpse challenges you'll face during the years 2001 and 2002. Use this preview to discover requirements that must be answered and to shoulder responsibilities with the understanding that they are part of your master plan.

The slower-moving planets—Uranus, Neptune, and Pluto—also offer particular challenges. Most notable is the continuation of Pluto traveling in opposition to your sign. The purging represented by this cycle takes a while, with the intensity increasing when Pluto makes the exact opposition to your Sun. You can check your birth date below to find out if this is the year you will experience the exact opposition, but even if you've completed the "exact hit," or if it's arrival is sometime in the future, you're feeling the stimulus to clear out destructive and unnecessary elements from your life. That's especially important this year, since you'll feel eager to exercise those wings and can ascend to greater heights if you're carrying a lighter load, particularly in regard to your personal relationships! Uranus and Neptune continue their transits through the Ninth House of your solar chart, opening your consciousness to new perspectives on spirituality and higher law.

There are four solar eclipses this year, bringing heightened awareness of your needs to balance your values with those of others and to reach a connection of heart and mind with those who share the circle of your life. Philosophical issues require your attention during the solar eclipse in February, and you may feel optimistic about making plans to improve your education or expand your business. During the summer months, there are two eclipses. On July 1 you're challenged to examine your values and personal worth, but by the time of the eclipse on July 30, your attention is drawn to delivering an important message. The last of the four eclipses occurs on December 25, when joint resources, inheritance, or debt issues can loom large.

If you were born on May 21 or 22, you're feeling the impact of Saturn's transit in conjunction to your Sun. This cycle will continue next year and marks a time of self-evaluation and the need to set reasonable limitations. Carrying burdens that are not yours to shoulder can be an act of futility, especially if you find that others are not appreciative of your support. However, those responsibilities that are yours must be satisfied, and your attitudes will determine whether or not you see this as a difficult test or a strengthening challenge. Initiate a long-term educational plan or pursue a worthy career challenge. You may feel that you're undergoing more intensive criticism and can also be more critical of others. In teaching, research, or study, these attributes have a positive outlet. Commitments you make now will be taken seriously—by you and by others, so try not to make promises unless you intend to do everything in your power to keep them. It's a wonderful time to make a promise to take care of yourself, and giving extra attention to your physical health now will help to strengthen your sense of personal power.

If you were born from May 23 to 29, you're feeling inspired to surrender to your creative muse. Neptune's transit in trine aspect to your Sun alters your perspective and lifts your awareness above the ordinary into the realm of compassionate understanding. Your spirituality blossoms when integrated into your daily life. Charitable outreach, community involvement, or volunteer service can present a means to give back and make a difference in the quality of life. Your imaginative and creative sensibilities are enhanced, and you may feel a strong impulse to develop or fine-tune your talents and artistic abilities as a means of expressing the compassion stirring in your soul. You're aware of a more natural flow and profound sense of peace, and you may find it easier to synchronize your actions with the rhythm of your inner self. It's time to forgive past hurts, to let go of pain, and to surrender to the guidance of your higher self.

If you were born from May 30 to June 6, you're feeling the impact of Pluto transiting in opposition to your Sun. This may be one of the most challenging periods of your life as you face the need to eliminate outworn attitudes or clear out unnecessary elements as a means of inviting true healing. You may meet confrontational, power-based situations that force you to re-evaluate your priorities, your goals, and your sense of self. Relationships can be exceptionally challenging, but can also be the source of your evolution. Becoming involved in restorational projects or activities can be a natural outreach of this cycle, and whether you're refinishing furniture, revising a manuscript, or getting your body into shape, you'll find that your ability to clear out the unnecessary elements works like a charm. Think of this as a period of pruning and transplantation. With proper care, the experience can lead to revitalization and amazing growth. You may not welcome outside interference now, although there are certainly outside influences playing a significant role in the changing circumstances of your life. The key issues are those revolving around power and its use and abuse. Your test is to determine the source of your own strength and to utilize it for constructive, healing transformation.

If you were born from June 6 to 13, you're uplifted while Uranus transits in trine aspect to your Sun. However, you're also challenged by Chiron transiting in opposition to your Sun. These two influences operating at the same time stimulate significant questions about your sense of purpose, and you may feel more courageous about stepping outside your old boundaries and onto a more fulfilling life path. Your intuitive instincts are operating in overdrive, and by blending your flashes of insight with data and logic, you may be able to arrive at conclusions that are not only unique, but innovative and trendsetting. However, if your ego gets out of control and you become too full of yourself, there's the potential of gaining notoriety instead of honor—a wounding that can certainly be a setback to progress. It's time to break free of restraint, inhibition, and self-doubt and to give your special genius room to operate. Travel can be especially enlightening, but you're also in an excellent cycle to explore cultures or philosophies that are quite different from your own. Educational pursuits, writing, publishing, or teaching provide unusual opportunities to broaden your horizons.

If you were born from June 10 to 13, you're feeling a tendency toward self-doubt and confusion since Neptune transits in sesquiquadrate to your Sun. The influence of this cycle can be rather subtle, although you may be aware of an undercurrent of uncertainty that may be difficult to pinpoint. The purpose of the cycle is to help you release concepts or prejudices that act as a barrier to expanded consciousness, but in the process, you may feel that you're traveling blindly through unfamiliar territory. By grounding yourself and maintaining your inner balance, you'll discover that it's easier to get your bearings, and you'll feel more secure. Then, the exploration becomes one of initiation into heightened awareness.

If you were born from June 14 to 21, you're taking steps to stabilize your future. Saturn transits in semisextile to your Sun, a period of deliberate focus and increasing clarity. In many ways, this period is like completing a series of prerequisites in school. With your eye on a particular goal, those requirements make sense and also strengthen your ability to meet your goals with confidence and authority. However, if you've failed to identify where you're going, you may become exhausted walking uphill toward an uncertain end. Career progress may be a key element of this cycle, although that progress may not be speeding along at the clip you prefer. On a personal level, this is an excellent time to make an assessment of your physical health and to follow a regimen that supports the balance of physical, mental, emotional, and spiritual qualities.

Tools to Make a Difference

To honor the energy of Jupiter transiting through your sign, take actions that help you identify the best directions for improving your life without overdoing it. Showing appreciation for the abundance granted to you works like a tonic to strengthen your life and stabilize your good fortune. You can do this by donating time or resources to support a worthy cause and by extending yourself to those who love you.

Your physical health may improve dramatically, and you can be particularly receptive to the incorporation of holistic and alternative healing methodologies. Treating symptoms will seem unsatisfactory if you are under the weather, and fortunately you are experiencing a cycle that allows you to probe beneath the surface for solutions. You may respond especially well to the use of aromatherapy, since you are, after all, an air sign! To help maintain strong airways, use the essential oils of basil, marjoram, lavender, frankincense, or eucalyptus in a vaporizing solution; or add the fragrances of lavender, melissa, and geranium to a massage oil. You might enjoy wearing sandalwood and ylang ylang to help lift your spirits in times of stress.

To maintain your mental clarity and focus, regular periods of meditation can be quite effective. During your meditations, certain visualizations can have a profound effect upon your attitudes. Particularly helpful are images that allow you to rise above the ordinary. Imagine that you are traveling through space in a ship that also warps time. You can easily travel to the future and choose a time into the future to return to the earth. While you travel, imagine the kind of world you want to see when you step onto the planet, and then set your course for home. Be specific, and then allow yourself to experience that return to a more ideal life. When your visualization is complete, bring your consciousness back into the present, and know that you can indeed alter your future by changing the quality of your thoughts.

Initiating the Millennium

You may feel that you are truly ready for the next century and are in the perfect space to help usher in changes that will improve your life and the lives of those who look to you for support and guidance. If you sense that there is unfinished business, determine the nature of things that require completion, and get them out of the way. You're in a frame of mind that propels you toward fresh and inspirational change, but cannot fully enjoy it unless you've released unnecessary baggage.

Ⅱ

Affirmation for the Year

Sharing my joy and resources magnifies
the power of the circle of life.

Gemini/January

In the Spotlight
You're driven to accomplish the realization of an important aim. Support from your partner helps smooth rough edges, but it's your philosophical ideals that form the basis of your strength.

Wellness and Keeping Fit
Tension mounts due to professional stress. Stay active, but avoid high-risk situations or circumstances for which you are ill-prepared. Be attentive to your limits.

Love and Life Connections
Show appreciation for the strengths your partner brings into your life, finding ways to revitalize your relationship from the New Moon on January 6 through January 14. Looking for love? It may find you in the course of your travels or academic pursuits near the time of the Moon's eclipse on January 20! Sending the right signals speeds the pace of romance. Consider a retreat to an extraordinary place to breathe life into a close relationship.

Finance and Success
Plans already set in motion show progress through January 4, and then, after January 6, you're eager to press your agenda. Watch reactions since you may alienate those who could be helpful allies if you're zooming past while blazing your trail. Contracts and legal matters bring everything into focus after January 18, with your ideas forming the basis for progress. Joint finances improve this month.

Cosmic Insider Tip
Everything heads toward a grand climax during the lunar eclipse on January 20, when you're in the perfect place to bring the right people together to assure success for all concerned.

Rewarding Days
8, 9, 12, 13, 14, 17, 18, 22, 25, 26

Challenging Days
3, 4, 10, 11, 23, 24, 30, 31

Affirmation for the Month
My faith in higher ideals lights the path toward true success.

Gemini/February

In the Spotlight
While others may seek your influence or support, your motivation may derive from your desire to assure the longevity of an important project. The Sun's eclipse on February 5 marks an awakening.

Wellness and Keeping Fit
To bring your energy up to more acceptable levels, team sports or a fitness class can fill the requirements after February 13. You'll appreciate taking on a challenge.

Love and Life Connections
Transcendent experiences can arise through love, or a spiritual retreat, vacation, or a meeting of the minds can lead to romance stimulated by the Sun's eclipse on February 5. You're waking up to all sorts of possibilities and may finally feel ready to let go of old ideals. Experimenting feels safer than making a commitment, since for a while you're in love with love—especially after February 20.

Finance and Success
Semantics can be a problem, or you could be facing a pure language barrier. Fortunately, you can find a way to bridge the gap from February 3-10, but watch for manipulators whose influence can drain your resources from February 6-16. The Full Moon on February 19 marks a time when your career path takes a turn toward the most innovative fork in the road. Watch for detours during Mercury's retrograde from February 21-29.

Cosmic Insider Tip
If you're willing to go out on a limb during the solar eclipse on February 5, you may discover that you gain the right kind of acknowledgment. Others seem receptive to your unique ideas.

Rewarding Days
4, 5, 9, 10, 13, 14, 17, 18, 22, 23

Challenging Days
6, 7, 8, 19, 20, 26, 27

Affirmation for the Month
My intuition is the source of absolute genius!

Gemini/March

In the Spotlight
Communication breakdowns, mechanical problems, and misunderstandings are the sources of potholes in the path of life. Although Mercury's retrograde ends on March 13, the effects continue all month. Exercise patience along with caution.

Wellness and Keeping Fit
Your physical energy level is strong, but your motivation to stay active may lag behind. Look for alternatives to your regular routine, or consider taking up a new sport.

Love and Life Connections
An unusual person or unexpected circumstance sparks your interest from the New Moon on March 6-13. It's an excellent time to explore issues with your partner, particularly if you've gotten bogged down with mundane problems. Watch for parental interference near the Full Moon on March 19, when outworn ideals can strangle progress in a relationship.

Finance and Success
Hammering out the details of a contract progresses from March 1-13, but a final decision concerning long-range deals may not be in the works. Instead of pushing against the tide, use this as a period of discovery and explore different options for investments. Career pressures mount midmonth, then gradually subside. Work behind the scenes to gather support for your projects after March 23.

Cosmic Insider Tip
You may be caught in a very sticky situation that requires you to define your loyalties. If making a choice compromises your ideals, think again before making your statement.

Rewarding Days
2, 3, 7, 8, 11, 12, 16, 20, 21, 30, 31

Challenging Days
1, 5, 6, 18, 19, 25, 26

Affirmation for the Month
My friends are my golden treasures.

Gemini/April

In the Spotlight
You thrive in community activities, particularly if your efforts are directed toward educational programs. Working cooperatively with others gives you a chance to lead, but you're also eager to use your influence on another's behalf.

Wellness and Keeping Fit
It's your month for inner fitness. You need more time for exercises like meditation and yoga that give you a chance to reflect on your drives and deeper needs.

Love and Life Connections
The attributes of unconditional love are at your fingertips. A friendship may even blossom into a romantic connection after the New Moon on April 4. Watch for traps midmonth, since you may jump into a situation that takes a surprising turn into bizarre territory. Allow true love to guide your path during the Full Moon on April 18.

Finance and Success
Political activities can upstage the reasons you're involved in a project, although you can use this to your advantage after April 7. Sign contracts from April 14-28. Meetings and conferences give you a chance to shine, although you may resent being "categorized" by those whose viewpoints limit your options. Investments gain momentum, peaking on April 18.

Cosmic Insider Tip
Conservative and liberal factions are defining their positions, and you may discover that you don't fit either of them. Stay out of skirmishes that are not your own from April 1-21.

Rewarding Days
8, 9, 12, 16, 17, 26, 27

Challenging Days
1, 2, 14, 15, 19, 21, 22, 29, 30

Affirmation for the Month
I can bring peace to a hostile situation.

Gemini/May

In the Spotlight

Mars moves into your sign, adding its thrust to your willpower and stimulating your drive to accomplish the realization of your dreams. Focusing your energy on your priorities brings amazing results.

Wellness and Keeping Fit

Although you may feel energized, pacing yourself is crucial if you are to avoid the effects of burnout. Strength-building exercises are appropriate, as long as you remember to stretch.

Love and Life Connections

The power of your secret desires can be overwhelming, and you may be drawn to a situation that requires secrecy or cover. You may simply be experiencing the awakening of long-held dreams, yet if they appear in the form of the apparently perfect person, you may not feel ready to act. Love is easier to express after May 24, when Venus moves into your sign, but significant communication may begin around May 15.

Finance and Success

During the New Moon on May 3 you may feel that you're witnessing the emergence of priceless possibilities. By the Full Moon on May 18, a change in your routine creates improved productivity at work. Presentations or written communications provide excellent opportunities to advance your career after May 14. By May 28, you're leading the way toward certain progress.

Cosmic Insider Tip

Careful preparation makes all the difference, and by concentrating on details, completing old business, and opening your imagination, you'll be on the brink of unprecedented success.

Rewarding Days

1, 2, 5, 6, 13, 14, 15, 23, 24, 25, 28, 29

Challenging Days

11, 12, 18, 19, 20, 26, 27

Affirmation for the Month

I carefully consider the effects of my words and actions.

Gemini/June

In the Spotlight
Your ability to gain the best reception for your efforts and ideas continues to gain momentum. If you've been hoping to find a good time to make a significant change, it has arrived! Exceptional progress occurs during the first half of June.

Wellness and Keeping Fit
You need a diversion from work. Whether you're taking vacation time or just rearranging your schedule, you'll benefit from experiences that take you away from the action.

Love and Life Connections
Initiating a significant love relationship during the Gemini New Moon on June 2 lifts your spirits in the most remarkable fashion. You're more expressive and can even be comfortable in emotionally intense circumstances. An existing relationship can be revitalized, but an unhealthy connection reaches its demise from June 1-6, and you may say good-bye to such a partnership during the Full Moon on June 16.

Finance and Success
Conservative attitudes abound, so if you are to make headway incorporating changes, you must consider the demands of the traditional or existing situation. Innovative technologies offer promise from June 1-4, and your finances undergo a positive turn from June 8-13. Sign long-term contracts before June 7 and short-term agreements prior to Mercury's retrograde on June 23.

Cosmic Insider Tip
Turn your attention to finances after June 17, when making the most of your resources can turn around a precarious financial situation.

Rewarding Days
1, 2, 5, 6, 10, 11, 20, 21, 25, 29, 30

Challenging Days
7, 8, 14, 15, 16, 22, 23

Affirmation for the Month
My thoughts and actions flow from a heart of pure love.

Gemini/July

In the Spotlight

Eclipses, eclipses...everywhere! Money matters require more attention, and giving in to emotional pressures leads to poor financial decisions. Jupiter enters your sign, increasing your confidence, but caution may be required to save the day.

Wellness and Keeping Fit

Concentrate on building your endurance and strengthening muscles. Maximize your body's strength as a means of improving your immune system. Nervousness can lead to digestive problems.

Love and Life Connections

You're feeling generous now that Jupiter is in Gemini, but may be questioning your values during the Sun's eclipse on July 1. Letting someone know how you feel can seem risky, but failing to express yourself feels really awful. Intimacy issues can arise during the lunar eclipse on July 16, when old problems surface. Dealing with them now leads to healing. By the second solar eclipse on July 30, you're more focused on the future and may feel uplifted by the spiritual union you share with a partner or special friend.

Finance and Success

The potential of more volatile money markets definitely exists, and your personal investments require careful review. Eliminate debts wherever possible, and avoid signing contracts this month. Mercury's retrograde is over on July 17, but the fallout continues all month.

Cosmic Insider Tip

Completion—that's the key concept. Leaving too many things undone is too precarious. You're on the brink of fresh opportunities, and now is the time to make room for them.

Rewarding Days

3, 7, 8, 17, 18, 22, 23, 26, 27, 30

Challenging Days

1, 5, 6, 12, 13, 16, 19, 20, 21

Affirmation for the Month

My values are reflected in my choices and actions.

Gemini/August

In the Spotlight
You'll find the most significant gold mines close to home this month. Although you may philosophically extend yourself globally, your security becomes your top priority, and you're feeling the importance of close family ties.

Wellness and Keeping Fit
Outdoor activities beckon. Early morning tennis, bike rides, jogs, or walks can be your salvation, providing a fresh perspective while strengthening your body. Plus, you can enjoy the neighborhood!

Love and Life Connections
An old relationship may come back to roost. If anything is unfinished, it's time to reach closure. Since you're on fire with ideas, you may be able to propel a relationship toward the direction you desire by opening lines of communication during the Full Moon on August 15. By the New Moon on August 29, you're feeling a need to focus on your nest. You might get around to making overdue repairs!

Finance and Success
Your ideas and communicative abilities are in demand from August 7-21, when meetings, presentations, or publications boost your career and solidify your reputation. Launching an important project around the Full Moon on August 15 draws a lot of attention, and the momentum can be powerful. However, there can be hidden loopholes or competitive undermining around the corner, so stay alert.

Cosmic Insider Tip
Saturn sneaks into Gemini for a brief period, so look for sources of pressure, guilt, or frustration. You're uncovering potential tests and can get ahead by realigning your priorities.

Rewarding Days
3, 4, 13, 14, 18, 19, 22, 23, 24, 27, 31

Challenging Days
1, 2, 8, 9, 15, 16, 29, 30

Affirmation for the Month
My words can heal or hinder. The choice is mine!

Gemini/September

In the Spotlight
Philosophical disputes rock the boat, and you may discover that a long-held belief or ideal is no longer relevant to your life. Ethical concerns can play a significant role in contractual negotiations.

Wellness and Keeping Fit
Obligations at home and at work can rob you of the time you need to devote to fitness. Stress increases after September 17. Relaxation and stretching make a huge difference!

Love and Life Connections
With the Full Moon on September 13 generating an echo between your career and personal life, you may feel that you're struggling with a deep-seated desire to gain parental approval. A fascinating love relationship alters your perceptions and can provide the support you need to break away from traditions that inhibit your free self-expression. Fresh directions emerge during the New Moon on September 27. Celebrate!

Finance and Success
Speculative ventures, artistic pursuits, and investments generate wonderful rewards. You may break away from a partnership or find that it's necessary to completely revamp your role in joint ventures. Unexpected opportunities arise from September 14-22 that can certainly improve your bottom line, but be aware of those who might take unfair advantage of your good fortune and kind heart.

Cosmic Insider Tip
While Jupiter and Pluto travel in opposition, you may be stuck between the proverbial rock and hard place in contractual negotiations. Setting limits requires courage and insight.

Rewarding Days
1, 9, 10, 11, 14, 19, 20, 23, 27, 28

Challenging Days
4, 5, 6, 12, 13, 25, 26

Affirmation for the Month
I trust my higher self to guide me in all things.

Gemini/October

In the Spotlight
Power struggles continue, and the action moves clearly into the work place. Unreliable support can result from poor communication, but could also be linked to jealous undermining. Situations you control may seem few and far between.

Wellness and Keeping Fit
Stress shows its impact on your health. Isolating yourself from difficulties through activities like meditation can shift your perspective. Get a massage!

Love and Life Connections
Tense situations surface. Sometimes you may wonder if you're in Geyser National Park! Family matters expose core problems. This unsettled period could be due to a move or changes in the family you cannot control, but you can control your reactions, and to heal a situation you may have to let go. Resolve to make healthy changes in your partnership with the New Moon on October 27.

Finance and Success
Confusion from October 1-3 can be the result of mixed signals, but it could also be part of a manipulation. Step away from the action to gain a perspective on the power plays, since they escalate to a peak during the Full Moon on October 13. If everything around you is in a state of flux, you may fare well, since you are, after all, adaptable. Quick-fix solutions ring hollow. Look for long-term resolution.

Cosmic Insider Tip
High-tension aspects are unsettling for everyone, but just knowing that Mercury's in retrograde after October 17 will help you understand the situation. It's actually time for things to fall apart!

Rewarding Day
7, 8, 12, 13, 16, 20, 25, 26

Challenging Days
1, 2, 9, 10, 22, 23, 29, 30

Affirmation for the Month
With a happy heart I let go of the things I no longer need.

Gemini/November

In the Spotlight
Inspired to exercise your creative abilities, you're likely to be recognized for your special talents. Children's activities can offer an exceptional opportunity to inspire others.

Wellness and Keeping Fit
Take full advantage of your favorite winter sport. Staying active generates the energy you need to do all the things on your long list, and you just might meet a fascinating person in the process.

Love and Life Connections
Mars energizes your Fifth House of love and pleasure during the next eight weeks. Awakening the spiritual and emotional bonds of love allows you to transcend the ordinary and experience the true ecstasy of sharing your soul. Romance intensifies from November 6-13, and during the New Moon on November 25 your adoration is literally on fire. Go for it!

Finance and Success
While Mercury completes its retrograde (through November 7), you're working on unfinished business. However, your eagerness to get on with an important project ignites the support of others during the Full Moon on November 11. Investments are most productive from November 13-20, although vague information can create questions about the best direction to pursue. Work toward new agreements after November 25.

Cosmic Insider Tip
Unpredictable changes can be destabilizing around the Full Moon on November 11, but clarifying plans through open discussions helps to resolve uncertainty. Employ unique innovations.

Rewarding Days
3, 4, 8, 12, 13, 16, 21, 22, 30

Challenging Days
5, 6, 7, 11, 19, 20, 25, 26, 27

Affirmation for the Month
Expressions of love open new pathways for fulfillment.

Gemini/December

In the Spotlight
Principles of universal law and a higher moral code alter the course of agreements, and your vision about the future inspires hope for true peace and understanding. Academic pursuits, publishing, advertising, or travel advance your career.

Wellness and Keeping Fit
A vacation might be just what you need to revitalize your spirits and strengthen your body. If you cannot travel, seek inspirational alternatives.

Love and Life Connections
Love gains momentum, and you may feel that you cannot wait any longer to express how you feel. The Full Moon on December 11 brings your focus to partnerships, and defining what you need seems only natural. You're willing to set aside problems in favor of nurturing love; after all, love is the supreme healer. A soulful quality emerges on December 9, reminding you that love also defies time.

Finance and Success
Teaching and learning play a significant role in advancing your career, with conferences and communications providing an opportunity to showcase your ideas from December 4-22. Adjustments that satisfy others' demands may be necessary from December 14-18, following disagreements about the best ways to use joint resources. Put innovations to work after December 26.

Cosmic Insider Tip
The solar eclipse on December 25 emphasizes issues of attachment, but can bring up problems with inheritance and joint finances. Watch your vulnerability!

Rewarding Days
1, 2, 10, 11, 14, 15, 18, 19, 28, 29

Challenging Days
3, 4, 16, 17, 22, 23, 25, 30, 31

Affirmation for the Month
Through love, all things are possible.

Gemini Action Table

These dates reflect the best—but not the only—times for success and ease in these activities, according to your Sun sign.

	JAN	FEB	MAR	APR	MAY	JUN	JUL	AUG	SEPT	OCT	NOV	DEC
Move								22-31	1-7			
Start a class		5					31	1				
Join a club				4								
Ask for a raise						2, 3						
Look for work		7-20	14-31	1-13					29, 30	1-17	11-30	1-3
Get pro advice	3-4, 30-31	26, 27	25, 26	21, 22	18-20	14-16	12, 13	8, 9	4-6	2-3, 29-30	25-27	23, 24
Get a loan	5-7	1-3, 29	1, 27, 28	23-25	21, 22	17, 18	14-16	10-12	7, 8	4, 5, 31	28, 29	25-27
See a doctor				30	1-13				28-30	1-31	1-30	1-4
Start a diet	27-29	24, 25	22, 23	18-20	16, 17	12, 13	9-11	6, 7	2-3, 29-30	27, 28	23, 24	20, 21
End relationship						16						
Buy clothes									8-27			
Get a makeover						2, 3						
New romance									27			
Vacation	7-9	4, 5	2-3, 30-31	26, 27	23-25	19-21	17, 18	13, 14	9-11	7, 8	3, 4, 30	1-2, 27-28

Cancer
The Crab
June 20 to July 21

Element:	Water
Quality:	Cardinal
Polarity:	Yin/Feminine
Ruler:	Moon
Meditation:	"I am in touch with my inner feelings."
Gemstone:	Pearl
Power Stones:	Moonstone, chrysocolla
Key Phrase:	"I feel"
Glyph:	Breasts, crab claws ♋
Anatomy:	Stomach, breasts
Colors:	Silver, pearl white
Animal:	Crustaceans, cows, chickens
Myths/Legends:	Hecate, Asherah, Hercules, and the Crab
House:	Fourth
Opposite Sign:	Capricorn
Flower:	Larkspur
Key Word:	Receptivity

Positive Expression:	**Misuse of Energy:**
Intuitive	Defensive
Sympathetic	Smothering
Nurturing	Manipulative
Protective	Distrustful
Patriotic	Brooding
Domestic	Crabby
Sensitive	Isolationist

Cancer

Your Ego's Strengths and Shortcomings

You love to encourage growth, and you're the one with the soothing touch when someone needs support. The cyclical rhythms of life have an integral link to your inner being, and you innately understand that life has its ebbs and flows. As "The Nurturer" of the zodiac, you project an energy of solace and genuine concern, and even those who are not related to you may think of you as family.

The evolutionary processes reflected in nature fascinate you, and as an outpouring of your connection to the energy of the Moon you may enjoy the experience of gardening, cooking, or domestic activities. Another expression of this energy is seen through your creation of a home—you need a nest! Even at work you'll fashion a comfort zone, and others may gravitate toward it when they need a "security" boost. Your psychic awareness and emotional sensitivity are powerful, although you may have trouble maintaining your emotional boundaries some of the time. In your attempts to protect those you love, you can become overbearing and smothering if you're not watching the signals from others. Cutting the emotional umbilical cord can be painful for you, even when you know it's time to let your fledglings fly on their own.

Your reverence for tradition is woven into your security platform, although it's often tough to let go of the past. As a result, you can insulate yourself from the impact of the emotional vulnerability that emerges when you bid someone or something good-bye. After all, your empty nest can be filled with new and imaginative growth experiences! Allow your intuitive prompting to tell you when it's time to open your arms with love and care or if you need to gracefully back away to give another space. Above all, invite your connection to the divine feminine to flow freely through the knowledge that "for everything, there is a season."

Shining Your Love Light

There's no doubt when you're in love, since your passion and dedication are crystal clear. However, until you find a partner worthy of your trust, you may send mixed messages to those who are attracted to you, since you're trying to keep your heart safely protected. Old hurts may have formed a barrier, and even if you want to let down your walls it may be difficult. Your intuitive sensibilities signal when it's time to drop your defenses. In the right situation, you have the capacity to enjoy a relationship that matures through mutual care and understanding.

Most at ease with the other water signs—Cancer, Scorpio and Pisces—you appreciate others who accept your emotional sensibilities. You may be most magnetized by Capricorn, your zodiac opposite, whose steadfast drive helps strengthen your security.

Aries is very attractive, but may seem immature and selfish. Delighting in the earthy strength of Taurus, you'll find it easy to build a stable future together if you can see eye to eye. You'll enjoy Gemini's playfulness and wit, but must remember to give him or her plenty of personal space. With another Cancer, you may share a devotion for creating strong family ties and building a real nest together. Leo loves your attention, but you may feel that you do not get as much as you give. With Virgo, you're encouraged to build a relationship based on cooperation and communication.

Libra is fascinating, but his or her air of detachment leaves you feeling uncertain. Shared sensuality and passion fuel a breathless relationship with Scorpio, and you may be eternal lovers. Sagittarius is fun, although he or she may seem unpredictable. Intimate surroundings may not fit with Aquarius, who, for you, may be a more reliable confidante than lover; but Pisces' spirituality and imagination can carry you into the realm of ecstasy.

Making Your Place in the World

Through your work in the world you're capable of attaining the assets and possessions required to build your security base. You need a career that offers emotional fulfillment, and by using your easy flow with the rhythms of life, you may be drawn to professions like counseling, social work, medicine, midwifery, or teaching. History, anthropology, archaeology, or the antiques business can also be rewarding endeavors.

You're comfortable in positions of prominence and may enjoy politics. Businesses like real estate, investments, the hotel industry, the restaurant or food industry, or home furnishings can be right up your alley. You can be persuasive in sales or might enjoy positions in human resources. You might decide to put your green thumb to work in landscaping or floral businesses.

Power Plays

To feel powerful, you need a secure base. Although storing enough food for a famine might seem like a reasonable proposition, your drive is to create growth for yourself and for others. When you're bonded with those you love, you feel whole and nurtured, and this is the core of your vitality. While family is part of this picture, your connection to the human family as a whole may be your most ideal goal. As a result, you may forever encourage others to develop their talents and fulfill their destinies.

Building a bridge between the past and the future enhances your sense of power, and as you find a way to modify traditions from the past within the framework of current trends you can clearly see hope for the future. When you and those you love are sheltered and safe, you feel strong; but to continue that strength, you must maintain an awareness of your changing needs and continue to find ways to stay connected to the Source that sustains you through every season of your life.

Famous Cancerians

Giorgio Armani, Arthur Ashe, Kathy Bates, Mel Brooks, Barbara Cartland, Harrison Ford, Bob Fosse, Ernest Hemingway, Helen Keller, Carl Lewis, Christine McVie, Nancy Reagan, Meryl Streep, Twyla Tharp, Liv Tyler, Robin Williams.

The Year Ahead
for Cancer

While creating a stable platform from which to manifest the realization of your hopes and dreams, you're experiencing a year of positive challenges. Your sense of confidence is stimulated by a more profound sense of spiritual unity, and you're finding ways to incorporate the lessons of the past into your current actions and decisions. Breakthroughs are happening in the realms of work and relationships.

The cycles of Jupiter during the year 2000 bring an influence of expansive energy to your goals and strengthen your connection to your inner self. During the first half of the year, Jupiter transits through the Eleventh House of your solar chart, and it is this period that draws your attention to personal and professional aims. This cycle stimulates optimism, and you may feel more satisfied with the rewards of your career. Most importantly, your ability to clarify and fulfill your goals is empowered. Your generosity toward your friends and within your community works like a magical elixir, since the more you do for others, the more support you attract. From July through December, Jupiter travels through your solar Twelfth House, lifting your spirits and opening your awareness of the more subtle spiritual realms. Your dreams and imagination are fueled, and you may feel a sense of spiritual protection that instills a deep confidence in the natural order of things. It's necessary to distinguish between those things that are currently possible and those things that are the experience of creative reverie, since your enriching fantasies may be mesmerizing!

Saturn's energy emphasizes the necessity of setting reasonable goals as a means of fulfilling your destiny. You're seeing a direct correlation between the disciplined and responsible actions that act as building blocks and your career advancement, and will find that the more clearly you define what you want, the more likely you are to accomplish it!

The planets Uranus and Neptune continue their longer cyclical influence over your intimate relationships and act as awakeners to the potentials of healing in every area of your life. You may be breaking down barriers and eliminating fears as you experiment with the possibility of accomplishing true intimacy. Pluto's influence in your sector of work and service is reflecting the upheaval and transformational change in your job. Your health may also be a matter of concern, especially the relationship between health and work. It's time to eliminate situations that are destructive to your physical well-being.

There are four solar eclipses and two lunar eclipses during the year 2000. It is rare that so many solar eclipses are happening in one year, and this can be indicative of a year of significant alterations in the collective experiences that affect us as a whole that result from crisis events. These events may not necessarily be devastating, but are, nonetheless, periods of intensity. Since the Moon's nodes are transiting through your sign this year, you may feel the impact of the eclipses more strongly than everyone else. By paying attention to your underlying motivations—the things that are driving you at an almost unconscious level—you can gain better control over the fulfillment of your life purpose.

If you were born from June 21 to July 6, you're taking a very serious look at your long-range plans. You're experiencing the transit of Saturn in semisquare to your Sun, and the tension from this cycle can actually be quite beneficial. By using your experience as a springboard into new developments, you can move your career forward by, literally, leaps and bounds! You may feel a little fearful about what the future holds if you cannot see precisely what to expect, but this is one of those times when you may have to take a leap if you are to progress. Think of it as a leap of faith. Your part is to prepare yourself, get your obligations squared away, and to focus on where you want to go next. Flexibility in your attitudes helps immensely, since if you're too tense, your ability to extend yourself will be severely limited! For those of you born from June 21 to 30, there's the complication of dealing with innovative changes that may leave you in an uncomfortable quandary. You're under the influence of Uranus transiting in sesquiquadrate to your Sun, an unsettling period when unexpected or unusual changes can throw you out of balance. This influence, coupled with Saturn's cycle, presents quite a challenge. You may want something you do not feel ready to attain. If that's the case, clarify the requirements, and then mull it over again before you act. However, if changes happen and you must act immediately, then the leap of faith you're taking is reminding you that, for the moment, you are safe, and you have what it takes to make a success out of the altered circumstances of your life.

If you were born from June 25 to 29, you're influenced by the confusing energy of Neptune transiting in quincunx to your Sun. This cycle challenges you to explore your spirituality and to find ways to incorporate your spiritual needs into your everyday life. It's like weaving a new color into a tapestry that at first seems to throw off the design, but as you work with it, you realize that there's a new quality emerging. There can be a problem with vague direction or uncertainty due to things you cannot control, and if this is happening in the realm of career, you may feel mistrustful of your company or employer. Your spiritual beliefs and ideals are changing, and you may be drawn to teachings that are quite different from those you experienced as a child. You may also feel a stronger impulse to escape from the pressures of life, but need to find healthy outlets. Falling victim to addictive behavior patterns can happen during this period. Blindly following without questioning is the danger of this cycle. Go with the flow when you can—but keep your eyes open!

If you were born from July 1 to 7, you're feeling a series of transformational changes while Pluto transits in quincunx aspect to your Sun. This period of empowerment brings you in touch with the parts of your life that need to be altered. It's a challenge to determine whether or not you can eliminate destructive or outworn elements from your life in an attempt to become a whole person. Some relationships may need to end, others may require revisions in order to survive, or your job may undergo changes. Your health can be a core issue: if you're feeling unwell, could it be that you need to get rid of a habit or lifestyle that is counterproductive? In some respects, this cycle is like a cosmic tag sale: it's time to clear out your closets, pantries, and attics and get rid of the clutter. You may be doing just that, or may see that these things are symbolic of what's happening to you on an internal or psychological level. Trying to keep everything the same will become a ridiculous process. It's time for change.

If you were born from July 6 to 15, the transit of Uranus in quincunx aspect to your Sun can be extremely unsettling. If you're resisting alterations that bring you into the twenty-first century, then you may feel quite out of place. Now, this does not mean that you have to junk your sentimental favorites and adapt to communicating only by e-mail! But you may find that you can actually use technological advances to streamline your work or alter your life in a positive manner. You may also be drawn to unusual people and can become fascinated by someone who represents a departure from what you know as the "norm." However, Saturn's cycle in sextile aspect to your Sun during the first half of the year can help you maintain your bearing. You can carefully evaluate what fits and what does not. By setting your priorities, you can incorporate the innovative changes that lead to growth. Some things may happen beyond your control that require you to make adaptations you had not anticipated, but even in these situations, it's important to remember that you always have a choice about how you respond to change. If you try to resist, you may feel something like the voice of Big Brother echoing, "Resistance is futile." The inner adaptations work best: alter your attitudes to make room for the innovative. You might actually discover that you like it!

If you were born from July 15 to 22, your life may seem to be settling into a reasonable routine, and you can feel a clear sense of direction. Saturn transits in sextile aspect to your Sun, adding a sense of lucidity and purpose. You're seeing evidence of acceptance for your hard work and may have a chance to take on new responsibilities that advance your career or standing in the community. This is an excellent time to step into a position of influence or a period in which you may realize a long-held dream. Commitments made this year are likely to be upheld, since it's easier to make appropriate judgments. If you're involved in academic pursuits, it's an excellent time to complete educational requirements, to teach, or to write. Your knowledge and expertise may be sought after, and taking advantage of the chance to guide others, you can assure that an important work will continue into the future.

Tools to Make a Difference

As you're building a bridge toward future growth, you're also trimming away the excesses represented by the things, people, and situations you've outgrown. To accomplish all you hope to achieve, you may need to undertake extraordinary measures to assure your success. Time-tested tools like creative visualization can be especially helpful to you during the year 2000. By creating goals that reflect your deepest hopes, and by concentrating on the inner and outer work necessary to accomplish these tasks, you'll not only reach those goals, you may even surpass them!

First, visualize the kind of life you want to have. No holding back now....Really think about it. Let yourself dream, and from that space, get in touch with your feelings about the dream. With a little practice, you'll learn to distinguish between the images that are an outflow of your inner truth and those that are simply illusion. When you find the images that leave you feeling hopeful and creatively powerful, you're seeing the potentials you can create. Write affirmations that help you focus on these goals. You'll also run into your own resistance and may need to use affirmations to help you overcome that resistance. This is where the work gets interesting!

There are tools to use to help in the process. Surprisingly, some of the subtle things are most effective. Using aromatherapy to help you release anxiety or clarify your focus is quite helpful. Try inhalations of frankincense or jasmine; or use oils of geranium, lavender, or rose during a massage. If you're feeling tense from all the hard work required every day, try relaxing with a cup of herbal tea made from chamomile, valerian, and spearmint in the evening. (Chamomile can also help soothe an upset tummy.)

During your meditations, spend extra time on stress-relieving visualizations. Simple techniques can be highly effective—like counting backward from ten to one as you imagine you are walking down a stairway into a quiet space. When you reach the bottom step, visualize a zero. Then, imagine that you are looking into that zero, and as you peer more deeply, it becomes a mirror. In the mirror you can see yourself as you want to be. Merge with this image. Once you return to your normal consciousness, remember that your true self is ready to be reflected through your words, actions, and thoughts.

Initiating the Millennium

This is an empowering year for you—a time of recognizing your place in the overall scheme of things. Coordinating your hopes and efforts with others who share your interests and attitudes, you'll experience an opportunity to show leadership. Your compassionate desire to make a difference in the quality of life needs a place of expression. On a personal level, you're ready to release your fears of intimacy, but may have to let go of old hurts through forgiveness and understanding. Begin the century with an attitude of healing—for yourself and for the world.

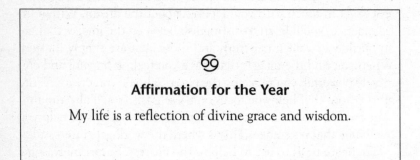

Affirmation for the Year

My life is a reflection of divine grace and wisdom.

Cancer/January

In the Spotlight
Feeling optimistic about plans for expansion, you're ready to take advantage of educational or promotional activities. Advertising, teaching, publication, or broad-scale networking provide excellent forums to let your voice sing out.

Wellness and Keeping Fit
Engaging in physical activities that incorporate philosophical or metaphysical concepts may be more interesting, and since boredom squashes your enthusiasm, you'll tend to stick with the program.

Love and Life Connections
While your attention may be drawn to partnerships and your commitment to a relationship, you're concerned about avoiding past mistakes and ready to turn over a new leaf. Initiate conversations during the New Moon on January 6 that allow you to uncover the issues undermining the integrity of an intimate relationship. Your spirituality forms the basis of renewal.

Finance and Success
Circumstances at work can become more harmonious, although you may have to communicate diligently to reach agreements that improve productivity and cooperation. The lunar eclipse on January 20 emphasizes finances and marks a time when joint resources can be a source of dispute. Agreeing upon goals, you will improve your ability to attract sufficient resources.

Cosmic Insider Tip
Exploring value differences helps you reach more workable agreements. At first you'll see the impasse, but solutions emerge around the time of the Moon's eclipse on January 20.

Rewarding Days
1, 10, 11, 16, 19, 20, 28, 29

Challenging Days
5, 6, 12, 13, 14, 25, 26, 30

Affirmation for the Month
I see the common thread that leads to peaceful resolution of problems.

Cancer/February

In the Spotlight
Research or investigation may expose a gem, and although you may uncover something of value, you're also facing your fears. Ethical issues may arise, and you'll be most inclined to take the high road.

Wellness and Keeping Fit
You need a positive vent for escalating competitive energy. Team sports, whether you're participating or spectating, can be an excellent choice. Travel can be rejuvenating, too.

Love and Life Connections
Your relationship grows stronger as you show more appreciation for your partner. Unrealistic expectations can lead to disappointments, and during the solar eclipse on February 5 issues of trust can arise. Unhealthy relationships are unlikely to survive this cycle. By the Full Moon on February 19, communication improves, and talking about your feelings while sharing your visions and hopes breathes new life into a strong connection.

Finance and Success
Finalize contractual agreements before February 6. Although negotiations are favorable after that time, formal contracts may be difficult to accomplish. Budget overruns can be a source of concern from February 11-23. Joint finances can be filled with pitfalls, and unless you have no alternative, it's best to avoid taking on additional debt. It's time to clear out obligations, not to create new ones.

Cosmic Insider Tip
Mercury begins a retrograde cycle on February 21, but for two weeks prior you may think it's already happening. Unstable situations unravel, and technical difficulties can create delays.

Rewarding Days
7, 8, 12, 14, 15, 19, 20, 24, 25

Challenging Days
1, 2, 9, 10, 22, 23, 29

Affirmation for the Month
My ambitions are in harmony with my highest needs.

Cancer/March

In the Spotlight
While you're facing a competitive challenge in your career, you're also exploring positive ways to expand your options and advance your reputation. Educational pursuits or travel provide the impetus for growth.

Wellness and Keeping Fit
To keep your energy strong you need an outlet. An adventurous vacation or even a long weekend will make a difference.

Love and Life Connections
An old love may enter the picture, or you may have a second chance with a relationship in need of repair. If you're free, the New Moon on March 6 can stimulate a fresh connection with someone who shares your spiritual ideals. Love ripens quickly, and by the Full Moon on March 19 you may be declaring intentions that before seemed to be the stuff of dreams. When you're ready, you're ready!

Finance and Success
While Mercury continues its retrograde through March 14, you're in an excellent position to reclaim lost contacts, review terms of agreements (or disagreements), and continue ongoing discussions. Legal proceedings fare quite nicely after March 15, when colleagues who share your interests may be standing in line to show their support. Conferences, meetings, or publication are perfect avenues to expand your influence.

Cosmic Insider Tip
Exaggeration leaves confusion in its wake from March 1-15, and during this time it's best to let circumstances reach their own level. Acting too quickly can undermine your reputation.

Rewarding Days
5, 6, 10, 13, 14, 18, 19, 22, 23, 24

Challenging Days
1, 2, 7, 8, 20, 21, 27, 28, 29

Affirmation for the Month
Truth is the light upon my path.

Cancer/April

In the Spotlight
Career takes front and center stage. Professional associations or community concerns give you a chance to influence growth and change, although much of your focus may be on revitalizing something of lasting value.

Wellness and Keeping Fit
Now it's time to become actively involved in shared activities. Whether you're on the office team or working out in aerobics class with your best buddy, you'll be inspired to continue if others are cheering your progress (and you'll be happy to return the favor).

Love and Life Connections
Interactions with friends can go further than the occasional lunch date. There are significant things to accomplish together. Sudden changes can leave you in shock, although some things may emerge that lead to you think, "I should have known that!" A love interest can arise through work who you may be tempted to pursue. Family matters need your attention around the Full Moon on April 18.

Finance and Success
Unusual opportunities can dawn in your career near the time of the New Moon on April 4, and by taking well-defined steps to show your interest you can assure your advancement. Recognition for past achievements leads to an interesting series of developments. The actual costs and rewards of making a change can be unclear, so you may prefer to wait before making a major change in your job.

Cosmic Insider Tip
Watch out for a partner's or investor's hidden agenda from April 1-6 and then April 21-28.

Rewarding Days
1, 2, 7, 10, 11, 14, 15, 19, 20, 29, 30

Challenging Days
3, 4, 16, 17, 23, 24, 25

Affirmation for the Month
My words and actions are a reflection of my true goals.

Cancer/May

In the Spotlight
Revising your long-range plans puts you on a steady path toward success. You can establish solid connections with your community that carry your ideas and efforts well into the future.

Wellness and Keeping Fit
Maintaining a steady pace helps conserve your energy. You may feel like giving up habits counterproductive to your health. Extra rest and rejuvenation may be required.

Love and Life Connections
Corroborating with friends, you can build a powerful network that serves the best interests of everyone. Talk over ideas during the New Moon on May 3 to confirm your commitments. Your affections for someone can undergo a radical change around the time of the Full Moon on May 18, when you may realize a need for deeper affection. A friend may awaken you to elements of a relationship that need careful scrutiny.

Finance and Success
Gaining substantial rewards from your career, you're seeking the best ways to preserve your success and to use your position as a stepping stone for lasting security. Emotionally charged situations midmonth can prompt you to spend for the wrong reasons. Since this is counterproductive to your plans, keeping a firm rein on your expenses might be advisable.

Cosmic Insider Tip
With a lineup of planets in your Eleventh House, you're in an outstanding position professionally. The manner in which you use your influence will have long-lasting repercussions.

Rewarding Days
3, 4, 7, 8, 11, 12, 16, 17, 26, 27, 31

Challenging Days
1, 2, 13, 14, 15, 21, 22, 28, 29

Affirmation for the Month
My hopes and dreams are created from pure love.

Cancer/June

In the Spotlight

Active communication propels you into the forefront, although there's a lot to do behind the scenes before you're ready to launch your ideas. The value of networking is quite apparent, since combining resources places you in a stronger position.

Wellness and Keeping Fit

Increase your expertise in a sport by applying the principles of visualization. Forge a bond between body, mind, and spirit.

Love and Life Connections

Your secret desires are active, and you may be fascinated by a clandestine romance. Integrating fantasy into your love life adds a special zing, and others may wonder about that smile you're wearing! More openness emerges after June 18 when Venus and Mars are both in your sign for a while. Expressing your feelings and desires is much easier, although starting an entirely new relationship can be frustrated by logistical problems.

Finance and Success

Putting the finishing touches on a special project requires patience with others who may seem distracted. You may also need extra time to go over details before you feel confident. Mechanical or technical problems can plague you after June 16, and once Mercury enters its retrograde on June 23 you may finally discover the weak link. Creative projects simply require more time than you anticipated.

Cosmic Insider Tip

Unraveling problems can be frustrating, but may be the only way to assure continuity. Your supportive and understanding nature places you in the foreground from June 17-30.

Rewarding Days

3, 4, 7, 12, 13, 22, 23, 27, 28

Challenging Days

10, 11, 16, 17, 18, 25, 26

Affirmation for the Month

I know when to be protective and when to pull away.

Cancer/July

In the Spotlight
On July 1, the Sun's eclipse in Cancer marks a period of intense focus. Your initiative can easily put you in the lead, but you must remember that your intentions are apparent. Pure motives result in powerful metamorphoses. Ulterior motives can get you into trouble!

Wellness and Keeping Fit
Any physical troubles are likely to escalate, giving you a chance to get to the core of problems. Altering your approach to diet and daily routine can make a huge difference in your sense of well-being.

Love and Life Connections
Relationships are a primary focus, and if you need to make alterations to improve an existing relationship or initiate a new relationship, your attentions will not go unnoticed. The lunar eclipse on July 16 emphasizes partnerships, and a healthy connection can grow more powerful while a destructive relationship falters. If you're facing an ending, this is a prime time to achieve closure.

Finance and Success
Initiating a project or taking on leadership roles advances your reputation and assures your long-term success. Your finances improve, but from July 13-21 it's easy to be drawn into a situation that drains your resources. Your attention to your budget will pay off; otherwise you can feel pretty stuck when expenditures intensify during the solar eclipse on July 30 and you need to tap into your reserves.

Cosmic Insider Tip
While Mercury retrogrades through July 17, you may feel that you're taking one step forward, two steps back. Careful maneuvering and alertness can keep you in a position of strength.

Rewarding Days
1, 2, 5, 6, 9, 10, 11, 19, 20, 21, 25, 28, 29

Challenging Days
7, 8, 14, 15, 16, 22, 23

Affirmation for the Month
I trust my higher self to guide my motives, thoughts, and actions.

Cancer/August

In the Spotlight
Put your resources to work. By making the best use of your time and energy, you'll assure growth on several fronts. Wasted efforts can result from becoming involved in disputes that are not yours to resolve.

Wellness and Keeping Fit
Extend your endurance through exercises that develop your muscles and improve your aerobic condition. Getting outside might feel great, and starting a fitness program at the beginning of the month can be as simple as walking around the block!

Love and Life Connections
Every relationship undergoes transformation, and to get beyond old fears or issues arising from past hurts you may be struggling with trust. Near the Full Moon on August 15 you're confronting these problems, and they can emerge in the guise of arguments over money. A loving relationship gives you a place to say, "I'm afraid." Then, you can move forward.

Finance and Success
Money matters—from balancing your accounts to planning a budget for a large project—require creative attention. Calling in your network of experts after August 6 will help assure that your requests and plans are well-documented and adequately supported. Business travel, meetings, or presentations offer exciting options, although conservative factions must be satisfied before you can move ahead.

Cosmic Insider Tip
Strong momentum from August 1-15 helps to assure your progress, but you're in a great position to launch another action on or after the New Moon on August 29.

Rewarding Days
1, 2, 6, 7, 16, 17, 21, 25, 26, 29, 30

Challenging Days
3, 4, 5, 10, 11, 12, 18, 19, 31

Affirmation for the Month
My life is filled with abundance in all good things.

Cancer/September

In the Spotlight
You may encounter resistance to your attempts to make changes at work, particularly if your ideas are seen as threatening. To avoid undermining your own position, review policies before you take action.

Wellness and Keeping Fit
If you feel like you're the world's biggest tension-attractor it could be because you're not letting go of stress on a regular basis. Exercise helps, but you may also benefit from a good massage.

Love and Life Connections
Prompted to beautify your nest, you may also feel like inviting good friends to dinner. Social time at home helps strengthen your emotional connections to those who are your true family. Your spiritual ideals can inspire powerful change during the Full Moon on September 13, as soul-level needs transform a love relationship. Romantic encounters after September 18 may stimulate deeper emotions that you usually keep hidden (even from yourself).

Finance and Success
To avoid depleting your resources too quickly, find ways to recycle. Increasing your productivity helps speed progress on a project at work, too, although you may have to be careful about political implications. Acting without full support of authorities can be costly. Review plans with the powers that be, and if you have to wait, then plan to initiate procedures after the New Moon on September 27.

Cosmic Insider Tip
Jupiter and Pluto are in opposition in the heavens, stressing the power of philosophical ideals that can be used like weapons. Be aware of this influence on the job.

Rewarding Days
2, 12, 13, 17, 21, 22, 25, 26, 29, 30

Challenging Days
1, 7, 8, 14, 15, 27, 28

Affirmation for the Month
I carefully consider the effects before I speak or take action.

Cancer/October

In the Spotlight

Intensive creative energy propels your reputation and career. Others may call upon you because of your expertise and talents, and by carefully choosing your opportunities you can exercise strong influence over the outcome of situations.

Wellness and Keeping Fit

Your physical vitality grows stronger. There's a potential for accidents from October 10-21. Delve into the root causes of health concerns after October 18.

Love and Life Connections

Your fascination with a romantic relationship may be based more on fantasy than fact. True love grows, but infatuation burns out by midmonth. To bring an existing relationship out of the doldrums, you might enjoy a more experimental attitude with your sexuality. A mutual love can reach an amazing plateau near the New Moon on October 27.

Finance and Success

Your special talents give you an advantage, and investing your resources in a creative endeavor before the Full Moon on October 13 can lead to advancement. Speculative ventures may entice, but are not to your advantage if they require you to dig into reserves. Investigate these situations during Mercury's retrograde after October 18. Avoid signing obligatory financial contracts this month.

Cosmic Insider Tip

Your reputation and honor may depend upon your ability to judge a financial situation. Seek authoritative advice, but trust your intuitive judgment to aid your final decision.

Rewarding Days

9, 10, 15, 18, 19, 23, 27, 28

Challenging Days

4, 5, 11, 12, 13, 21, 24, 25, 26, 31

Affirmation for the Month

I can initiate change while holding tradition in high regard.

Cancer/November

In the Spotlight
Your competitive buttons are activated, and although you may not be overtly donning armor, in your mind you may be drawing battle lines. You have all the resources to meet challenges with confidence.

Wellness and Keeping Fit
Dealing with situations that create anger or frustration in a healthy manner may require that you adopt a more committed attitude to your fitness activities.

Love and Life Connections
Although you're more open about expressing your feelings, you may be more easily hurt if others are too direct or harsh. Turmoil at home can definitely escalate, but it may be due to increased holiday activities. Your partner offers more caring support, and reminding him or her of your appreciation around the time of the Full Moon on November 11 makes a huge difference. Make time to share your favorite pleasures.

Finance and Success
Confusing or misrepresented facts create contractual problems through November 16. Although Mercury turns direct on November 7, uncertainty remains for a while. You'll be more confident about agreements signed after November 18, when everybody's intentions are more clear. Initiate changes at work designed to increase productivity after the New Moon on November 25.

Cosmic Insider Tip
Family pressures can fly in the face of your partner's needs from November 13-22. Determine what you can do to ease the tension, but stay out of battles that belong to others.

Rewarding Days
5, 6, 11, 14, 15, 19, 20, 23, 24

Challenging Days
1, 2, 8, 9, 21, 22, 28, 29, 30

Affirmation for the Month
Love always finds an answer.

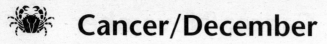 # Cancer/December

In the Spotlight
Although you might prefer to avoid confrontation, you may need to take a stand. Relationships evolve, but not without work on the part of everyone involved. Remember: you do not have to do it alone!

Wellness and Keeping Fit
To solve the mystery of a physical concern, consult a trusted health practitioner. You're eager to take action to create a sound body, and, armed with understanding, can make significant headway.

Love and Life Connections
Love dissolves barriers, and trusting your commitments is the first step toward becoming intimate. Friction at home can distract you from your primary aim, but may also escalate if you're ignoring the need to delve into the promise of intimacy. The agitation of not following your desires can be unsettling. Partnership issues reach a peak around the solar eclipse on December 25, when communicating your sincere feelings is your only option if you desire a healthy outcome.

Finance and Success
Talk over grievances at work if you want to withstand the pressure from your competitors. Cooperation during the Full Moon on December 11 can turn around a tense situation, while undermining exposes the weak links in the system. Avoid taking on additional debt from December 10-26, when your joint resources may be weakened by rash or unwise actions.

Cosmic Insider Tip
To rectify long-standing problems in a relationship, the situation may have to reach a peak. The Sun's eclipse on December 25 intensifies a crisis that can lead to healing a breech of trust.

Rewarding Days
3, 4, 12, 13, 17, 20, 21, 30, 31

Challenging Days
5, 6, 7, 18, 19, 25, 26, 27

Affirmation for the Month
I am a compassionate and understanding partner.

Cancer Action Table

These dates reflect the best—but not the only—times for success and ease in these activities, according to your Sun sign.

	JAN	FEB	MAR	APR	MAY	JUN	JUL	AUG	SEPT	OCT	NOV	DEC
Move									8-27			
Start a class		1, 2, 29	6					29, 30				
Join a club					4							
Ask for a raise				13-29			1, 2					
Look for work	5-6											4-21
Get pro advice	8, 9	1, 2, 29	1, 27, 28	23-25	21, 22	17, 18	14-16	10-12	7, 8	4, 5, 31	1-2, 28-29	25-27
Get a loan		4, 5	2-3, 30-31	26, 27	23-25	19-21	17, 18	13, 14	9-11	7, 8	3, 4, 30	1-2, 28-29
See a doctor					14-29							4-22
Start a diet	3-4, 30-31	26-28	25, 26	21, 22	18-20	14-16	12, 13	8, 9	4-6	2-3, 29-30	25-27	23, 24
End relationship							16					
Buy clothes									28-30	1-17	9-30	1-3
Get a makeover							1, 2					
New romance										27, 28		
Vacation	10, 11	6-8	5, 6	1-2, 28-30	26, 27	22, 23	19-21	15-17	12, 13	9, 10	5-7	3-4, 30-31

Leo
The Lion
July 22 to August 21

♌

Element:	Fire
Quality:	Fixed
Polarity:	Yang/Masculine
Ruler:	The Sun
Meditation:	"My energy glows with light from the Source."
Gemstone:	Ruby
Power Stones:	Topaz, sardonyx
Key Phrase:	"I will"
Glyph:	Lion's tail ♌
Anatomy:	Heart, upper back
Colors:	Gold, scarlet
Animal:	Lions, large cats
Myths/Legends:	Apollo, Isis, Helius
House:	Fifth
Opposite Sign:	Aquarius
Flower:	Marigold, sunflower
Key Word:	Magnetic

Positive Expression:	Misuse of Energy:
Benevolent	Pompous
Dramatic	Pretentious
Self-confident	Domineering
Vigorous	Dictatorial
Regal	Chauvinistic
Loyal	Insolent
Bold	Self-absorbed

Leo

Your Ego's Strengths and Shortcomings

With a powerful radiance that shines from the love in your heart, you don't have to be the center of attention, but when you are, you certainly know what to do there! Your dramatic creativity is an outpouring of this quality, assuring that you leave a lasting impression. Through your deep sense of conviction, you function as "The Loyalist" of the zodiac, radiating confidence in your strong opinions and ideas and providing encouragement to others in need of hope.

You have a playful spirit and relish opportunities that bring you into the middle of the action. Like the Sun, your ruler, your countenance can be brilliant, and your warm generosity is rarely forgotten. Others can count on you to keep your loyalty, and you expect the same from those who share the circle of your life. You need lots of room to exercise your creative talents and purr with delight when you're the object of adoration and praise, but if you feel unappreciated you can become dejected and may show insolent or demanding behavior.

When you take a stand for yourself or someone dear to your heart, your courage is unmatched; but sometimes your pride can be blinding, and if you feel betrayed, you can be completely unyielding and unforgiving. Once you surrender your ego to the guidance of your higher self, your life can become a brilliant light, luminous with the power of divine love.

Shining Your Love Light

When you love, your ardent devotion and passion can be unforgettable. The game of love and all its pleasures inspires you to express your most confident and generous qualities, but if you're deeply hurt, you may forever withdraw your affections. However, it takes more than a few faltering steps on the path toward true love to discourage you, and once you've found your match, you can create an enduring love. Your heart sings when you make others happy—this is the trigger of your generosity.

Contact with the other fire signs—Aries, Leo and Sagittarius—is most inspiring to you. You may have an instant attraction to

Aquarius, your zodiac opposite. For that relationship to last, you'll both have to learn about true autonomy and the freedom that comes from a deep commitment.

With Aries, your attraction can end as quickly as it began if you are not devoted to one another. Taurus is certainly pleasing, but you may dislike the feeling that you've become a possession. Gemini's intelligence stimulates your imagination, and you may be lifelong friends. You're comfortable with Cancer, but not always romantically inclined. With another Leo you'll feel tremendous bursts of creative passion, but ego conflicts can emerge if you each do not have a chance to shine.

Virgo's attention to perfection is appealing, but you may be better working partners than lovers. Libra's exceptional refinement and beauty is purely enticing. Although Scorpio's sensuality can be absolutely breathtaking, you may feel throttled by emotional intensity. Sagittarius appeals to your sense of adventure while stimulating your heart to open to a capacity you may not have deemed possible. Capricorn can make you work too hard to sustain a relationship. Fascinated by Pisces' mystical qualities, you can feel rather uncomfortable with the sense that you've lost control.

Making Your Place in the World

You need a career that can last a lifetime and that offers a chance for you to receive adequate recognition for your efforts. In the entertainment fields, you might excel as a director, performer, musician, actor, model, or producer. And if you're interested in politics, you can do well as a candidate or campaign director.

Once in a position of leadership, you can influence lasting changes, and whether you're foreman, CEO, president, or general, your ability to delegate and direct can be exceptional. As a teacher or promoter, your ability to inspire can bring a sense of self-importance to others. Since you like to be where others are enjoying themselves, you might successfully develop businesses like theaters, night clubs, amusement centers, or restaurants. Whatever your choice, you need to work in a field that keeps your creativity alive.

Power Plays

Just as the sun stimulates and sustains the life force, you are closely connected to the power of life, and by tapping into the divine Source, you are strengthened and inspired. Shining your light for the sheer reason of self-importance can be a misuse of this power, but by learning to direct your ego in harmony with a sense of higher purpose, you can become a convincing authority figure and person of influence. Walking along the path of power, you will encounter those who would try to push you aside in favor of their own greed, and your greatest lessons may arise from encountering a blatant misuse of power.

You can be a benevolent ruler or a dictatorial tyrant: the difference depends on your values and sense of self-worth. Opening your heart is easy when you feel good about yourself; otherwise, you may remain in a position of defensive power and can be tempted to steal the power of others in an attempt to maintain your own. Maintaining an awareness of the efforts and talents of others helps to keep your ego in a healthy place. Working in concert with those who are meeting the challenge of using their talents to the fullest may become your most cherished experience of the power to create feelings of hope, love, and joy.

You may be most interested in assuring that the best of life can be sustained over the course of the centuries. To this end, uniting your energy with that of your higher self illuminates a path that will lead others to know that you are, indeed, the keeper of the flame of the heart.

Famous Leos

Princess Anne, Neil Armstrong, Antonio Banderas, Angela Bassett, Wilt Chamberlain, Coco Chanel, Wes Craven, Alexander Dumas, Mata Hari, Whitney Houston, Carl Jung, Monica Lewinsky, Madonna, Martha Stewart, Cindy Williams, Alicia Witt.

The Year Ahead for Leo

By embracing the challenge to honor your priorities while incorporating innovations and adapting to change, you're seeing true progress. The rewards for your efforts can be quite tangible—from improvements in finances to recognition and advancement in your professional endeavors. To shoulder your responsibilities, you're also letting go of the things that no longer fit into your life.

The expansive energy of Jupiter highlights your reputation and honor and leads to a cycle that indicates that you're becoming quite familiar with the spiritual laws of abundance. You're in a position to share much of what you've learned, while at the same time your influence allows you to enter thresholds that lead to improvements in your own understanding and expertise. Through the end of June, Jupiter travels through your solar Tenth House, increasing your ambition and the drive necessary to accomplish those aims. The things you do professionally can have a lasting effect upon your success, and if you wear your accomplishments well, you'll endear the right kind of support. However, too much ego or pride during this cycle can damage your reputation and lead to unnecessary competition later on. From July through the end of the year 2000, Jupiter's energy highlights your hopes, goals, and friendships. From professional associations to personal ties, the value of your friendships cannot be understated, and by showing your appreciation, these connections grow stronger.

Saturn's cycle completes its transit through your solar Tenth House, and this influence presents the challenge of maintaining your priorities as you continue toward the realization of your long-range ambitions. You may gain greater recognition during this period, but with that recognition comes more responsibility. Even your expertise, which is likely to increase, can become a challenge, as you work even more diligently toward your personal goals of creating a true standard of excellence.

The travels of Uranus bring awakening to your relationships, and your ideas about your place in society can undergo significant changes. This cycle takes time to fully manifest, but the effects of the changes are usually apparent for quite some time. The very slow-moving transit of Neptune continues through your solar Seventh

House, marking a time of forgiveness and a desire to contribute something intangible to the world. Pluto's transit continues to emphasize your creative drive, and you're feeling comfortable breaking through barriers in order to express the depths of your talents.

There are four solar eclipses during the year 2000. It's unusual to experience this number of eclipses in one year, and the indicators of these celestial events mark a greater opportunity for humanity to experience awakening through crisis. Getting in touch with your deepest yearnings may be easier this year, since the eclipses of the Sun and Moon emphasize the Leo/Aquarius axis, strengthening your awareness of your potentials and needs. You may also become more aware of your mind/body link, and can become more dedicated to taking care of your health so that you have the energy necessary to fulfill those creative drives.

If you were born from July 22 to 25, you're experiencing a period of stable focus while Saturn moves into a sextile to your Sun this year. Although this cycle is not fully effective until the summer, you'll see the effects of your efforts gradually taking shape, and by targeting the months of August through November to launch significant plans, you'll see the greatest success. This cycle will also repeat itself early next year, so getting started now will put you ahead of the game when it comes to advancing your career and realizing your goals. Educational pursuits are favored, whether you're teaching or learning, and you may also take on more responsibilities in community projects or special interests. Your leadership definitely needs a target!

If you were born from July 26 to 31, you're undergoing an initiation in consciousness while Neptune transits in opposition to your Sun. The influence of Neptune can have the effect of dissolving many of your attachments, allowing you to release and forgive so that you can move onward; but sometimes this influence is also confusing, since your old security base may seem to disappear and you may not feel that you have a stable foundation. In many ways, you're simply more sensitive. That sensitivity functions on multiple levels, and you may even discover that you're more physically sensitive to environmental or dietary influences than you once were.

Eliminating toxic situations is important, and you may find it necessary to isolate yourself from influences that undermine your health. Emotionally, your increased sensitivity can lead you to let go of barriers that have kept you from fully enjoying the experience of compassionate love. If you've been struggling with a difficult relationship, this influence is helpful for releasing your attachment to keeping everything the same, as you let go of the negative elements. A strong relationship can become more spiritually enhanced now, but an unhealthy relationship can be problematic unless you're keeping very careful personal boundaries. It's easier to be deceived by what you want, and you can blind your objectivity unless you make a real effort to remain honest with yourself and with others.

If you were born from July 31 to August 2, you're developing your talents more easily. Saturn's transit in quintile to your Sun marks a very interesting cycle. If you have been hoping for the right situation to allow your creativity to blossom, this is the time when it can manifest. Whether that occurs through a change in environment, the introduction of better information, or the guidance of a powerful mentor, you're ready to tap into your resources and become more expressive. A quiet confidence emerges that can attract positive attention, and by becoming more disciplined your artistry can improve in a significant manner.

If you were born from August 3 to 7, you're experiencing a period of powerful healing while Pluto transits in trine aspect to your Sun. This rare cycle energizes a period of profound insight into your strengths and weaknesses. Your awareness can be directed toward several ends, but you may feel most oriented toward finding the true drives residing deep within your heart. Trimming away excesses that slow your progress is much easier, but you'll have to make a determined effort to first decide where you're going if you want to make the most of the "pruning." Developing your creative self-expression may take top priority, and by clarifying your wishes you'll attract the best circumstances. Some of the barriers that have prevented you from actualizing your potential may seem to drop away, and the relief can free you to be more expressive. If you choose to simply ride along during this period, life seems to be generally easier; but if you put the gift of this energy to work for you, you can progress at a rate that is truly amazing.

If you were born from August 7 to 16, the disruptive energy of Uranus transits in opposition to your Sun. You may feel that you can hardly wait to get out of one situation and be free, but life is rarely that easy! This is a time when you may feel plagued by tradeoffs, since Saturn's restrictive and realistic influence in square to your Sun reminds you that you can't just wipe the slate clean and move on. You're seeing the truth that freedom does rely upon taking responsibility for yourself and your actions, and since freedom is your ultimate goal, then by embracing your obligations and making every effort to satisfy them, you'll be able to use your wings to their fullest. That may require you to complete a course of study or finish one project before you can go on to another. It can also manifest in your relationships by honoring the needs of others as you extract yourself from situations that are no longer healthy. So before you light that torch and drop it on the bridge, make sure you're not standing in the middle, or determine whether or not you may need to cross back one more time to finish. Rash actions can be extremely costly. Prudent consideration of the best ways to carry out revolutionary change can lead to an exceptional period of growth and self-realization.

If you were born from August 15 to 23, you're feeling the tension of Saturn transiting in square aspect to your Sun. This cycle prompts you to take a very serious look at where you're heading, and you may have a very clear awareness of the effects of your life circumstances upon the realization of your dreams. Think of this time as a test. You're testing the validity of your aims, and if you truly want something, you may have to go the extra mile to get it. You may also need to examine your motivations carefully, since if you're driven toward a goal to satisfy somebody else, it may have lost its luster (and you may be losing your momentum). The responsibilities you currently carry can be quite demanding, and taking on burdens that are not yours to shoulder can lead to your collapse. Determine what you need to release, complete what must be finished, and fine-tune your aims. Your physical health can also be demanding, and wherever your weak links exist, they'll be exposed. It may be impossible to ignore physical problems, but by dealing with them and taking a responsible attitude toward healing, you can actually become stronger. The purpose of this cycle is to fortify your foundations, and part of that fortification involves eliminating destructive elements. The manner in which you meet these challenges will determine the types of opportunities you'll encounter during the next two years.

Tools to Make a Difference

Developing mindfulness can be the most profound tool you'll put to use this year. Since you enjoy the feeling of being in control—the master of your destiny—taking steps to assure that you are more aware will enhance your awareness of how effectively you are in charge of your life. Of course, some situations are beyond your control, while your responses are almost always up to you! Mindfulness is an experience of seeing who you are and how you are responding to life situations as you bring your conscious and unconscious processes together. A good exercise in mindfulness is to simply attempt to watch yourself more carefully, as though a part of you is sitting on your shoulder as an observer. It can be an intriguing exercise!

Goal setting is another tool that can have a significant impact on your accomplishments, since by defining your goals, you're setting priorities and outlining parameters that help you manifest your dreams. You may need to concentrate on one area at a time, although your larger goals this year may include most every part of your life—from physical health to relationships to financial success.

To enhance your physical well-being, you may decide to revamp your schedule so that you have more time to care for your body. You might also want to incorporate aromatherapy, and there are lots of products now on the market that you can access. Whether you're using essential oils to scent your room, changing your perfume, or adding fragrances to massage oils, the effects of different aromas can be powerful. Cypress and pine can help strengthen your circulatory system, while clary sage can be a good muscle relaxant. Ylang-ylang, neroli, patchouli, and rose help to lift your spirits, and may be the perfect aromas when you're feeling stressed. Although you may not want to wear it, eating more garlic has been shown to improve circulation.

During your meditations, strive to find the place inside your consciousness that is the heart of peacefulness. You may want to concentrate on your breathing to relax your mind and allow the tension to float away from your body. Envision a place where everything is calm, beauty, and harmony. Hear the music and let the images fill your mind, while the warmth embraces your spirit. Remind yourself that wherever you go, the essence of this peace travels with you.

Initiating the Millennium

As you step into the new century, your attitudes can have a profound effect upon your sense of contentment. Even though you're facing challenges, you may relish the experience of bringing the improvements and alterations to your life that will give you a chance to show the world what you can do and who you are. By consciously removing the barriers of self-doubt and adopting an attitude of courage and hope, you'll not only feel more confident, but may find that others are enthusiastically following your lead. It's time to find the core of your power and to create a way to allow that power to manifest.

♌

Affirmation for the Year

I surrender my desires to the guidance of my higher self.

Leo/January

In the Spotlight
While you may be focusing most of your energy on work, your creativity is fortified and you're facing a welcoming horizon. Applied effort, coupled with your special talents, advances your aims.

Wellness and Keeping Fit
A careful assessment of your health provides the information that helps you determine a better daily regimen. You'll be most comfortable with a holistic approach.

Love and Life Connections
You may question your commitment to a partnership, and if you're in love but afraid to take the next steps, it's crucial to explore your fears. The depths of your passion increase from January 1-13, when eliminating your inhibitions strengthens your expression of love. The Leo lunar eclipse on January 20 can bring your situation to a critical point, when uncertainty can be costly to your relationship. Maintain open lines of communication.

Finance and Success
Your efforts lead to enhanced productivity at work and can impress your superiors, although others may balk if your suggestions include budget increases. Illustrating benefits wins support from January 6-15, but fear of change (or a loss of power) can undermine your progress from January 17-22. Tax or insurance problems can create friction, but accurate records help clarify misunderstandings.

Cosmic Insider Tip
Emotionally biased judgments can create difficulties in business and personal relationships around the time of the Moon's eclipse on January 20. Open-mindedness strengthens your position.

Rewarding Days
3, 4, 12, 13, 18, 21, 22, 25, 30, 31

Challenging Days
1, 2, 8, 9, 15, 16, 27, 28, 29

Affirmation for the Month
Acknowledging the needs of others aids my capacity to love fully.

Leo/February

In the Spotlight
Unexpected changes in social circumstances or partnerships can keep you on your toes, especially if issues like shared liability are involved. As a result, you're likely to be juggling your priorities.

Wellness and Keeping Fit
Getting to the core of physical problems speeds healing from February 1-12. After February 13, your vitality improves, and increasing activity levels helps you keep up with your commitments.

Love and Life Connections
The solar eclipse on February 5 stimulates lively interaction with your partner. Staying in a rut may be virtually impossible. Revolutionary change in your roles adds a fresh quality to your commitment. An unhealthy relationship may not survive, with issues escalating near the Full Moon on February 19, but a spiritually empowered love grows more intense.

Finance and Success
Practical considerations may override innovations that seem too futuristic for conservative thinkers, although a breakthrough in negotiations can open the way for new options from February 5-11. Contractual negotiations completed before February 12 promise longevity, but if you're uncertain, use Mercury's retrograde starting on February 21 to investigate your concerns. Speculative investments can be too costly after February 17.

Cosmic Insider Tip
Overestimating the potential of a situation can lead to problems from February 14-29, and waiting can be your most prudent option. Hidden factors undermine stability.

Rewarding Days
9, 10, 17, 18, 22, 26, 27

Challenging Days
4, 5, 6, 11, 12, 19, 24, 25

Affirmation for the Month
My words and actions create support and healing.

Leo/March

In the Spotlight
Academic endeavors, travel, and promotional activities advance your career and enhance your reputation. Emphasizing your unique qualities works to your advantage only if tempered with good taste.

Wellness and Keeping Fit
Getting outside can be invigorating. Adventurous travel helps alter your perspective, and your change in attitude goes a long way toward helping to heal your mind, body, and spirit.

Love and Life Connections
Fascinated by an unusual person, you may stray outside of your normal boundaries from March 1-6. You're seeing possibilities you may not have previously considered, and during the New Moon on March 6, you may feel ready to release inhibitions standing in the way of experiencing a deep love. If you're in over your head, you'll find out from March 19-23, when a test of trust can emerge.

Finance and Success
Mercury's retrograde through March 14 is only part of the picture complicating business deals. Vague promises can leave you wondering exactly where you stand, and, as a result, you may be unwilling to commit to anything long-term until you get the facts. Making sensible choices may require that you spend more time investigating options, although you may be highly intrigued. Funnel intrigue into your artistry, not into your bank account.

Cosmic Insider Tip
The square between Jupiter and Neptune radiates an energy of propaganda and promise, but there may be little substance. Define the differences between teacher and the teaching.

Rewarding Days
7, 8, 11, 16, 17, 20, 21, 25

Challenging Days
2, 3, 9, 10, 19, 22, 23, 24, 30, 31

Affirmation for the Month
My intuitive guidance arises from the wisdom of my higher self.

Leo/April

In the Spotlight
Interaction with others in your field helps preserve your influence while providing a chance to incorporate more wide-ranging ideas. Sustained effort is necessary to your success.

Wellness and Keeping Fit
Stress levels are on the rise, particularly if you're in a competitive situation or facing tough deadlines. Staying active helps, but you may need the added benefit of a massage before month's end.

Love and Life Connections
Spiritual and philosophical connections forge a powerful bond, and it is through a meeting of the minds that you may encounter a kindred spirit near the New Moon on April 4. Love blossoms after April 6, and sharing a vacation, retreat, or inspiring experience with your sweetheart helps to strengthen your union. If an extended trip won't work, a romantic rendezvous between April 16 and the Full Moon on April 18 could suffice.

Finance and Success
In order to fulfill career obligations, you'll need a combination of persistence and understanding. Changes can seem threatening from April 14-30, but may offer solutions to an impasse or a situation that's grown stale. Conferences and presentations provide a chance to share knowledge after April 14, and incorporating innovation into an existing situation may be the only way to preserve it.

Cosmic Insider Tip
Mars, Jupiter, and Saturn transiting together present a challenge, and you may feel driven to prove yourself. The measure of your success depends on who you're trying to please!

Rewarding Days
3, 4, 8, 12, 13, 16, 17, 21, 22

Challenging Days
5, 6, 7, 18, 19, 20, 26, 27

Affirmation for the Month
My steps are sure and certain along the path of accomplishment.

Leo/May

In the Spotlight

Rewards for your efforts can come in the form of recognition, and others may look to you for leadership if they feel you can be influential. Authorities can present a significant challenge.

Wellness and Keeping Fit

Tension mounts—and you thought last month was intense! The good news is that a fitness class, team sport, or regular workouts with a good buddy fuel your vitality.

Love and Life Connections

Dealing with family matters can take a lot of time, especially if the power base is shifting or if there's a crisis brewing. Changes you're making can break with tradition, and you may feel alienated from your family as a result. Conflicts between your career and your personal life can also loom large, and identifying your priorities will help you avoid a potential crisis during the Full Moon on May 18.

Finance and Success

Your reputation leads the way, and if you're at the door with your honor intact, your success takes a solid step forward. However, if you've alienated a person of influence or ignored the rules, you'll find out about that, too—big time! Conservative factions may present resistance during the New Moon on May 3, but with the help of strong alliances, you're making headway. Investments fare best from May 15-22.

Cosmic Insider Tip

Power struggles between those afraid of change and those insistent upon revolution can threaten the status quo. By clarifying your goals, you'll know which options fit best for you.

Rewarding Days

1, 2, 5, 9, 10, 14, 18, 19, 28, 29

Challenging Days

3, 4, 15, 16, 17, 23, 24, 25, 30, 31

Affirmation for the Month

Honor and truth guide my path.

Leo/June

In the Spotlight
Your persistence pays off, with unusual situations providing ripe opportunities to further your aims. Responsibilities may remain heavy, but you have more help and can utilize your position to make a difference in your community.

Wellness and Keeping Fit
You'll benefit from a change of pace by midmonth. Devoting extra time to rejuvenating activities strengthens your creative drive. Meditation provides wide-ranging support.

Love and Life Connections
Your friends add excitement, although there are changes in a friendship you may not have anticipated. A love interest draws your attention, and initiating contact during the New Moon on June 2 can lead to fast-paced interaction. Romantic involvement fuels your self-esteem. During the Full Moon on June 16, activities encouraging spontaneous joy are highly recommended.

Finance and Success
Professional alliances and community concerns provide an excellent forum for your leadership, and if you've been hoping for the right time to institute a new project, launching it on June 2 or 3 can garner positive attention. Sign long-term contracts before June 11. Mercury's retrograde on June 23 marks a great time to reconsider an idea that's been brewing on the back burner.

Cosmic Insider Tip
Situations that provide an arena to showcase your talents or ideas can advance your reputation from June 2-6. Surrender the spotlight after June 17.

Rewarding Days
1, 2, 5, 6, 10, 14, 15, 16, 25, 29, 30

Challenging Days
12, 13, 19, 20, 21, 27, 28

Affirmation for the Month
My heart is filled with joy!

Leo/July

In the Spotlight

You may be plagued with old situations that seem to hang on like a badger. Forgiveness is the key to your progress, since carrying an old grudge can act like a lead weight.

Wellness and Keeping Fit

Physical weaknesses can be quite bothersome, and underlying health problems can surface. Seek out their deeper causes near the lunar eclipse on July 16.

Love and Life Connections

An old lover can enter the picture, just in time to confuse the issue! Your fascination with someone can be rather addictive, but is it based upon realistic possibilities, and do you care? With Venus in your sign from July 13 onward, your best attributes become highly attractive. Add fantasy to your love life! If you're not "available," stay out of the game to avoid getting into trouble during the Leo solar eclipse on July 30.

Finance and Success

The Sun's eclipse on July 1 emphasizes imaginative activities that need work behind the scenes before they're released in a public forum. Since Mercury's retrograding until July 17, you'll have more success completing an ongoing project. Safeguard investments, avoiding unknown circumstances. After July 23, you'll feel more confident, and an imaginative, artistic endeavor can become profitable.

Cosmic Insider Tip

With solar eclipses at the beginning and end of the month, everything can feel more intense. Unless you're comfortable with lots of attention, play down your efforts.

Rewarding Days

3, 4, 7, 12, 13, 22, 23, 26, 27, 30, 31

Challenging Days

1, 9, 10, 11, 17, 18, 24, 25

Affirmation for the Month

With compassion and understanding, I extend a hand of forgiveness.

Leo/August

In the Spotlight

Taking the initiative works to your advantage, and others may eagerly follow your lead. You can make a fresh start in situations that have grown stale, and you may decide to head toward new horizons with courage and imagination.

Wellness and Keeping Fit

Mars enters your sign, fueling your verve. It's a good time to build strength, tone muscles, increase endurance—as long as you pace yourself! Avoid high risks after August 25.

Love and Life Connections

The signals you've been sending pay off, but now you're eager to get on with the passionate side of romance. Infatuation can leave you vulnerable from August 2-9, when you can get in over your head, though you may feel satisfied as a result! Partnership issues loom large during the Full Moon on August 15. Excitement beckons after August 21, when you're eager to experiment with more open attitudes.

Finance and Success

Restrictions on finances from August 1-6 provide an indicator of the weak links that require fortification. Clarify misconceptions before August 11, and solidify agreements from August 13-22, allowing room in the budget for renovation or repair. Eliminating situations on the job that undermine productivity maximizes your resources, although you may alienate some people in the process.

Cosmic Insider Tip

While Mars is in your sign for six weeks, you can become overbearing and not even realize it. Being attentive to other's responses helps you gauge how far to go, personally and professionally.

Rewarding Days

3, 4, 8, 9, 18, 19, 23, 27, 28

Challenging Days

6, 7, 13, 14, 15, 20, 21

Affirmation for the Month

My actions are tempered by heartfelt compassion.

Leo/September

In the Spotlight
Interaction with others to share your ideas and interests helps to build a platform of support benefiting the good of the whole, while providing an opportunity for you to assert your leadership. Accountability is crucial to your success.

Wellness and Keeping Fit
Continuing to take on physical challenges adds confidence while helping to improve your overall sense of well-being. Team sports can be fun, although it's tempting to take the game too seriously.

Love and Life Connections
Expressing your thoughts and feelings with ease, your ideas can have a powerful influence. Your dreams and vision for the future inspire trust from your partner. Loving energy flows freely, and your experiences with children and family make you feel alive. Embarking upon a journey with your love alters the course of your relationship after the New Moon on September 27.

Finance and Success
Humanitarian ideals may drive your actions, and your concerns for making improvements in the quality of life inspire others. Fund raising may not be easy, but your vigorous persuasion during the Full Moon on September 13 succeeds if your appeal gives someone a sense of power! Mergers provide an option for speculation, but watch for the cutbacks before you sink your resources into anything.

Cosmic Insider Tip
Your ideals may run headlong into the nasty politics of greed, but by taking the high road you can be in a position to share information that empowers others to do the right thing.

Rewarding Days
1, 4, 5, 14, 15, 23, 24, 27

Challenging Days
2, 3, 9, 10, 13, 17, 18, 29, 30

Affirmation for the Month
I am honest with myself and with others in all matters.

Leo/October

In the Spotlight
The manner in which you use your resources has profound implications, since prudent expenditures may be required to restore the true value of a project or situation.

Wellness and Keeping Fit
Emotional stress takes its toll on your physical health, and if you're feeling tired it could be that you've lost your enthusiasm. Playful time out after October 20 helps to restore your energy.

Love and Life Connections
Improvements on the home front test your patience, particularly if your partner balks at your suggestions or overtures. Turning to your spirituality for inspiration during the Full Moon on October 13 promotes a feeling of hope and allows you to rise above petty issues. Heartfelt bonds grow more profound after October 20. Put expectations aside in favor of savoring the joy of the moment.

Finance and Success
Your budget may need a complete overhaul, and liquidating costly elements from October 1-6 helps you get rid of situations draining your assets. Your partner may take actions that counter your own from October 6-10, prompting you to reconsider the value of your shared resources. An established investment shows substantial revitalization after the New Moon on October 27, but new speculation could prove excessively expensive.

Cosmic Insider Tip
Mercury enters its retrograde cycle on October 18, when communication breakdowns can undermine your position and influence. Clarify misunderstandings as quickly as possible.

Rewarding Days
2, 3, 12, 16, 20, 21, 25, 29

Challenging Days
7, 8, 9, 13, 14, 15, 27, 28

Affirmation for the Month
I surrender the power of my ego to the control of my higher self.

Leo/November

In the Spotlight
Stubborn ideologies surrender to common sense. Getting involved with others who understand your drives and ideals helps to shape a network that can benefit your family or community.

Wellness and Keeping Fit
Keep moving to help release stress. Working to release emotional tension has a positive effect on your physical health. Pamper yourself after November 13, and allow more time for yourself.

Love and Life Connections
Bringing the passion back into your partnership from November 1-6 can be the result of simply spending more time together doing things you love. Everyday tensions and problems have been taking their toll, and family issues can be problematic near the Full Moon on November 11. Honor your relationship's strengths. Spending time with children inspires your creativity.

Finance and Success
Vague directions leave you wondering exactly what's expected of you from November 1-16, and since Mercury retrogrades until November 10, clarification will require extra effort. Meetings and presentations generate an enthusiastic reception of your ideas after November 5. The talents of others add to productivity after November 13, and implementing your plan of action on or after the New Moon on November 25 helps to assure success.

Cosmic Insider Tip
Misjudging the value or cost of a situation can undermine your confidence, but by uncovering the details you'll feel you've learned a lesson worthy of your attention.

Rewarding Days
8, 9, 12, 13, 16, 17, 21, 26

Challenging Days
3, 4, 10, 11, 19, 23, 24, 30

Affirmation for the Month
I am an effective and knowledgeable communicator.

Leo/December

In the Spotlight
Feeling more alive and optimistic, your self-assurance goes a long way toward reinforcing your self-expression. Interactive circumstances enhance your reputation and advance your career, and networking is a major asset.

Wellness and Keeping Fit
Sports and recreational activities can be invaluable. Travel could be invigorating, particularly if you're with someone you love.

Love and Life Connections
An intriguing encounter sparks your interest from December 1-6 and may lead to a dynamic romance by the Full Moon on December 11. To breathe new life into an existing relationship, do something out of the ordinary or change the scenery. Let your sense of drama work to your advantage from December 11-23. After December 24, family matters require your attention, but love keeps the glimmer in your eyes!

Finance and Success
Your ability to dazzle others with your expressive tones and gestures works to your benefit. By creating images that draw others into their most imaginative frame of reference, you'll enjoy tremendous success. Speculative interests can be extremely rewarding, although you're somewhat vulnerable to emotional ploys from December 9-13, when it's best to keep your cash in your pockets.

Cosmic Insider Tip
The solar eclipse on December 25 stimulates a period of introspective analysis of your life circumstances and needs. Reflect on areas that can use improvement. Start with your health!

Rewarding Days
5, 6, 10, 11, 14, 15, 18, 19, 23, 24

Challenging Days
1, 2, 8, 9, 20, 21, 27, 28, 29

Affirmation for the Month
My thoughts and actions are a reflection of pure love.

Leo Action Table

These dates reflect the best—but not the only—times for success and ease in these activities, according to your Sun sign.

	JAN	FEB	MAR	APR	MAY	JUN	JUL	AUG	SEPT	OCT	NOV	DEC
Move									28-30	1-17	9-30	1, 2
Start a class				4					27, 28			
Join a club						2						
Ask for a raise								30, 31				
Look for work	1-18				1-14							24-31
Get pro advice	8, 9	4, 5	2-4, 30-31	26, 27	23-25	19-21	17, 18	13, 14	9-11	7, 8	3, 4, 30	1-2, 28-29
Get a loan	10, 11	6-8	5, 6	1-2, 28-30	26, 27	22, 23	19-21	15-17	12, 13	9, 10	5-7	3-4, 30-31
See a doctor	1-17				31	1-30	1-31	1-7				24-31
Start a diet	5-7	1, 2, 29	12, 27, 28	23-25	21, 22	17, 18	14, 15	10-12	7, 8	4, 5, 31	28, 29	25, 26
End relationship								13-15				
Buy clothes												4-22
Get a makeover								30, 31				
New romance											25, 26	
Vacation	12-14	9, 10	7, 8	3, 4	1-2, 28-29	24-26	22, 23	18, 19	14, 15	11-13	8, 9	5, 6

Virgo
The Virgin
August 22 to September 21

♍

Element:	Earth
Quality:	Mutable
Polarity:	Yin/Feminine
Planetary Ruler:	Mercury
Meditation:	"I experience love through service."
Gemstone:	Sapphire
Power Stones:	Rhodochrosite, peridot, amazonite
Key Phrase:	"I analyze"
Glyph:	Greek symbol for containment, virgin ♍
Anatomy:	Abdomen, intestines, gall bladder
Colors:	Taupe, gray, navy
Animal:	Domesticated animals
Myths/Legends:	Astraea, Demeter, Hygeia
House:	Sixth
Opposite Sign:	Pisces
Flower:	Pansy
Key Word:	Discriminating

Positive Expression:	Misuse of Energy:
Methodical	Intolerant
Humble	Tedious
Practical	Nervous
Conscientious	Skeptical
Helpful	Hypercritical
Efficient	Superficial
Meticulous	Hypochondriacal

Virgo

Your Ego's Strengths and Shortcomings

You know quality when you see it and strive for perfection in yourself and whatever you produce. As a result of this drive, your sharply developed observational skills rarely rest, and your analytical abilities are second to none. Your connection to the energy of Mercury, the planet of communication, shines through your love of intelligent people, intellectual pursuits, and the development of your mind. Learning is a lifelong quest, and sharing what you know through guidance and teaching can be an unmatched pleasure.

Your studious approach to life and practical efficiency can place you in high demand in the working world, particularly since you have a knack for bringing complex information into a workable format. You're a "fixer," driven by the feeling that almost anyone or anything can benefit from improvement, and this quality is reflected in your role as "The Modifier" of the zodiac; but you have a secret: you're not the neatness freak some think you are, since you can just as easily stuff things into a junk drawer or closet in favor of concentrating on whatever you perceive to be more important (priorities, you know!). You do prefer cleanliness and have a penchant for staying healthy. Nothing escapes your scrutiny, which is why you may be rather picky about your diet, and just as critical of your relationships. Finding positive ways to apply your critical analysis to people and situations may be one of your greatest challenges.

As you strive for spiritual perfection, you encounter the lesson of acceptance. From self-acceptance to tolerance for others and their differences, you realize that the only hope for humankind rests in the opportunity for each individual to develop his or her own proficiency, and from this point you will find it easier to fine tune your own life path.

Shining Your Love Light

Your soul yearns for a love that can endure the test of time, and as a result you may have a very long list of qualifications for potential partners. Some are quickly eliminated, but once you've opened your heart to love, your romantic dreams awaken. Your loving touch can be pure enchantment, and your lover may be surprised at your intense sensuality. When you're committed, you prefer to surrender body, mind, and soul to create the perfect relationship, and you will blossom in an atmosphere of true love.

The comfortable pace and stable energy of the other earth signs—Taurus, Virgo and Capricorn—allow you to feel right at home. You may have a strong attraction to your zodiac opposite, Pisces, even though there can be a battle between practicality and idealism unless you work toward a common bond.

Aries is definitely exciting, arousing your sexual energies, but can also be too distracting. You'll adore Taurus' sensuality and endurance, while appreciating his or her conservative practicality. Gemini's mentality, curiosity, and intellectual levity are amusing, although you can be confounded by this sign's lack of focus. Physical attraction and friendship abound with Cancer. With Leo, that warm embrace can be the stuff of your dreams, but you may feel uneasy unless you're good friends. Life with another Virgo can be comfy, as long as you learn how to funnel your critical natures into constructive arenas.

Libra stimulates your objectivity, but you may have to continually clarify where you stand with one another. Scorpio can be ideal, since passion and deep love are a natural outflow of this connection. Although you readily share private pleasures and favorite pastimes with Sagittarius, you may not spend much time together. Capricorn's dry wit stimulates your sense of playfulness and feels very stable when it comes to love. With Aquarius, both spiritual strength and fireworks abound, but you may feel alone when you're ready to settle into a sweet embrace.

Making Your Place in the World

Work that provides a feeling of accomplishment while challenging your mind can be the perfect choice. You might enjoy running your own business. Occupations requiring manual dexterity can be rewarding. Drafting, design, graphic arts, crafts fields, or detail work in the building industry can answer you need to keep those hands busy.

Your planning abilities are in demand in office managements, desktop publishing, secretarial and administrative services, accounting, systems analysis, and scientific research. Your desire to share knowledge can be fulfilled in teaching, writing, speaking, or broadcasting. Service-oriented fields—counseling, social services, and health professions—can be prosperous. You may even develop skills in more than one career and can probably do more than one job at a time. Whatever your choices, you will do your reliable best.

Power Plays

Holding a position of power will only interest you if you feel you can use your influence to alter the course of events or bring about wide-ranging improvements. The power of the mind is something you readily embrace, and in shaping the course of your own life or the lives of others, you may strive to make honest use of wisdom and information. Since you may not seek power for its own sake, others may be amazed when they realize the scope of your accomplishments. After all, your proficiency sometimes leaves the impression that what you've done has been effortless; but when you walk away, there's always a big gap to fill. Learning to appreciate your own worth helps restore the balance of power in your life.

You can become caught in the quagmire of codependency since you're frequently drawn to serve the needs of others. Knowing when to take charge and when to allow someone to fail or succeed on their own is part of the proper use of your power. You're challenged to use the power of service to help improve the quality of life for yourself and for the world in which you live.

Famous Virgos

Agatha Christie, Marcia Clark, Patsy Cline, Sean Connery, David Copperfield, Hugh Grant, Julio Iglesias, Sophia Loren, Bill Medly, Dee Dee Myers, Seiji Ozawa, Keanu Reeves, Claudia Schiffer, Peter Sellers, Ione Skye, Oliver Stone.

The Year Ahead for Virgo

Your expertise and reputation open the way for advancement of your career, but in typical Virgo fashion, that may mean you'll have to adapt to even more changes if you are to see the full measure of your success. It's the kind of challenge you like: learning new things, incorporating innovation, and experimenting with fresh ideas. Your practical sensibilities are in demand, and by applying your analytical mind to the ever-changing options in the world around you, you'll know exactly which opportunities to accept and which to decline.

Increased confidence in your professional skills, prompted by Jupiter's transit through your solar Ninth and Tenth Houses this year, gains notice. Publishing, promotional activities, academic pursuits, or public speaking can help to further your growing reputation. From January through July, while Jupiter highlights your Ninth House, travel will be significant, and whether your journeys are personally or professionally motivated, the effect of expanding your understanding and increasing your confidence can be highly inspiring. After July, Jupiter transits through your Tenth House, marking an exciting period of professional growth. The last time Jupiter highlighted this part of your chart was twelve years ago, and many of the things you set in motion at that time will move ahead by leaps and bounds. The downfall of this transit is knowing when to say "no," since you may be tempted to think that unless you take advantage of every opportunity, you'll lose out. Setting reasonable limits that help fulfill your larger goals makes these decisions easier. Remember throughout this period of prosperity and growth to keep your ego in check, since you'll go much further with an attitude of humble pride than one of arrogant self-importance.

Saturn's energy of discipline, focus, and determination travels in a complimentary position to your Sun this year, emphasizing the importance of obtaining credentials through education, publication, or exercise of professional expertise to help build your reputation. Extended travel is often a feature of this cycle, particularly if it's related to your profession. Teaching can also be exceptionally rewarding since you may discover that your own knowledge is strengthened through the experience of sharing or mentoring.

The slower-moving cycles of the planets Uranus, Neptune and Pluto have their most noticeable impact when they are exactly aspecting your Sun or other energies in your natal chart. (To determine if your Sun is undergoing an exact aspect from these planets, follow the paragraphs in the next section of "The Year Ahead" according to your birth day.) However, the particular sectors of your chart undergoing the transits of these planets will be powerfully emphasized. Uranus and Neptune highlight your house of work and health, marking a period when making room for innovation and creativity on the job will work to your benefit. Pluto's cycle continues its impact in your house of security, home, and family, and the transformations in this area are definitely noteworthy. Eliminating excess strengthens your security base.

The four solar eclipses and two lunar eclipses during the year 2000 draw your attention to the flow of love and feelings of satisfaction in your life. Your ability to open yourself to receiving love, confirmation, and acceptance is tested, and this can be an exceptional time of clearing old inhibitions. The impact of these eclipses on society and the world centers around nationalism, family, and human rights, and you'll see these issues filtering into your own work and life experience.

If you were born from August 23 to 24, you're feeling the restraint of Saturn transiting in square aspect to your Sun. This cycle is most powerful during the summer and fall months and will surface again next year. You will feel the full effects of this cycle for a little more than a year, with the early impact happening in the last half of the year 2000. You'll need to pay very careful attention to the temptation of overdoing it during July (stimulated by a square aspect from Jupiter to your Sun), since excesses accumulated then will slow you down for the following six months! It's easy to worry when Saturn squares your Sun since the feeling that you're running out of time, doing things inefficiently, or are overburdened with too many obligations can get you down. By eliminating some of your obligations you can more fully embrace the responsibilities that support your personal growth. You may also run into your fears, shrinking from opportunities because you feel inadequate. It's quite likely that you simply need to fulfill requirements in order to move forward.

Since you'll be setting new priorities, remember to put a niche in your routine for your health. This cycle brings with it an awareness of your physical needs and limitations, and by dealing with problems directly and taking a responsible attitude toward your health, you can improve your sense of well-being.

If you were born from August 25 to 31, you may be feeling more confused. Neptune's transit in quincunx aspect to your Sun increases your sensitivity on every level. From health issues to concern about your relationships, you're feeling things that before may have gone unnoticed. You may be more in touch with your environment, including the people surrounding you, but that increased sensitivity can leave you scrambling to make adjustments. Creative energy is enhanced, but can be distracting if you fall into addictive patterns with your creativity (e.g. doodling at your desk because your images are fascinating, but not getting your work done as a result!). This cycle involves a shift in your awareness, and although you may ultimately welcome it, getting used to it requires patience. You may also feel that you're out of touch due to changing circumstances beyond your control, but by shifting your focus, you can incorporate these alterations without losing your connection to the things that really matter most.

If you were born from September 1 to 3, it's time to refine your artistic and creative sensibilities. Neptune's transit in biquintile aspect to your Sun can have a very subtle effect, but you may discover that your yearning to pull out those unfinished craft projects, take up the study of an instrument, or dust off your talents in other areas is haunting you. The influence of this cycle can be missed if you're not looking for it, but if you're interested in developing your skills and artistry, then this period can allow you to open to levels of expression that are truly beautiful. Your ability to translate the stuff of your imagination into a physical reality is strengthened, but you'll have to apply the focus and discipline necessary to make it happen.

If you were born from September 3 to 8, you're experiencing the transformational challenges of Pluto. Pluto's transit in square aspect to your Sun helps to bring old issues to the surface during what is, essentially, a cycle of healing and rebirth. This can be a very difficult cycle if you're fighting it. Some of the issues surfacing can be downright unpleasant, since they were repressed for a reason! However, by addressing old trauma, disappointment, guilt, or shame, you're creating the mechanism to reclaim your personal power. You may also be face to face with a power struggle. Always remember that even when you are not initiating changes, you always have a choice about the way you respond. Unhealthy circumstances that you've tolerated out of fear or lack of courage may now seem completely untenable, and eliminating these unhealthy elements from your life can feel like the lifting of a terrible weight. You may realize that it's time to leave something behind, but some changes may only require altering your attitudes and your responses so that you're capable of maintaining your course toward growth. Your spirit is yearning for release from the things that are inhibiting your full and free expression, clearing the way for you to become whole, perfect, strong, and powerful! Just remember that if it were easy, it would not be called transformation.

If you were born from September 6 to 16, you're experiencing the unsettling influence of Uranus transiting in quincunx aspect to your Sun. However, Saturn's supportive trine aspect to your Sun from March through May of 2000 helps you determine how far you need to go in making adjustments, and will add a stabilizing element to this period of evolutionary or revolutionary change. The temptation to burn your bridges can be overwhelming at times during this cycle, since losing your patience with yourself and with your circumstances can bring out your most impatient qualities. It's definitely time to release the things you no longer need in favor of a more free self-expression—whether you're eliminating bad habits, a sick relationship, an unrewarding job, or a negative attitude. You're also realizing that you can no longer hold on to anybody in your life who needs to be free of you, and this may mark a period of change in your relationship with a child, friend, parent, or spouse. The most significant revolution is the one going on inside your soul: you have the power to bring forth your most profound and endearing qualities. They've been sleeping too long!

If you were born from September 17 to 23, you're experiencing the stabilizing influence of Saturn transiting in trine aspect to your Sun. The decisions and commitments you make this year are designed to last, and if there are changes to make, you may feel you're in a safe cycle to implement them. Now is the time to become seriously involved in academic pursuits, to finish a dissertation, write your novel, buckle down in your career by taking on the responsibilities that give your talents a place to shine, or to gain credentials. You may also become involved in teaching others, and through teaching may confirm your own knowledge while surrendering to learning even more. This is a time of work, but it's work that pays off through stability and confirmation. For once you may feel that you're finally in charge of fulfilling your destiny!

Tools to Make a Difference

To fully welcome the gifts of Jupiter and Saturn, reflect on the things you want to learn that strengthen your understanding of the mysteries of life. Others are likely to seek your guidance, and by graciously acknowledging the respect being shown to you, you are also acknowledging the power that has provided for your abundance. Teaching may be one of the best ways to say "thank you," and in many cases, provides the most fertile ground for learning. Taking a sabbatical could be a wonderful gift for yourself and can provide the tool of a more reflective mental and emotional space from which to embrace understanding and wisdom. If you cannot take months away from your work, incorporate periods of reflection and contemplation into your routine.

Holistic health concepts make perfect sense to you, and if you've not investigated complimentary or alternative health care options, this is a good time to open those doors and to employ that knowledge as part of your health maintenance. Tools like acupuncture, body work, chi gung, yoga, or tai chi can help you keep your energy flowing freely. If you want to incorporate aromatherapy, you'll appreciate the effects of inhalations of frankincense, bergamot, or geranium. In the evenings, you might enjoy relaxing with a cup of herbal tea containing chamomile, kava kava, hops, and valerian. Soaking in a tub fragrant with rosemary or lavender can be just what you need to take the edge off a busy week.

During your meditations, visualizations that bring a sense of connection to the earth can be comforting, but you may also feel that you need to balance your earthly contact with a link to divine intelligence. Envision that you are hiking through a perfectly serene forest. Listening to the gently running stream, you follow an old trail into a clearing, where you come upon what appears to be an ancient structure built of large stones and rocks. You're drawn to a flat rock in one quadrant of the structure, and when you sit on the rock you can feel the warmth of the sun shining directly over your head. Closing your eyes, allow this energy to permeate your body and soul. Time seems to stop in this place, but you are somehow aware of the connection of past, present, and future in a profound way. You can see yourself as a child, adult, and ancient wise one, and feel the links of divine wisdom through every age. Embrace your own timeless soul.

Initiating the Millennium

You're in an excellent place to begin a new century since you're filled with a powerful mix of confidence, responsibility, and excitement. While technological innovations will play a significant role in the evolution of your work, you're also recognizing the awakening of your own intuitive and visionary sensibilities. Assimilating your visions for the future into practical reality is very much your style, and through your guidance, others may learn to welcome change as much as you have embraced it.

℧

Affirmation for the Year

I welcome the experience of growth and healing!

Virgo/January

In the Spotlight
Initiation of fresh creative ideas sets the stage for renewal in relationship to your children, artistic expression, or affairs of the heart. Sound judgment supports your ability to make wise choices when it comes to speculation.

Wellness and Keeping Fit
You need a competitive challenge. Whether you're setting fitness goals in class or joining a team, you're aiming for excellence. Probe psychological issues connected to your physical health.

Love and Life Connections
You may be feeling more assertive and can feel that your partnership has become a battle zone if you disagree on fundamental issues, although you're breaking free of old patterns. Breathing life into an existing connection is the theme of the New Moon on January 6, when resolution of conflict is also easier. Gatherings at home, surrounded by loved ones, remind you of life's true values.

Finance and Success
Investments show progress, although costs for a project may absorb your profits. Beneficial support from a partner is helpful, but only if you agree on your limitations. Contracts signed from January 6-17 hold the greatest potential. Your talents may gain acknowledgment, but before you decide to exercise them, be sure you're comfortable with proposed schedules, since you may already be obligated.

Cosmic Insider Tip
The lunar eclipse on January 20 emphasizes the importance of striking a balance between emotional and physical needs. Reflection or meditation helps sharpen your perspective.

Rewarding Days
5, 6, 15, 16, 19, 20, 23, 24, 28, 29

Challenging Days
2, 3, 4, 10, 11, 17, 18, 30, 31

Affirmation for the Month
I trust my intuitive insights.

Virgo/February

In the Spotlight
Improvements capture your attention, and whether you're making them in regard to your health, lifestyle, or work circumstances, you're ready to apply your analytical and practical creativity to the processes of evolutionary change.

Wellness and Keeping Fit
Bringing your mental, emotional, and physical needs into harmony can require extra work. Incorporate imagery and fitness activities, but still allow time for reflection and rest.

Love and Life Connections
Conflict with your partner may be the result of repressed anger, and if you're openly airing your grievances with compassionate understanding, you'll see progress. Hurt feelings seem to be the order of the day around the Virgo Full Moon on February 19, although your philosophical ideals may prompt you to seek solutions that lead to realistic resolutions, even if it's not what everybody wants.

Finance and Success
The Sun's eclipse on February 5 stimulates unprecedented change, and you may be scurrying about trying to keep up. Fortunately, you're an adaptable soul, and you may even welcome innovation, but only if your productivity is enhanced. It's finally time to get rid of non-productive elements on the job. Joint finances and tax matters can be unsettling after February 13, but expert advice is helpful.

Cosmic Insider Tip
On February 21 Mercury enters its three-week retrograde period, and by using this time to revisit a situation or reopen negotiations, you may see progress where there was once an impasse.

Rewarding Days
1, 2, 11, 12, 15, 16, 19, 20, 25, 29

Challenging Days
6, 7, 8, 13, 14, 26, 27

Affirmation for the Month
I seek the guidance of higher wisdom in all my decisions.

Virgo/March

In the Spotlight
Communication glitches, misinformation, and uncertainty inhibit progress, especially in the midst of situations that have political implications. Staying above the fray requires patience and tolerance for different styles and backgrounds.

Wellness and Keeping Fit
Bring stress down to a manageable level by maintaining your dedication to your fitness activities. A visit to a massage therapist or acupuncturist can help keep your energy flowing harmoniously.

Love and Life Connections
It's crucial that you assess your deep feelings about your relationships. Aligning your honest feelings with your actions can lead to major change, and initiating dialogue during the New Moon on March 6 may be the first step. From the Virgo Full Moon on March 19 until March 25, you may be struggling with the realization that you've had a change of heart. It takes courage to make the healthy choice.

Finance and Success
Legal wrangling may seem to be going nowhere fast, and there's a red herring complicating matters in contract negotiations. Use this time to research, but realize that progress may not occur until after Mercury turns direct on March 14. Until then, it's a rehash of the same problems. Conferences or business travel offer promising connections after March 23. The spotlight is flattering on March 27-28.

Cosmic Insider Tip
Separating fact from fiction or prejudice from truth can be quite a challenge since Jupiter and Neptune are transiting in square aspect to each other. Trust your philosophical understanding to guide you.

Rewarding Days
1, 9, 10, 13, 14, 18, 19, 23, 27, 28

Challenging Days
4, 5, 6, 11, 12, 25, 26, 30

Affirmation for the Month
Truth opens my mind and heart to ultimate wisdom.

Virgo/April

In the Spotlight
Publishing, advertising, and convening with others in your field provide the perfect situations to share your ideas and strengthen your reputation. Forming connections with partners adds credibility.

Wellness and Keeping Fit
Probing into your psyche aids your quest to locate the core elements of physical complaints. Your spirituality also plays a significant role in altering your health.

Love and Life Connections
An intimate relationship prospers as you eliminate your fears, and the key to growing closer may reside in your spiritual ideals. Whether you're involved or single, you may have felt stuck, but the New Moon on April 4 stimulates courage to release your inhibitions and allow a higher love to heal your heart. Banish guilt and concentrate on stepping onto a path of optimism for yourself and your future.

Finance and Success
Endorsements of your accomplishments may arise through academic or cultural recognition. Conferences or business travel provide exceptional connections to others who appreciate you and your work. If you need funds to continue a project or further your education, the pathway arises near the Full Moon on April 18. Legal matters take an unusual turn from April 14-22, when your practicality helps determine the outcome.

Cosmic Insider Tip
Intractable attitudes can be frustrating midmonth, but by shining light on the larger picture you can get past the personal prejudices involved. Concentrate on long-range impact.

Rewarding Days
5, 6, 10, 11, 14, 15, 19, 20, 23, 24, 25

Challenging Days
1, 2, 8, 9, 21, 22, 29, 30

Affirmation for the Month
I honor and respect the higher principles of the law.

Virgo/May

In the Spotlight
Manifesting your professional goals can work like magic. Travel and education play a powerful role, and your insights may be widely sought by others who appreciate your expertise.

Wellness and Keeping Fit
A well-defined time to get away has a positive effect on your well-being, even though taking a real vacation might be difficult. Maybe you can sneak extra down time into that business trip.

Love and Life Connections
If your heart is ready for love, you may feel inspired to make a serious commitment. The New Moon on May 3 ushers in a powerful period of hope, and you may meet the person of your dreams in the course of your travels or professional activities. Testing the situation confirms whether or not you're in the right place emotionally, and by the Full Moon on May 18, you'll feel more secure about your choice.

Finance and Success
While you're sometimes a bit shy in the spotlight, stepping onto the podium to accept your rightful place seems quite natural now. Your influence makes a huge difference, and using your position to bring about changes in the world feels like a fulfillment of your destiny. Your ideas are golden, and by exercising your talents you can produce significant work as your path diverges from the ordinary and into the realm of the extraordinary.

Cosmic Insider Tip
The powerful alignment of energies this month influences your need to broaden your horizons. It's definitely time to go beyond your own backyard and connect on a more global level.

Rewarding Days
3, 4, 7, 8, 11, 12, 16, 17, 21, 22, 30, 31

Challenging Days
5, 6, 18, 19, 26, 27

Affirmation for the Month
I surrender my will to the will of the source of all power.

Virgo/June

In the Spotlight
With so much activity surrounding your career you may have little time to yourself, but that should not stop you from enjoying this very productive period! Be aware of your attitudes, since others may see you as predatory if you're not careful.

Wellness and Keeping Fit
Staying active strengthens your vim and vigor and is necessary if you are to accomplish everything on your busy agenda. Ignoring physical needs can lead to problems or injuries. Check your speed.

Love and Life Connections
Family members may not agree with your personal choices, and although you want to keep the peace you're not likely to give up something you truly need. Sharing your dreams for the future helps clarify your actions and brings resolutions near the Full Moon on June 16. Love blossoms after June 19, when allowing time for amorous play enriches your life. Reconnect with friends after June 22.

Finance and Success
Career moves can include changes in your work environment or even a job change, and alterations made on or after the New Moon on June 2 can make room for growth. Technological assistance improves your productivity, but may lead to overwork if you're not careful. Business associates offer endorsement for your work, and your leadership can influence long-range changes after June 16.

Cosmic Insider Tip
Another Mercury retrograde beginning on June 23 can actually be rather helpful since solutions come to light for problems previously unresolved—finally!

Rewarding Days
3, 4, 7, 8, 12, 13, 17, 18, 27, 28

Challenging Day
1, 2, 14, 15, 16, 22, 23, 29, 30

Affirmation for the Month
I celebrate my success and those who have helped me achieve it.

Virgo/July

In the Spotlight
Defining new goals stemming from a rising tide of creative energy, you may feel that you have a fresh perspective on your options and possibilities. Community activities give you a place to shine!

Wellness and Keeping Fit
The pleasure of fitness may be heightened through a class, sport, or teaming up with a good buddy to stay in shape. If you prefer singular activities, meet with a trainer to streamline your routine.

Love and Life Connections
Friends warm your heart during the Sun's eclipse on July 1, when a relationship may take a new turn. If the situation's right, friendship can turn to romance, particularly if you've harbored feelings for one another. During the lunar eclipse on July 16, a child can be the stimulus for powerful change, but a romantic love may also take flight. If you're feeling overwhelmed by the intensity of it all, pull away to reflect on your needs during the second solar eclipse on July 30.

Finance and Success
Taking the bull by the horns, so to speak, makes a huge difference in career. Waiting for someone else to make the first move tries your patience, and revitalizing a project on July 1 generates amazing momentum. Investments peak near July 16, but fresh opportunities inspire you to take creative risks. Focus on preparatory work after July 23, getting ready for the next wave.

Cosmic Insider Tip
Two solar eclipses and Mercury retrograde—that's a lot of cosmic news! Crises activate stalemates, but until Mercury turns direct on July 17, the path of progress may be uncertain.

Rewarding Days
1, 2, 5, 6, 9, 14, 15, 16, 24, 25, 28, 29

Challenging Days
12, 13, 19, 20, 21, 26, 27, 30

Affirmation for the Month
I welcome new directions in the pursuit of my true destiny.

Virgo/August

In the Spotlight
Balance your life by taking it easy. You're realigning your priorities, and in the process you may feel more inclined to allow yourself to savor the fruits of your considerable labors.

Wellness and Keeping Fit
Mars energizes the need to strengthen your inner being. Dedicating more time to physical activities that require contemplative focus is rejuvenating. Your dreams may be more active. Explore them!

Love and Life Connections
Venus in Virgo from August 6-30 stimulates your most attractive qualities and makes it easier to open your heart to love; but expectations and changes from August 11-17 challenge you to come to grips with your true feelings. Talking over your concerns without excessive criticism is the challenge from August 22-24. Then, with the Virgo New Moon on August 29, you'll be ready for a fresh start.

Finance and Success
Reorganizing your work environment, including clearing away that stack of stuff that's no longer a priority, makes room for better productivity. Frustrations reach their peak near the Full Moon on August 15, when you may also decide that you need to do something about your finances. This could include reviewing your salary, but altering your budget will also help. Meetings speed career progress after August 23.

Cosmic Insider Tip
Finish things that have suffered due to procrastination since you'll be eager to follow a different direction under the stimulus of the Virgo New Moon on August 29.

Rewarding Days
1, 2, 6, 7, 11, 12, 20, 21, 25, 29, 30

Challenging Days
8, 9, 15, 16, 17, 22, 23, 24

Affirmation for the Month
Relaxation and rest are a valuable part of my life.

Virgo/September

In the Spotlight
Maintaining a positive attitude in the midst of changes that threaten your security tests your ideals. It's easy to become cynical in the face of hypocrisy, but your integrity can raise the standards.

Wellness and Keeping Fit
Keeping a reasonable pace is a challenge, since stressful situations can lead you to exceed your physical limitations. Mars enters Virgo on September 16, stimulating your dedication to fitness.

Love and Life Connections
Although you may have concerns about your partnership, dealing with them is another thing. Articulating your needs is easiest from September 1-7, but major philosophical differences can block progress. The Full Moon on September 13 brings matters to a critical point, and family or career can create obstacles. If you want to salvage a situation, try again after September 25 when romance moves back into the picture.

Finance and Success
Organizational changes at work that are beyond your control can undermine your sense of direction. Stepping back to redefine your priorities helps you determine where to start. Fortunately, your resources can carry you through, and improvements are on the horizon with the New Moon on September 27. By isolating problems, you'll cut things down to size and get productivity back on track.

Cosmic Insider Tip
Building tensions, symbolized by the opposition of Jupiter and Pluto, can create a climate of change in economic or political arenas. Keeping your boundaries intact levels the playing field.

Rewarding Days
2, 7, 8, 17, 18, 21, 22, 25, 26, 29, 30

Challenging Days
4, 5, 6, 12, 13, 19, 20

Affirmation for the Month
The light of truth illuminates my path.

Virgo/October

In the Spotlight
Your words and actions can influence significant changes, and you may issue the challenge that sets in motion a series of improvements. Power struggles abound: choose your battles with care.

Wellness and Keeping Fit
Stress intensifies. Avoid high-risk activities from October 1-17, but do stay active. Police your cravings after October 26 when it's easy to overindulge.

Love and Life Connections
The bonds of love grow stronger and your sense of self-worth is enhanced. Getting away for a romantic rendezvous between October 9-15 can deepen intimacy. Trust issues can emerge during the Full Moon on October 13 when you're releasing your own blocks and fears. By the New Moon on October 27 your outlook is refreshed, and you're ready to let love transform your life.

Finance and Success
The rules seem to be changing, and certainly there's reorganization. Jockeying for position, you could be caught in the crossfire from October 1-7, so take an appropriate stand. Explore details of financial contracts and finalize agreements prior to October 17, when Mercury enters its retrograde phase. After that, dedicate your time to completing projects or investigating options that you can later implement.

Cosmic Insider Tip
Meetings, conferences, and communications offer the best forum for progress from October 1-20. Just remember that words can wound as easily as weapons.

Rewarding Days
4, 5, 14, 15, 18, 19, 22, 23, 28, 31

Challenging Days
2, 3, 9, 10, 16, 17, 29, 30

Affirmation for the Month
My principles are guided by universal law and wisdom.

Virgo/November

In the Spotlight
By making connections with others who share your interests, you advance your career and establish important links. Your artistry shines its light on the commencement of an important life change.

Wellness and Keeping Fit
Target activities that extend your endurance. Complimenting strength training with activities like yoga or dance adds to your vitality. The social benefits can be pretty exciting, too!

Love and Life Connections
Social gatherings close to home can be the stimulus for loving interactions with friends and family, and beautifying your personal surroundings lifts your spirits. Declarations of love will be most welcome after November 12, although you may feel a bit insecure if your finances are uncertain. Remind yourself that your worth goes beyond money! Initiate positive changes at home with the New Moon on November 25.

Finance and Success
Manipulative and confusing communication from November 1-16 tests your patience, especially if you feel powerless against forces bent on self-interest. Your common sense takes charge, and by focusing on a creative project after the Full Moon on November 11, you'll enjoy increased productivity. Investments pay off after November 18, but excess expenses can blow your budget.

Cosmic Insider Tip
Mercury's retrograde cycle is not complete until November 7, although the fog of confusion due to misinformation or communication breakdowns may not lift until the end of the month.

Rewarding Days
1, 2, 10, 11, 15, 19, 20, 23, 28, 29

Challenging Days
5, 6, 7, 12, 13, 25, 26

Affirmation for the Month
My words and actions reflect pure and loving intentions.

Virgo/December

In the Spotlight

You're juggling several priorities. Your primary focus centers around creative endeavors and may involve children or their activities. You're happily devoting significant time to home and family matters.

Wellness and Keeping Fit

Staying active is your best assurance that you'll have ample energy to get everything done; but you do need a spiritual recharge, so make time for contemplation.

Love and Life Connections

Affairs of the heart are reassured by actions like exchanging vows from December 1-9. Love takes another turn after December 24 when your need for experiences that confirm your true worth and deeper yearnings prompts you to speak from your soul. The Sun's eclipse on December 25 turns your attention to children, and appropriate to the yule season, you may feel that your inner child deserves more time to play as well!

Finance and Success

Speculative investments—ranging from stocks to your own creative endeavors—offer substantial rewards through December 8. You may decide to reapportion your assets after reviewing them from December 24-31. At work, you're seeing progress through improvements in technology. Unique and immediate approaches resolve most problems that arise.

Cosmic Insider Tip

Although the energy of the Full Moon on December 11 may prompt you to reconsider your career, you may feel that making adjustments is more suitable than a complete change of course.

Rewarding Days

8, 9, 12, 13, 16, 17, 21, 25, 26

Challenging Days

3, 4, 10, 11, 23, 24, 30, 31

Affirmation for the Month

I am happiest when my talents are put to good use!

Virgo Action Table

These dates reflect the best—but not the only—times for success and ease in these activities, according to your Sun sign.

	JAN	FEB	MAR	APR	MAY	JUN	JUL	AUG	SEPT	OCT	NOV	DEC
Move												4-23
Start a class					4, 5					27, 28		
Join a club							1, 2					
Ask for a raise								29, 30				
Look for work	19-31	1-5			14-29							
Get pro advice	10, 11	6-8	5, 6	1-2, 28-30	26, 27	22, 23	19-21	15-17	12, 13	9, 10	5-7	3-4, 30-31
Get a loan	12-14	9, 10	7, 8	3, 4	1-2, 28-29	25, 26	22, 23	18, 19	14, 15	11-13	8, 9	5-7
See a doctor	18-31	1-4						8-21				
Start a diet	8, 9	4, 5	2-4, 30-31	26, 27	23-25	19-21	17, 18	13, 14	9-11	7, 8	3-4, 30	1-2, 28-29
End relationship									12, 13			
Buy clothes	1-18											
Get a makeover								29, 30				
New romance	6, 7											
Vacation	15, 16	11, 12	9, 10	5-7	3-4, 30-31	27, 28	24, 25	20, 21	16-18	14, 15	10, 11	8, 9

Libra

The Balance Scales
September 22 to October 21

♎

Element:	Air
Quality:	Cardinal
Polarity:	Yang/Masculine
Planetary Ruler:	Venus
Meditation:	"I am creating beauty and harmony."
Gemstone:	Opal
Power Stones:	Tourmaline, kunzite, blue lace agate
Key Phrase:	"I balance"
Glyph:	Scales of justice, setting sun ♎
Anatomy:	Kidneys, lower back, appendix
Colors:	Blues, pinks
Animal:	Brightly plumed birds
Myths/Legends:	Hera, Venus, Cinderella
House:	Seventh
Opposite Sign:	Aries
Flower:	Rose
Key Word:	Harmony

Positive Expression:	Misuse of Energy:
Refined	Indecisive
Objective	Critical
Logical	Argumentative
Impartial	Distant
Artistic	Conceited
Gracious	Unreliable
Sociable	Inconsiderate

Libra

Your Ego's Strengths and Shortcomings

Your love of beauty is apparent. From the people in your social circles, to the charm of your surroundings and artistic nature—your life is an expression of the energy of Venus, your planetary ruler. When courtesy and refinement are needed, you're the person called upon to act as a planner or an impartial intermediary.

Your role as "The Judge" of the zodiac arises when logical alternatives, harmony, and symmetry are important. You're a natural diplomat and possess the power of objectivity, but sometimes in your own life you may feel that it's difficult to find it when you need it (one of those gifts that seems destined to be applied to help others). This is especially true in your relationships, since sometimes you can go overboard trying to ensure that everyone else is happy. By keeping a clear measure of your deeper values, your self-esteem remains strong and your decisions reflect a balanced perspective. If you measure your worth by the wishes of others, you'll feel unstable.

Setting goals that lead to attaining personal security helps you maintain a strong sense of self in the midst of an ever-changing world. As long as you feel a sense of balance between your inner self and the world around you, you'll feel safe. After all, the harmony you feel with your inner partner radiates the peaceful, loving energy you hope to see reflected in the eyes of others around you.

Shining Your Love Light

Oh, the tales you could tell of love, broken hearts, and victorious conquests! Whether you're speaking about your dreams of the perfect partner or from your personal experiences, you are the most likely sign to think in terms of an "ideal" mate and eternal love. In your heart of hearts, you hope for a relationship filled with equality, but may have trouble either allowing yourself or your partner to be truly autonomous. The natural, evolutionary processes of love and relationship will strengthen your confidence that your ideals may, after all, be fully realized—in one lifetime!

The air signs—Gemini, Libra and Aquarius—share and understand your appreciation for communication, socialization, and fascination with the mind and ideas. For a relationship to survive in your life, shared ideas is a requirement.

Aries, your zodiac opposite, can be powerfully attractive, but you may feel there's a lack in the fairness department. Your love for the aesthetic is shared by Taurus, although financial control issues can be problematic. Gemini's mental acrobatics are delightful, and you may adore learning and traveling together. With Cancer, you'll enjoy the nurturing until you've had enough, and may not know how to say "back off!" Leo stimulates an opening of your heart, and his or her laughter, passion, and drama can be unforgettable.

With Virgo, you feel comfortable and appreciate his or her attention to detail and quality, but you may not always be romantically inclined. Another Libra may share your love of beauty and you may have a strong meeting of the minds, but stability can be lacking. It's easy to feel overtaken by Scorpio's intense tidal wave of energy, and you can lose track of your personal boundaries if you've been swept off your feet. The fun and excitement of adventures with Sagittarius can fill your diary for years. With Capricorn, you can feel a connection that is sometimes overpowering, but control issues can try your patience. Aquarius is creatively inspiring and you may have an unmatched romantic bond. Pisces' mystical energy swirling around can carry you into fanciful escape, but you may feel smothered by the tide of emotions.

Making Your Place in the World

An expressive career path that puts you in touch with people can be right up your alley. Public relations, personnel management, advertising, or sales can be lucrative. Diplomatic service, politics, or the law may also draw your interest. Counseling others, including image consulting, could be rewarding.

Putting your artistic abilities to work can lead to a wide range of possibilities, from the arts and literature, to design, costuming, or interior design. You might also enjoy teaching or promoting the arts through museums, conservatories, or galleries. Whatever your choice of career, you'll add a touch of class to your work.

Power Plays

You may bristle at the mere thought of unfairness, and a misuse of power can be repugnant to you. As a result, you may act as though you care little about power, but from a position of leadership or strength, you can become exceptionally influential. Your ideals of justice and humanitarian treatment for all have a very logical basis, and when you apply your impartiality to your logical assessments, your opinions can spearhead revolutionary change. However, you can appear cold or uncaring to those under your scrutiny if you lose your balanced perspective to emotionally prejudicial choices.

You're a person of high ideals, and your image of perfection may be second to none. These attitudes can undermine your power base if you apply unrealistic ideals to a person or situation, including yourself, during the times when your self-esteem is wavering. Finding ways to affirm your own value as an individual while keeping positive personal boundaries allows you to create life on your own terms while sharing with those who know your love and care.

By blending the beautiful qualities glowing within yourself with the energy that flows from the light of the Source, your life reflects an unmatched beauty that whispers the truth of love on the winds of eternity.

Famous Libras

Toni Braxton, Montgomery Clift, Divine, Brett Favre, F. Scott Fitzgerald, Jim Henson, Annie Leibovitz, Thomas Moore, Olivia Newton-John, Gwyneth Paltrow, Luke Perry, Scottie Pippen, Susan Sarandon, Bernie Siegel, Christine Todd Whitman.

The Year Ahead for Libra

While you may be eager to throw caution to the wind, you're experiencing the value of persistent, patient efforts directed toward your true goals. On the extraordinary side of things, you're filled with ideas and open to expressions that take you further toward personal realization than you may have dreamed possible. By allowing your creativity to emerge in full force, you can change the entire course of your life, although you're realizing that it could mean more work than you anticipated. Some things are worth it!

Jupiter's expansive power emphasizes your connections to others from January through June. During this period, you may find that others are more generous and that you're gaining a new appreciation for your relationships. This can be an exceptional time of healing and rebirth, lifting hopes that help you move beyond the obstacles in your path. Take care to avoid accumulating unnecessary debts during this cycle, since they could hang on longer than you anticipate. In July, you're feeling a stimulus to open to new horizons. Throughout the second half of the year 2000, you're thinking about the future and may be moving as fast as you can to get there. Travel, publishing, or broadcasting can have exceptional effects on your life, and you may also become more involved in academic pursuits. Setting limits can be extremely difficult during this time, and if you push too far beyond your limitations, you could inhibit your ability to fully enjoy the growth promised by making prudent choices.

The disciplined, clarifying energy of Saturn turns its focus on your need to eliminate unnecessary attachments, old fears, and mistrust in favor of healing. In the process, you're likely to confront those skeletons in your closet. The funny thing about them is that they take up usable space! By consciously eliminating the psychological blocks standing in the way of your happiness, your relationships and entire life experience take on a new light.

Uranus and Neptune highlight the sectors of your life that involve your creative self-expression, and these energies may stimulate you to invite evolutionary qualities of love and loving while also altering your tastes. Things you may never have considered to be beautiful or valuable can capture your attention. It's also possible that you've never even looked into these dimensions because you've not had the time, inclination, or opportunity. Pluto's energy of transformation trains its intensity on the way you think. You're seeing profound implications of your thoughts and mind processes. Not only can this be an amazing time to develop your intellect, but your consciousness itself is undergoing breakthroughs.

There are four solar eclipses during the year 2000. This phenomenon occurs about every twenty years, usually marking a period of more intensified crisis. On a personal level, crisis frequently accompanies profound growth, but there can be difficulty associated with what you would perceive as a life passage of some sort. The emphasis of the eclipse cycles centers around your feelings about your life work, and many of the changes you're prompted to make may stem from this concern. Vocation, calling, life work—these terms reflect a bond between your inner purpose and the opportunities in the outside world. Allowing the love that flows from the core of your being into your artistry and your career path to direct your choices and life course can be difficult if you resist the process or try too hard to control it. Flowing with changes, using your characteristic grace, you can enjoy a sense of reassurance and hope.

If you were born from September 23 to 25, you're experiencing the supportive energy of Saturn in trine aspect to your Sun. This cycle is most powerful from July through October, and can help offset some of the restless energy provoked by another cycle, Uranus transiting in sesquiquadrate to your Sun, which lasts all year. Fortunately, if you're paying attention, you'll realize that it's time to break away from old ways of doing things in favor of increased productivity or gaining more enjoyment. In either case, you're seeking to get more for your efforts, and are less likely to compromise. By trimming away excess, you're most of the way past the challenges of these cycles. Your need to eliminate the things, situations, or people weighing you down, although some changes in circumstances may be beyond your control; yet welcoming the changes and redirecting your energy toward more satisfying situations can have a remarkable effect.

If you were born from September 26 to 30, you're feeling an enhanced sense of compassion, artistry, and spirituality. Neptune is transiting in trine aspect to your Sun, stimulating expanded awareness and a strong sense of inner peace. This is one of those cycles that can slip by unnoticed, since you'll feel that life is basically good and that things are naturally falling into place. However, you're also feeling a kind of "needling" energy from Uranus traveling in sesquiquadrate to your Sun, prompting you to consider whether or not you should make some changes. These two cycles together can work quite nicely, since you can direct some of your energy to developing a more profound connection to your inner self, and when you're wondering where those changes should occur or if you need to wait or move forward, your inner guidance can be an exceptional resource. Devoting time and energy to the development of your spirituality is an excellent focus, and you may find that your intuitive sensibilities are more reliable. To keep your physical body strong, listen to those intuitive promptings that may be quite valuable in regard to altering your physical energy and vitality. Your spirituality can have a remarkable effect on your health this year.

If you were born from October 1 to 7, you're experiencing an opportunity for healing and rebirth. Pluto's transit in sextile aspect to your Sun can bring deep-felt transformation, and it might not even hurt! This is particularly true if you're focusing the energy of your mind in such a way as to alter the quality of your life (what you think and become). If you've been hoping to develop skills or understanding that will allow you to exercise your creativity or improve your career, this is the perfect cycle. Saturn's transit in sesquiquadrate to your Sun adds a bit of intensity to the process of change and growth and may be the factor manifesting when you feel that others are being too critical or that situations are somehow standing in the way of your progress. Before you point a finger of blame, it's a good idea to stop and reassess the situation since you may be confronting your own fears or anxieties. One of the side effects of transforming the way you think is confrontation with your old mindset! It's not easy to give up old habits. Your task is to convince yourself that you're capable of making the changes you desire and need to make. The rest is as simple as walking the talk!

If you were born from October 7 to 15, you're feeling the impact of Uranus transiting in trine aspect to your Sun. This may be one of the most exciting periods of your life since circumstances may be changing in a magical way. It's the perfect time to exercise your talents and to express the parts of your individuality that have been itching to show themselves. Relationships can have a remarkable impact and may be the key to your growth and self-expression. Sometimes the presence of a child or lover can awaken qualities that have been slumbering for years or that have needed a new catalyst in order to manifest. Consciously inviting the presence of love into your life can make a remarkable difference. It's time to open your heart to the pure power of love, and to allow your devotion to this light to awaken the truth of yourself.

If you were born from October 16 to 23, the transit of Saturn in quincunx aspect to your Sun brings a period of adjustment and fine-tuning. You're testing your limits and may feel that you're sometimes doing the cosmic three-step: one step forward, two steps back. The frustrations of this cycle are usually tied to situations you cannot control, and by releasing your desire to direct things (or people) beyond your influence, you're halfway past the test! Even more significant is the potential for changing your health. This is the time when destructive habits can be a real problem, but when you can apply your energy to change them. Weak links in your body make themselves known, which may require making alterations you had not intended (like actually adding daily workouts to your routine in order to strengthen your lower back). The purpose of this cycle is to eliminate situations that undermine your stability since in another year you'll be building new structures, and you will want your foundation to be strong enough to support them!

If you were born from October 19 to 22, you're breaking away from old patterns in order to move onto a new platform. Pluto's transit in semisquare to your Sun marks a significant period of breakthrough. You may feel that it's time to launch major changes, but getting from point "A" to point "B" can be tricky. You could be traveling in uncharted territory, discovering parts of yourself that have suffered from lack of use. Think of this as a time when you're learning a dissimilar language or developing concepts that will form a fresh paradigm. At first you may feel that you're completely out of control—airborne; but by uncovering the connections from your present circumstances to your intended target, you can begin to see how to get there. Part of it is just the experience of taking the uncharted path and enjoying the discoveries along the way. In the process, something called serendipity can manifest, and this brings the healing, empowerment, and awakening that may have eluded you in the past. Embrace the chance to uncover the core of your being. It's the source of your power.

Tools to Make a Difference

While dancing with the knowledge flowing directly from the Source, amazing things can happen. Welcome the qualities emerging from your creative spirit by finding situations that give you a chance to employ your talents. You may want to spend some time volunteering or doing work for charitable foundations devoted to the arts. Since you're eager to further your understanding and develop your mind, you might enjoy enrolling in classes that suit your special interests or traveling to places that support your learning.

Studying metaphysics, psychology, or healing may hold special interest for you this year, since your focus on looking beneath the surface for answers may prompt you to probe into subjects that were previously intimidating. You're also exploring your own psyche for answers to questions that invoke your inhibitions: looking into your personal taboo areas allows you to uncover the shadowy aspects of yourself as you strive for true healing.

Since you're an air sign, you may gain significant benefits from using aromatherapy as a means to balance your energies. Inhalations of jasmine, frankincense, or patchouli can help lift your spirits, or you might enjoy a massage using oils scented with rosemary or sandalwood. For attracting others, the fragrance of ylang ylang might be just what you need. You're also in touch with the subtle energy fields of your body and will benefit from therapies like acupuncture or learning chi gung.

During your visualizations, center your consciousness on the experience of probing into the deeper recesses of your memory. Imagine that you are traveling across clear waters on a sailboat. You can feel the sea breeze, the warm sun, and the exhilaration of sailing. Steering from open waters into a cove, you drop anchor, and looking over the edge of the boat, see a beautiful mermaid beckoning you. It seems natural that you dive into the water, and you follow her deeper into the ocean toward a cave. Inside, everything seems rather surprising. You can breathe freely, and are walking through open corridors. You stop to reflect on the translucent colors of the walls of the underground cave, and see a reflection of yourself, but it is another you. Exploring this image, you realize you have found a reflection of an ancient lifetime. Investigate the memory—who you were and what you learned—and forgive.

Initiating the Millennium

As you step into the year 2000, you may feel that you're ready to fly, and to some extent you are! Spiritually, you're reaching planes that may be difficult to describe in contexts other than the abstract, but the effect of integrating your spiritual awareness into your everyday life becomes a truly transformative process. Developing your intuition through exercises in mindfulness helps to create the perspective and clarity that allow you to surrender your artistry to the divine.

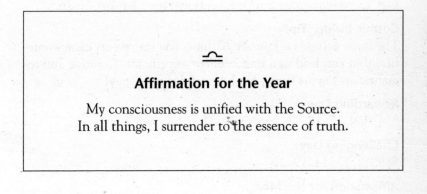

Affirmation for the Year

My consciousness is unified with the Source.
In all things, I surrender to the essence of truth.

Libra/January

In the Spotlight
Even though you might prefer staying close to home, your work may require extra time. Your ideas garner appeal and approval, assuring the support you need to do the job with class—and on time!

Wellness and Keeping Fit
If you're feeling drained, exercising will help to build your endurance. Watch for a tendency to overdo it (especially if you're guilt-ridden). Take care to avoid accidents from January 14-21.

Love and Life Connections
Attending to family concerns can stave off a misunderstanding from January 1-9. You may be trying too hard to please and could alienate someone who misunderstands your intentions from January 5-19. During the Moon's eclipse on January 20, you're vulnerable to the experience of ecstasy—not a bad choice! Your heart can sing with love, although you may have to let go of an old attachment before the harmony rings forth.

Finance and Success
You're in an excellent position to influence others, but if you're trying to do someone a favor from January 6-18, you could mismatch the job and the person. Your artistic and diplomatic faculties are back in the groove after January 19, when cooperative ventures and speculative investments are showing amazing progress. Travel, meetings, or presentations can be exceptional from January 16-26.

Cosmic Insider Tip
The lunar eclipse on January 20 draws you into a very clear awareness that can lead to a transcendent experience. Creative and romantic endeavors shine, but be careful with money!

Rewarding Days
3, 4, 8, 9, 17, 18, 21, 25, 26, 30, 31

Challenging Days
5, 6, 12, 13, 14, 19, 20

Affirmation for the Month
My words are inspired by a loving heart.

Libra/February

In the Spotlight
Exciting directions emerge with the Sun's eclipse on February 5, marking a period of innovative change that allows you to express the essence of your artistic and creative spirit. Your part is to do the work!

Wellness and Keeping Fit
The only thing that might motivate you is a challenge, and unless you're into competitive sports, you may have to create that challenge by setting new fitness goals.

Love and Life Connections
While the solar eclipse on February 5 can precipitate a crisis in a love relationship, you may also feel that it's time to break out of a monotonous rut and try something (or somebody!) different. Whether it's through your connection to your kids or involvement with a significant other, you're feeling forgiving after February 19 and may be willing to step over fear-based boundaries and trust your heart.

Finance and Success
Investing time, energy, or resources in an entrepreneurial endeavor can be successful from February 4-18. However, your schedule may require adjustments to accommodate everything during or after the Full Moon on February 19, when part of your support system may seem to be falling apart. You may simply need to regroup, and keeping a careful watch on your budget is necessary, although some expenditures may be unavoidable after February 25.

Cosmic Insider Tip
Mercury turns retrograde on February 21, when other astrological aspects combine to indicate the potential for monetary losses or lack of clarity. Investigate, negotiate, or repair after this time.

Rewarding Days
4, 5, 13, 14, 18, 21, 22, 26, 27

Challenging Days
1, 2, 3, 9, 10, 11, 15, 16, 19, 29

Affirmation for the Month
My creativity is an expression of my inner strength.

Libra/March

In the Spotlight
Confrontation from the outside may cause you to question your own motivations or commitments, and as a result you may make plans to alter your course. Completing unfinished tasks takes top priority before you can move ahead.

Wellness and Keeping Fit
Psychological dilemmas can drain your physical vitality, and if you're wrangling with some old issues, you may find it easier if you're keeping your body flexible. A massage can do wonders!

Love and Life Connections
If you really want a love relationship to grow, you may have to take the initiative. Your partner may be angry or frustrated, and you could be feeling that the blocks to intimacy run deeper than you realized. Playful time together from March 1-13 helps break the tension, but the biggest problem you face could be unrealistic expectations of each other. Honesty can seem like a cruel taskmaster.

Finance and Success
If financial circumstances are creating a block to your success, you may need to regroup. Productivity could be falling, and if you're feeling burned out, then you've found the cause! Take a look at your work conditions and institute improvements between the New Moon on March 6 and the Full Moon on March 19. Budget overruns can get out of hand midmonth, prompting you to cut back for a while.

Cosmic Insider Tip
Review policies and procedures during Mercury's retrograde, through March 14. Expansion and idealism are battling for attention, and the battleground may be your joint resources.

Rewarding Days
2, 3, 11, 12, 20, 21, 25, 26, 30, 31

Challenging Days
1, 7, 8, 13, 14, 19, 27, 28

Affirmation for the Month
I strive to be realistic and responsible when making promises.

Libra/April

In the Spotlight
You're going beyond old issues and moving toward positive, evolutionary change. Social situations provide a marvelous arena for networking with others who can enhance your reputation.

Wellness and Keeping Fit
Treating symptoms will not satisfy your needs, and you may be inclined to step outside traditional methods and into alternative therapies to find solutions to health problems.

Love and Life Connections
Your need to break away from inhibiting situations may prompt you to consider a period of separation, but if you're in a healthy relationship, building trust and exploring your deeper needs can lead to a powerful alchemy during the New Moon on April 4. You may feel that you're requiring an unusual mix of stability and experimentation. Strengthen your commitment to your true needs during the Libra Full Moon on April 18.

Finance and Success
Taking on a business partner or investor can provide the resources necessary to your success, but before you agree to a contract, make sure to review your obligations. Certainly, it could be worthwhile, but you can easily get in over your head and later have regrets if realizing a profit takes longer than you anticipated. Regulations can be a problem after April 23, so explore the laws before you decide.

Cosmic Insider Tip
Although you can certainly feel appreciative for another's help or support, knowing what they expect will determine whether or not you're happy with the arrangement. Potential traps abound!

Rewarding Days
8, 9, 13, 16, 17, 21, 22, 26, 27

Challenging Days
3, 4, 5, 10, 11, 23, 24, 25

Affirmation for the Month
I am grateful for the support and love others extend to me.

Libra/May

In the Spotlight

Financial concerns take center stage. Your energy and enthusiasm can prompt others to be generous with their resources, although it's tempting to get in over your head and obligate yourself for a longer period than you intended.

Wellness and Keeping Fit

Natural surroundings can have a remarkably rejuvenating effect. To break the tension, consider morning walks, tennis, bicycling, or take a long weekend—but most effective is the human touch.

Love and Life Connections

Breaking through the barriers of fear or inhibition is part of the magical alchemy of love. Surrender to your deeper yearnings during the New Moon on May 3, releasing your attachment to old pain existing as shame or guilt. Exploring your hopes and fears with your love from the Full Moon on May 18-27 can open new vistas. After May 26, travel or retreat may stimulate a meeting of minds and souls.

Finance and Success

The balance between assets and liabilities needs careful examination. You may benefit immensely from another's resources, but will not enjoy the association if your freedom or individuality are limited because of your obligations. Inheritance or tax matters can be at issue. After May 15, conferences, publication, or academic endeavors provide an excellent avenue for advancing your career.

Cosmic Insider Tip

The thin line existing in transformation—leaving one experience behind as another takes on life—is sometimes difficult to cross, but it is your challenge during the Full Moon on May 18.

Rewarding Days
5, 6, 9, 10, 13, 14, 15, 18, 19, 23, 24

Challenging Days
1, 2, 7, 8, 21, 22, 28, 29

Affirmation for the Month
I release my attachment to the things I no longer need.

Libra/June

In the Spotlight
The remarkable thing about breakthrough is the experience of flight that can follow. It's your turn to feel the energy of inspiration, anchored in your spirituality and expressed through your creativity.

Wellness and Keeping Fit
An adventurous vacation could be the perfect healing tool. If you can't travel, seek other escapes. Chronic problems can be bothersome, but an innovative therapy can lead to healing.

Love and Life Connections
The New Moon on June 2 sparks your interest in exploring an ideology, culture, or place, and in that context you may meet someone just as fascinating as your subject! If you enjoy writing, you may be filled with marvelous ideas, and conversations with those you admire can be the catalyst for your creativity. The Full Moon on June 16 invites your wanderlust, although a romantic rendezvous could seal your love.

Finance and Success
Contractual matters help solidify an important career move from June 1-16. Sign final documents prior to Mercury's retrograde on June 23. Your career is on fast forward, and since your influence is expanding, you may be able to accomplish several feats at once. Conferences or promotional activities are most effective through June 21. Even in the face of competition, your talents shine brilliantly.

Cosmic Insider Tip
Exposure to different philosophies or ideals can be like a breath of fresh air, although you may run headlong into an old prejudice from June 1-11. There's nothing like transformation!

Rewarding Days
1, 2, 5, 10, 11, 14, 15, 19, 20, 21, 29, 30

Challenging Days
3, 4, 17, 18, 24, 25, 26

Affirmation for the Month
I welcome truth in all things!

Libra/July

In the Spotlight
The eclipses—two solar and one lunar—underscore the importance of listening to your inner voice in matters of your life path, career, and future hopes. You're perched on the brink of expansive growth and have the power to direct its course.

Wellness and Keeping Fit
To stay on top of the tension that can arise from your drive, funnel part of the energy into your fitness routine.

Love and Life Connections
A family crisis can ensue between the Sun's eclipse on July 1 and the lunar eclipse on July 16, particularly if you're making changes at home. As you alter your course, others may be unsure of how they fit, and you can show them by including them in your plans. Contact with friends after July 12 helps you refine your goals. Open to the vision of life as you desire it to be during the Sun's eclipse on July 30.

Finance and Success
Changes in your career may leave you feeling uncertain, although your ability to direct those changes grows stronger as you allow your talents to shine. It's time to determine what you want and what you're worth. If you need to enhance your professional value, you know now what you must do to get there. Professional alliances open doors after July 23, when your diplomacy may be the key to resolving problems.

Cosmic Insider Tip
Mercury's retrograde until July 17 makes it difficult to finalize plans. It's time to make repairs and to devise new goals. Set them in motion after July 30.

Rewarding Days
3, 4, 7, 8, 12, 17, 18, 26, 27, 30, 31

Challenging Days
1, 2, 14, 15, 16, 22, 23, 28, 29

Affirmation for the Month
I am open to the vision of a future filled with everything I need.

Libra/August

In the Spotlight
Whether your inspiration is romantic or born of your spiritual ideals, you're eager to channel it into your work. Community concerns and political or special interest activities allow you to broaden your focus and feel that you're making a difference.

Wellness and Keeping Fit
Getting involved in a fitness class, team sport, or working with a personal trainer can be just what you need to meet a personal fitness goal. Encourage a friend to join you.

Love and Life Connections
The joys of love fill your heart, and the more you open to the experience, the easier it becomes to share your feelings, desires, and outpourings of affection. Sharing a memorable experience, your favorite pastime or entertainment can be a milestone near the Full Moon on August 15. Friends play a significant role, and inviting them to celebrate with you reminds you of the true value of life itself.

Finance and Success
The promise of advancement is fulfilled, although there can be a delay until after August 12 due to red tape. Curb your expenses, trim excess, and eliminate debt. Then you can funnel your increasing resources into new avenues from August 11-15. From August 23 onward, you'll be most successful devoting your attention to a project behind the scenes, carefully planning your next move.

Cosmic Insider Tip
Your intuitive promptings can be the most powerful indicators of the best directions to pursue. Devoting time to your spirituality and becoming more mindful alters your perspectives.

Rewarding Days
3, 4, 8, 9, 13, 14, 22, 23, 27, 28, 31

Challenging Days
10, 11, 18, 19, 25, 26

Affirmation for the Month
All things in harmony with my highest needs are possible!

Libra/September

In the Spotlight
You're attracting the people and situations that allow you to radiate your most beautiful qualities. This period of abundance is accompanied by the energy and drive to make your dreams come true, and others cheer you on!

Wellness and Keeping Fit
The philosophical elements of your fitness routine make an important difference in your health. Spirituality applied to healing can work true miracles.

Love and Life Connections
With Venus and Mercury in your sign, it's easier to express precisely how you feel and to show your affections. Romantic encounters from September 1 through the Full Moon on September 13 can be truly exhilarating, and you may meet that special someone in the course of your travels or professional pursuits. Initiate changes or a fresh relationship during the Libra New Moon on September 27.

Finance and Success
Recognition or advancement are only part of the rewards from your career. Your finances gain momentum. Your portfolio expands to include powerful professional credentials, and through your influence you can alter certain facets of your profession. Avoid untried financial "opportunities" after September 25, since you could be tempted by something with more hype than substance

Cosmic Insider Tip
Jupiter and Pluto are in opposition, testing the limits of credibility. Your logical abilities allow you to see through the propaganda, and your leadership can help others do the same.

Rewarding Days
1, 4, 5, 9, 10, 19, 20, 23, 24, 27, 28

Challenging Days
7, 8, 14, 15, 16, 21, 22

Affirmation for the Month
In the light of truth I can clearly see the best course of action.

Libra/October

In the Spotlight
Making the best use of your resources may include a revision of your budget, but you're also considering the importance of your time. You may prefer to spend time enjoying the fruits of your labors instead of just laboring!

Wellness and Keeping Fit
Retreat rejuvenates, and it's time to devote your attention to your inner self.

Love and Life Connections
Conflicts between your values can threaten the stability of a close relationship, although the arguments may revolve around control of resources. Look deeper, since you may be worried about commitment or trust, and money could merely be a "symptom." A relationship turns a corner with the Full Moon on October 13, and if there's no room for growth, you may abandon your commitment in favor of seeking a new path.

Finance and Success
Misleading information can create havoc with your investments. Unless you must make changes, you might be more successful riding the waves instead of making major alterations to your portfolio. The political climate is definitely affecting the economy, and you may be able to make gains as a result, but you must be patient. Direct your energy toward an artistic endeavor that is personally meaningful.

Cosmic Insider Tip
Take a second look at an opportunity during Mercury's retrograde beginning on October 18 and continuing into next month. Your investigation yields important discoveries on October 27.

Rewarding Days
2, 7, 8, 16, 17, 20, 24, 25, 26, 29

Challenging Days
4, 5, 11, 12, 13, 18, 19, 31

Affirmation for the Month
My intuitive insights offer clarity in times of confusion.

Libra/November

In the Spotlight
Initiating changes or making headway with projects is motivated by your need to strengthen your security base. Whether you're making improvements at home or stabilizing your relationship with your boss, you're thinking long-term.

Wellness and Keeping Fit
Mars moves into Libra on November 3, and for the next seven weeks you may feel more energetic. Pace yourself to avoid setbacks.

Love and Life Connections
Waiting for the other person to make a move is not an option. Your eagerness can open the way for true understanding if you're also sensitive to signals. A getaway with your sweetie can relieve pressure from November 1-12, and you're eager to feel the power of love during the Full Moon on November 11. Adventurous romance is promising after the New Moon on November 25.

Finance and Success
Clear directions for financial solidity may not emerge until a week after Mercury leaves its retrograde on November 7. You may be trying for the wrong reasons, and if you're fascinated by an option that holds little substance, you could undermine your worth by pursuing it. Meetings or presentations after November 23 lead to interesting developments when your talents put you in the spotlight and you're garnering excellent reviews.

Cosmic Insider Tip
Developing your artistry pays off, and if you're in a situation to showcase your abilities after November 19, you may be surprised at who's taking notice!

Rewarding Days
4, 12, 13, 17, 21, 22, 25, 26, 27, 30

Challenging Days
1, 2, 8, 9, 14, 15, 28, 29

Affirmation for the Month
My values are strengthened by an awareness of my true self.

Libra/December

In the Spotlight

After a series of developments, you're finally making headway with a loving relationship. Your artistry is shining brightly and may be the factor that attracts the love you've longed to experience.

Wellness and Keeping Fit

Social activities take time away from your personal routine, but you'll maintain your energy if you're at least keeping up with some physical activity. Recreation gives you a boost after December 9.

Love and Life Connections

Time spent close to home helps confirm your feelings of affection, and you're in the mood for romance during the Full Moon on December 11. Sharing your hopes and dreams, you may realize that you're closer to a sense of fulfillment than you've experienced for quite some time. Children can be especially enjoyable after December 9. The solar eclipse on December 25 marks a powerful time of appreciation for your family. Let it show!

Finance and Success

Interactive support with others who share your way of thinking can be affirming from December 3-22. Schedule meetings, attend conferences, and make an effort to stay on top of correspondence or writing, since your ideas can interject important qualities which help assure the success of a project. Investments can be lucrative from December 4-23.

Cosmic Insider Tip

Creating traditions of your own can be a result of realizing that you're finally in a position to have a truly positive and loving influence within your family—a nice stimulus of the eclipse.

Rewarding Days

1, 2, 10, 11, 14, 15, 18, 19, 23, 24, 28, 29

Challenging Days

5, 6, 7, 12, 13, 20, 25, 26

Affirmation for the Month

My actions and words are tempered by true love.

Libra Action Table

These dates reflect the best—but not the only—times for success and ease in these activities, according to your Sun sign.

	JAN	FEB	MAR	APR	MAY	JUN	JUL	AUG	SEPT	OCT	NOV	DEC
Move	1-18											24-31
Start a class						2					25, 26	
Join a club							31	1				
Ask for a raise									27, 28			
Look for work		5-20	14-31	1-12	31	1-22	18-31	1-7				
Get pro advice	12, 13	9, 10	7, 8	3, 4	1-2, 28-29	24-26	22, 23	18, 19	14, 15	11-13	8, 9	5-7
Get a loan	15, 16	11, 12	9, 10	5-7	3-4, 30-31	27, 28	24, 25	20, 21	16-18	14, 15	10, 11	8, 9
See a doctor		5-29	1-31	1-12				22-31	1-6			
Start a diet	10, 11	6-8	5, 6	1-2, 28-30	26, 27	22, 23	19, 20	15-17	12, 13	9, 10	5-7	3-4, 30-31
End relationship										12, 13		
Buy clothes	19-31	1-4										
Get a makeover									27, 28			
New romance		5										
Vacation	17, 18	13, 14	11, 12	8, 9	5, 6	1-2, 29-30	26, 27	22-24	19, 20	16, 17	12, 13	10, 11

Scorpio
The Scorpion
October 22 to November 20

♏

Element:	Water
Quality:	Fixed
Polarity:	Yin/Feminine
Planetary Ruler:	Pluto (Mars)
Meditation:	"I achieve mastery through transformation."
Gemstone:	Topaz
Power Stones:	Obsidian, pearl, citrine, garnet
Key Phrase:	"I create"
Glyph:	Scorpion's tail ♏
Anatomy:	Reproductive system
Colors:	Burgundy, black
Animals:	Reptiles, scorpions, birds of prey
Myths/Legends:	Phoenix, Hades and Persephone, Shiva
House:	Eighth
Opposite Sign:	Taurus
Flower:	Chrysanthemum
Key Word:	Intensity

Positive Expression:	Misuse of Energy:
Healing	Caustic
Passionate	Extreme
Regenerating	Obsessive
Sensual	Destructive
Creative	Lascivious
Transforming	Jealous
Incisive	Overbearing

Scorpio

Your Ego's Strengths and Shortcomings

Others are fascinated by your charisma, yet mystified by your enigmatic nature, and you like it that way! You're usually aware of much more than you share, and your love of intrigue and mystery coupled with your keen perceptive abilities prompts you to probe beneath the surface. Your creativity may stem from your discoveries of the mysteries of life, and you play the role of "The Catalyst" of the zodiac when your actions or words bring about transformational change.

Protective of your needs, you only rarely expose the details of your own life or your feelings, and only once you've established a bond of trust. Keeping the volcano of your emotions under control, you may project a cool quality that contrasts sharply with your deeper feelings. You're secretive for a reason: your intuitive and psychic sensibilities frequently alert you when a person has something to hide. You may also have your own hidden agenda, and until you bridge the gap created by hurt or mistrust, circumstances can be a tangled web indeed.

Your planetary ruler is Pluto, and when you're flowing with this power, you can experience an amazing connection to the deeper qualities of human nature. You may feel that you are called to walk the path of the shaman, creating regeneration and healing and, in the process, experiencing the extremes of life—from despair to joy. Directing your energy toward higher principles, you can rise to heroic action, but when you're hurt, you can be consumed by vengeful feelings. Forgiveness will bring ultimate spiritual and emotional rebirth as you release guilt, shame, and disappointment and move toward renewal.

Shining Your Love Light

In truth, you are a sensitive soul and may yearn to bond with your soulmate. Your sensuality is highly attractive, and when you want to turn on your enticements, others may find it difficult to resist. Through your erotic sensibilities you may develop lovemaking into an art form as you open the gates to ecstasy with your lover. Although unlocking the doors to your heart may not be easy, your life transforms through trusting love. Despite your tendency to close the doors to your heart if you've been hurt, your ability to heal your feelings can set you free.

Finding a partner with the other water signs—Cancer, Scorpio and Pisces—can lead to an experience of shared desires and emotional compatibility. Your zodiac opposite, Taurus, may be the most intensely attracting, and his or her sensuality and steadfast devotion can match your own; but in the face of disagreement you can both be monumentally stubborn.

Aries teases and can be fun, but you may be frustrated. Gemini's witty intelligence is entertaining, but you may not feel that your deeper longings are fulfilled. Cancer is sensitive and may share your ideals while inspiring your own feelings of security. Leo's magnetism can leave you feeling weak in the knees, but you may tire of this sign's tendency to be self-absorbed. Developing a relationship with Virgo can be a powerful blend of friendship and passion. With Libra, you may feel at ease, but can resent the fact that you seem to be the one making most of the decisions.

Another Scorpio can feel like your soulmate, although the relationship can go from one extreme to another, including volatile power struggles. Sagittarius is fun, but his or her self-reliant attitudes can seem too noncommittal. Capricorn's supportive energy goes a long way toward helping you accomplish success while confirming your security needs. Even though you may feel intrigued by Aquarius, the emotional distance makes it difficult to achieve a sense of union. Pisces may be your ultimate lover, stimulating your romantic creativity while providing imaginative sensitivity.

Making Your Place in the World

A career that provides an opportunity to exercise your strategic skills and ability to restore or renovate can be exceptionally rewarding. The healing arts, including counseling, may draw your interest, and you're also well-suited to a career in science, history, anthropology, archaeology, or research. You might even enjoy working as a detective or special agent.

In the arts you may excel as a painter, musician, or writer, and your works can have a healing effect. You could become an excellent performer, producer, or director, and may be drawn to science fiction or mystery. Positions of influence can fit you quite nicely, and you may be gifted at making the most of others' resources. Investment banking, financial counseling, career management, politics, corporate law, or the insurance industry can be your cup of tea.

Power Plays

There's no question that you know the meaning of power. Scorpios exude power. Your fascination with powerful people and superheroes may have begun during childhood, and of course you identified with the hero or heroine. Those who misuse their power or influence draw your resentment, and when someone does not own his or her power, you can sense that, too. You might feel most at ease when the total extent of your potency is not open to scrutiny or prying eyes, and you function best when you surrender to the higher nature of power itself. Because you embrace the totality of life experience—from birth to sexuality to death—you've grown to accept the ultimate changes that shape the circle of life. Yet your desire to hold onto life's richest treasures may be driven by a feeling the you want to control these natural processes in some way.

The essence of healing contains the clues to true power, and by reaching deep within your soul to embrace your true needs, your strength and power emerge as your life is healed. The warrior spirit residing at the core of your being constantly guards you from harm; but it is compassion that sustains your strength and a desire to bring about changes that impart hope and growth, now and for the future, that fill your cup to overflowing.

Famous Scorpios

Lisa Bonet, Michael Crichton, George Eliot, Calista Flockhart, Larry Flynt, Grace Kelly, Billie Jean King, Garry Marshall, Johnny Mercer, Dennis Miller, Pablo Picasso, Hilary Rodham Clinton, Maria Shriver, Ted Turner, Yanni.

The Year Ahead
for Scorpio

While your challenges during the year 2000 may come from re-lationships or outside changes, you're experiencing a series of inner changes that are a result of personal awakening. You're discovering the importance of eliminating unnecessary restraints to your self-expression, and may find that striking a delicate balance between freedom and responsibility holds the key to your success during this first year of the millennium.

The expansive energy of Jupiter ushers in new levels of support from your associations with others. From partnership or marriage to projects that involve multiple participants or investors, you're seeing the importance of joining forces with others. While Jupiter highlights your house of partners and social connections from January through July, you can experience positive growth through strengthening your social circle. If you're seeking a partner, it's an excellent time to attract potential mates, and an existing partnership can accelerate. After July, Jupiter's energy moves into an area of your chart that deals with healing, and you may finally get to the core of a physical or psychological problem or discover resources that can play a significant role as you continue your quest for wholeness. The temptation of this cycle is to spend beyond your resources or to jeopardize joint finances by being too indulgent, but the gift of this cycle is an awareness that you are attracting true abundance and prosperity. It's the way you use it that's important!

Saturn's energy tests your social commitments and personal relationships, and you may be carrying greater responsibilities in these areas. Since Jupiter and Saturn are transiting in conjunction to one another for part of the year, you may find that your desire to expand is inhibited by those responsibilities. Saturn's transit in the sign opposite of your own can bring a feeling of weightiness and an impatience with the slow-moving pace of true progress. However, the intensity of this cycle is strengthened when Saturn makes the exact opposition to your Sun. Check the birthdates below to determine if you fall into that category.

The energies of Uranus and Neptune are influencing the personal security sector of your chart, and the changes you're feeling in this area can be disruptive and unsettling. Knowing when to let go and when to forgive can enhance your ability to flow with the nature of these cycles. Pluto's influence in your solar Second House of personal resources brings transformation to your values and attitudes toward money. At a fundamental level, this cycle challenges you to make the most of all your resources, even the intangibles, and to eliminate waste and wasteful attitudes.

There are four solar eclipses during this year, something that happens only rarely every century. The emphasis of each solar eclipse and the two lunar eclipses will be outlined in the monthly forecast sections, but the underlying nature of these eclipses is defined by the transit of the Moon's nodes. Striking a balance between your desire and need to explore higher-minded issues like spirituality or philosophy and the fundamental things you learned as a child can be an interesting dilemma. You may feel that your spirituality must take top priority in all your dealings this year, and that focus is certainly apparent in the cycle of the Moon's North Node.

If you were born from October 23 to 25, you're experiencing a year of self-control and positive self-esteem. There are no long-lasting transits aspecting your Sun, and the tests you've experienced during the last two years are finally complete. There is a period of adjustment from August through October when Saturn transits in quincunx aspect to your Sun, and during this time you may feel that progress is slowing down while you make alterations or repairs. The primary thing to watch for involves your health, since physical problems that have lain dormant can surface during this cycle, or you may find that it's necessary to eliminate some things from your life while making time for others if you are to have the ultimate satisfaction you desire.

If you were born from October 26 to 31, you're feeling the influence of Neptune transiting in square aspect to your Sun. This can be a confusing period when determining your priorities may be troublesome. The desire to escape what you may consider "ordinary" life in favor of a more peaceful or spiritually focused lifestyle is the crux of the issue this year. Finding healthy outlets for your creativity can be your salvation, since your artistic drive may be almost addictive in its intensity. Physically, you can also fall into addictive patterns, or may become more physically sensitive than you've been in the past. You may have difficulty determining the full effects of medications, drugs, or alcohol, but supportive advice from a trusted source can be helpful. Although your intentions may be honorable—a desire to make a difference or to reach out to others—you may actually attract others who are less than honest or who would take advantage of you. Developing your intuitive or psychic abilities now may be easier, although maintaining a balance between your need to be grounded in reality while exploring your inner self will enhance this development. All in all, this is a cycle of increasing sensitivity on every level, and accepting the challenge of maintaining your boundaries will help you navigate less turbulent waters.

If your birth occurred from November 1 to 7, you may be eliminating a lot of clutter from your life—emotionally and physically. Pluto's transit in semisextile aspect to your Sun presents a significant challenge. It's time to move forward, stepping onto a different platform, but that means you're leaving an old security base behind! In most respects, you may sense that these changes are like a series of stair steps, instead of an attempt to climb Mt. Everest. You may encounter barriers, but they are likely to involve the elimination of negative attitudes or removing yourself from situations you've outgrown. This is a great time to clear out attics, closets, pantries, or drawers in the name of freeing up space. Emotionally, you're ready to release negative programming in favor of strengthening your self-esteem.

If you were born from November 7 to 14, you're feeling the cycle of Uranus traveling in square aspect to your Sun. The restless nature of this cycle can be rather disturbing since it has a kind of roller coaster effect. From January through April, Saturn transits in opposition to your Sun, complicating the process and marking a time when you may definitely see a period of endings overlapping with new beginnings. However, the longest influence this year is that of Uranus square your Sun, marking a time of personal revolution.

You're eager to change, to let go of the things that are in the way of your individual self-expression, but you may encounter resistance from others who seem to lack an understanding of your motivations. Although you may have felt the need to make changes brewing on an inner level for some time, the actualization of those changes may just now seem possible. There is also the potential that forces from the outside will create changes, and that your challenge will be to determine how to deal with them. The unexpected nature of these changes can test you. Are you really happy with your life choices? If you need to maintain your course, the challenge may exist as a test of your conviction and devotion to your responsibilities. Health problems surfacing now are more likely to be a result of fighting against the need to make changes. Your emotional attachment to keeping things the same may be at the core of your issues. Life is filled with change; it's how you deal with it that determines whether or not you're growing!

If you were born from November 14 to 17, your creative sensibilities are enhanced while Neptune transits in quintile aspect to your Sun. This cycle can come and go with little notice, but since you're now aware of it, you have the advantage! Whether you feel the need to strengthen your artistic abilities, fine-tune your intuitive perceptions, develop a more satisfying career situation, or simply spend time with a hobby that's been gathering dust, the integration of a more mindful quality and your ability to go with the flow of the energy can be wonderfully rewarding.

If you were born from November 15 to 22, you're experiencing the trials of Saturn transiting in opposition to your Sun. You may face tremendous adversity or tests of your abilities with your initial response falling in the category of feeling discouraged. Although you may be eliminating some situations from your life or facing endings, you may not have the energy to undergo new beginnings. It's a time of completion, examination, and clarification. You may feel that you're on a proving ground, and the things that you started about fourteen years ago are the subject of your test. If you're confident and shouldering your responsibilities in a healthy manner, you're more likely to weather this period of endings gracefully; but if you've been slacking off, failing to meet obligations, or pushing the limits of acceptable behavior, you may find that you're paying a substantial price. This is a cycle of karma—you're reaping what you've sown. Some things will be apparent—you'll see the cause and effect. Others may seem to have their roots in distant memories. Take care of health issues now, since finding ways to accommodate your physical needs can actually strengthen your body. You may feel weary, emotionally and physically, and if you sense that you're depressed, seeking treatment for depression can make a difference in your ability to cope. Now is not the time to take on more, start new projects, or begin a new career path. It is time to finish what you've started, and then, when the storm clouds subside, the bright light of change will illuminate a new path.

Tools to Make a Difference

Taking care of business: that may be what seems the first order of priority, and to be effective you need to keep your priorities in a well-defined order. Using affirmations that help to strengthen your focus and resolve and that remind you that you deserve the good things life has to offer can be a very helpful tool. Since Saturn's energy plays a major part in the cycles you're experiencing this year, you may have an opportunity to teach or learn. These activities are excellent ways to honor the energy of Saturn in a positive way.

You may also be concerned about your physical health and may feel that your body has a mind of its own! Becoming more conscious of the connection between spirit, mind, and body can have an amazing effect on the way you feel. If you're dealing with feelings of depression or anxiety, the beneficial effects of herbs like kava kava and St. John's Wort might help you stay more emotionally centered and feel more physically alive. Bodywork can also be an exceptional tool: massage, rolfing, shiatsu, or acupuncture can all be effective healing agents. Adding the essential oils of ylang ylang, patchouli, rose, frankincense, geranium, or jasmine might also help you relax and let go of tension, anxiety, or sadness. Staying physically active is also important, but remaining flexible needs to be at the top of your list. Whether you prefer dance, swimming, or yoga, the effects of maintaining flexibility can be seen physically, mentally, and emotionally.

During your meditations, bring your consciousness to a space that gives you a feeling of connection to the flow of your energy. Imagine that you are walking along the shores of a beautiful ocean, watching the waves tugging away at the sand and then crashing against the shoreline. The relationship between receding inward and the explosion of letting go creates a natural rhythm. You can feel your own power connected to this eternal ebb and flow. As you merge with this rhythm, you are transported to a place that feels like your true home. Even there, nestled in comfort, you can hear the sounds of the sea and feel the rhythm. Take this awareness with you to remind you that your life can ebb and flow—it's all part of the same thing.

Initiating the Millennium

The millennium marks a series of endings for you, in many ways. It's your time to recognize what is required for you to feel complete, and since some of your attachments are being eliminated, you're taking a serious inventory of your current needs. By gathering together your resources and maintaining your focus, you can initiate this period with a feeling of confidence. Knowing that life is filled with periods of completion and times to say good-bye is something you've always understood. During this time, some things seem dormant, almost like the experience of winter—resting in anticipation of the burst of energy that accompanies spring.

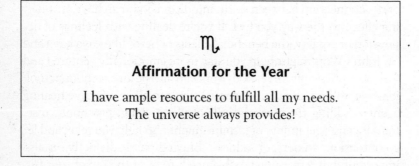

♏

Affirmation for the Year

I have ample resources to fulfill all my needs.
The universe always provides!

Scorpio/January

In the Spotlight
Your creativity and passion grow stronger, and the impulse to focus most of your energy on an artistic project can lead to rewards. You may also take a more active role in pursuit of a love relationship.

Wellness and Keeping Fit
Finding a physical activity you truly enjoy will keep you interested. It's a good month for an active vacation and time to consider a new daily routine.

Love and Life Connections
Your confidence in expressing your deeper feelings can lead you to pursue a love interest on or after the New Moon on January 6. Sending a clear message about your intentions will go a long way toward assuring whether or not a relationship can grow. Home and family matters require extra attention on and after the lunar eclipse on January 20.

Finance and Success
Conferring with others may require travel, but you can also be effective sharing written messages, phone calls, or cyberspace conferences. The important thing is to get your ideas and creations out there, since you're in the right place to garner support. Finances can be troubling through January 18, and you may be stretching your resources. By putting sufficient energy into your work, you'll see positive rewards by January 24.

Cosmic Insider Tip
The lunar eclipse on January 20 is accompanied by the impulse to follow visionary ideas, and charismatic messages can be misleading unless you're trusting your own mind and intuition.

Rewarding Days
1, 2, 5, 10, 11, 19, 20, 24, 27, 28, 29

Challenging Days
3, 8, 9, 15, 16, 21, 22

Affirmation for the Month
I communicate my feelings and ideas.

Scorpio/February

In the Spotlight
Your expressive creativity continues to gain momentum, and you may reach the stage when you're ready to revise or review as part of your fine-tuning. Investments grow, adding to your self-confidence.

Wellness and Keeping Fit
After February 11 you may feel restless energy building unless you channel it into some form of physical activity. Enroll in fitness class, join a team sport, or work with a personal trainer.

Love and Life Connections
The solar eclipse on February 5 can be an indicator of family crisis, although you may also be dealing with changes like a move or shift in family structure. Expressions of affection help to solidify an amorous relationship. A getaway can be wonderful from February 2-9, and during the Full Moon on February 19 you're eager to give your sensuality free reign.

Finance and Success
Networking with others pays off with shared resources working to your advantage. Interviews or conferences are most promising from February 3-10, although you may have a chance to follow up during Mercury's retrograde from February 21 to March 14. Social connections can boost your career opportunities after February 14. A review of your investments sheds light on the changes you need to consider in the future.

Cosmic Insider Tip
Unexpected changes can accompany the solar eclipse on February 5 and may leave an unsettled security base. However, you possess the fortitude and insights necessary to restore order.

Rewarding Days
1, 6, 7, 8, 16, 19, 20, 24, 25, 29

Challenging Days
4, 5, 11, 12, 17, 18

Affirmation for the Month
I am safe in the face of change.

Scorpio/March

In the Spotlight
While your creative flow remains strong, tensions can arise in the work place that pour over into your personal life. Unclear messages or a lack of direction can be problematic in your career and may result from changes you cannot control.

Wellness and Keeping Fit
Although staying active is important, gauging your limits is necessary since you could be more prone to illness or injury if you misjudge a situation. Avoid high-risk circumstances.

Love and Life Connections
Frustrations in a close relationship can leave you feeling out of touch, and if you pull away from March 1-4, it could be because you're afraid of dealing with the changes. By the New Moon on March 6, opening your heart to the right person can lead to an important relationship development. Romance fares best from March 6-23, and the Full Moon on March 19 can be purely delightful.

Finance and Success
Mercury's retrograde continues until March 14, and power plays over budgets and positions of influence can interfere with your productivity. You're becoming keenly aware of the power of words and contrived agreements, particularly if they're creating financial problems for you! Postpone signing contracts since there is likely to be hidden language or problems with the deal you cannot foresee.

Cosmic Insider Tip
While Jupiter and Neptune are in a tense aspect all month, many things are undergoing change, and stabilizing anything may be virtually impossible. It's good for creativity, though!

Rewarding Days
5, 6, 14, 18, 19, 22, 23, 27, 28

Challenging Days
2, 3, 4, 9, 10, 16, 17, 30, 31

Affirmation for the Month
My intuitive insights provide clarity in uncertain circumstances.

Scorpio/April

In the Spotlight
Partnerships and social activities take center stage, although everything associated with them may not be entirely pleasant. Necessary changes may provoke tension or anger, although improvements can be readily implemented.

Wellness and Keeping Fit
Tension can exhaust your energy unless you're making a conscious effort to remain flexible. Your fitness activities may become a high point in your day.

Love and Life Connections
Your commitment to a partnership can become an issue, and if you're interested in strengthening your relationship, finding ways to build trust will be a major focus. If the relationship is unhealthy or you've outgrown it, you may be struggling to find a resolution. Striking a healthy balance between personal freedom and responsibility to family requires honest communication of your needs.

Finance and Success
Changes at work or within your work-related relationships can open the way for increased productivity after the New Moon on April 4. You may need to pare down certain activities in favor of concentrating on areas that need more intense focus or that are undergoing upgrades in equipment or procedures. Trying to keep everything exactly the same will waste energy and may jeopardize your career.

Cosmic Insider Tip
The planetary aspects this month spell high tension within political and economic frameworks. You must determine the most responsible action to help you maintain your security.

Rewarding Days
2, 10, 11, 15, 18, 19, 20, 24, 30

Challenging Days
5, 6, 7, 12, 13, 22, 26, 27

Affirmation for the Month
I am aware of the impact of my actions upon the lives of others.

Scorpio/May

In the Spotlight
Work closely with others to find solutions that will serve the good of the whole. Individual considerations may have to be set aside.

Wellness and Keeping Fit
Getting to the core of physical distress or reaching an understanding of the multifaceted elements involved in a physical problem can help you find a workable remedy. Getting rid of unhealthy habits can be the first step toward healing.

Love and Life Connections
You may feel more confident about making a serious commitment or renewing vows in a relationship and, stimulated by the New Moon on May 3, may feel that you have to make a decision one way or another. Waiting will be too painful; you need to know! The intensity builds, and by the Scorpio Full Moon on May 18, you're either in or out, and there's no doubt about it. Period.

Finance and Success
Contractual negotiations may run into a snag if you feel you're being placed in a situation that can have its benefits, but at the cost of your individuality or personal freedom. Defining the limits of your freedom may be the first step toward determining if you're in the right position. Getting involved with the wrong people can be costly—short-term and long-term. Use your penetrating intuition when making your determinations.

Cosmic Insider Tip
The world requires interaction and defining your position becomes crucial if you are to feel that you are a real player or if you're simply a pawn in the game. It's time to eliminate doubt.

Rewarding Days
7, 8, 11, 12, 16, 17, 21, 22, 26, 27

Challenging Days
3, 4, 5, 9, 10, 18, 23, 24, 25, 30, 31

Affirmation for the Month
I am clearly aware of the kind of partner I want and need to be.

Scorpio/June

In the Spotlight
Solidifying your position can result in advancements, although you may have to do some promotional work before you're assured of your place. Convening with others who share your ideals has a powerful impact on your reputation.

Wellness and Keeping Fit
Time away from your regular routine can be rejuvenating, and your body responds nicely to a change of pace. Schedule a massage or body work session from June 1-16.

Love and Life Connections
Your impatience with others can be damaging to an intimate relationship, although your intentions may be honorable. The spiritual connection you feel with someone leads to transformation of your relationship, and you may be more willing to explore possibilities after June 15, although you've been considering them for a while. Rekindling love after June 18 confirms your sense of hope.

Finance and Success
Investments, inheritance, and joint finances require a fresh approach, and initiating change with the New Moon on June 2 can lead to satisfactory results. Legal matters fare best after June 18, when revisiting a case that's been in a stalemate can uncover information previously overlooked. Mercury's retrograde from June 23 to July 17 can be advantageous for negotiations.

Cosmic Insider Tip
Details of a difficult situation come to light as the Full Moon approaches on June 16, when you can determine the things you need to eliminate in order to strengthen your finances.

Rewarding Days
3, 4, 7, 8, 12, 13, 17, 18, 22, 23

Challenging Days
5, 6, 16, 19, 20, 21, 27, 28

Affirmation for the Month
My actions and words are guided by truth and understanding.

Scorpio/July

In the Spotlight
The eclipses make front page news. Your focus centers around the best means of expanding your professional horizons. Your reputation may hang in the balance of ethical or moral dilemmas and your confidence in your principles.

Wellness and Keeping Fit
Your physical energy may be exceptionally strong. Making changes to your environment to enhance the flow of energy makes a huge difference. Try feng shui.

Love and Life Connections
Awakening to a spiritual union during the solar eclipse on July 1, you may feel inspired to reach far beyond the ordinary in a close relationship. If you're not with your soul mate, you may be longing for that connection. Look inward to determine the true nature of your partnership during the Moon's eclipse on July 16, when you're also realizing the influence of your past on your current choices.

Finance and Success
Despite Mercury's retrograde that lasts until July 17, you're experiencing a positive period of recognition, and publishing, broadcasting, or advertising can advance your career. Legal matters fare best through July 12, although you may be reviewing contracts throughout the month. Your questions about your life work and true vocation can loom large during the solar eclipse on July 30.

Cosmic Insider Tip
Everything seems more intense. Even where you're experiencing good fortune, you can feel overwhelmed. That's okay. You're actually one of the few who might survive a tidal wave!

Rewarding Days
1, 2, 5, 6, 9, 10, 11, 14, 15, 16, 19, 20, 21, 28, 29

Challenging Days
3, 4, 17, 18, 24, 25, 30, 31

Affirmation for the Month
I am united with the energy of my higher self.

Scorpio/August

In the Spotlight
Challenges in career can seem more like rivalry, and you may face what seems to be an unfair disadvantage. What you can count on are your connections, personal and professional, since your community of friends gives you strength.

Wellness and Keeping Fit
Try participating in sports, taking on the challenge of a race, or getting into shape with a friend. A buddy can provide the right balance of support and competition.

Love and Life Connections
Power struggles in personal relationships can result from pressures at home. Trust can become an issue. Misunderstandings can thwart your attempts to communicate. Seeking counsel can help you gain objectivity. You may feel better equipped to deal with everything after August 22, and you're breaking away during the New Moon on August 29. Rash action can be damaging.

Finance and Success
The rewards you've anticipated from career efforts may fall short of expectations from August 1-10, when you can also have trouble getting a straight answer from anybody. Your frustrations can build to a peak during the Full Moon on August 15, when self-control may be difficult to maintain. Using legal or contractual means to get to the core of a financial dispute may be your best strategy.

Cosmic Insider Tip
While misleading or deceptive situations can be difficult, you can stay on top of them by researching the facts and pulling together realistic and informative sources.

Rewarding Days
2, 6, 7, 11, 12, 16, 25, 26, 30

Challenging Days
13, 14, 20, 21, 23, 27, 28

Affirmation for the Month
Truth is my ultimate ally.

Scorpio/September

In the Spotlight
Power plays can be unsettling, and you may be disturbed about changes in your finances. Rewards are just as likely as losses, but the real concerns arise from uncertainty about the best ways to use and protect what you have.

Wellness and Keeping Fit
A fun-oriented, competitive outlet can have an amazing effect on your stamina and attitude. Fitness classes or regular workouts with a buddy keep you on your toes and in top shape.

Love and Life Connections
Any turmoil within the family may have its origins in your different philosophies. Fortunately, your love life can be a source of exceptional satisfaction, and declarations of love near or on the Full Moon on September 13 help to confirm your commitment to one another. Children may also be a great source of joy. Venus enters your sign on September 24, increasing your powers of attraction.

Finance and Success
Proving yourself in your career may seem like a contest, but you could also be challenging the old order to adopt necessary alterations. Professional endorsements are helpful from September 1-7, although you may have trouble convincing investors to participate. Before signing loans or agreements, make sure you're willing to pay the price. After September 18, friends may join your efforts.

Cosmic Insider Tip
While you're seeing progress professionally, you may feel the urging of your creative muse drawing you toward development of a soulful project. Tie up loose ends so you have the time!

Rewarding Days
2, 3, 7, 8, 13, 21, 22, 25, 26, 29, 30

Challenging Days
4, 9, 10, 16, 17, 18, 23, 24

Affirmation for the Month
I use all my resources wisely.

Scorpio/October

In the Spotlight
Your insights about the best ways to break through barriers can lead to exceptional resolutions. Your creative expression and artistic abilities garner positive attention.

Wellness and Keeping Fit
Your vitality is strengthened through your commitment to taking care of your health. You're seeking solutions to discomforts or illnesses that get to the core of problems.

Love and Life Connections
Love relationships are highlighted. Your feelings can shift radically, since you're less likely to fall victim to illusion and are more drawn to an experience that is closer to an emotional epiphany. An attraction from October 1-12 may be only fleeting, but it can open doors to your heart. Embark upon a different approach to loving during the Scorpio New Moon on October 27.

Finance and Success
By knowing what you want from a contractual negotiation or meeting with superiors, you can be very impressive with your presentation or requests. Initial requests fare best from October 1-12 and after October 27, although Mercury's retrograde on October 18 can draw you back into unfinished business and may make it more difficult to initiate anything new. Changes in your investment strategy are best left for a more settled time.

Cosmic Insider Tip
The opposition of Jupiter and Pluto intensifies financial concerns. Joint finances, inheritances, or taxes can be a source of runaway disputes. Your values tell you when to stand firm.

Rewarding Days
4, 5, 9, 10, 18, 19, 23, 27, 28, 31

Challenging Days
2, 7, 8, 14, 15, 20, 21, 22

Affirmation for the Month
I deserve true abundance in all things!

Scorpio/November

In the Spotlight
Clarifying misunderstandings or repairing breakdowns may take more time and attention than you prefer to give, but if left undone, these things can undermine your progress. Your insights can be highly sought after by others needing guidance.

Wellness and Keeping Fit
Inner fitness takes top priority. Devoting more time to spiritual practices rejuvenates your spirit.

Love and Life Connections
Healing a breech from the past may be necessary if you are to move on with your life. An old resentment can get in the way of what might be a productive relationship. The Full Moon on November 11 emphasizes partnership, although you may also be involved in making amends with a sibling. You forgive not because it is "deserved," but because it is necessary if guilt and shame are to be eliminated.

Finance and Success
Working behind the scenes on a project not yet ready for launch is more comfortable than exposing your ideas to critical eyes. Using what you've learned, you'll then be ready to release a more complete product next month. Meetings fare best after November 18, since prior to that time you may spend most of your energy "explaining" things! Your ideas may still stir controversy, but you can handle it.

Cosmic Insider Tip
Although Mercury completes its retrograde cycle on November 7, the confusion stirred during the last four weeks may take most of the month to clarify. Patience may be your best ally!

Rewarding Days
1, 6, 7, 14, 15, 20, 23, 24, 28, 29

Challenging Days
3, 4, 10, 11, 16, 17, 18, 30

Affirmation for the Month
I honor the differences between myself and others.

Scorpio/December

In the Spotlight
Laying the groundwork for significant changes may take most of your time, and you're aware that pushing anything before it's ready will jeopardize the potential for success. Safeguard your resources.

Wellness and Keeping Fit
You may be drawn into a desire to understand your dreams more fully. Psychological probing can also play a significant role in improving your overall sense of well-being.

Love and Life Connections
Family relationships provide the greatest rewards, but may also be a source of inner turmoil. The conflicts arise from realizing that there's a need to let go of unhealthy patterns, even if they are "traditions." The solar eclipse on December 25 can mark a new understanding, but only if you're willing to communicate your needs honestly. If you're holding back or in denial, you'll feel extremely dissatisfied.

Finance and Success
Meetings or conferences aid your plans from December 1-7 and after December 25. The Full Moon's stimulus on December 11 can open the core issues over budget or joint financial agreements, and you may feel that you have to give way on some of your demands in order to accomplish true consensus. After December 24 you're more comfortable taking the initiative to launch your pet project, but even then may not share details with just anybody.

Cosmic Insider Tip
Keeping private things private may be an important quality you intend to preserve, since eyes prying into the wrong areas can undermine your sense of security.

Rewarding Days
3, 4, 12, 13, 16, 17, 20, 21, 25, 26, 30, 31

Challenging Days
1, 2, 8, 9, 10, 14, 15, 28, 29

Affirmation for the Month
I have everything I need to make my life complete.

Scorpio Action Table

These dates reflect the best—but not the only—times for success and ease in these activities, according to your Sun sign.

	JAN	FEB	MAR	APR	MAY	JUN	JUL	AUG	SEPT	OCT	NOV	DEC
Move	19-31	1-4										
Start a class	6, 7						1, 2					
Join a club								29, 30				
Ask for a raise				13-29						27, 28		
Look for work								7-21				
Get pro advice	15, 16	11, 12	9, 10	5, 6	3-4, 30-31	27, 28	24, 25	20, 21	16-18	14, 15	10, 11	8, 9
Get a loan	17, 18	13, 14	11, 12	8, 9	5, 6	1-2, 29-30	26, 27	22-24	19, 20	16, 17	12, 13	10, 11
See a doctor				13-29					8-27			
Start a diet	12-14	9, 10	7, 8	3, 4	1-2, 28-29	24-26	22, 23	18, 19	14, 15	11-13	8, 9	5, 6
End relationship											10, 11	
Buy clothes		5-20	15-31	1-12								
Get a makeover										27, 28		
New romance			5, 6									
Vacation	19, 20	15, 16	13-15	10, 11	7, 8	3, 4	1, 2, 29	25, 26	21, 22	18, 19	14, 15	12, 13

Sagittarius
The Archer
November 21 to December 20

♐

Element:	Fire
Quality:	Mutable
Polarity:	Yang/Masculine
Planetary Ruler:	Jupiter
Meditation:	"All things in harmony with higher law are possible."
Gemstone:	Turquoise
Power Stones:	Lapis lazuli, azurite, sodalite
Key Phrase:	"I understand"
Glyph:	Archer's arrow ♐
Anatomy:	Hips, thighs, sciatic nerve
Color:	Royal blue, purple
Animal:	Fleet-footed animals
Myths/Legends:	Athena, Chiron
House:	Ninth
Opposite Sign:	Gemini
Flower:	Narcissus
Key Word:	Optimism

Positive Expression:	**Misuse of Energy:**
Understanding	Bigoted
Tolerant	Condescending
Wise	Opinionated
Adventurous	Foolish
Jovial	Self-righteous
Philosophical	Extravagant

Sagittarius

Your Ego's Strengths and Shortcomings

Continually searching, your quest for wisdom and understanding is fueled by a spirit of hope. You are "The Adventurer" of the zodiac, and through faith you carry the torch of truth, inspiring others who are charmed by your sincerity and disarmed by your direct manner. Striving for honesty, you appreciate natural order and admire those who possess genuine insight.

Educational pursuits, travel, and a fascination with culture may inspire you to keep an open mind in a changing world. You may have a voracious appetite for reading and a love of languages, and are usually happy to open your life to diverse friendships spanning many backgrounds. Influenced by the energy of Jupiter, your need to expand leads you to set your aims high, particularly within the context of your spirituality, understanding of universal law, and desire to attain a higher level of consciousness. This energy also impels you to push your limits, and sometimes you can go too far, overextending your time or resources.

Generosity seems natural for you and stimulates trust from others. Since you're always looking forward, you can grow impatient when the pace of life fails to keep up with your ideals and expectations, including your expectations of others. It's easy to become too judgmental of those whose beliefs are different from your own, but as you redirect your zeal toward developing true tolerance you can avoid the traps of self-righteousness.

Shining Your Love Light

The grand adventure of romance may capture your heart and your imagination. Although you can be happy on your own, you're enticed by the pleasures of sharing life with a companion whose ideals support your own. Over the course of your lifetime, you may leave several old loves behind in the confusing wake of your sudden disappearances created by your desire to follow another quest! Until you're ready to surrender some of your independence, you may resist becoming entangled in the lair of love. You'll feel more in love when your mate gives you room to exercise your individuality, when finally, breathing freely, you can become a steadfast partner.

You're most at ease with the fire signs—Aries, Leo and Sagittarius—whose needs for illumination and passion for life are much like your own. With Aries, love can remain strong and is constantly charged with romantic excitement. You may be comfortable with Taurus, but can feel frustrated by the slower pace. Gemini's attraction (after all, this is your zodiac opposite!) stimulates your mind and desire to communicate your most profound desires, but you do have differences to bridge if you are to develop trust. You may adore Cancer's great cooking and safety net, but can resent being overprotected. Leo's dramatic and demonstrative manner can transport you into bliss. Virgo can definitely be interesting, but may feel too much like your mother with all those directions for doing things the "right" way.

Libra's refined grace is enticing and fascinating, and you adore the artistry. Watch out for the allure of Scorpio, since you can be overcome and momentarily lose your sense of independence! Your own philosophies and ideals can mesh beautifully with another Sagittarian, and you can become excellent traveling partners. Capricorn's steadfast security is inviting, but if you sense you're being controlled, you may bolt and run. With Aquarius, you can honor your mutual needs for independence, and you may adore his or her unique approach to life. Pisces' mysticism and imagination are different and intriguing, but you may have a gap in understanding one another.

Making Your Place in the World

For a career to hold your interest it must offer unlimited potential, lots of freedom, and provide room to exercise your enthusiasm. Your ability to influence and inspire others can be used in fields like politics, the ministry, the law, promotions, advertising, sales, or acting as an agent for the talents of others. Also, careers in diplomatic service or the travel industry, publishing, journalism, or writing offer good outlets for sharing your thoughts while gathering information and expanding your mind.

Your desire to continue learning may lead you to seek an academic or educational profession where you can inspire and empower your students while reaching higher levels of personal mastery. You might be physically adept in sports and can lean toward a career in the sports industry. Business and speculative investments can capture your attention—whether in stocks, real estate, banking, sports, racing, or gambling. Regardless of your choice, you think big!

Power Plays

Defining power can be an active philosophical exercise, but in your heart of hearts, liberty and power are innately linked. You quest for right and truth, inspired by your freedom to think and act in accordance with higher law in a true expression of the power ordained by a higher source. Your abhorrence of the idea of using power to limit human potential goes hand in hand with your views that power without wisdom is wasted. The achievement of enlightenment may equal the highest level of power, and you're willing to work to get beyond all the useless double talk and blind alleys of belief systems in order to get there. You know that truth will set you free.

While material abundance may appear to symbolize power, you may not have an appreciation for the abundant life until your actions and thoughts are harmonized with your highest needs. Maintaining an open mind is a key to uncovering power, and you're learning that narrow-minded thinking is an obstacle. Your study, writing, teaching, and travels light the fires of inspiration, allowing you to reach toward others, realizing the power of understanding as the architect of a healthy future for all humankind.

Famous Sagittarians

William Blake, Kenneth Branagh, Larry Byrd, Winston Churchill, Noel Coward, Jane Fonda, John Fitzgerald Kennedy, Jr., Don King, Howie Mandel, Stone Phillips, Giacomo Puccini, Bhagwan Shree Rajneesh, Tina Turner, Dionne Warwick.

The Year Ahead
for Sagittarius

You're filled with optimism and inspiration about stepping onto new paths and exercising your originality and independence. There's definitely work to do, and your diligence about fulfilling obligations or obtaining necessary credentials can carry you a long way toward accomplishing your aims. While partnerships or associations with others can offer exceptional benefits, you may struggle with your personal desires to feel unfettered.

Jupiter, your planetary ruler, is transiting in the signs Taurus and Gemini this year, enhancing your desires to make improvements and take the steps that will allow you to feel integrated into society in a meaningful way. This does not mean that you're giving up your individuality; in fact, it is your uniqueness that will attract significant opportunity. From January through July, you'll gain momentum by finding ways to work more cooperatively with others. Improvements to your health may also take precedence, and increasing your physical activity level can have amazing results. After July, Jupiter moves into your house of partnerships, and for the remainder of the year you may feel more inclined to work in tandem with others on important projects and issues. If you're married, this cycle can bring improvements in your marriage, and if you're looking for a mate, your choices may be better than they've been in the past!

Saturn's transit emphasizes your need to take care of business, paying special attention to the details and responsibilities of the tasks associated with your work. Not only is your job demanding more of your time and energy, but if it's the wrong job, you'll find that it's draining your vitality. Making adjustments that will allow you to move into a more fulfilling position can give you a new lease on life. Special attention to health may also be necessary.

The slower-moving cycles of Uranus and Neptune are accentuating your mental curiosity and desire to learn, but you may feel drawn to explore extraordinary subjects that can expand your understanding in ways you've never entertained. Your imaginative ideas are also running in high gear, and although every brainstorm you experience may not be as brilliant in practice as it seems when your first think of it, you're very likely to come up with some real gems of ideas. Pluto continues its cycle in your sign, marking a very long period of transformational change and ability to surrender to the processes of rebirth. The years in which Pluto is exactly conjunct your Sun are the most significant periods of this transit, and if this is your year, it will be noted in the paragraphs below, designated by birth day.

We're experiencing four solar eclipses and two lunar eclipses during the year 2000. The exact influences of each eclipse will be defined in the monthly forecast sections that follow. The underlying influence of the eclipse cycles is shown by the transit of the Moon's nodes, which are bringing your emphasis to deeper issues like emotional attachment, fears, inhibitions, and issues surrounding trust. The external changes in the world may trigger these emotionally sensitive areas for you, and, in your personal life, the crisis points you're experiencing may relate most significantly to the process and experience of true healing. Releasing old anxieties, dealing with the past by letting go of hurt, shame, guilt, or resentment, and moving toward a deeper understanding of your motivations, you're given a chance to become whole.

If you were born from November 22 to 23, you're feeling the impact of Saturn transiting in opposition to your Sun. This transit begins during the summer months, gaining momentum through October, and returns in 2001. The thrust of this cycle is discipline, focus, and restraint, and during the time you're experiencing Saturn's influence you may feel inhibited by excessive responsibilities or tests. It's not easy to move into new situations, but instead you may feel that you are constrained by your current circumstances, forced to remain until you've completed your obligations. In many ways, this is a period of endings, but it can also be a time when you're more aware of the strictures of time. No matter what your age, you may feel old, or you may be concerned that you're "running out of time," and in some instances, if you fail to meet a deadline, it could definitely be a setback. If you're happy with your life choices, then you may experience this as a time of reality testing. Since Uranus is also transiting in quintile aspect to your Sun, your creative capacities are strengthened throughout the year. This cycle blended in harmony with Saturn's influence can indicate that you can apply the discipline to bring your talents into their full expression.

For Sagittarians born from November 22 to 30, Uranus is transiting in quintile aspect to your Sun. While this cycle operates on a subtle level, if you work to access and incorporate the energy of this time you'll find that your special talents grow significantly. It's time to access the unique gifts that set you apart from the crowd and to develop your talents so that you can make better use of them. Studying with a respected teacher or working with a mentor can also be especially helpful, since a master can help you access qualities that may be dormant or underdeveloped. Technological advances may also play a part in enhancing your creative capacities.

If you were born from November 24 to 29, you're experiencing the influence of Neptune transiting in sextile aspect to your Sun. Your spirituality may become a more significant priority, and working in cooperative situations with others to reach out and make a difference in the world can give your life new meaning. You're more sensitive to everything, and if you're involved in creative or artistic expression, your flow can certainly be strengthened. Letting go is also easier, and if you've been dealing with hurtful situations or losses, you will feel that you're finally ready to forgive and move on. Your quest for inner peace may be more easily satisfied as your sense of vision and ability to connect with your intuitive awareness also grow stronger. The work you do now to strengthen the connection between your inner self and the Source will be rewarded on many levels, including enhanced creativity and more profound psychic awareness. By embracing life and surrendering to the rhythm pulsating from a pure heart, you may finally feel that you're on the path of truth and understanding.

If you were born from December 1 to 6, you're experiencing the life-altering cycle of Pluto transiting in conjunction to your Sun. This cycle has been building for several years and now reaches its peak; the transformational changes you undergo can modify the remainder of your life. This once-in-a-lifetime cycle makes it a good year to work with a therapist or to consult a competent astrologer, since you're undergoing major changes. On many levels, you're leaving behind the "old you" in favor of opening to an experience of regeneration. While you may feel that many changes are happening beyond your control, you're also capable of producing broad-scale changes by consciously releasing the things you no longer need. Perhaps it's time to change jobs, move, or end a relationship. If you know in your heart that you've completed a situation or have grown beyond it, hanging on now will become painful. Your job can be filled with unusual power plays, your house may become a burden, or an unhealthy relationship can become an immense drain on your energy. It's time to determine where you want to go from here and to develop positive ways to use your power and influence. Physically, make a very careful evaluation of your health and eliminate anything that can undermine your well-being. Cultivating bad habits now will definitely work against you! On the most basic level, you are being healed. Chiron's transit over your Sun helps assure that this is true healing—an experience that means that the unhealthy elements in your life are eliminated so that you are empowered. Make special note of the period from August through November, since during this time the transit of Jupiter in opposition to Pluto has a direct impact on your life. While on a collective level this cycle represents power struggles on the political or economic front, in your life the power struggle may be directly related to breaking out of situations that have pushed you beyond your limits.

If you were born from December 6 to 14, you're feeling the stimulus of Uranus transiting in sextile to your Sun, energizing your need to express your individuality while exercising independent thought and applying your talents. This can be an exciting year, since you're forging new pathways and may feel that you have a new lease on life. Travel, learning, developing your understanding, or honing your skills—all can have a significant influence in changing your life. You may become more adept at utilizing technological support or may even be instrumental in developing new technologies or experimental models. These models can be literal, or you may forge into new territory in the realms of learning, creativity, or communication. If you're interested in fields such as broadcasting, television, computer science, or education, your opportunities in these areas can skyrocket. It's time to let the real you emerge with full force and to gain positive recognition for what makes you special.

If you were born from December 14 to 21, Saturn is transiting in quincunx aspect to your Sun. Now is the time to finish obligations, fulfill educational requirements, or work harder to make your dreams a reality. Slacking off will work against you, and taking on nonessential burdens will slow you down too much. To make the most of this year, you'll need honesty and must be willing to make a conscious evaluation of the potential outcome of your choices. It's also crucial that you pay attention to your body's needs, since any weaknesses are likely to be exposed. The good thing is that you know what you're dealing with. The hard part may be changing schedules, habits, or attitudes so that you're focused more on well-being and less on indulgences (or denial). It's time to pare down excess in favor of feeling focused and effective.

Tools to Make a Difference

Since you're excited about the possibility of trying unusual solutions to problems or exploring people, situations, and information that fall into the realm of " the unprecedented," you may have more success employing nontraditional methods. Additionally, you're finding all sorts of uses for technological advances, and taking advantage of areas like computer technology, Internet access, and satellite communications can put you on the leading edge professionally. Forging a wide-ranging communication network can make a difference, since no matter what type of information you're seeking, you'll be at an advantage if you have more choices.

Getting your physical body in top condition is likely to involve a wide-ranging series of therapies and changes. Although you may be tempted to push your body past its limits without giving yourself the rewards of time off, massage, a positive health routine, or reasonable maintenance, you'll only be able to sustain abuses for a limited period of time. Taking advantage of therapies like acupuncture, rolfing, or shiatsu can be regenerating. If you're interested in using aromatherapy, try inhalations of rose, frankincense, geranium, or jasmine to help lift your spirits. You might also benefit from adding supplements like ginkgo biloba to your diet to improve your memory.

During your meditations, let yourself open to the experience of freeing your mind. Once you've begun to relax, simply concentrate on your breathing for awhile. With each inhalation, feel your energy growing stronger as your mind opens to an expanded awareness. With each exhalation, feel tension releasing from your body and consciously let go of the thoughts cluttering your mind. Once you feel that your mind is open and free, you feel lighter and more connected to the Source. Throughout the day, take time to clear your mind and let go, since constantly filling your mind with tasks clutters your thinking.

Initiating the Millennium

As you step into the year 2000, you may feel a sense of excitement and anticipation, but you also realize that there's work to be done. Create a set of priorities that will help you realize your goals, but keep an understanding that these priorities may have to change if situations beyond your control provide alternatives or challenges you had not anticipated. Your natural ability to adapt to change works to your advantage, and your ability to pinpoint the opportunities that are in harmony with your needs works like a charm; but you have to put these attributes into action if they are to make a difference in the quality of your life.

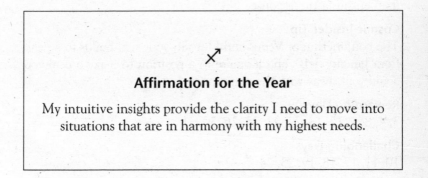

↗

Affirmation for the Year

My intuitive insights provide the clarity I need to move into situations that are in harmony with my highest needs.

Sagittarius/January

In the Spotlight
While your powers of attraction are rather potent, challenges or obstacles in your path can upset your sense of stability. Maintaining open lines of communication helps your maintain a more even keel in the midst of control issues.

Wellness and Keeping Fit
Competitive situations can tempt you to push past your limits. You may also be dealing with simple burnout! Staying active is important, but take extra care in sports or in high-risk situations.

Love and Life Connections
Venus transits in your sign until January 25, and if you've been hoping to make the right impression, it's easier to emphasize your positive attributes. Your intensity can be overwhelming from January 5-18. The lunar eclipse on January 20 stirs your imagination, and expressing the depths of your feelings can turn the tide.

Finance and Success
Dealing with the details of a budget keeps you on track in negotiations, and if you're considering making a major investment you'll need to know exactly where you stand. You may accomplish a financial coup from January 7-14, when an unusual change of events can put you in line for prosperity. Schedule meetings, interviews, or conferences from January 20-31, when your imaginative ideas elicit an enthusiastic response.

Cosmic Insider Tip
The conjunction of Venus and Pluto in your sign builds to a peak from January 3-10, and if you're in a position to make a deal you could walk away with the major prizes.

Rewarding Days
3, 4, 8, 9, 12, 13, 21, 22, 25, 26, 30, 31

Challenging Days
10, 11, 17, 18, 19, 23, 24

Affirmation for the Month
I am worthy of true and abundant love.

Sagittarius/February

In the Spotlight
Your ideas for improvement or change can be trendsetting, but the problem with being on the leading edge resides in those who are stuck in the old ways. Tests of your patience may keep you on edge.

Wellness and Keeping Fit
Tension on the job and pressure at home may leave you feeling that you're a stress magnet. Activities like yoga or tai chi may be beneficial. Recreation and sports take up the slack after February 13.

Love and Life Connections
Friction at home can be uncomfortable until February 13, but talking over your concerns during the Sun's eclipse on February 5 can help alleviate much of the turmoil. You're feeling more romantic after February 13, when your attraction to an enchanting individual can be consuming. Fortunately, your humor, intelligence, and charm are in top form from February 15-29, and if a meeting of the minds has opened the door, you'll be in business!

Finance and Success
Taking a conservative approach to spending or investing feels best, and you may do well with an investment from February 13-19. Since Mercury is in retrograde from February 21-29, you'll be more successful signing contracts prior to that time, and if you've not completed negotiations, use the retrograde to probe trouble spots or to investigate your concerns. Property purchases are not advised.

Cosmic Insider Tip
While meetings and presentations can keep the momentum going from February 1-5, you may be more at ease developing an ongoing project after that time.

Rewarding Days
4, 5, 9, 10, 18, 22, 23, 26, 27

Challenging Days
6, 7, 8, 13, 14, 19, 20

Affirmation for the Month
My creativity is an expression of pure love.

Sagittarius/March

In the Spotlight
Heightened enthusiasm shines through your attitude, and your ability to instill hope can influence others to support your ideas or projects. Innovations may be more promising in theory than in practice, but that's unlikely to stop you!

Wellness and Keeping Fit
Your favorite sports may beckon, and dedicating time to enjoyable forms of recreation adds vitality and helps you sustain your energy during a busy period. Concentrate on building your endurance.

Love and Life Connections
You may feel most loving when you're spending quiet time together in your personal surroundings. Changes at home during the New Moon on March 5 can take the pressure off a tense situation. After March 21 you may feel more confident about declaring your intentions, although during the Full Moon on March 19 you may hesitate because of security issues or value differences.

Finance and Success
Conferences work to your advantage from March 1-14, even though Mercury is retrograding until then. Listen to the ideas of others and interject your thoughts primarily when you think your ideas will keep conversation moving. Promises made on the job may be more hot air than substance, particularly if the resources to make changes are scarce. Next month is better for contracts.

Cosmic Insider Tip
The tension between Jupiter and Neptune can leave you feeling ill at ease since you may sense that you're being manipulated by propaganda. Know your own opinions!

Rewarding Days
2, 3, 7, 8, 15, 20, 21, 25, 26, 31

Challenging Days
5, 6, 11, 12, 13, 18, 19

Affirmation for the Month
In all things I seek the honest and truthful path.

LLEWELLYN PUBLICATIONS
P.O. BOX 64383
ST. PAUL, MN 55164-0383

Sagittarius/April

In the Spotlight
Expressing what's in your heart is your first priority, and whether you're targeting a love relationship or becoming more involved with the development of a creative venture, your passion can be contagious—and very attractive!

Wellness and Keeping Fit
Staying active keeps your energy at a peak, although it's easy to concentrate more on building strength and too little on flexibility. Techniques like Reiki and acupuncture may be highly effective.

Love and Life Connections
You may be drawn into a captivating relationship, and the power of love can turn your life around. Speaking from your heart during the New Moon on April 4 can open pathways to understanding. You're also feeling an urge to surrender to the soulful qualities of a special relationship. Romantic experiences from April 14 through the Full Moon on April 18 can be simply amazing!

Finance and Success
The rewards of hard work are definitely evident, and your productivity may be on the increase from April 1-15. Unexpected changes can arise after April 16 when procedural alterations can interrupt your normal routine. Your talents are in high demand, and you may finally feel that you're garnering respect for your abilities. Finances improve, and investments fare best from April 15-24.

Cosmic Insider Tip
Investing your time and energy into situations that allow you to use your most creative sensibilities is rewarding and profitable! Showcase your talents and ideas after April 7.

Rewarding Days
3, 4, 12, 13, 16, 17, 21, 22, 26, 27

Challenging Days
1, 2, 8, 9, 14, 15, 28, 29, 39

Affirmation for the Month
Listening to the song of my heart I hear the voice of true love.

Sagittarius/May

In the Spotlight
Answering the demands you're feeling from your work can shift your attention from a personal project to a cooperative endeavor. Tension within your partnership can escalate if your work becomes too time-consuming.

Wellness and Keeping Fit
Tension and stress may be at an all-time high, particularly if you're trying to keep everyone happy. A challenging fitness routine helps take the edge off stress. Schedule a couple of massages this month.

Love and Life Connections
Conflicts with your partner can occur if you feel you're being over-controlled or if you sense that your needs are constantly taking a back seat. Dealing with tense issues is a necessity, although you do not have to wage a full-scale war! Communication improves after May 15, but problems with semantics can lead to petty disagreements from May 19-22. Romance fares best after May 27.

Finance and Success
The question about your job may loom large: are you in the right position, and is your situation offering you a chance to be as productive as you desire to be? Tension in the work place can escalate between the New Moon on May 3 and the Full Moon on May 18, and may be secondary to changes in policy designed to create "improvements." Your direct approach can be a breakthrough after May 18.

Cosmic Insider Tip
Your physical energy and emotional state are very clearly tied together, and the parts of your life that are creating a sense of unhappiness need attention before May 18!

Rewarding Days
1, 2, 9, 13, 14, 18, 19, 23, 24, 29

Challenging Days
3, 5, 6, 7, 11, 12, 26, 27, 30, 31

Affirmation for the Month
I am committed to fulfilling my highest needs.

Sagittarius/June

In the Spotlight
Partnerships move into the spotlight, and the amount of energy you're directing toward your relationships will be in direct proportion to the progress you feel you're making. Contract negotiations may be heated, but progressive.

Wellness and Keeping Fit
Whether you're changing your routine, altering habits, or beginning a new commitment to fitness, it's time to take charge of your health.

Love and Life Connections
If you're initiating a new course in a relationship, taking action during the New Moon on June 2 adds emphasis to the points you desire to make and helps underscore the roles you're most comfortable playing. By the time the Sagittarius Full Moon occurs on June 16, you may run into another set of issues that are at the heart of your fears of intimacy. Old hurts can haunt you, but you're the only one who can banish those ghosts!

Finance and Success
Legal matters may take on a life of their own, although your participation in negotiations or introduction of solutions can be instrumental in creating a successful agreement. At work, productivity becomes the motto, and you may feel that you've become a slave to obligations. To deal with the onslaught on responsibility, you'll be juggling priorities and eliminating wasteful situations.

Cosmic Insider Tip
The build-up of convoluted communications preceding Mercury's retrograde that begins on June 23 can lead you and others astray. Fortunately, your direct manner insists on clarity!

Rewarding Days
5, 6, 10, 11, 14, 15, 16, 20, 21, 24, 25

Challenging Days
1, 2, 3, 7, 8, 9, 22, 23, 29, 30

Affirmation for the Month
I honor the value of others who are a significant part of my life.

Sagittarius/July

In the Spotlight
It's the diminishing light that takes center stage: the lunar eclipse and two solar eclipses pinpoint the potential for crisis. A new understanding helps you heal, but requires that you let go of an old attachment if you are to fully test your wings!

Wellness and Keeping Fit
The psychological and spiritual dimensions of healing are almost glaring, and it is crucial that you embrace and utilize your spiritual strength. Faith works miracles.

Love and Life Connections
An impasse in a close relationship on July 1 (a solar eclipse) may have money as the external argument, but resentment or mistrust may be at the core. You may discover that you are not as connected as you thought you were. By the lunar eclipse on July 16, you're more comfortable speaking up in situations that affect your self-esteem. The final solar eclipse on July 30 sparks your imagination and hope for the future: you're ready to let wisdom guide your steps.

Finance and Success
Inheritance, debt, or tax matters can put the kibosh on a business deal, and since Mercury is in retrograde until July 17, you're better off postponing new purchases and dealing with unfinished business. It's time to address debts realistically and change your spending patterns. After July 23 career opportunities open new doors.

Cosmic Insider Tip
An exciting month! You're dealing with matters that once would have given you reason to lock the doors and hide the key! It's time to try on the mantle of your power and see how it fits.

Rewarding Days
3, 4, 7, 8, 12, 13, 17, 18, 22, 23, 30, 31

Challenging Days
1, 5, 6, 16, 19, 20, 21, 26, 27

Affirmation for the Month
I surrender what I no longer need and celebrate my newfound freedom!

Sagittarius/August

In the Spotlight
All the housecleaning you've been doing pays off. Now you're in the perfect position to step into a more challenging career or to initiate a significant change in your life path. You may even welcome new responsibilities.

Wellness and Keeping Fit
Your physical vitality improves, and you may feel more inclined to get involved in a fitness class or work with a personal trainer.

Love and Life Connections
The respect you garner from your family means a lot, although you may be challenging certain family traditions that seem out of place. New dimensions of an existing relationship are nurtured by traveling or retreating into experiences that strengthen the spiritual basis of your union during the Full Moon on August 15. Meeting your soulmate can happen, but this person may not be your current partner!

Finance and Success
Your career opportunities grow through academic accomplishments, promotional activities, publishing, or conferences. Others are acknowledging the value of your work, and your work itself shines on its own merits. Defining expectations of superiors during and after the New Moon on August 29 helps to keep you from becoming overwhelmed, and gives you a chance to align your priorities with your current situation.

Cosmic Insider Tip
Breaking with traditional or established procedure works to your benefit from August 7-15, when your enthusiasm enlists exceptional support, allowing you to set new standards.

Rewarding Days
3, 4, 5, 8, 9, 13, 14, 18, 19, 27, 28, 31

Challenging Days
1, 2, 15, 16, 17, 22, 23, 29, 30

Affirmation for the Month
In all matters I follow the path of truth and integrity.

♐ Sagittarius/September ♐

In the Spotlight
The rewards from your career can be exceptional, ranging from growing recognition to increased financial remuneration. The way you exercise your influence makes a difference in what happens next.

Wellness and Keeping Fit
You might enjoy integrating several disciplines into your workouts. A competitive situation can be an excellent reason to be more diligent.

Love and Life Connections
It's time to open your heart and allow love and tenderness from others to pour into your life. Then, by returning the affection you're feeling from friends, children, and loved ones, the flow of love lifts you to new heights. Family matters may require more attention through the Full Moon on September 13, although you can feel gratified by the connection you share. Affairs of the heart gain momentum during the New Moon on September 27.

Finance and Success
Business travel and meetings with colleagues provide the perfect situation to showcase your products or ideas, and may even lead to a job offer. The competition gets hotter after September 18, but that's not likely to stop you if you're on the path toward accomplishment. Your talents shine brightly, and from September 1-25, your connections give you an advantage that others lack, and your moral values may also give you an edge.

Cosmic Insider Tip
While the planets Jupiter and Pluto transit in opposition all month, you may be faced with a dilemma that puts you right in the middle of a power struggle. Choose your battles carefully.

Rewarding Days
1, 4, 5, 6, 9, 10, 14, 15, 23, 24, 27, 28

Challenging Days
12, 13, 19, 20, 25, 26

Affirmation for the Month
My principles help me determine the best course of action.

Sagittarius/October

In the Spotlight

Competitive situations escalate, and you may have to deal with issues you'd prefer to avoid. It's time to test your mettle, and the associations you choose can make a difference in the outcome of a tricky conflict.

Wellness and Keeping Fit

To release some of the tension building from your career or within your family, you need to remain committed to your fitness routine.

Love and Life Connections

Your actions and plans may run up against objections from your family or your partner, particularly if the changes you're making will threaten an old security base. It may be time to break out of a rut that has become an excuse. Listen to your heart during the Full Moon on October 13, when your true feelings guide you. A change in relationship made in January is tested from October 27-31.

Finance and Success

Maintaining your course may be difficult if your company or career path is under renovation or construction. Looking out for the detours, which may center around ethical disputes, helps you avoid falling by the wayside. You're moving onto a more stable platform after October 21, although you may feel like you're revisiting issues that you thought were resolved. Reconsider your investment strategy, but don't change it yet.

Cosmic Insider Tip

Mercury retrogrades after October 17, so finish a current project. Then, from October 26-29, Venus and Pluto once again conjoin in your sign (see January). How do you want to handle it this time?

Rewarding Day
2, 3, 7, 8, 11, 12, 13, 20, 21, 25, 26, 29, 30

Challenging Days
9, 10, 16, 17, 18, 22, 23

Affirmation for the Month
My evolving needs lead to growth and positive change.

⚑ Sagittarius/November ⚑

In the Spotlight
Financial situations and personal values take top priority, and the decisions you're making now may be centered around making sure you're being paid what you're worth. Campaigning may be required!

Wellness and Keeping Fit
To keep your interest in fitness, enlist a buddy to join you in workouts or get into team sports or a fitness class. Associating with others who have positive and healthy goals helps you stay on track.

Love and Life Connections
You may be fascinated by the prospects of a new love from November 1-11, or you may be seeking to breathe new life into an established relationship. The one thing you're trying to avoid is the death knell of boredom. Fortunately, the Sagittarius New Moon on November 25 spurs you to go after whatever you desire, so if you need a change, then it is time to make it! It's easy to send mixed signals, so keep your message crystal clear.

Finance and Success
Complex negotiations can leave you frustrated if you're trying to finalize a contract, and until Mercury ends its retrograde on November 7, you might prefer to keep expectations to a minimum. Professional associations provide healthy outlets for competition after November 4, and innovative developments can spur your interest after November 23. Launch projects after November 25.

Cosmic Insider Tip
Behind the scenes planning works best until November 23, and after that time, you may feel much more confident about your choices and actions. Satisfying results follow thorough homework.

Rewarding Days
3, 4, 8, 9, 17, 21, 22, 25, 26, 27, 30

Challenging Days
5, 6, 7, 12, 13, 19, 20

Affirmation for the Month
I choose my friends wisely.

♐ Sagittarius/December ♐

In the Spotlight
You're moving along at such a consistent pace that others may have trouble keeping up, and you might be quite happy about outdistancing the competition! Fully developing and initiating an idea or project positively influences your reputation.

Wellness and Keeping Fit
You're appreciating the value of staying active, but may enjoy the social aspects of a class or workout schedule just as much. Participating in your favorite sport is especially rewarding.

Love and Life Connections
You may be quite comfortable taking the initiative in a love relationship. A rather intriguing prospect for new love enters the picture after December 9. Make time for romance near the Full Moon on December 11, when you may also feel like indulging a fantasy or sharing delightful pleasures with your sweetheart. Time with friends and family works best before December 25.

Finance and Success
Your leadership keeps a project moving through December 13, and after that, you might prefer to take a back seat and allow someone else to spearhead things while you sort through details and put things in order. The solar eclipse on December 25 emphasizes your financial and material affairs, and marks an excellent time to set out a new plan of action or to devise a realistic budget.

Cosmic Insider Tip
You need a break from the action, although you may not be able to get away until after December 24. Meanwhile, maximize what you can accomplish at meetings or through correspondence.

Rewarding Days
1, 2, 5, 6, 14, 15, 18, 19, 23, 24, 28

Challenging Days
3, 4, 10, 11, 16,1 7, 30, 31

Affirmation for the Month
I am willing to put forth the effort to manifest my goals.

Sagittarius Action Table

These dates reflect the best—but not the only—times for success and ease in these activities, according to your Sun sign.

	JAN	FEB	MAR	APR	MAY	JUN	JUL	AUG	SEPT	OCT	NOV	DEC
Move		5-20	15-31	1-12								
Start a class		5					30, 31					
Join a club									27, 28			
Ask for a raise											25-27	
Look for work				30	1-13			22-31	1-6			
Get pro advice	17, 18	13, 14	11, 12	8, 9	5, 6	1-2, 29-30	26, 27	22-24	19, 20	16, 17	12, 13	10, 11
Get a loan	19, 20	15, 16	13-15	10, 11	7, 8	3, 4	1-2, 28-29	25, 26	21, 22	18, 19	14, 15	12, 13
See a doctor					1-24				28-30	1-18	8-30	1-3
Start a diet	15, 16	11, 12	9, 10	5-7	3-4, 30-31	27, 28	24, 25	20, 21	16, 17	14, 15	10, 11	7-9
End relationship												11
Buy clothes				13-29								
Get a makeover											25-27	
New romance				4								
Vacation	21, 22	17, 18	16, 17	12, 13	9, 10	5, 6	3-4, 30-31	27, 28	23, 24	20, 21	16-18	14, 15

Capricorn

The Goat
December 21 to January 19

♑

Element:	Earth
Quality:	Cardinal
Polarity:	Yin/Feminine
Planetary Ruler:	Saturn
Meditation:	"I am mastering the challenges of the physical plane."
Gemstone:	Garnet
Power Stones:	Diamond, quartz, onyx, black obsidian
Key Phrase:	"I use"
Glyph:	Head of goat, knees ♑
Anatomy:	Skeleton, knees, skin
Color:	Black
Animal:	Goats, thick-shelled animals
Myths/Legends:	Chronos, Vesta, Pan
House:	Tenth
Opposite Sign:	Cancer
Flower:	Carnation
Key Word:	Structure

Positive Expression:	Misuse of Energy:
Conscientious	Miserly
Disciplined	Controlling
Patient	Repressed
Ambitious	Machiavellian
Prudent	Fearful
Responsible	Severe

Capricorn

Your Ego's Strengths and Shortcomings

There's no doubt about the fact that you aim for the top. Through your determination and persistent effort you are assured the achievement of your ambitions. Whether you're making your way up the ladder to success in your career or seeking to master anything that's important to you, you know how to make the most of the materials at hand and when to put your talents to work. As "The Pragmatist" of the zodiac, you hope to keep everything running at utmost efficiency.

You prefer to keep moving forward, and when you marshal your discipline you're capable of meeting most challenges. Your common sense and dry humor draw the admiration of others, and you may be sought as an authority by those who appreciate your sense of structure and clarity of focus. Through your affinity with the energy of Saturn, you understand the importance of creating a solid foundation for your dreams. Once you've set out on the path toward accomplishment or have established your target, you are not likely to take "no" for an answer, a trait that can sometimes be exceptionally irritating to others. You may even buck authorities if arbitrary rules are standing in the way, and may have to learn some hard lessons about taking responsibility and honoring social limitations. At times, your desire to have what you want can prompt you to ignore the needs of others who may complain that you're taking unfair advantage of them, but by sharing responsibilities you may be able to accomplish goals beyond your own vision. Although you are happiest when you're in charge, you may enjoy relinquishing control when a student, partner, or friend takes the driver's seat. This gives you a chance to alter your perspective and refine your dreams. When you need to clear your energy, getting back to basics always helps. By connecting with the simple joys of life, it's easier to create a pattern for success that serves you well and that may be emulated by others eager to reach their own pinnacle.

Shining Your Love Light

Your reserved, matter-of-fact manner can give others the mistaken impression that you are not romantic, but that's far from the truth! Your guard may remain in place until you know it's safe to let someone see your tender side, but once you open your heart, your playful spirit emerges. Looking for a love that can withstand the tests of time, you may feel that a fling is a waste, and may even be reluctant to experiment with romance until you feel you've satisfied a certain level of material stability. When you do surrender to love, you can become a steadfast, sensual, and supportive partner.

The earth signs—Taurus, Virgo, and Capricorn—will make you feel most at ease, and you'll share a mutual appreciation for practicality and common sense. However, your most powerful attraction may be to Cancer, your opposite, with whom you can create a partnership based on family values and a mutual desire for security. Aries stimulates your teasing qualities, but you can lock horns with your mutually headstrong attitudes. Taurus engages your earthy sensuality and can hold the key to your heart's eternal love. Gemini can get on your nerves, and you may be equally frustrating to him or her. Your attraction to Leo can be strong, but determining who's in charge can lead to disputes. With Virgo you may share mutual values and ideals and may find the perfect companion for life's journey.

Libra holds a legendary attraction, but getting close emotionally can take on vestiges of an epic quest. Scorpio promises the potential for magical alchemy and passionate devotion. Sagittarius inspires you to seek the best life has to offer, but the relationship will not last if you try to limit his or her freedom. Getting close to another Capricorn may be easy, but you can get stuck in stale routines that tarnish your love. Aquarius can be an eternal friend, and Pisces' romantic mysticism invites you to share the magical escape of love.

Making Your Place in the World

One of your priorities centers around developing a high-quality career, and you may feel most content when your life work promotes your self-respect. You operate well in positions of authority that allow you to exercise your executive abilities and delegate tasks. In politics or the ministry, your ambition supports your desire to reach for the heights. As a teacher you may be drawn to the life sciences, geology, physics, the healing arts, or life skills.

Metaphysical studies seem natural, and working in the healing arts as an herbalist, naturopath, chiropractor, holistic physician, or counselor can be practical applications of your understanding of energy and healing. The construction industry can be appealing, and you might excel in contracting, development, or design. Managing a farm, ranch, zoo, or forest can answer your need to stay in touch with nature. In any choice, you're determined to become a success.

Power Plays

When you're in control of something, your heart sings! Determining the nature of control and power can be an arduous task since you can become too rigid in your quest to be in charge. Flexible attitudes and tolerance for the needs of others allow you to improve your understanding and exercise of true power. In many ways, power may be more a means than an end, since once you accomplish the position you desire, your influence over others becomes readily apparent. You're a natural leader and role model, and may become an icon if you allow your sense of power to be tempered by a loving heart.

When you exert excessive control over the lives or ideas of others, you can actually undermine your power base, and hanging on to traditions or archaic concepts can thwart your growth. Because others tend to look up to you, when you're taking full responsibility for yourself and holding a responsible attitudes toward others, you can help them shape their own destinies. Surrendering your ego to a higher power keeps everything in its proper perspective.

Famous Capricorns

Muhammad Ali, Rowan Atkinson, Joan Baez, Jim Bakker, Larry Csonka, John Z. DeLorean, Wyatt Earp, Heidi Fleiss, Dave Foley, Cuba Gooding, Jr., Johannes Kepler, L.L. Cool J, Kate Moss, Floyd Patterson, Cokie Roberts, Albert Schweitzer.

The Year Ahead
for Capricorn

Your creative sensibilities continue to provide the basis for your personal and professional growth, and by developing your talents and abilities you may gain greater recognition while enhancing your personal worth. Job opportunities and work circumstances may undergo improvements, but to improve your finances you may have to make radical changes in the way you handle your resources.

The expansive energy of Jupiter emphasizes abundance in the realms of pleasurable relationships, creativity, and better work circumstances. From January through the end of June, Jupiter's influence aids your ability to attract the kind of love that frees your heart and allows your true creativity to shine forth. Then from July through the end of the year, Jupiter moves through the Sixth House of your solar chart, bringing health improvements and emphasizing positive changes at work. The test of these cycles rests in your ability to say "no" when you've reached the limits of your capacities to give your energy to others, and to know when to limit your work. You can push beyond your capacities before you know it unless you make a conscious effort to be attentive to your physical limitations.

Your planetary ruler, Saturn, is transiting in a supportive cycle to your Sun this year, aiding your ability to keep your priorities in order as you focus on your responsibilities. Strengthened productivity is a positive side effect of this cycle, and you may also feel much more confident about your commitment to an intimate relationship. In some instances this cycle indicates meaningful associations with children through your work or personal life, and your ability to guide and inspire others can be empowered by Saturn's influence. The long-term effects indicated by the cycles of Uranus and Neptune impact your material worth and value systems. Letting go of outmoded values can be a freeing experience, but first you may have to address your fears associated with changes occurring beyond your control. Pluto's transit through the Twelfth House of your solar chart stimulates a deep release of the things from your past that are no longer relevant to your life. You may become more aware of the workings of your inner self, and can use your dreams and periods of insightful reflection as guideposts of your spiritual and psychological growth.

During the year 2000, there are two lunar eclipses and four solar eclipses. It is unusual to experience this number of solar eclipses in one year, and the result can be an escalating potential for crisis through global events. On a personal level, the influence of each of the eclipses will be explained in your monthly forecast section. The underlying effects of the eclipse cycles are measured by the transit of the Mood's nodes, and this year your emphasis centers around what you need from partnerships and your roles in relationships. Your feelings about your partner may require honest appraisal, and if you're dealing with buried resentment or guilt, then this is the year to release negativity in favor of allowing a new quality to emerge. The changes you make in relationships can have far-reaching effects on other parts of your life.

If you were born from December 21 to 29, you're adapting to a series of changes, some unexpected, while Uranus transits in semisquare aspect to your Sun. You may be leaving behind a tried-and-true situation in favor of an unknown circumstance, although the change may be something you welcome. To some extent, this period can leave you feeling that your feet are not quite on the ground, and establishing a solid foundation may be virtually impossible. This is a cycle of flux and marks a time when you're challenged to break away from an old security base as you move toward untried possibilities. For example, in relationships, you may be moving from dating to a serious commitment, or saying good-bye to a partner and starting a new life. On the career front, you could be moving out of a corporate environment into owning our own business, or might be entering the work force after completing your educational requirements. Either way, the scene you're facing is quite different from what you've come to know as familiar and reliable. To counterbalance the effects of Uranus, establishing a method of keeping yourself grounded can be extremely beneficial. Additionally, if you were born from December 21 to 23, you may feel somewhat stymied while Saturn transits in quincunx aspect to your Sun from August through the end of October, a time when your plans and the effects of your changes will be tested.

If you were born from December 26 to 30, you're feeling the stimulus of Neptune transiting in semisextile to your Sun. Your imagination and sensitivity are enhanced by Neptune's influence, and if you're involved in any type of creative or artistic pursuit, you may expand your expression or feel more in touch with your artistic muse. Your spirituality may take on a more significant role, and integrating your spiritual practices into your daily life can alter the way you perceive yourself and your life choices. Because Saturn is also transiting in biquintile aspect to your Sun, your natural tendency toward practical considerations can be helpful, and in order to fine-tune your creativity you may attract a mentor or teacher whose influence encourages you to develop your skills more fully. A spiritual teacher can also manifest, but may arrive through an unusual source, such as a coworker or even a child, whose influence and different way of viewing things opens your mind to fresh possibilities.

If you were born from December 31 to January 5, you're feeling the need to leave behind the things you no longer need since Pluto is transiting in semisextile to your Sun. Your underlying motivation stems from a desire to experience healing on many levels, including the physical level. Altering your attitudes and daily routines may come naturally as you uncover valuable information or discover core-level problems, giving you a specific target for changing your life. Eliminating relationships, lifestyle choices, or job situations can be the focal points of your transformation, and you may also feel impatient if everyone else around you is not changing at your rate. Fortunately, Saturn's transit in trine aspect to your Sun adds a measure of stability as you step from one platform onto another. (Although Saturn's cycle will be complete in April, the positive influence can extend for years.) Pluto's cycle is the stronger of the two, and you may feel that you're finally ready to say good-bye to your old support system as you grow into a more powerful expression of your true self.

If you were born from January 6 to 13, you're experiencing the disruptive influence of Uranus transiting in semisextile aspect to your Sun. You may be tempted to step into a new situation before you've completed your obligations to another, and can feel that your timing is off in general. The underlying impatience associated with this cycle can also stem from a fear that if you don't change quickly enough you'll lose valuable time, or you may feel that outside changes are destabilizing the way you've always done things. Technological changes can prompt you to consider alternatives to your old ways of doing things, or you may feel that it's time to incorporate some modifications of your own. You're not adverse to change, but prefer to be the initiator, and since some of the changes you're experiencing will be the result of circumstances you cannot control, you can feel an uncomfortable level of uncertainty. Since you can always be in charge of your responses, you can formulate alternatives that will be most suitable to your particular needs.

If you were born from January 14 to 21, you're feeling the supportive transit of Saturn in trine aspect to your Sun this year. The choices you make now and the foundations you're creating will serve as your primary security base during the uncertainties of the future. It's your year to make the most of educational opportunities or to develop career situations that allow you to pursue your talents. Whether you're a teacher or a student, you may relish the fact that you're attracting valuable knowledge and experience. Love relationships can grow into trustworthy commitments if you feel you're ready to make a long-term promise. Knowing when to relinquish burdens you've carried for others is a positive feature of this cycle, and you may finally be able to bid your birds farewell as they leave the nest, or you may cut the support cords to someone you've been mentoring professionally.

If you were born from January 17 to 21, you're experiencing the unsettling influence of Pluto transiting in semisquare aspect to your Sun. Fortunately, Saturn's influence (noted above) can add a positive measure of stability during this period of transformational change. However, you may no longer be able to maintain situations that are counterproductive to your growth, and even if you try to hang onto something you no longer need, you may find that you cannot bear the pressure. Cooperating with this cycle makes life easier, because, in effect, you are being challenged to eliminate or leave behind the things, people, and attitudes you've outgrown. The problem lies in the fact that you may feel you're being led into unfamiliar territory in the process and may have difficulty maintaining your course. Since your life course is also being altered, your trusty sense of direction will help, but you may end up taking a few detours!

Tools to Make a Difference

This year you're recovering your power, and many of the tools that will be most effective can arrive in the guise of pleasurable or entertaining experiences. Allowing your heart to open has an amazing effect upon your sense of self and can heal old wounds while inviting new experiences. Honor the energy of Saturn by recalling the treasures you've swept aside as responsibilities have taken their toll. It's time to recall the dreams of your childhood and to rediscover simple joys that may be eagerly waiting to return. Your creative sensibilities are awakening, and you're gaining a new appreciation for the value of such an "intangible" asset. After all, by embracing your creativity you are allowing yourself the chance to do, think, say, or experience something that could awaken all sorts of possibilities—and *that* has a truly practical value! Embrace creativity. Dust off your hobbies. Go to an inspiring movie in the middle of the afternoon. Buy tickets to a concert and take someone you adore. Enroll in an art class, a local chorale, or a theater group. Help your kids with their major homework projects, or pull out your musical instrument, art supplies, favorite cookbooks, garden planners, etc.

To help heal your body, make this the year you consult a holistic health practitioner, and determine that you'll finally take a serious look at your habits. At least once each season, schedule a massage or a visit an acupuncturist, chiropractor, or reflexologist to help redirect and balance the flow of your energy. Use the aromatherapy oils of clary sage, jasmine, ylang ylang, pine, eucalyptus, or patchouli to help lift your spirits, or apply lotions or body oils scented with sandalwood to help soothe dry skin.

During your meditations, reclaim your joy and enthusiasm. Imagine a time when you were blissfully happy. Focus only on that time. See yourself enjoying the moment, and allow that joy to permeate every breath. As your body and soul absorb joy, imagine that you are standing before a reflective pool. Peer into the pool, seeing your own image. Then, as you open your mind, see yourself and your image changing as you think about the things you want to do that will make you happy. When you return to your waking consciousness, remind yourself that you can always choose to reflect joy.

Initiating the Millennium

As the master or mistress of your own destiny, you are entering the millennium with a powerful sense of hope. Even though you may feel somewhat frustrated with changes that seem to carry your life into directions you are not controlling, you will aid your progress by embracing the possibilities represented by these changes. To cope with the need to break away from outworn structures, make an effort to ground yourself, and then the changes will feel more like a breeze than a windstorm. Get back to nature, work in your garden, walk in the woods—touch the earth! This is your power base, and it will serve you well.

VŜ

Affirmation for the Year

I deserve to have my needs fulfilled. My life is filled with prosperity on every level!

Capricorn/January

In the Spotlight
Eager to make connections with others whose interests, ideas, and support may be beneficial, you may be spending more time on the road, in meetings, or performing writing projects. Keeping an open mind speeds progress.

Wellness and Keeping Fit
Increasing your activity level spurs your mental alertness. If you enjoy winter sports, getting into nature can be invigorating. Avoid pushing past your limits from January 16-21.

Love and Life Connections
Your feelings of love are transforming, and from January 1-10 you may be reluctant to explain why you prefer to withdraw. Talking over your concerns with a friend during the Capricorn New Moon on January 6 helps clarify your priorities. Words can be wounding from January 15-19, but after the lunar eclipse on January 20 you may feel that you can talk more openly without fear of negative reprisals.

Finance and Success
An unfinished project is vulnerable to budget cuts through January 12, and even though you may wonder how you can operate with diminishing funds, you're also resourceful. Your connections can provide assets that go beyond money, allowing you to produce satisfactory results. Finances improve after January 25, but conferences and presentations offer rewards throughout the month.

Cosmic Insider Tip
The Moon's eclipse on January 20 emphasizes creative use of your resources, and while some help may be dwindling, a visionary supporter emerges and renews your confidence.

Rewarding Days
5, 6, 7, 11, 15, 16, 23, 24, 29

Challenging Days
12, 13, 14, 19, 20, 25, 26

Affirmation for the Month
I carefully consider my words before I speak.

Capricorn/February

In the Spotlight
Attracting better circumstances and more enjoyable people lifts your spirits. You may take on a challenge that requires you to sharpen your competitive edge, but your determination can easily overcome most obstacles.

Wellness and Keeping Fit
Your attitudes are upbeat, helping you handle stress more effectively. Setting new fitness goals may be in order after February 12.

Love and Life Connections
While Venus transits in your sign through February 17, you're radiating your best attributes, and others may also extend their appreciation. Extraordinary expressions of affection during the solar eclipse on February 5 allow a special someone to know exactly how you feel. However, romance is notable on and after the Full Moon on February 19, when a romantic rendezvous can be the answer to a dream.

Finance and Success
You may be in an entirely new ball game after the Sun's eclipse on February 5, when unexpected changes prompt you to seek alternatives instead of following the same path or tradition. Your matter-of-fact approach garners positive attention from February 1-11, although someone may misunderstand your plans or intentions from February 12-16. Your efforts to clarify things will pay off, but letting it slide can be a costly error.

Cosmic Insider Tip
Beginning something new after the eclipse on February 5 can be beneficial, but be sure all contracts and agreements are signed before Mercury turns retrograde on February 21.

Rewarding Days
1, 2, 7, 8, 11, 12, 19, 20, 25, 29

Challenging Days
9, 10, 15, 16, 17, 21, 22

Affirmation for the Month
My thoughts and actions are motivated by a pure and caring heart.

Capricorn/March

In the Spotlight
To avoid feeling that you're being outdone by the competition or that your security is being undermined by conflicts, you'll need to maintain open lines of communication. Your support network is there—but you have to activate it!

Wellness and Keeping Fit
Stressful situations can exhaust your vitality, and you may be plagued by a tendency to worry about things you cannot control. Practice conscious relaxation techniques and supplement with a massage.

Love and Life Connections
Talking about problems at home helps smooth over conflicts. A fresh approach may be suggested during the New Moon on March 6, when bringing issues to the table is beneficial. Trust can become a bone of contention, and you may run into difficulties over differences in your values. The spiritual connection you feel invites a deeper love to develop during the Full Moon on March 19.

Finance and Success
Study investment options, but avoid sinking your valuable resources into anything untried for the time being. You may be motivated to spend for the wrong reasons and can also fall victim to unscrupulous individuals who seem to know your weaknesses. At work, be attentive to communication problems since the effects of Mercury's retrograde (ending on March 14) last until the end of the month!

Cosmic Insider Tip
Although you're feeling creatively inspired and may even feel that you've fallen in love, taking it slow and easy will ensure a better outcome. Commitments fare better later.

Rewarding Days
1, 5, 6, 9, 10, 18, 19, 23, 27, 28

Challenging Days
7, 8, 13, 14, 15, 20, 21

Affirmation for the Month
I am honest with myself and with others.

Capricorn/April

In the Spotlight
Increasing confidence in your talents stimulates you to put them to use. As a result, your reputation and career are undergoing progress, and you may feel that you have a much firmer foothold on success.

Wellness and Keeping Fit
Your dedication to fitness improves when you find something you really enjoy, and this is the time when the right situation emerges. Your vitality and endurance grow steadily stronger.

Love and Life Connections
At home, you're feeling more satisfied that things are working out and may decide to make improvements or move during the New Moon on April 4. You're feeling the impulse to let your heart guide your choices. An existing love ripens, and if you're ready for a new love, the potential is powerful. You could take unnecessary risks that could injure your self-esteem. The signals tell you when to pull back.

Finance and Success
Meetings from April 1-13 provide valuable information about which directions to pursue at work, and if you're planning to launch a pet project, you'll be more confident by forming a strong support network. Uncertainty dissipates after April 24, when your plans seem to have a more solid foundation. Bucking the system will be too costly, but employing worthwhile innovations puts you on the fast track to success.

Cosmic Insider Tip
Battle lines seem to be drawn between conservative and liberal factions, and by maintaining a reasonable pace you can set the standards for resolutions after the Full Moon on April 18.

Rewarding Days
1, 2, 6, 14, 15, 19, 23, 24, 25, 29, 30

Challenging Days
3, 4, 10, 11, 16, 17, 20

Affirmation for the Month
I use my talents wisely.

Capricorn/May

In the Spotlight
Continuing to benefit from employing your talents, you may feel that it's time to take your artistic expression to another level or to shift your resources so that they're producing better results. Working cooperatively with others makes a huge difference.

Wellness and Keeping Fit
Increasing your activity level helps build your endurance. Pleasurable experiences also have a beneficial effect on your sense of well-being, so remember to play!

Love and Life Connections
Love is definitely in bloom. Taking a healthy relationship to the next level of intimacy feels natural during the New Moon on May 3, when love can be an absolutely sweet justification for being alive! An old love can enter the picture (or someone who seems like a soulmate), or a friendship may transform into much more during the Full Moon on May 18. You're ready to let love work its magic.

Finance and Success
Investments of time, talent, and money pay off nicely and can stimulate new directions you had not previously considered. Whether you're starting a new project, beginning a job, or working with new people, you're on very solid footing, even though you may be in unfamiliar territory. Unexpected developments give you reason to carefully evaluate your choices from May 1-19.

Cosmic Insider Tip
With almost every planet stimulating your self-expression, you may feel an overwhelming surge of confidence. The tangible qualities of love are sweet. Enjoy every moment!

Rewarding Days
3, 4, 11, 12, 16, 17, 21, 22, 30, 31

Challenging Days
1, 2, 7, 8, 13, 14, 15, 28, 29

Affirmation for the Month
The light of love burns brightly in everything I do and say.

Capricorn/June

In the Spotlight
Work relations can be a bit frustrating, particularly if you have different ideas about the best ways to get things done. A battle of wills can ensue if you are demanding too much of others or if their requirements encroach on your sense of control.

Wellness and Keeping Fit
You need a healthy, competitive challenge, and continuing your endurance-building program will help keep your energy strong. Ignoring your body's needs will quickly drain your vitality.

Love and Life Connections
Partnerships, marriage, or social relationships can be a source of friction, and you may feel that others are trying to bend your will to their own. You could be projecting your own frustrations into your relationships, and you may find that you've been projecting more hostility than you intended. Find the source of tension and direct your energy there! Your love life will improve immediately.

Finance and Success
You're eager to have something to show for your efforts and will resent anyone who's not pulling his or her weight. While you're feeling more committed to a significant project, you also may have more invested. To make the most of it, review plans with coworkers during the New Moon on June 2 and set your targets. Cooperative ventures fare best after June 16. Sign contracts before June 22.

Cosmic Insider Tip
Mercury's three-week retrograde begins June 23, indicating a need to investigate a situation before proceeding. You'll do yourself a favor by waiting to sign long-term agreements.

Rewarding Days
7, 8, 12, 13, 17, 18, 22, 27, 28

Challenging Days
3, 4, 10, 11, 23, 24, 25, 26

Affirmation for the Month
I am patient and understanding.

Capricorn/July

In the Spotlight
Relationships take center stage, and with the eclipses adding intensity to your relationships, you may feel more certain of your affections and needs. A strong relationship endures and prospers; an unhealthy bond can wither.

Wellness and Keeping Fit
If you're feeling emotionally out of sorts, you may experience repercussions in your health. The reverse also applies: a strong connection to your inner self aids healing.

Love and Life Connections
The Sun's eclipse on July 1 brings your attention to your underlying feelings. You may feel you've grabbed the tail of a comet if you initiate a relationship now, but you may experience a powerfully compelling attraction. By the time the Capricorn lunar eclipse arrives on July 16, you're feeling more balanced. Intimacy issues arise around the Sun's eclipse on July 30, indicating that a committed relationship may be facing the challenge of letting go of the past.

Finance and Success
Partnership agreements may be tempting, but because Mercury is retrograding until July 17, you're better off negotiating, then finalizing after July 18. Selling or ending an agreement can be a profitable option, though. Inheritance and taxes require attention after July 23, when emotional judgments can cloud the best alternatives.

Cosmic Insider Tip
By addressing your concerns in partnerships now, you can accomplish life-enriching changes. Failing to deal with your needs can leave you feeling absolutely miserable.

Rewarding Days
5, 6, 10, 14, 15, 16, 19, 20, 24, 25

Challenging Days
1, 2, 7, 8, 22, 23, 28, 29, 30

Affirmation for the Month
I show appreciation to others and respect their needs and concerns.

Capricorn/August

In the Spotlight
Making the most of joint assets becomes a primary focus, and you can be highly effective if you're seeking an investor. Defining your aims not only helps you determine a target, but can attract the right resources from others.

Wellness and Keeping Fit
Probing into the underlying causes of a physical problem may lead you to a chronic weakness. It's time to eliminate destructive elements and make room for regeneration.

Love and Life Connections
The question of who's in charge of the finances can arise, and working out a compromise may be necessary in order to keep the peace. Money may not actually be the problem. The hidden issues emerge during the Full Moon on August 15. Your spiritual bond and faith in love can be the keys to getting through a tough time. Fresh options emerge with the New Moon on August 29.

Finance and Success
Special care with finances is necessary through August 10 if you wish to avoid getting caught in a frustrating financial maze; things (or people!) are not what they appear to be. Convene with others to share ideas after August 7, although the best time to initiate a new academic or promotional endeavor is after August 23. Travel, publish, or make presentations on August 29 or 30.

Cosmic Insider Tip
You may be fooled by what glitters and fail to notice the weak points of a proposal, purchase, or personal encounter. Enjoy the thrill, but keep your credit cards in your wallet.

Rewarding Days
1, 2, 6, 10, 11, 12, 20, 21, 29, 30

Challenging Days
3, 4, 5, 18, 19, 25, 26, 31

Affirmation for the Month
I am willing to let go of unnecessary attachments.

Capricorn/September

In the Spotlight
Emphasis on your career goals prompts you to take a careful look at your workload and the best ways to satisfy requirements that will advance your position. Ethical dilemmas can leave you feeling uncharacteristically insecure.

Wellness and Keeping Fit
Using alternative methods or complimentary therapies can speed healing, and you're certainly eager to feel in tip-top shape. Make a conscious effort to relax in order to remain balanced.

Love and Life Connections
Family and career obligations can demand most of your energy, leaving little time for play or romance. Taking some time for yourself can make a huge difference in your state of mind, and whether you opt for an afternoon at the gym or spa, a weekend retreat, or a day away from the regular grind, a break will feel great near the Full Moon on September 13. Romance fares best after September 25, when there are fewer restraints.

Finance and Success
Making a good impression is easiest if you know what someone expects, and your superiors will be more forthcoming from September 10-22. Business meetings or publishing give your career a boost after September 17. Undermining situations at work can put you face to face with a moral or ethical dilemma, and it is crucial to articulate where you stand or to step aside if the battle is not yours to fight.

Cosmic Insider Tip
If someone is not doing his or her job, you may end up as the scapegoat unless you're careful. Concentrate on your obligations.

Rewarding Days
3, 7, 8, 12, 18, 25, 26, 30

Challenging Days
1, 4, 14, 15, 21, 22, 27, 28

Affirmation for the Month
My sense of purpose is guided by my higher self.

Capricorn/October

In the Spotlight

You're experiencing substantial rewards for your hard work and may gain recognition in addition to seeing an increase in your finances. Fresh opportunities arise, allowing you to expand your horizons personally and professionally.

Wellness and Keeping Fit

Your physical energy gets a boost, and you may feel inspired to engage a good friend to join you in your fitness activities or consider joining a class or team sport.

Love and Life Connections

You're ready for a true meeting of the minds. Your common ground may be a special interest, or you might sense that your spiritual paths are complimentary. An existing relationship can be reborn or a new relationship successfully nurtured from October 1-20. Special time together during the New Moon on October 27 leads to more profound intimacy.

Finance and Success

Interactions with your colleagues help you forge a solid coalition that can assure the success of a significant project from October 1-17. Mercury turns retrograde on October 18, when re-evaluating your plans and troubleshooting can be valuable if you wish to continue making progress. However, for the remainder of the month, you're better off waiting to initiate new business deals.

Cosmic Insider Tip

Your inspiration keeps you moving, and even though you may withdraw from the action after October 18, you can still be positively involved. The glare of the spotlight can be uncomfortable.

Rewarding Day

4, 5, 6, 10, 14, 15, 22, 23, 28, 31

Challenging Days

11, 12, 13, 18, 19, 24, 25, 26

Affirmation for the Month

I use my influence wisely.

Capricorn/November

In the Spotlight
Your driving ambition grows, and although you may have a clear idea about your aims, you can lose sight of the impact of your actions if you're not careful. Watch for sensitive reactions from others and make appropriate alterations.

Wellness and Keeping Fit
Work can have you tied in knots if you're not careful! A massage after the New Moon on November 25 can give you a new lease on life!

Love and Life Connections
Sharing fantasies with your sweetheart can result in memorable romantic encounters. By the Full Moon on November 11, your passion about expressing your affections can make a strong impression, and you may even decide that it's time to make a commitment or renew your vows. Venus moves into Capricorn on November 12, adding to your capacities for love and increasing your magnetism. However, work can interfere with love after November 25.

Finance and Success
Mercury's retrograde is complete on November 7, but the potential for misunderstandings continues until November 15. Maintaining careful attention to your finances is crucial to avoid losing money or assets, and if you're traveling, take special care to avoid loss. Career progress is most outstanding after November 18. Reconsider your options during the New Moon on November 25.

Cosmic Insider Tip
Convening with colleagues and friends is fine, but mixing business and pleasure can be very costly. After all, a friendship might be worth saying "no" when it's appropriate!

Rewarding Days
1, 2, 6, 10, 11, 19, 20, 23, 28, 29

Challenging Days
8, 9, 14, 15, 21, 22

Affirmation for the Month
My love for my true friends enriches my life immeasurably.

Capricorn/December

In the Spotlight
You're tying up loose ends, not just because it's the end of the year, but because you have new dreams ready to launch. Put the finishing touches on a project, reconnect with old friends, and set goals that give you a chance to grow.

Wellness and Keeping Fit
If you're feeling on edge it could be that you need to be more active. Exercise helps alleviate tension, and a challenging fitness class may be just what you need to release the stresses of everyday life.

Love and Life Connections
Clarifying your intentions from December 1-8 can seem to be the next natural step in a love relationship. You may also feel good about sharing social events, although you may be busy with work until December 24. The Capricorn solar eclipse on December 25 marks a significant period of self-realization—a time when taking a personal inventory of your life is not only appropriate, but empowering.

Finance and Success
Getting everything done that's expected of you can keep you moving at a steady pace from December 1-16, and you're quite capable of accomplishing everything on your agenda. Investments fare best from December 1-8 and then after December 24, when you may want to adjust your portfolio. Schedule meetings from December 3-7 and 26-31. Your leadership can inspire significant changes.

Cosmic Insider Tip
The impact of the Capricorn solar eclipse centers around your ability to initiate new growth while letting go of the past. Just remember that old saying about the baby and bath water...

Rewarding Days
3, 4, 8, 9, 16, 17, 21, 25, 26, 30, 31

Challenging Days
5, 6, 7, 12, 13, 18, 19

Affirmation for the Month
My ego is aligned with my highest needs.

Capricorn Action Table

These dates reflect the best—but not the only—times for success and ease in these activities, according to your Sun sign.

	JAN	FEB	MAR	APR	MAY	JUN	JUL	AUG	SEPT	OCT	NOV	DEC
Move				13-29								
Start a class			6, 7					29, 30				
Join a club										27, 28		
Ask for a raise	6, 7											25-27
Look for work					14-29				8-27			
Get pro advice	19, 20	15, 16	13, 14	10, 11	7, 8	3, 4	1-2, 28-29	25, 26	21, 22	18, 19	14, 15	12, 13
Get a loan	21, 22	17, 18	16, 17	12, 13	9, 10	5, 6	3-4, 30-31	27, 28	23, 24	20, 21	16, 17	14, 15
See a doctor					14-29							3-22
Start a diet	17, 18	13, 14	11, 12	8, 9	5, 6	1-2, 29-30	26, 27	22-24	19, 20	16, 17	12, 13	10, 11
End relationship	20											
Buy clothes				30	1-13							
Get a makeover	6, 7											25-27
New romance					4							
Vacation	23, 24	19, 20	18, 19	14, 15	11, 12	7-9	5, 6	1-2, 29-30	25, 26	22, 23	18, 19	16, 17

Aquarius
The Water Bearer
January 20 to February 18

≈

Element:	Air
Quality:	Fixed
Polarity:	Yang/Masculine
Planetary Ruler:	Uranus
Meditation:	"I create new paths by focusing my mind."
Gemstone:	Amethyst
Power Stones:	Aquamarine, black pearl, chrysocolla
Key Phrase:	"I know"
Glyph:	Currents of energy ≈
Anatomy:	Ankles, circulatory system
Color:	Iridescent blues, violet
Animal:	Exotic birds
Myths/Legends:	John the Baptist, Ninhursag, Deucalion
House:	Eleventh
Opposite Sign:	Leo
Flower:	Orchid
Key Word:	Unconventional

Positive Expression:	Misuse of Energy:
Altruistic	Thoughtless
Friendly	Aloof
Humanitarian	Anarchistic
Progressive	Extremist
Autonomous	Subversive
Ingenious	Detached
Unconditional	Undirected

Aquarius

Your Ego's Strengths and Shortcomings

You like being different! Willing to step outside the boundaries of the mainstream, you appreciate the extraordinary and seek out unusual people and situations. Getting stuck in the past is not your style, and as "The Reformer" of the zodiac, you may be instrumental in the creation of innovation on many fronts. You can be an individualist in the purest sense of the term, capable of marching to the beat of your own drum, guided by the light of intuitive inspiration.

Your best qualities emerge when you express true friendship, opening to the boundless flow of unconditional love. From this space, your creativity emerges in full force, allowing you to tap into the untamed energy of your planetary ruler, Uranus. The expression of your unique qualities can be seen in your ideas, which may at first seem revolutionary, but you can also be a trendsetter! You can be frustrated by the restrictions imposed by the "traditions" others use as an excuse for lack of progress, and in some instances your ability to pierce the veil of future possibilities runs in clear counterpoint to the establishment. This tendency to rebel can create an estrangement from the world, yet you sometimes need that remoteness in order to tap into the realms of possibility that are home to your genius. You simply view life from a different perspective, taking into account a more universal and futuristic frame of reference.

When others accuse you of being aloof, they may be responding to the distance they feel when you're light years away in your mind as you attempt to forge a connection to higher consciousness. Once you've integrated your energy and perceptions with the flow of unconditional love, your creativity emerges in full force, illuminating your true path as you pour the rays of divine light and wisdom into a world facing a new dawn.

Shining Your Love Light

Before you allow yourself to develop a love that transcends the ordinary, you must first feel true friendship. You need a loyal and equal partner, someone who values autonomy and supports your individuality. However, you can be more possessive than you realize! Even when you feel that you've finally found true love, your need for logic can lead you to talk yourself out if it. Yet once you surrender to the urging of your intuitive voice whispering that you've discovered the right person, love itself will open the doors to your heart, and your loyalty can invite you to become a truly committed partner.

As an air sign, you prefer relationships centered around shared ideas, and will function most easily with those who are openly communicative. Gemini, Libra, and Aquarius, the air signs, can be most at ease with you, and vice versa. Aries stimulates your passionate need to express yourself and keeps you on your toes. Taurus holds on to everything, including you, and that may feel too restrictive. You'll find Gemini's intelligence engaging and charming, allowing you to open your mind and heart. Cancer's need for constant contact can dampen your need for independence. The magnetic warmth and drama expressed by Leo, your zodiac opposite, can be extremely attractive, but if you become too detached you may feel wounded by his or her claws! Virgo inspires your soul searching, although you may disagree when it comes to intimacy.

Libra touches your spirit, and you'll enjoy exploring culturally rich avenues and sharing beautiful experiences. Scorpio's intensity can make you feel that you're drowning in a sea of wordless complexities. Sagittarius' adventurous joie de vivre entices you to enjoy life more fully. While Capricorn can become a good friend, you may disappear in a puff of smoke in the face of control issues! If you forge a true connection with another Aquarius, you can create a remarkable life, although you can short circuit before you accomplish intimacy. Your affinity with Pisces centers on universal ideals, but you can become lost in the vapors if you're in different planes of reality.

Making Your Place in the World

In order to feel happy, you need a life path that allows you to express your creativity and where you can be instrumental in bringing about transformational change. You may be most suited to fields that are mentally stimulating, encouraging you to express your originality. You can excel in fields like writing, advertising, public relations, broadcasting, sales, or the communications industry. Scientific fields like meteorology, computers, electronics, aviation, the space industry, or theoretical mathematics can be excellent.

You may also be a natural in fields like psychology and astrology that require you to blend rational and intuitive insights.

Owning your own business can provide a chance to market your incomparable creations, but you might also prefer a career in fine arts, ranging from original music to visionary art. Political service can be a positive challenge, or working in nonprofit endeavors focused on humanitarian outreach can be perfect. Your trademark uniqueness will be outstanding in any career you pursue.

Power Plays

Understanding that what benefits all benefits one, you hold the power of universal humanitarian principles in highest regard. You may go out of your way to avoid power struggles, particularly since abuses of power seem to be everywhere. Yet if there is a cause tugging at your soul, you can harness an exceptional level of revolutionary energy and create a ripe climate for change. You can be a champion for those crushed by greed or abuse or thwarted by hate-mongers whose actions diminish the flame of human integrity. While you may not want power for the sake of personal recognition, you may seek it in order to make a difference in human evolution. However, you must be aware of your inner shadow that craves the spotlight and can become overwhelming if your motives are selfish. Your visionary creations can become a lightning rod for evolutionary transformation in your family, company, or even your nation.

Famous Aquarians

Evangeline Adams, Buzz Aldrin, John Belushi, Garth Brooks, Carol Channing, Sam Cooke, Christian Dior, Farrah Fawcett, Peter Gabriel, Benny Hill, Jimmy Hoffa, Eartha Kitt, Jennifer Jason-Leigh, Franklin D. Roosevelt, Cybill Shepherd.

The Year Ahead
for Aquarius

Forging a steadfast security base while reaching into ground-breaking territory is quite a challenge, and if anybody is up to it, it's you! You may feel that you're being transplanted, uprooting old situations, leaving behind the familiar and moving into the exciting realm of possibility springing from your creativity. The goals you set now may seem lofty, but you have at least one toe on the ground, and your enthusiasm about fantastic possibilities gives you the fuel to launch plans that will carry you well into the century ahead.

Uranus, your planetary ruler, continues its transit in your sign, aiding your ability to fully embrace your individuality and exercise your sense of autonomy. Since this is a slow-moving cycle, the restlessness generated by the stimulus can leave you feeling that progress requires too much time, but when you look back on this period, it may seem that time itself has literally flown. The most intensive years of the Uranus transit are marked by the time when the planet is exactly conjunct your Sun, and if this is your year, it will be noted in the birthdate categories following. Neptune is also transiting in your sign for another eleven years, opening your sensitivity and imagination to realms that were previously beyond your grasp. You may be having an experience of expanded consciousness that can be difficult to describe or explain.

Pluto's slow-moving cycle continues to influence your goals, hopes, and wishes. As you realize many of your previous goals, you may recognize the need to completely revamp your plans. Eliminating targets that are no longer relevant frees your creativity for other more significant projects and actions.

Jupiter's expansive energy highlights your need to broaden your security base and increase your creative self-expression this year. From January through July, Jupiter's emphasis can stimulate your desire to give yourself more room to move, and you may do just that—move! At the very least, you'll feel an impetus to have more space at home and may decide that it's time to get rid of clutter. From July through December the influence of Jupiter moves into the realm of your heartfelt desires, vitalizing your creative drive and increasing your opportunities to experience and express feelings of love. Your family may get bigger this year, bringing more reasons to manifest true joy.

Saturn's influence adds intensity to your evaluation of your security needs, and you may feel that you are somewhat restrained in realizing all your desires because of your responsibilities. Satisfying your responsibilities is absolutely necessary, since failure to meet your obligations will result in long-term setbacks.

The eclipse cycles this year are quite significant, in that there are four solar eclipses and two lunar eclipses during the year 2000. While the effect of each eclipse is described in the monthly forecast section for your sign, the significance of the eclipses and what you may be feeling can be described by the transit of the Moon's nodes. The nodal transit draws your attention to health issues, work conditions, and your desire to bring improvements into your life. As a result, during each eclipse period you may feel that your motivations in response to the eclipse are driven by your need to feel that you're making things better. That may mean that you need to evaluate your habits, change your routine, or make new commitments to yourself!

If you were born from January 20 to 22, you're feeling a stabilizing influence while Saturn transits in trine aspect to your Sun. This cycle's influence will be strongest from July through the end of October, and you can take full advantage of it by targeting this time period to begin significant projects or make long-term agreements. Making the preparations necessary may require several months, and knowing the most significant time to target major change can help assure your success. Many of the things you may have dreamed of doing last year or that began to take shape then may finally come into form during the summer, allowing you to take advantage of your more influential status. Love relationships may be more fulfilling and your connections to children more meaningful. This is the time to let your talents shine, to teach others who wish to learn from you, or to make lifelong commitments. You're ready to embrace the responsibilities that will help you realize your fullest potential.

If you were born from January 23 to 28, you're experiencing the spiritual force of Neptune transiting in conjunction to your Sun. This once-in-a-lifetime cycle can help you feel more in tune with the true nature of energy, spirituality, imagination, and the transcendent power of these expressions. In many ways, every part of your being will seem more sensitive. Your attunement to your physical body is likely to change, and by balancing your spiritual, emotional, and physical energies you can feel light, free, and more alive. Taking care of your health may not be the highest priority, although you may seek a more "pure" existence, since your body may be more sensitive to foods or environmental influences during this time. Your response to subtle or vibrational influences such as music, art, or healing touch is heightened, and your capacity for compassion expands. If you feel prompted to devote more time to your spirituality, then integrating your spirituality into your daily life can be rather easy. However, you may also feel that it's time to withdraw from the intensity of the outside world and devote more time to your creative expression or spiritual path. While complete isolation may not be the best idea, you are hungry for the experience of unity between your inner self and a higher power. Psychologically, you're ready to forgive and release old traumas, and may have a greater capacity to express your feelings of love and devotion to those who share your life. It's your turn to transcend the ordinary in exchange for an experience of profound insight and a feeling of true inner peace.

If you were born from January 29 to February 3, you're feeling the impact of Pluto transiting in sextile aspect to your Sun. This cycle has the magnificent effect of allowing you to eliminate unnecessary elements from your life as you experience a period of rebirth and healing. Those things that disappear during this time may seem to fall away naturally, but if there is a healthy change you feel compelled to make, it will also be easier to accomplish. Additionally, from January through March you'll be feeling the disciplined restraint of Saturn traveling in square aspect to your Sun, frustrating your desire to break free while you deal with responsibilities or obligations. Getting those things out of the way may not be easy, but after March you'll be free to fully exercise and express the potential for growth promised by Pluto's transit. Especially noteworthy are the months of September and October when Jupiter also travels in a trine aspect to your Sun, amplifying your need and increasing your opportunities to exercise your artistry and creativity. This is your time to feel whole, alive, and complete, and by making choices that illustrate your sense of personal power and provide a feeling of accomplishment, you may finally feel the true essence of your identity as an individual.

If you were born from February 3 to 11, you're in for a powerful ride while Uranus transits in conjunction to your Sun. Since this cycle occurs only once every eighty-seven years or so, it's unlikely that you'll experience it again. The impulse of Uranus to your Sun can feel like an electrical charge, and if you're ready to embrace your sense of autonomy and to exercise your individuality, that charge can be more like a stimulus to get up and get on with it! The inhibitions in your life, whether imposed as internal fears or external restraints, seem to fall away under this cycle, and your natural revolutionary energy can emerge with full force. You're ready to break free. From January through April you'll also feel the restraints of Saturn in square aspect to your Sun, making that breakaway more challenging. Think of this time period as your homework phase, getting your obligations out of the way so you can feel the true freedom promised by Uranus' influence. You might also appreciate the safety that accompanies this "braking" stage, particularly if the slope seems a bit steep. Other people may respond to you with surprise that you're changing so much, but the changes you're exercising may be things you've thought about for a long time. It's just that now is the time to make them. Additionally, outside influences can stimulate change—things you cannot control, but to which you can respond creatively. All in all, this will definitely be a year to remember!

If you were born from February 4 to 19, you're feeling the restrictive energy of Saturn transiting in square aspect to your Sun. While you may feel that you're nearing the tip of an iceberg, you may also be facing a series of challenges that seem to slow your progress. This is your year to satisfy obligations, review your priorities, and deal with the results of your previous decisions and promises. The manner in which you handle your obligations now will have a definite effect on the opportunities that will present themselves in the future. Everything about this cycle is not "bad," in fact one of the good things is that you're finally feeling ready to let go of burdens that are not yours to carry. Allowing others to stand on their own two feet can be one of the challenges of this time, since you may really want to jump in there and take over—but if it's not your test, then you're not supposed to take it! Dealing with health concerns is important, too, and getting to the real core of physical problems is necessary. This is no time to mess around, and the role you play in staying healthy cannot be understated. Destructive habits and attitudes need to be eliminated so you can become whole, healthy, and feel more alive!

Tools to Make a Difference

Since your awareness and consciousness may seem to be expanding by leaps and bounds, you may feel that it's time to reach beyond conventional into more experimental methods of creating change and healing in your life. You've always been an innovator, and now, more than ever, you may be inclined to compliment your life with alternative approaches to healing, working, and living. By developing trust in your intuitive abilities, you can allow your visionary abilities to shine.

In addition to working toward expanding your consciousness through such methods as meditation, you may also be attracted to brain-mind techniques that allow you to transcend ordinary consciousness. To heal your body, working with magnetic therapy, polarity therapy, crystal energy therapies, or acupuncture might produce the results you desire. Subtle work with your chakras, ranging from chakra balancing to Reiki, could provide an alteration in your flow and balance of energy. As an air sign, you might also respond very powerfully to aromatherapy. Adding essential oils of lavender, eucalyptus, frankincense, or clary sage to your massage oil could be just what you need to help you let go of tension. You might also enjoy inhalations of rosemary to help improve your memory, or melissa and marjoram to help balance your blood pressure. In the evening, unwinding with a cup of chamomile, valerian, and kava kava tea can help alleviate anxiety and aid your relaxation.

During your meditations, allow your mind to relax as your visionary abilities open. Focusing on your breathing can be a helpful way to let go and allow your energy to flow freely. Once you feel that you're in a deeper state of relaxation, invite your creative imagination to come forth. Simply ask for a vision, and follow it until you feel the story has come to a logical stopping place. You're ready to move into dimensions of awareness that may be beyond description, but that you can translate into a creative masterpiece. It's up to you to find the vision, embrace it, nurture it, and allow it to change your life.

Initiating the Millennium

You may have a sense that this is *your* century, and you are probably right! At the very least, you can be instrumental in setting trends or standards that can lead humanity into a more functional society. Yet you know that the path will not be an easy one to follow, and the struggle you face echoes the struggle humanity must endure: forging fresh pathways through responsible thought and action. Your desire may be to move as quickly as possible, allowing innovation, new technology, and fresh ideas to revitalize society. Your challenge is to set forth with your vision, knowing that humanity is at an important crossroads and that a clear awareness of cause and effect must accompany your choices.

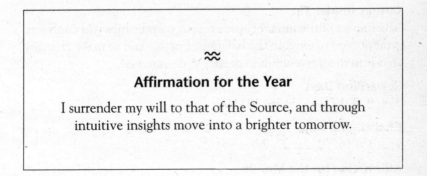

≋

Affirmation for the Year

I surrender my will to that of the Source, and through intuitive insights move into a brighter tomorrow.

Aquarius/January

In the Spotlight
To make the most of your resources, you may have to mobilize the forces of your professional connections. Fortunately, your ideas capture the imagination of others, and they may be happy to offer whatever is necessary to create the magic you inspire!

Wellness and Keeping Fit
Until January 20, you may feel that you need more private time in order to maintain your focus. Use this time for rest and rejuvenation so that you will be prepared for the challenges ahead.

Love and Life Connections
Time with friends warms your heart. However, a power struggle can emerge from January 14 through the lunar eclipse on January 20, when different value systems can alienate you from someone you previously trusted. Talking out problems leads to a new understanding after January 19. Invite the spiritual essence of your partnership to emerge by sharing your most cherished vision.

Finance and Success
You may also run into financial woes if you fail to allow sufficient funds or energy to cover repairs or necessary improvements. However, your reputation for ingenuity and your network of resourceful and talented people work to your advantage. Politically sensitive issues can make things difficult at work after January 7, but your ideas inspire healing change from January 20-31.

Cosmic Insider Tip
The impact of the lunar eclipse on your partnerships and contracts prompts you to explore the balance of power and to make changes that lead to forgiveness and deeper understanding.

Rewarding Days
3, 4, 8, 9, 17, 18, 25, 26, 30, 31

Challenging Days
1, 2, 15, 16, 20, 21, 27, 28

Affirmation for the Month
I invite healing change into every facet of my life.

Aquarius/February

In the Spotlight
The Aquarius solar eclipse leaves a definite impression: it's time to seriously evaluate your needs and your yet-unfulfilled dreams. You're primed to make headway, but an unexpected crisis can force you to see something you may have missed.

Wellness and Keeping Fit
Making your health priority number one can prevent setbacks due to hidden health problems that could emerge later.

Love and Life Connections
If you're questioning your affections, it could be that you're determining whether or not a relationship fits your current needs. Before you throw away something valuable, explore your own inner evolutionary change. The Aquarius eclipse on February 5 may have the feeling of a lightning bolt, awakening needs you've ignored. A healthy relationship will survive changes, but it's time to bid farewell to a demoralizing bond.

Finance and Success
Extra care with your expenditures can help you salvage a potentially difficult monetary situation. Negotiations can open the way for new agreements, but you may not reach a final decision this month, or may feel that further research is necessary before a commitment is worthwhile. Your creativity is peaking, and employing your special talents can lead to unanticipated career advancements.

Cosmic Insider Tip
Mercury enters its retrograde on February 21, two days after the Full Moon. Emotions are running high and can interfere with decisions requiring objectivity. Postpone contract decisions.

Rewarding Days
4, 5, 9, 10, 13, 14, 22, 23, 26, 27

Challenging Days
11, 12, 17, 18, 19, 24, 25

Affirmation for the Month
I welcome the release of the things I no longer need.

Aquarius/March

In the Spotlight
An overly idealistic approach to your commitments can get you into trouble. Making a determination of realistic goals and promising only what you can confidently deliver keeps your reputation intact.

Wellness and Keeping Fit
A change of scenery may be what you need to enliven your spirits, and getting outdoors more often can have an amazing effect on your psyche. Staying in a stale environment can lead to waning energy.

Love and Life Connections
Your enticement from March 1-6 can be the result of your need for a diversion, but you may also be more open to the experience of a purely exciting encounter! Although it's not a good idea to change your life just yet, experimenting to determine what's really happening can be rather enjoyable. The course of love is rarely smooth and straight! However, an inappropriate choice can damage your reputation.

Finance and Success
Making a clear judgment can be difficult since you may be receiving mixed signals from your superiors, or there can be factors in operation that alter the course in ways you cannot anticipate. Taking carefully measured steps is absolutely necessary; otherwise, you could fall victim to misguided decisions or manipulative circumstances. You're on more solid ground after March 21.

Cosmic Insider Tip
Not only is Mercury in retrograde until March 14, but Jupiter and Neptune are in an unfriendly aspect, indicating that there are potential land mines. Dealings with the media require extra care.

Rewarding Days
3, 4, 7, 8, 11, 12, 20, 21, 25, 30, 31

Challenging Days
2, 9, 10, 16, 17, 19, 22, 23, 24

Affirmation for the Month
My intuitive insights provide valuable clues to unanswered questions.

Aquarius/April

In the Spotlight
Clarity emerges through improved communication. Conferences, interviews, and correspondence help spur progress but may also be the keys to stabilizing uncertainty resulting from recent modifications.

Wellness and Keeping Fit
Although you may feel a lack of motivation, staying active may be the only way to keep up with your own agenda. Address stress by scheduling time out for healthy options like a massage.

Love and Life Connections
Obligations on the home front or with family can absorb your time. If you're moving or making other changes in your personal environment, costs can get out of hand or you may change your mind about your preferences in the middle of the project. Keeping things simple is helpful, and taking a break around the New Moon on April 4 helps clarify your options. Romance fares best through the Full Moon on April 18.

Finance and Success
You attract a more receptive audience for your ideas and talents after April 5, and working together with colleagues can provide the support you need to influence innovative changes. Conservative factions may be resistant to your ideas from April 16-28, and if your plans threaten to disrupt the status quo, you'll meet with opposition. Read the signals from influential superiors before you take action.

Cosmic Insider Tip
You need a safety net, and it may come from the foundation you've created through your past successes. Knowing how far to stretch your limits can be the tricky part!

Rewarding Days
3, 4, 8, 9, 16, 17, 21, 26, 26

Challenging Days
5, 6, 12, 13, 18, 19, 20

Affirmation for the Month
The changes I create now help to stabilize my security base.

Aquarius/May

In the Spotlight
Although you may be stuck close to home, the influence of your ideas can extend further than you realize. Concentrating your energy on a creative project can lead to amazing expressions. You may feel perfectly synchronized with your muse.

Wellness and Keeping Fit
Staying active will be easier if you're doing something that seems more like fun than work.

Love and Life Connections
While your passions may lead you to express your heartfelt desires to one you adore, you may feel that taking a slow-paced course is best. Moving too quickly can undermine your progress, and the most significant changes initiated during the New Moon on May 3 may be those that illustrate just how stable you are. A family crisis can emerge during the Full Moon on May 18. However, romance gains momentum after May 21.

Finance and Success
If your ideas are interpreted as "too revolutionary," you may open the way for your more conservative competitors to take the lead in important negotiations for advancement. Illustrating the value of your ideas by showing a working model or offering testimonials from those who've succeeded can sway the open-minded, but those who fear change may sit, arms folded, just waiting for you to finish.

Cosmic Insider Tip
A definite battle line has been set between those who invite change and those afraid to move forward. You're attracting progressive thinkers and may become part of a brewing revolution.

Rewarding Days
1, 2, 5, 6, 14, 19, 23, 24, 25, 28, 29

Challenging Days
3, 4, 9, 10, 16, 17, 30, 31

Affirmation for the Month
I can create necessary change within the established order.

Aquarius/June

In the Spotlight
Your leading-edge ideas chip away at the resistance, although you may discover that you've overstepped your boundaries if you move too fast. Planting seeds in fertile soil works, but sowing them in a wasteland will bring poor results.

Wellness and Keeping Fit
Recreational activities that elicit your enthusiasm are an excellent fitness resource, but an overly structured class or fitness challenge that leaves you feeling tense is not a good idea.

Love and Life Connections
With Venus and Mars stimulating your need to express feelings of love and affection from June 1-16, you may feel that you are definitely primed for romance! Initiating a relationship during the New Moon on June 2 can lead to fast-paced changes. By the Full Moon on June 16, you may be talking about the future, although certain things about commitment may seem premature.

Finance and Success
Showcase your talents, giving others a chance to see what you have to offer from June 1-18, emphasizing your unique qualities. You may discover that someone from your past is quietly promoting your efforts, while you're also attracting significant new options. Mercury enters its three-week retrograde on June 23, when reviewing procedures at work will help streamline your productivity.

Cosmic Insider Tip
Although you may feel inclined to explore fresh territory, basing your actions and projects on home turf can give you a stronger foundation. Expansion might be easier later.

Rewarding Days
1, 2, 10, 11, 14, 15, 16, 19, 20, 21, 29, 30

Challenging Days
5, 6, 12, 13, 17, 27, 28

Affirmation for the Month
Expressing the pure love flowing from my heart makes me feel alive!

Aquarius/July

In the Spotlight
The buzz about the three eclipses—one lunar and two solar—may have you wondering what's up. You may feel creatively inspired to use the changes happening now to bring widespread improvements to your health and work.

Wellness and Keeping Fit
Addressing physical ailments during the Sun's eclipse on July 1 can lead you directly to the core of a problem. The spiritual link to a health concern can be very illuminating.

Love and Life Connections
While the time you're spending with your lover may be limited due to work commitments or family matters, you may find that love is the source of your vitality. Your feelings for your partner or about your roles in marriage are changing, with most changes centered around the need for mutual autonomy. A more playful approach to expressing intimacy allows you to release old inhibitions, and by the solar eclipse on July 30, you may feel you're ready to turn over a new leaf.

Finance and Success
Addressing work issues may be like opening Pandora's box, and plans for improvement can result in some people being forced to make changes they resent. Stepping away from conflicts that do not concern you during the lunar eclipse on July 16 can keep you from taking an arrow meant for someone else.

Cosmic Insider Tip
In addition to eclipses, Mercury continues its retrograde until July 17. Getting anything straight may fall in the category of miraculous. Patience and love get you through it all.

Rewarding Days
7, 8, 12, 13, 17, 18, 22, 23, 26, 27

Challenging Days
1, 3, 4, 9, 10, 16, 24, 25, 30, 31

Affirmation for the Month
I am sensitive to the needs and feelings of others.

Aquarius/August

In the Spotlight
Activity centers around partnerships and social situations. Cooperative ventures can be exceptionally rewarding as long as everybody carries his or her own weight.

Wellness and Keeping Fit
Competitive situations offer a personal challenge. Whether you're involved in a team sport or have decided to work with a personal trainer, a target goal enhances your drive and vitality.

Love and Life Connections
While your desire may be to express love, your actions can be taken the wrong way and lead to open conflict! Knowing the limitations of others helps, but defining your own limits will get you through the extra stress during the Aquarius Full Moon on August 15. By the New Moon on August 29, you may experience a conflict between your need to be with your friends and the demands of your lover.

Finance and Success
Legal wrangling can take on a surrealistic quality from August 1-8, particularly if you feel that someone is presenting misleading information. To avoid getting caught in an undermining scheme, address the truth of the matter. Give extra attention to your investment strategies, since you may discover that an old reliable resource is no longer viable. New options need careful consideration from August 13-23.

Cosmic Insider Tip
You may wonder why some people are so easily manipulated, only to realize that you, too, have fallen victim to propaganda. Probing beneath the surface can lead to fascinating discoveries.

Rewarding Days
3, 4, 8, 9, 13, 14, 22, 23, 31

Challenging Days
6, 7, 16, 20, 21, 26, 27, 28

Affirmation for the Month
I am releasing my attachment to the things I no longer need.

Aquarius/September

In the Spotlight
While a general "truth-stretching" experience seems to be happening around you, you're more interested in pushing the limits of your creativity, concentrating instead on manifesting the powerful vision inspiring you.

Wellness and Keeping Fit
It's tempting to push past your limits after September 18. Eliminating unhealthy habits and attitudes can lead to increased vitality after the Full Moon on September 13.

Love and Life Connections
Bringing issues of trust into the open may be the only way to get beyond an impasse. Your desire to merge on spiritual, emotional, and physical levels will not be satisfied unless the barriers drop away. Examining your own fears will require courage. The New Moon on September 27 brings a rush of hope arising through a new relationship or fresh vitality returning to an existing connection.

Finance and Success
To get beyond contractual disputes, the decision of ownership or rights comes into play. The Full Moon on September 13 marks a turning point, when nonproductive situations must be addressed in an honest manner so that progress can begin. Whether it's a change in your schedule or employing different methods, adapting can try your patience. Improvement is on the horizon after September 27.

Cosmic Insider Tip
You will not appreciate problems resulting from the misleading actions or attitudes of others and may decide to withdraw your support if you feel a trust has been violated.

Rewarding Days
2, 3, 7, 8, 16, 17, 25, 26, 29, 30

Challenging Days
1, 14, 15, 20, 21, 23, 27, 28

Affirmation for the Month
I am honest with myself about my true needs and feelings.

Aquarius/October

In the Spotlight
While your career may gain favorable reviews, you can also ruffle a few feathers in the process if your ideas or actions run contrary to those of your superiors or the established order. Of course, being different looks good on you!

Wellness and Keeping Fit
Delving into the links between mind, spirit, and body, you may uncover old emotional trauma at the core of a physical ailment. You're ready to eliminate unhealthy elements, even if it does hurt a little.

Love and Life Connections
Intimacy can prove to be a challenge, particularly if your manner of expressing your affections is misunderstood. If you feel like withdrawing, it could be because your partner has hit a nerve. A healthy relationship responds to honest communication during the Full Moon on October 13, when your shared spiritual ideals go a long way toward healing a breech.

Finance and Success
Career issues are complex. You may gain positive recognition for your creativity and ingenuity, although the conditions at work can be filled with disagreements over budget. Tax matters and joint resources can be a source of concern from October 1-8, with improvement after October 20. Be wary of pursuing untried directions during the New Moon on October 27, since they may lead to traps.

Cosmic Insider Tip
Tense ethical issues can arise, and when Mercury enters its retrograde cycle on October 18, you may feel that the same problems you considered to be resolved surface with a vengeance!

Rewarding Days
2, 3, 7, 8, 12, 16, 17, 25, 26, 29, 30

Challenging Days
1, 13, 14, 15, 20, 21, 27, 28

Affirmation for the Month
I stand confidently on a platform of truth and integrity.

Aquarius/November

In the Spotlight
Conferences, academic pursuits, and promotional activities help advance your reputation and career. Establishing new goals may be high on your agenda, particularly if you feel that you've realized an important milestone.

Wellness and Keeping Fit
Solicit a good friend to join you in your quest for better health. A retreat can be a positive healing option after November 13.

Love and Life Connections
Getting together with good friends can give you just the boost you need. A reunion with those you love helps strengthen your bonds, but also encourages you to rely more on your foundation for support. Untried pathways emerge with the New Moon on November 25. While romance may be part of the picture, it's more likely that a fresh direction with an old love will surface.

Finance and Success
Misunderstandings can dampen your enthusiasm, although your professional allies may come to your rescue. Complex issues can become muddled by vague communication, with conflicts reaching a peak during the Full Moon on November 11. Although Mercury leaves its retrograde cycle on November 7, a cloud of mistrust can linger until November 24. Your ideas are best received after November 25, when you have every reason to feel hopeful.

Cosmic Insider Tip
Sharing your dreams, hopes, and ideas with those you trust can lead to amazing progress from November 22-28. It's best to sign contracts from November 25-27, when momentum is highest.

Rewarding Days
3, 4, 8, 9, 12, 13, 21, 22, 25, 26, 27, 30

Challenging Days
10, 11, 16, 17, 17, 23, 24

Affirmation for the Month
I am completing unfinished business.

Aquarius/December

In the Spotlight
You may feel that you're almost glowing with happiness! Allowing your best attributes to shine forth, you're attracting well-deserved recognition for your efforts and may rise to a more influential position in your career.

Wellness and Keeping Fit
It's your turn to enjoy the fruits of your labors. A vacation between December 9-23 can be most relaxing. Opening your heart and sharing love has a positive effect on your health.

Love and Life Connections
Travel or cultural or academic pursuits can lead to romance. A meeting of the minds can open the path to a deep understanding on more than the mental level, and by the Full Moon on December 11, love is in bloom! Your ability to surrender to the flow of love allows you to express a purely unconditional quality of acceptance. By the solar eclipse on December 25, you might crave absolute privacy.

Finance and Success
Presentations, conferences, or business meetings can offer the perfect forum to illustrate your ideas or share your talents, and promotional activities can spark progress from December 1-22. You're capable of taking action that stirs the imagination and generates powerful support from an influential camp after December 9. Your leadership can inspire others to risk stepping onto the path of progressive change.

Cosmic Insider Tip
You may possess precisely what's needed to institute important evolutionary change. Trust your vision and talents to light the path.

Rewarding Days
1, 2, 10, 11, 18, 19, 23, 24, 28, 29

Challenging Days
8, 9, 14, 15, 20, 21

Affirmation for the Month
I surrender my actions and thoughts to the wisdom of divine love.

Aquarius Action Table

These dates reflect the best—but not the only—times for success and ease in these activities, according to your Sun sign.

	JAN	FEB	MAR	APR	MAY	JUN	JUL	AUG	SEPT	OCT	NOV	DEC
Move				30	1-13							
Start a class				4					27, 28			
Join a club											25, 26	
Ask for a raise		5										
Look for work					30, 31	1-23	18-31	1-6	28-30	1-17	9-30	1, 2
Get pro advice	21, 22	17, 18	15-17	12, 13	9, 10	5, 6	3-4, 30-31	27, 28	23, 24	20, 21	16, 17	14, 15
Get a loan	23, 24	19, 20	18, 19	14, 15	11, 12	7-9	5, 6	1-2, 29-30	25, 26	22, 23	19, 20	16, 17
See a doctor	1-17				30, 31	1-22	18-31	1-6				23-31
Start a diet	19, 20	15, 16	13, 14	10, 11	7, 8	3, 4	1-2, 28-29	25, 26	21, 22	18, 19	14, 15	12, 13
End relationship	21, 22											
Buy clothes					15-29							
Get a makeover		5										
New romance						2						
Vacation	25, 26	21-23	20, 21	16, 17	13-15	10, 11	7, 8	3, 4, 31	1, 27, 28	24-26	21, 22	18, 19

Pisces

The Fish
February 19 to March 19

♓

Element:	Water
Quality:	Mutable
Polarity:	Feminine/Yin
Planetary Ruler:	Neptune
Meditation:	"I surrender to the heart of divine compassion."
Gemstone:	Aquamarine
Power Stones:	Amethyst, bloodstone, tourmaline, sugilite
Key Phrase:	"I believe"
Glyph:	Two fish joined, swimming in opposite directions ♓
Anatomy:	Feet, lymphatic system
Color:	Violet, sea green
Animal:	Fish, sea mammals
Myths/Legends:	Aphrodite, Buddha, Jesus of Nazareth
House:	Twelfth
Opposite Sign:	Virgo
Flower:	Water Lily
Key Word:	Transcendence

Positive Expression:	Misuse of Energy:
Visionary	Confused
Mystical	Escapist
Idealistic	Confused
Flexible	Susceptible
Poetic	Codependent
Empathetic	Unconscious
Imaginative	Addictive

Pisces

Your Ego's Strengths and Shortcomings

You have a very special way of looking at life: you perceive what can be through your imagination and feel the essence of everything happening around you through your heightened sensibilities. Mystical, visionary, and magical, your perceptive self-expression can range from that of concerned world server to whimsical artist. You can be devoted to high ideals, and through the energy of Neptune, your planetary ruler, can forge a profound connection to the spiritual plane.

When facing the storms of life, surrounded by others who may be trapped by apathy, your faith can lift you to a higher level. In your role as "The Illusionist" of the zodiac, you can project much-needed hope and true compassion into a world in need of healing. Trusting your inner senses, you may escape into your creativity as a means of strengthening your own security. Your sensitivity invites others to seek your insightful support, but drawing personal boundaries may not be easy. In your attempts to rescue another you can, yourself, become a casualty! You may also fall victim to illusion or deception, since the delicate line between the many levels of reality can be difficult to define. You need time and room for personal reflection or seclusion to rejuvenate and must safeguard against unscrupulous individuals who would misuse your sympathetic understanding. Even if you are involved with the public, you may relish a quiet life. You need time and space to surrender your daily burdens; however, it is tempting to fall into addictive or abusive escapes, like drugs or alcohol. Following the transcendent beauty of your inner light, you can connect your spiritual power to your physical existence, and from this source can express the real magic of changing the world.

Shining Your Love Light

The quest for your soulmate can fill your dreams, and even if you've experienced disappointment through romance, you're not likely to give up on true love. Without love, life would be meaningless to you! You can see potential and beauty in the eyes of almost everyone, yet the unique experience of surrendering to a true and complete love is your ultimate goal for a partnership. Once you make the promise to love, you can create a spellbinding space where you and your partner can retreat together into ecstasy.

With the water signs—Cancer, Scorpio, and Pisces—you may feel an instant kinship through a mutual understanding of the nature of emotion. Aries stimulates your love of spontaneous passion, but if romance withers you can be disappointed. Taurus can understand your needs, helping to build a foundation for your dreams. Gemini can keep you on your toes, and while that dizzy feeling can be enticing, you may not like it for long periods of time! Cancer nurtures your self-expression and encourages you to express the fullness of love. With Leo, you may feel that you rarely have a chance to express your own needs, and that he or she demands all your energy.

Virgo, your zodiac opposite, can be engaging and frustrating at the same time, but if you develop understanding you can become partners in building a magnificent dream. Libra's refined elegance is intriguing, but you may feel ill at ease if demands for perfection get in the way. With Scorpio, your thirst for passion is filled, and sharing sensual moments can launch you into another dimension. Keeping up with Sagittarius is a challenge, since what seemed real yesterday may not even happen today. With Capricorn, you can feel safe, stable, and trusting, as long as you maintain your personal boundaries. Although Aquarius can be a treasured friend, you may not be comfortable as lovers. With another Pisces you may feel you've come home to a place where your desires and dreams are embraced, but only if your spirits are in harmony.

Making Your Place in the World
While you may not see yourself as worldly or ambitious, you do need to develop a vehicle for expressing your imagination through your life's work. Your wide-ranging interests can make it difficult to pin down a single choice. You may be drawn to a career that brings beauty into the world—areas like landscaping, the floral industry, fashion design, the beauty industry, or interior design. With your ability to tap into the energy of the collective consciousness, you can be successful in ventures like the movies, television, or advertising, and you can also be a talented actor, musician, dancer, artist, or photographer.

Your hopes for uplifting the human spirit can lead you into counseling, social work, the ministry, medicine, or charitable work, and your special sensibility toward animals may prompt you to follow veterinary medicine or zoo keeping. The restaurant or club business can be a successful choice. The key to feeling happy with your work is knowing that you're in the flow.

Power Plays

When people start talking about power, you might feel like running for the hills. You prefer peace, harmony, and a vision of utopian society. In truth, you know a lot about power and understand the unlimited power that arises from joining with divine compassion, when you've tapped into the absolute energy of the Source. A tremendous sense of freedom emerges when you surrender to the radiant vision of love, faith, and hope, allowing your destiny to emerge and guide your path; yet seeing yourself is difficult, particularly if you feel you've lost your connection to the Source. You may feel powerless until you accomplish the task of self-acceptance, and this begins when you merge your inner and higher selves.

Your power wanes when others influence you in negative ways, pulling you into the morass of abuse or manipulation for their own desires. While you may feel that surrender is one key to your strength, unnecessary self-sacrifice robs you of your true power. The light you seek to guide you may be quietly shining in the depths of your own soul, evoking true peace, emanating the harmony you know as the true essence of power.

Famous Pisces

Prince Andrew, Tammy Faye Bakker, Drew Barrymore, Alexander Graham Bell, Karen Carpenter, Enrico Caruso, Kurt Cobain, Gordon Cooper, Ron Howard, Quincy Jones, Michelangelo, Jimmy Swaggart, John Updike, Tom Wolfe.

The Year Ahead for Pisces

While unraveling your attachment to the things from the past that are no longer part of your life, you're also strengthening your understanding, skills, and abilities to communicate your vision for the future during this first year of the century. By forging a strong network with those who understand your ideals and whose aims support your own, you may feel less isolated in your attempts to make a difference in the quality of life.

You're feeling the expansive influence of Jupiter in the arenas of enhanced communication and a broadening of your security base. From January through July, Jupiter's stimulus prompts you to develop your skills and connect with others whose resources and talents compliment your own. You've always been community-minded, and now, by developing a support network, you may feel that you are not alone in your attempts to accomplish your aims. After July, Jupiter's influence highlights your need for personal space and a more significant link to home and family. You may be feeling inclined to move, renovate, or make changes in your personal environment that give you a sense of space. With more breathing room, you may also feel open to inviting others into your life, and your family may grow larger this year! It's important to avoid over-obligating your time and resources, however, since increasing your burden can happen before you know it, and it's rarely a good idea to carry another's load unless they are simply incapable of the task.

Saturn's energy of clarity, discipline, and focus brings your attention to the need to strengthen your communication expertise and build your database. It's a good time to be in school, studying under the guidance of a mentor or master, or devoting more energy to refining your abilities and understanding in your chosen field. You may also be more aware of your shortcomings and realize that these will only serve as limitations if you fail to take the responsibility of dealing with them in some way.

The slow-moving cycle of Pluto continues to influence transformation of your life path, and the alterations you make to your career or basic lifestyle now can have far-reaching consequences. Challenged to eliminate choices that are not in harmony with your true needs can help you move beyond situations that are inhibiting or where you've denied yourself. Uranus and Neptune also take a long while in their effects, and the impact of these influences is likely to be felt as a kind of spiritual awakening, bringing you in touch with your deeper truth and helping you release the things from your past that are no longer part of your life.

During the year 2000, there are four solar eclipses and two lunar eclipses. With the impact of four eclipses, there are likely to be more crisis-oriented periods on the planet. From a personal level, it's important to understand the underlying influence behind these eclipses emphasized by the cycle of the Moon's nodes. The transit of the nodes brings your attention to the flow of love through your heart and the manner in which you give and receive love. While relationships are part of the test, the larger challenge may reside in whether or not you truly allow love to guide your actions and thoughts, whether expressed to a person or through your creativity. The specific impact of each eclipse will be explained in your monthly forecast section that follows.

If you were born from February 19 to 21, you're feeling the restraints of Saturn transiting in square aspect to your Sun. This cycle will have its greatest influence from July through the end of October, although you may sense that it's on its way before the actual high-impact period. During the beginning of the year you can make positive preparations for the late-year challenges by dusting off your talents and putting them to use. From January through March, Saturn will transit in quintile aspect to your Sun, providing clarification about the best ways to make use of your assets and abilities. By marshaling your resources during this time, you may feel more confident when you face the tests of Saturn in square aspect to your Sun during the summer months. While Saturn is squaring your Sun (July to October), you may feel a bit despondent over the fact that opportunities seem to be limited, or, if they arrive, that there are a lot of strings attached to them. This is a testing period, a time to review your choices, life circumstances, and responsibilities. It can also be a period of retribution. If you've been handling your obligations with care and putting forth your best efforts, this may simply be a time when you're working harder to fulfill your goals or meet a challenge. However, if you've been shirking your responsibilities or have failed to meet important requirements, you will feel that you're being held back as a result. Taking care of your physical health can be more challenging, too. If your body is giving you problems, it could be a result of the fact that you've failed to take care of your health. Now is the time to do something about it.

If you were born from February 22 to 26, you may feel that it's time to take the next steps in your spiritual evolution while Neptune is traveling in semisextile aspect to your Sun. Your devotion to your spiritual ideals can be an excellent beacon whether you're making career choices, determining the best course for a relationship, or uncovering the best ways to use your special talents. You may also feel that you're capable of separating beliefs based on truth from illusions based on false pretense, and as a result may break away from false principles that can serve to guide you only in circles! It's time to let go of the things that are inhibiting your growth and to forgive hurts from your past so that you can move forward.

If you were born from February 27 to March 4, you're experiencing the powerful challenge of transformation. Pluto's transit in square aspect to your Sun brings with it a reminder of the areas of your life that are in need of healing. This cycle may happen only once in your lifetime, and the changes you make will have far-reaching effects. You're breaking away from the "old you" and releasing your true power and creativity. Oppressive situations can become almost unbearable, particularly if you're resisting the need to let go or make necessary changes. Sometimes changes beyond your control can happen, like the dissolution of a company or a storm, leaving you to choose the most appropriate and creative response to the changes. Even though you may not understand why some changes happen, the fact that they are occurring is an indicator that it's time for you to move on. Trusting that you can find the power and resources may be the primary reason for the change—you must prove to yourself that you are worthy of a life filled with the things that echo your strengths. Since Saturn's cycle creates a supportive quintile aspect to your Sun during the late spring and late fall months of this year, you may feel more confident about your ability to effectively transform your life during those times. Take special care with your physical health since breakdowns can occur if you've been abusing your body (or soul!), or a congenital weakness can become troublesome. The key quality of this cycle is healing, but it is healing that requires you to say good-bye to the things, attitudes, people, and situations you no longer need.

If you were born from March 5 to 13, you're feeling the impulse to break free while Uranus transits in semisextile aspect to your Sun. In some ways this cycle can be like a natural evolutionary change, like going from childhood to adolescence. There is a contrast: you feel differently about yourself and your needs, but you can still recognize yourself! While you are ready to break out of inhibiting life situations, you may also feel that it's time to take on the challenge of allowing your true self to emerge. Because Saturn's stabilizing energy is transiting in a supportive sextile aspect to your Sun from January through May, you may be more confident about meeting the challenge to create or respond to evolutionary change during these months. Throughout the year you may see the old falling away as the new emerges to take its place. Think of yourself as a computer in need of an upgrade! You'll appreciate the effects of moving at a faster speed or processing change more effectively once you're used to the new system.

If you were born from March 8 to 12, you may feel less certain of yourself while Neptune transits in semisquare aspect to your Sun this year. This can be a confusing cycle, especially if you allow others to have an undue influence over your decisions or actions or to take control of your life. The commitments you make now may seem to fall short or may not materialize as you had anticipated. Although your impulse may be to shrink away from confrontation, you will find that by drawing from your spiritual strength you can meet challenges more effectively. It's time to learn how to incorporate the spiritual into your everyday life instead of feeling that you have to isolate these qualities or this time. By integrating your spiritual power, your creativity can be enhanced, and you may also feel better prepared to deal with the issues that emerge in close personal relationships.

If you were born from March 14 to 20, you're experiencing the steadying influence of Saturn transiting in sextile aspect to your Sun. This cycle is most influential from May through December and will continue into early next year. To a great extent, this is your year to build a solid foundation beneath your dreams. Educational pursuits are favored, and it may also be easier for you to develop your talents or strengthen your special skills. It's your turn to move forward based on your previous performance and current capabilities, and if you've been hoping to strengthen your reputation, the time is now. You may also find that changing habits or incorporating changes that aid self-improvement can be rather beneficial, giving you a sense that you have a new lease on life. You're definitely making positive preparations for the challenge of the new century!

Tools to Make a Difference

Welcoming the changes and challenges of this new century can be an exciting prospect for you. Developing your mind may be a top priority, and whether you're in school, studying another language, traveling more, or involved with a study or special interest group, strengthening your understanding and sharpening your mental skills can be among your most valuable tools. Honing your public speaking skills can also be helpful. However, one of your most cherished assets can be the creation of a pool of resources or a network of supportive individuals.

Developing a more profound quality of mindfulness can be a tool of immeasurable value. By strengthening your awareness of the more subtle things happening around you, you can better interpret these signals and make wiser choices. You will be more in touch with yourself and, instead of functioning on automatic pilot, you will also feel that you're more in control. To start, promise yourself that you will pay closer attention to your motivations and your inner dialogue. You might be amazed at what's happening in there! This will also enhance your awareness of your physical needs and allow you to read your body messages more clearly. Giving yourself time to retreat—whether you're taking a sauna at the gym, enjoying a hot tub at home, indulging in a spa experience, or just taking more bubble baths—you need to pull away and simply indulge your body and mind in the peaceful tranquillity of letting go. During baths, showers, or massages, add essential oils to heighten your senses. You might even like the benefits of cypress oil to help alleviate foot odor! Patchouli, jasmine, or rose can lift your spirits. Juniper added to your bath is an excellent detoxifier.

During your meditations, open your mind to the experience of truly letting go and feeling the power of tranquillity. Create an image of a gently flowing stream, allowing your thoughts to flow along with the stream into the infinite oneness. Feel your energy merging with the Source of ultimate power, surrendering your cares, sinking into the caress of pure energy. You are never truly apart from the Source, although sometimes life can convince you that you are. When that happens, take a deep breath, close your eyes, and flow with the stream!

Initiating the Millennium

By taking a more active role in the creation of your foundations, you're building the resources necessary for your success and happiness during the coming years. Your visionary capabilities may be in high demand during the initiation of this new century, and by fine-tuning your awareness you will have more confidence about sharing your insights. Innovative techniques that allow you to boost your brain power while heightening your awareness can be exceptionally valuable. It's time to incorporate your mystical sensibilities into your everyday life!

♓

Affirmation for the Year

My consciousness is focused on higher truth and wisdom.

Pisces/January

In the Spotlight
With an extra energy boost from Mars in your sign, you may feel that you're ready to take on almost any challenge. Community actions and politically focused efforts can be especially noteworthy.

Wellness and Keeping Fit
Pushing past your physical limits can result in problems ranging from fatigue to accidental injury. By listening to your body's signals and setting a reasonable pace, you can feel healthier. High-risk situations are best avoided.

Love and Life Connections
You may feel passionately about things that others do not understand, or can feel that you've been setup if you are unclear with your actions or words. The manner in which you direct your energy can make all the difference in whether or not some relationships emerge unscathed or if they fall as a casualty of emotional warfare from January 7-20. Romance fares best after January 24.

Finance and Success
Professional associates rally to offer their support, and during the New Moon on January 6 you can experience a strong sense of unity among your peers. A potential crisis is brewing and can affect your work. By the Moon's eclipse on January 20, most problems should be in the open. Until then, paying special attention to your reputation will be necessary.

Cosmic Insider Tip
Differences in values will be quite apparent from January 1-20, and taking a stand for your real values may be your only choice if you want to live with yourself later!

Rewarding Days
1, 5, 6, 10, 11, 16, 19, 27, 28, 29

Challenging Days
3, 4, 17, 18, 20, 23, 24, 30, 31

Affirmation for the Month
My words and actions are inspired by truth, love, and integrity.

Pisces/February

In the Spotlight

Your ability to tap into the wide-ranging effects of a situation may place you in a position of advisor when others need a perspective on the big picture. As the old order slips away, your visionary insights can be extremely valuable.

Wellness and Keeping Fit

Building endurance now can give you the energy reserves you need to stay healthy. Setting up a reasonable exercise program gives you a head start on the upcoming busy season.

Love and Life Connections

While your friendships need special care, a passionate relationship needs privacy if you are to share your fantasies. The Sun's eclipse on February 5 can stimulate especially meaningful dreams, providing valuable insights into your deeper feelings. Considering your commitment to a relationship during the Full Moon on February 19 helps you determine what you want and need from your partner.

Finance and Success

Negotiations fare best through February 18, and meetings occurring from February 5-18 can lead to career advancement. Your financial picture improves, although you may be tempted to spend impulsively after February 13, which can lead to problems if you fail to adhere to your budget. Take care in business communications after February 21 to avoid getting into a situation filled with land mines.

Cosmic Insider Tip

Mercury enters its three-week retrograde cycle on February 21, and while you may know what you want to say, others may seem to be talking in circles. Avoid signing contracts.

Rewarding Days

1, 2, 6, 7, 8, 15, 16, 24, 25, 29

Challenging Days

13, 14, 19, 20, 21, 26, 27, 28

Affirmation for the Month

My goals are clearly defined. I know what I want and need!

Pisces/March

In the Spotlight

Your thoughts can be a powerful magnet for the situations developing around you, and by training your focus on things that are in harmony with your needs, you may easily end up in the right place at the right time!

Wellness and Keeping Fit

The balance between mind, spirit, and body may need fine-tuning. Target a workout routine that incorporates a positive philosophy.

Love and Life Connections

Your sudden attraction to an unusual person can lead to infatuation from March 1-5. Before you become involved there may be barriers to overcome, including whether or not the situation offers realistic potential, although initiating contact can be intriguing during the Pisces New Moon on March 6. Venus enters Pisces on March 13, beginning a four-week period when love relationships can grow stronger.

Finance and Success

Exaggerated claims, even when you know they may be filled with pitfalls, may still be difficult to resist. Investing your time in something that is not yet tested can be costly. Exploration during Mercury's retrograde through March 14 can bring facts to light that clarify your options. You may have a change of heart around March 22 when you can see how your actions will affect your honor.

Cosmic Insider Tip

Completing negotiations or legal proceedings can be difficult before the Full Moon on March 19, since the remainder of the unseen facts may emerge at that time.

Rewarding Days

1, 5, 6, 9, 10, 13, 14, 23, 27, 28

Challenging Days

11, 12, 18, 19, 20, 25, 26

Affirmation for the Month

Love and understanding nourish my ability to be patient.

Pisces/April

In the Spotlight
Your talents gain acknowledgment and afford you the chance to strengthen your support network. Attracting others whose influence and abilities can aid your success, you're building your tangible and intangible assets.

Wellness and Keeping Fit
Take advantage of the grounding qualities of getting out of doors. Gardening can be especially enjoyable, but you might also feel energized by regular walks or strolling along the beach.

Love and Life Connections
Expressing your deeply-felt affections from April 1-5 can lead to a meeting of heart, mind, and soul. A journey with your sweetheart can stimulate a different perspective once you're away from daily pressures and focusing on your shared ideals and hopes. Fear of losing control can emerge after April 23 if you feel like things are moving too quickly, but you may just be experiencing a test of your love.

Finance and Success
Communing with others in your field can help you target your next steps in building your skills or amplifying your talents. Meetings or interviews fare best from April 1-12, although you'll enjoy what you learn from others after April 20, when leading edge experts can provide information or insights that can help you put a solid foundation under your dreams. Try to make good use of practical advice.

Cosmic Insider Tip
Determining the best ways to utilize your resources—time, money, and energy—from the New Moon on April 4 until the Full Moon on April 18, gives you a solid foothold on success.

Rewarding Days
1, 2, 5, 6, 10, 11, 18, 19, 20, 24, 28, 29, 30

Challenging Days
8, 9, 14, 15, 21, 22

Affirmation for the Month
I choose my words carefully in order to communicate my intentions.

Pisces/May

In the Spotlight
Unsettled situations on the home front can be distracting since you may be concentrating on educational pursuits, travel, or communication. Keeping an open mind is helpful since a change of direction will be easier if you're not stuck in one position.

Wellness and Keeping Fit
You may feel that you're being stretched beyond your capacities, and if that's the case, exercises that enhance your physical flexibility may go a long way toward opening your emotional flexibility.

Love and Life Connections
There are many ways to communicate, and you're ready to accentuate your viewpoints. Initiating a serious conversation with your sweetheart during the New Moon on May 3 can provide the perfect opening to clarify your feelings. By the Full Moon on May 18, you're ready for a more soulful experience, and an exotic vacation or a long weekend might be the perfect backdrop for an enchanting romance.

Finance and Success
Integrating your ideas with others can lead to a tremendous opportunity, especially if you're surrounded by like-minded people. Convening with those who share your interests can be self-confirming through May 13 and gives you a chance to showcase your talents. Avoid the temptation to alter your investment strategies from May 14-20, since you may need to ride out a change in the market.

Cosmic Insider Tip
An unanticipated event can shake the stability of your work situation, although your positive attitudes can place you in a position of influence and respect.

Rewarding Days
3, 4, 7, 8, 16, 26, 27, 30

Challenging Days
5, 6, 11, 12, 13, 18, 19, 20

Affirmation for the Month
I am an attentive listener and an excellent communicator.

Pisces/June

In the Spotlight
While others seem to be jockeying for position, you're comfortably situated in a creatively stimulating circumstance. By allowing your talents to emerge, you can realize the fulfillment of a cherished dream.

Wellness and Keeping Fit
Stressful circumstances at work or at home can drain your energy. You'll benefit from the rejuvenating effects of a massage near the Full Moon on June 16.

Love and Life Connections
Knowing when to stand firmly on your convictions and when to give someone the benefit of the doubt can be a tricky proposition. Watch for signals during the New Moon on June 2 that indicate the effects of your actions upon your security. You may need to make a fresh start on family matters. A love relationship grows more powerful after June 18, when you may feel more comfortable letting your passion lead the way.

Finance and Success
Competitive situations on the career front can feel threatening through June 16, and if your anxieties are triggered by events you cannot control, that can be a signal that you need to retreat and wait for the storm to pass. Showcase your talents after June 19, when you're likely to be met with glowing reviews by those who appreciate your efforts. Investments fare best from June 18-22.

Cosmic Insider Tip
While improvements are on the horizon after June 18, Mercury enters its three-week retrograde on June 23. Use this time for review, research, and finishing what you've started.

Rewarding Days
3, 4, 12, 13, 17, 18, 22, 23, 28

Challenging Days
1, 2, 7, 8, 9, 14, 15, 16, 29, 30

Affirmation for the Month
My heart is open to an experience of pure love.

Pisces/July

In the Spotlight
In the midst of potential crisis, you may be the one with your wits about you, offering support, care, and compassion. Changes in a love relationship can be foremost on your mind, and following your heart may be your first priority.

Wellness and Keeping Fit
You need a pleasurable distraction and may work harder to get in shape if it will help your "game."

Love and Life Connections
A love relationship can take a turn during the solar eclipse on July 1, and if you're in the right situation—one that fulfills your true needs—you may feel ready to change your life for love. The Moon's eclipse on July 16 challenges you to open your heart to receive love from others; after all, love grows when you let it flow into and out from your heart! Celebrate! Share your joy with others who laugh and smile along with you.

Finance and Success
Despite Mercury's retrograde (until July 17) you may be making real progress, since your talents, ideas, and projects place you an in advantageous position. Investments grow through July 13, and putting more energy into a speculative venture after July 23 can help you maintain the momentum; but if it's time to cut losses, take advantage of a chance to move forward after the Sun's eclipse on July 30.

Cosmic Insider Tip
The two solar eclipses this month add emphasis to the areas of your life that can be most productive. It's up to you to determine the best uses of your talents, but use them you must!

Rewarding Days
1, 2, 9, 10, 14, 15, 16, 19, 20, 21, 25, 29

Challenging Days
5, 6, 12, 13, 26, 27, 30, 31

Affirmation for the Month
I am ready for accelerated growth and positive changes!

Pisces/August

In the Spotlight
Your patience is tested when it comes to working cooperatively with others. If you feel that you're being saddled with responsibilities that rightfully belong to someone else, express your concerns. Being too nice can add to your burden.

Wellness and Keeping Fit
It's easy to get in over your head before you know it, and if you're in a new fitness program or trying a new sport, giving yourself time to gradually adjust can help you avoid a painful price.

Love and Life Connections
Your partnership can reach a crisis due to differences in the way you express affection. A conflict between your career and personal life can take its toll, and you may respond by pulling away for reflection during the Full Moon on August 15. Tension from family can also be the culprit. By exploring your roles and needs, you can set your partnership on a fresh course during the New Moon on August 29.

Finance and Success
Contract negotiations can be unpleasant if you're disagreeing over the budget or feel that your ideas are being ignored in favor of other priorities. You may be able to illustrate your point more effectively from August 1-7, but after that, you may feel you need an advocate in your corner. Address areas at work in need of improvement; innovations may be part of the problem after August 22.

Cosmic Insider Tip
By acknowledging the assistance you receive from others, you may avert a crisis, since anyone who feels you're taking unnecessary advantage may balk or withdraw support.

Rewarding Days
6, 7, 11, 12, 15, 16, 17, 25, 26

Challenging Days
1, 2, 8, 9, 22, 23, 24, 29, 30, 31

Affirmation for the Month
I am sensitive to the needs and concerns of others.

Pisces/September

In the Spotlight
It's time to get to the core of fears or inhibitions by working out the details of deeper issues, whether they involve contracts or personal matters.

Wellness and Keeping Fit
Staying on track with fitness may be a necessary part of staying sane in the midst of high-tension circumstances.

Love and Life Connections
Reaching a deeper stage of intimacy with your partner may be your ultimate goal, although it can be a test of your love to get there! Old issues, some of them stemming from early hurts, can get in the way, prompting you to mistrust your feelings. You may feel especially vulnerable during the Pisces Full Moon on September 13, although expressing emotions that arise from the depths of your soul can lead to healing.

Finance and Success
Hostilities at work can get out of control. Renovation or a change of command can prompt outrageous political posturing. You may want to stay out of it, although you may feel forced to take a stand if your own security is in question. Maintaining the ethical high ground can keep you from drowning in a sea of petty disagreements, and you'll be willing to fight for the larger issues. Hope emerges after September 25.

Cosmic Insider Tip
While the planets Jupiter and Pluto are transiting in opposition, you may feel caught in the squeeze of problems that easily escalate out of proportion. Keep your eye on the big picture.

Rewarding Days
2, 3, 12, 13, 21, 22, 29, 30

Challenging Days
4, 5, 6, 19, 20, 23, 25, 26

Affirmation for the Month
I surrender my will to the guidance of divine wisdom.

Pisces/October

In the Spotlight

Maintaining your objectivity in the midst of turmoil can be difficult, particularly if you feel you're under attack. Strengthened by your beliefs and ideals, your ability to draw attention to higher principles presents a worthy challenge.

Wellness and Keeping Fit

Physical activity can be a perfect balance to stressful situations. Martial arts, tai chi, or yoga may offer the mix of physical and spiritual disciplines you seek.

Love and Life Connections

Sometimes open disagreements are healthiest because you know what's on the table and can deal with them directly. Fundamental differences can separate you and your partner, but if your bond is positive, the spiritual essence of your connection will help you transcend any conflicts escalating during the Full Moon on October 13. You may have a change of heart by the New Moon on October 27.

Finance and Success

Competitive circumstances at work may arise due to political problems and are most intense from October 1-7. If moral or ethical standards are breached, you may lose faith in someone you had trusted. Legal negotiations can be tangled, but expectations are clarified after October 13, helping you determine the best choices. If you're uncertain of your commitment, it's probably best to wait.

Cosmic Insider Tip

In addition to the ongoing struggle about who's right, Mercury enters its retrograde on October 18, marking a three-week period when taking a second look can be illuminating and healing.

Rewarding Days

4, 9, 10, 18, 19, 27, 28, 31

Challenging Days

2, 3, 7, 12, 13, 16, 17, 22, 23, 29, 30

Affirmation for the Month

I am always open to the truth.

Pisces/November

In the Spotlight
Travel, cultural, or academic pursuits offer exceptional opportunities to advance your career while stimulating a sense of excitement about the future. Your search for higher meaning may be self-confirming.

Wellness and Keeping Fit
Cutting through the surface, you're ready to address physical problems at their core. Psychological connections offer a potential breakthrough in your sense of well-being.

Love and Life Connections
Your desires for intimacy can grow more intense as a result of transformations in your feelings. True love leads to an alchemy of souls, and getting past your old inhibitions or dealing with underlying problems can allow you to finally release the barriers to love during the Full Moon on November 11. You are opening your heart to an experience of unconditional love.

Finance and Success
Confusion over budget details or contractual agreements can slow progress from November 1-14, when trying to rush through anything will only lead to more delays. While this is not a good time to go into debt, it is an excellent period to release obligations, eliminate overstocks, or evaluate productivity. Formulate new plans after November 13, and launch your actions during or after the New Moon on November 25.

Cosmic Insider Tip
Mercury's retrograde ends on November 7, but the shroud of confusion resulting from a change of power can leave things in limbo until November 24.

Rewarding Days
2, 5, 6, 7, 11, 14, 15, 23, 24, 28, 29

Challenging Days
12, 13, 18, 19, 20, 25, 26

Affirmation for the Month
My strength and healing come from a higher source.

Pisces/December

In the Spotlight
Your reputation and career may be foremost on your mind, but you're also sorting through the details of repairs or renovation. In many ways, this is a time to determine what you can fix and what needs to be left behind.

Wellness and Keeping Fit
Continuing your probe into underlying problems, you're making headway. You are open to options that will help you eliminate unhealthy elements while you concentrate on true healing.

Love and Life Connections
Sharing special moments with friends lifts your spirits. Joining with those whose ideals are similar to your own, you're building your connections to your spiritual family. An amorous relationship takes a positive turn after December 24, when the luminous essence of your soul connection can guide you into ecstasy. Surrender to the truth of love during the solar eclipse on December 25.

Finance and Success
Meetings from December 1-8 can be the key to forging a positive agreement and may give you a chance to move up in the ranks. Your reputation can open doors during the Full Moon on December 11, although you may wonder if you're being tested in the process. Finances show improvement after December 23, when you may also feel more satisfied with the rewards of your work that go beyond money.

Cosmic Insider Tip
While a solar eclipse on December 25 may seem ominous, the impact in your life can be rather positive, since you're experiencing the value of opening your heart to fulfill cherished hopes.

Rewarding Days
3, 4, 9, 12, 13, 20, 21, 25, 26, 30, 31

Challenging Days
10, 11, 16, 17, 22, 23, 24

Affirmation for the Month
My mind and heart are open to the happiness of the moment.

Pisces Action Table

These dates reflect the best—but not the only—times for success and ease in these activities, according to your Sun sign.

	JAN	FEB	MAR	APR	MAY	JUN	JUL	AUG	SEPT	OCT	NOV	DEC
Move					14-29							
Start a class					4					27, 28		
Join a club	6											25, 26
Ask for a raise			6									
Look for work								7-21				4-22
Get pro advice	23, 24	19, 20	18, 19	14, 15	11, 12	7-9	5, 6	1-2, 29-30	25, 26	22, 23	19, 20	16, 17
Get a loan	25, 26	21-23	20, 21	16, 17	13, 14	10, 11	7, 8	3-5, 31	1, 27, 28	24-26	21, 22	18, 19
See a doctor	19-31	1-4						7-22				
Start a diet	21, 22	17, 18	16, 17	12, 13	9, 10	5, 6	3-4, 30-31	27, 28	23, 24	20, 21	16, 17	14, 15
End relationship		19, 20	19									
Buy clothes					31	1-22	18-31	1-6				
Get a makeover			6									
New romance							1, 2					
Vacation	27-29	24, 25	22, 23	19, 20	16, 17	12, 13	9-11	6, 7	2-3, 29-30	1, 27, 28	23, 24	20-22

The Twelve Houses of the Zodiac

You may run across mention of the houses of the zodiac while reading certain articles in the *Sun Sign Book*. These houses are the twelve divisions of the horoscope wheel. Each house has a specific meaning assigned to it. Below are the descriptions attributed to each house.

First House: Self-interest, physical appearance, basic character.

Second House: Personal values, monies earned and spent, moveable possessions, self-worth and esteem, resources for fulfilling security needs.

Third House: Neighborhood, communications, siblings, schooling, buying and selling, busy activities, short trips.

Fourth House: Home, family, real estate, parent(s), one's private sector of life, childhood years, and old age.

Fifth House: Creative endeavors, hobbies, pleasures, entertainments, children, speculative ventures, loved ones.

Sixth House: Health, working environment, coworkers, small pets, service to others, food, armed forces.

Seventh House: One-on-one encounters, business and personal partners, significant others, legal matters.

Eighth House: Values of others, joint finances, other people's money, death and rebirth, surgery, psychotherapy.

Ninth House: Higher education, religion, long trips, spirituality, languages, publishing.

Tenth House: Social status, reputation, career, public honors, parents, the limelight.

Eleventh House: Friends, social and community work, causes, surprises, luck, rewards from career, circumstances beyond your control.

Twelfth House: Hidden weaknesses and strengths, behind-the-scenes activities, institutions, confinement, government.

2000
Sun Sign Book
Articles

Contributors:

Skye Alexander

Alice DeVille

Sasha Fenton

Mark Kenski

Dorothy Oja

Leeda Alleyn Pacotti

Derek & Julia Parker

Kim Rogers-Gallagher

Kaye Shinker

Cathy L. Zornes

Locational Astrology
Where On Earth Should You Be?

By Sasha Fenton

We have all heard stories of how a change of location changed someone's life, but is there anything in astrology that confirms the notion that a change of place can bring you a change of luck? Well, yes, there is! Furthermore, can you choose the kind of destiny you would most like by picking the right location? The answer to this is also yes!

In order to make up your astrological chart, an astrologer first asks you for your date, time, and place of birth. The idea behind this is surprisingly close to that of navigation: a sailor or an airline pilot needs to know exactly where he or she is in relation to the face of the earth at any given moment in time. You know where and when you were born, but your astrologer needs to determine where the planets, stars, sunrise, and Midheaven were at that particular time and place. Once this is established, the astrologer can then interpret your birthchart accurately. The position of your birthchart features shows the pattern of your childhood experiences, describes your innate talents and abilities, and suggests where success in various spheres of your life might be found. By looking at the movement of these celestial features at any point in time, your astrologer can point out the trends and events that are emerging. If, therefore, a change of location alters the angles formed by the planets, and if it changes the position of the sunrise and the Midheaven, the theory is that this should also alter your lifestyle—and it could even change some aspects of your nature! In the search for answers, modern astrologers have gone right back to the early principles of navigation and have come up with several techniques, two of which seem to work extremely well.

Astro-Maps

The late Jim Lewis computerized one of these locational astrology systems which he called by the copyrighted name Astro*Carto*Graphy (or A*C*G as it is known in the trade). The name may be copyrighted, but the system is ancient, so astrologers like myself can use it—as long as we don't use the acronym A*C*G. In my book, I call this system Astro-maps.

If you want to see how the Astro-map system works, you need nothing more than a globe of the world and a torch. **(Figure 1.)** Shine the torch onto the globe somewhere close to the equator. The light from the torch will mimic the glow of the sun. The brightest area will be the spot on the earth where the sun shines brightest, while the other side of the globe will be in darkness. The area where day breaks will be to the left of the sunlight, and the encroaching night will be on the right. To see the effect of the sun rising and setting over the earth, give your globe a slight spin to the right (eastwards).

Now find the point where your imitation sunlight is shining brightest and draw an imaginary line northwards up and over the globe, through the North Pole, and down the other side. Continue onwards by drawing your line under the South Pole and back up again so that it bisects the globe just like a meridian line. The "front" part of the line, where the sun is shining, is called the MC line. (MC stands for Medium Coeli or Midheaven.) The part of the line that continues to bisect your globe around the "back" where there is no light is called the IC line. (IC stands for Immum Coeli or bottom of the sky.)

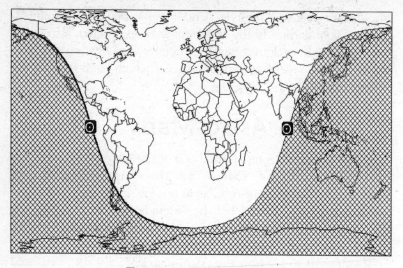

Figure 1. Day and Night

If you look at the illustration, you can clearly see an area where the sun is rising, to the left of the lighted area, called the rise line. *(Figure 2.)* The area to the right where the sun is setting is called the set line. You will notice that when the earth's globe is "flattened," as in the illustration, the daylight area appears to be bell-shaped.

We know that only the sun and moon can illuminate the earth, but if you imagine for a moment that every planet in the solar system has the same lighting and reflective ability as the sun and moon, you will see how the MC, IC, rise line, and set line for each planet on an Astro-map chart are determined. If you now ask your astrologer to make up your Astro-map chart, you will be able to see for yourself where all these lines occur in your own birthchart.

A move to any planetary line will bring changes to your lifestyle, although the type of change you experience will depend upon the planetary line in question. If you move to a place where two (or more) lines cross, your experiences in that location will be influenced by the effects of the two (or more) planets in question. There are further complications that can arise and other factors which astrologers take into account when reading an Astro-map chart, but they are a bit too advanced for this article.

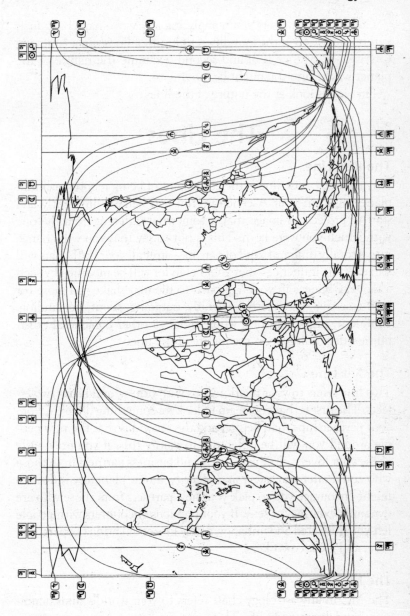

Figure 2. Astro*Carto*Graphy Chart

Consider two factors when analyzing an Astro-map chart: first, determine which of the four different kinds of lines you are moving to (rise, set, MC or IC); and second, examine the nature of the planet whose line you might be moving to.

First let us look at the nature of the lines.

The Lines

The Rise Line

Any move to a rise line is the equivalent of being reborn with that planet right on your Ascendant. You will behave differently and start to project an image that is somewhat different from the one with which you were born. This is not to say that you will change into a totally different kind of person—after all your birthchart will still exert its influence—but your behavior will be modified by such a move. Changes in your approach to life may make you more (or less) assertive, cooperative, friendly, outgoing, silent, demanding, confident, suspicious, or a whole range of other behavioral possibilities, depending upon the nature of the line.

The Set Line

This line refers to your relationships with others, and it has two effects. The first is that you begin to look for something different from your partnerships than before, and the second is that the new people around you will be different. To clarify this, if you previously chose your lovers, close associates, and business partners from those who could offer you safety and security, a new planetary influence might encourage you to pick your new partners from those who are dynamic, exciting, or sexy. If your previous encounters with people left you frustrated and unhappy, a new line could bring cooperation, love, and great coworkers.

The MC Line

The MC in any astrology chart refers to your worldly aims, ambitions, and direction in life. This is often taken to mean one's career path, but not everyone wants a career. You may change from being a laid-back, unambitious type to a real go-getter. You may suddenly decide to seek out spiritual experiences or to change your philosophical outlook on life in some way. You may throw your career aims out of the window in order to concentrate on building a successful domestic and family life—or the reverse may be the case.

The IC Line
The IC in astrology refers to one's home and family, and it can also reintroduce issues of the past. A move to a new location may take you back to an atmosphere that is similar to one that you have experienced before, or it can bring issues and experiences that are completely new. The kind of home and domestic setup in your new environment may be totally different from that which you are used to. For example, if you lived in a small city apartment that served as no more than a place to lay your head after a day's work, you may now find yourself living in a large home with plenty of open space around you.

The Planets

The nature of each of the planets is the key to the locational astrology system. A look at the brief outline that follows will show you how this works.

The Sun
The Sun brings success and achievement to any line, and it opens up creative energies. Children and young people may become a feature on any Sun line, and you could become closely involved with them in a way that didn't happen before. A father figure might enter your life here. Fun-filled activities, vacations, trips to places of interest, and having a good time will be important here, while sunshine and music could fill your day. Your sense of humor will improve and a kind of childlike attitude might take over, but you could become arrogant and intolerant of fools. Any Sun line is a great place for a holiday, a love affair, or for retirement.

The Moon
The Moon has a bearing on your internal feelings, your emotions, and your attitude to home and family life. A mother figure might enter your life here, or issues of motherhood could become important.

Your emotions will deepen and may actually become overwhelming. Your need for a home or family will become far stronger here, and you could easily feel as though you have "come home." Issues related to food or the production of food could enter your life here.

Mercury

This brings business, communications, and dealings with neighbors and friends sharply into focus. You will have more dealings with relatives of your own generation. In the unlikely event that you have never learned to drive, you will do so here, because short journeys will become part of your lifestyle. Phones, faxes, e-mail, and other communication techniques will become part of your daily life. You may learn to work with your hands, or you could get into writing at this location. Love and sex may become less important, while friendships and career issues take over.

Venus

The planet of love, relaxation, and beauty will enhance your life, bringing you to a place of beauty or to a place that is filled with people whose company you thoroughly enjoy. You will become more relaxed and self-indulgent at this location, and you may put on weight! Money should come your way, but you are also likely to spend freely. This would be a great place for a holiday, and you could fall in love here. Alternatively, you might develop your artistic or musical talents. For both sexes, new female friends and contacts will become important at this location.

Mars

If you have misplaced your energy or drive, it will come back here. You may take up competitive sports, or you may simply be surrounded by macho men. You could work as hard as you play and will become much more assertive, although you could overdo this by becoming aggressive. You could find yourself amongst dangerously aggressive people, or a war-like situation might even arise. However, this could also be a great place in which to improve your sex life!

Jupiter

If you do not have a strongly Jupiterian chart yourself, this will add an expansive element to your nature. If you are already strongly Jupiterian, you will seek more freedom than you really need, and you may turn to gambling or other risky behaviors. Your luck will increase here, and your horizons will expand as you begin to explore new ideas and get to know people who are different from those with whom you are accustomed to associating. Foreign interests, legal matters, and education could become important to you here. You will also re-examine your most deeply held beliefs and perhaps change some of your views.

Saturn

This planet brings hard work, limitations, poverty, and sadness, but it is not all bad. You can put some real structure into your life and make tangible achievements at this location. Ambition and career matters will come to the fore, and your status will rise. Life will not be easy here, but it will be productive. Father figures or authority figures may become part of your life here. Naturally, this one is better for a working environment than a home and family life.

Uranus

This is the "breakout" planet that revolutionizes your life, so if you feel the need to turn your world upside down, take a trip to a Uranus line! You will make new friends and connections with interesting and unusual groups of people here. You may decide to study astrology at this location!

Neptune

Do you remember the old hippie slogan "Turn on, tune in, and drop out"? Well, this is the place to do it. If you need a quiet fishing holiday or time off from the hurly-burly of your daily life, this is the place to come to. If you stay at this location for any length of time, you may lose all ambition, becoming lost in a world of dreams and impractical or escapist ideas, and you could even take to drink or drugs! However, your artistic, psychic, and creative faculties will increase at this location.

Pluto

Transformation is the key idea at this location, so if you have something deep and dark in your psyche that needs to be brought to the surface and examined, it will happen here. Self-awareness on a major scale is a possible outcome, as is a deeper awareness of the motives and nature of other people. Joint financial matters will be important here, and your own finances could increase or decrease greatly as a result of joint financial arrangements. If sex hasn't been an issue in your life recently, it will become so here, and any relationships that are formed at this location will be deep, meaningful, difficult, and sexy.

Chiron

I have heard Chiron referred to by astrologers as an asteroid, a planetoid, a comet, and an escapee centaur from the Kuiper belt. Astrology books suggest that the position of Chiron in a chart shows the area of life where one has been wounded and where one can find inner healing, thereafter using this experience to heal others. As a working astrologer who has used Chiron ever since it came into astrological existence, this is not what I have found. Chiron seems to bring accidents and the sudden onset of unpleasant illnesses. Perhaps the sick person does learn something from this experience—perhaps not. In many cases, the Chironic shock to the system coincides with other disasters such as sudden financial losses or the unexpected breakup of a relationship. If you think you would learn anything from such "fun-filled" experiences, take an extended visit to your Chiron line. My personal choice would be to stay as far away from it as possible!

The Nodes of the Moon

My experience of working with the nodes of the Moon suggests that they have something to do with the lunar issues of home, family, and motherhood, so a trip to one of these lines will have an effect on these aspects of your life. Both nodes seem to connect with our karmic cycle of birth, life, death, and rebirth, and the North Node appears to move us forward on our karmic journey while the South Node brings back issues of the past. If you want to take your soul's journey a step or two into its future, I guess a trip to your North Node line would do it.

A Fateful Meeting!

Early in 1996, I went to Johannesburg, South Africa to fulfill a book and lecture tour. I stayed with friends and had a great time in that beautiful country. This was not surprising because both Mercury and Venus move to my IC in the area where I was temporarily living. In addition to this, the Uranus rise line crossed my Mercury and Venus lines at exactly the spot where I was giving my lectures. Uranus breaks down an existing order, often with little or no warning, after which it can very quickly set a new situation into place. My marriage to Tony Fenton was not so much on the rocks as buried under them, but despite the fact that I knew it was over, the last thing I was looking for was a new love interest. However, Venus, Mercury, and Uranus had their own ideas of how my life should go.

One evening, a man who was driving home turned on his car radio in order to catch the regular Saturday night astrology program. Instead of hearing one of the usual local astrologers, he heard my voice. When he realized who he was listening to, his ears really pricked up as he had several of my books in his collection, and he loved them. The man was Jan Budkowski, and he was on the committee of the Astrological Society of South Africa. Jan found himself attracted to something about me that transmitted itself to him across the radio waves, and when he heard me announce that I would be giving an advanced astrology workshop the following Saturday, he decided to attend. The weather that day was atrocious and the turnout to the workshop was small. This stroke of fate gave us an opportunity to chat together, and well before the day's end, we knew that something important was brewing. After many trials and tribulations, Jan and I are now happily married, living in London, and publishing mind, body, and spirit books together.

Local Space Astrology

The Local Space system is the brainchild of Michael Erlewine, who took the idea from celestial navigation and applied it to astrology. Mr. Erlewine called this "Local" space because he thought it would only apply to distances of a few miles around one's place of birth. Later on Mr Erlewine realized that the system also works on much greater distances, and he went on to create and market the software for this technique. The name "Local Space" is a trademark, but it is not copyrighted, which has made it much easier for astrologers to use without having to hide behind dark glasses!

The Local Space Astrology system is amazingly simple. Try picturing a newborn baby who comes into the world, out in the open air on a clear night. (*Figure 3.*) This baby, being highly intelligent and forward in his development, sits up, looks around, and sees the planets as they come up over the horizon. He mentally draws a line in the direction of each planet, through himself, and onwards around the world, much in the same fashion as Astro-map lines, except that the lines all start from one's place of birth. (*Figure 4.*)

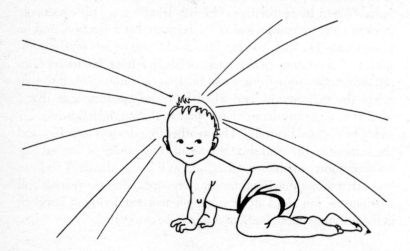

Figure 3.

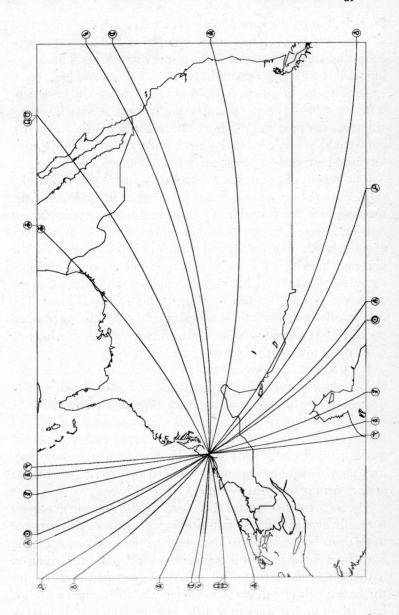

Figure 4. Local Space Chart

Each line carries the nature of the planet to which it belongs, thus a journey along or to a spot on any planetary line will bring experiences that are characterized by the planet in question. A move to a Jupiter line will bring opportunities for expansion and luck, but it could also bring litigation. A hop over to a Mars line will bring contact with men and energetic or sporting interests. A Mars line is exciting but not peaceful. A Saturn line might be a little depressing, but it could be very good for business, while a Neptune line is great for inward spiritual development or just a drunken weekend.

One benefit of Local Space Astrology is that it can be used locally. You can have a Local Space Astrology chart made up for the time at which you moved into your present home or your place of business. If you then place this simple pattern of lines over a map, aligning north, south, east, and west, you will soon see how the planetary lines work for you. Your happiest direction will be represented by pleasant Sun, Moon, or Venus lines, while those that energize you will be signified by Mars, Uranus, or even Pluto. The Neptune line may point to your local cinema or swimming pool, especially if you happen to enjoy visiting those places. A Mercury line could point towards the post office and local shops.

If you want to look inside your home in terms of Local Space Astrology, draw a rough plan of your house and place the chart over it, aligning north, south, east, and west. (*Figure 5.*) This will show you which parts of your house are lucky and which are not. If there is any place in your house that you are not happy with, you can improve matters by using Feng Shui techniques, such as carefully placing a plant there or by suspending a set of dangly chimes or a mobile arrangement of seashells over it.

The software that creates map charts for the Astro-map systems is readily available from most astrological software suppliers the world over. The ones I know best are Matrix for Windows and Solar Maps from Astrolabe, but there are others and more are coming on to the market all the time. My book *Astrology on the Move!* explains the system fully and shows you in detail how to interpret each line for yourself so that you can plot the best place for your holiday or business meeting, or so that you can unearth your soulmate in just the way that I did.

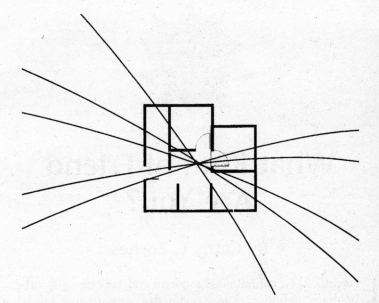

Figure 5. Local Space—House Plan Picture

What Kind of Friend Are You?

By Cathy L. Zornes

Everyone has a natural need to blend and associate with others. We have friendly exchanges every day of our lives and develop associations through daily contact at work, at social functions, in our neighborhood, and in our travels. We relate regularly to people on a superficial level, yet we are most attracted to those with whom we share a common thread. Friendships are formed between people who have a strong rapport and similar interests. Most of us desire deep connections in relationships that withstand the test of time. Some of us have "best" friends with whom we share a very special connection. In fact, life would be rather "lifeless" without friends to share it with. But do we really know what makes our friends tick?

Aries

Aries pals have a charming, witty personality that is long on enthusiasm and short on patience. There is a dynamic restlessness in their character; they want to capitalize on an idea the moment it enters their brain. Vibrant and enthusiastic at the start of any enterprise, they plan their actions and process their thoughts so swiftly that they appear careless and too quick to judge to others.

The Arien's role in life is to show others how to initiate action by taking the lead. They are logical and swift of mind, quick to offer ideas and make lightning fast decisions. They are anxious to act and often jump in without much forethought. They enjoy a wide variety of friends and interests; in fact, the Aries nature can seem a bit fickle due to its quick changeability. Ariens can alter their direction in a nanosecond, particularly if they become apathetic or if another item of interest captures their attention or better suits their needs.

In truth, the Arien's swift mind is capable of processing information instantaneously, eliminating unnecessary issues (like emotions) that only serve to inhibit progress. Friends are often intrigued by this admirable ability, yet it leaves the door open for misunderstandings; others periodically come to resent the seamless Arien efficiency. How would you like it if your Aries friend constantly beat you to the punch? Remember, Aries Suns don't take time to explain things to you, they expect you to keep up with them, and if you can't, oh well.

Ariens are highly self-conscious. They are likely to spend their energy on activities of personal interest, and when their interest wanes, they quickly become bored. They are not shy about asserting themselves and can be highly opinionated; they love any opportunity to express their viewpoints and beliefs. If you ask Aries friends for their opinion, be prepared, for they assume you are looking for an honest answer and will tell you exactly what they think without mincing words. You may perceive this as a bit insensitive, so if you are looking for someone to tell you what you want to hear, you may have to look elsewhere.

Ariens are friendly, open-minded, adaptable, and willing to work with others, but their energy is not necessarily made for cooperative efforts. This is something they have to learn if they want to be successful in social matters. They are naturally imbalanced in the area of cooperation with others and are frequently frustrated that other people simply don't move as fast as they do. With Aries, the name of the game is to continually move forward, so with every friendship or social situation, their goal is to expand their own realm. Don't take it personally if your Aries friend seems to have moved on to other interests, leaving you behind in search of new pastures. It isn't meant as a slight. Ariens rarely forget their friends—after all you never know who you'll meet up with again when you least expect it. They give their friends lots of space and expect the same in return. They are famous for having long-lasting friendships with infrequent contact. When you meet up again, the initial connection between the two of you will be instantaneously restored; in fact, they enjoy "catching up" with old friends. They will be more than happy to tell you about all the things they have been doing since they last saw you.

Ariens gravitate toward the center of action, and if the spotlight happens to shine a little on them, so much the better. They remain optimistic and often have unflappable faith in their own abilities, but long to have others recognize them as well. They are usually fun to be around, and their childlike enthusiasm naturally attracts others. They constantly seek greener pastures and are very open to change. They are willing to take gambles; in fact, walking through open doors often exposes them to new possibilities. Their goals constantly shift with their sights set on bigger and better things. In this regard, they can be rather unpredictable. Independence is very important to them; no moss gathers on this rolling stone. They are capable of uplifting others along the way with their own sense of excitement; yet when around them for too long, their driving energy can become a bit overbearing, and they can appear insensitive. For this reason, a little distance can serve a constructive purpose.

If your Aries friends seem too self-absorbed, try to understand that it is part of their nature to lead; their focus is on their own endeavors and they often leave others to fend for themselves. No slight is intended, just don't expect them to succumb to your expectations. Their impulsive acts can appear thoughtless and careless, but no malice is ever meant; in fact, they would be delighted to discuss the matter to clear the air and often use their quick wit to lighten the heaviness of the situation. If Arien friends don't seem to respond to your emotional ploys, it is because they are analytical creatures who are more eager to find a quick, logical solution. They don't have patience for overly emotional friends. They are good listeners but will be quick to suggest a few solutions, and you will be expected to either take their advice (or don't ask) or at least ponder their suggestions. Eventually, they will become impatient if you don't take some sort of action to correct your own situation; after all, that's what they would do.

Taurus

Taurus friends are without a doubt the most determined people in the zodiac. Above all, Taureans desire material gain, financial security, and some social status wouldn't hurt, either. Outwardly they are charming and accommodating, appearing rather easygoing with an added touch of surface sweetness. Their concern for their public image and reputation makes them conscious of social mores. They are careful to put their best foot forward and desire to be around others who exhibit good taste and social grace, as if their companions were a direct reflection on them.

The Taurean's role in life is to develop an appropriate consciousness regarding wealth, success, and abundance. They are attracted to tradition, substance, luxury, and quality—everything that constitutes good living. They gravitate toward upstanding people they admire and respect, judging them against their own standards of success or perfection. If they think well of someone, they practically idolize them, refusing to see their faults; yet they can also be critical of friends and acquaintances who choose to adopt a differing view. They are very aware of the "haves" and "have nots" and are drawn toward people who seem to have whatever they appreciate or aspire to attain. They can be quite envious of their friends' success and covet their possessions. They feel a sense of participation in a particular level of outward success by living vicariously through people of wealth and class who own nice things (even beyond their means, such as a lavish home or expensive clothing). However, their values tend to fluctuate and appreciate over time; they may desire something one week and want something else the next. They can be rather unrealistic about their own goals and aspirations, often wanting what others have, frequently looking sideways and comparing their own standing to that of their peers or to their own lofty ideals that they haven't yet achieved. After all, their goal in life is to acquire!

Taureans are fine hosts and hostesses. They enjoy entertaining at home in a comfortable and familiar environment, surrounded with good friends, good food, basic creature comforts, and their beautiful things. Their creative talents are often best expressed through earthy delights such as cooking, gardening, or home decorating.

They enjoy routine more than they may appear to on the surface. Change often makes them uneasy and doing things the "tried and true" way satisfies their fundamental need for stability and constancy. They are quite good at offering themselves in service to others and have a particularly creative flair for organizing social functions and coordinating activities. They possess endless patience to see things through to a successful conclusion. They are highly efficient organizers who find a sense of belonging through involvement in their church, school district, or neighborhood.

Friends often appreciate Taurus Suns' constancy, reliability, and readiness to help. Yet Taureans need to learn boundaries, for they often confuse true friendship with sympathetic support. Highly idealistic and trusting, they can experience deception through friends or associates. They are quite sensitive and easily caught up in the emotional whirlwinds of others. They can be unselfish and willing to help anyone in trouble, but may be easily drawn to unreliable people or into questionable situations.

Taureans desire friendships that are steady and reliable, and they prefer to cultivate lasting connections. They exhibit a nurturing and caring concern for their friends and family members and are able to murmur empathetic words of kindness when needed. This behavior, however, reflects their own sensitivity and desire to be loved and accepted. Their own fluctuating emotions come through loud and clear in conversation. Taureans often make emotional appeals and easily express their hurts and feelings to their friends. They are concerned about what others say about them. Their image is important, and they can be quite hurt or become resentful if they feel they have been slighted or mistreated. They have a tendency to view people through rose-colored glasses and can be somewhat naive, causing misunderstandings between friends and evoking sad stories of disillusionment due to unmet expectations.

Taureans are strongly attached to home and family, and many leisure activities will revolve around their personal arena. They strive to be model-perfect parents, have particularly high expectations for their children, and can be quite critical of other people's parenting methods. Being surrounded by material wealth makes them feel prosperous and secure. Although they may have a lazy streak, they desire abundance and will work relentlessly to get it, particularly if they see something as a means to an end. It is through their determination that you will witness their stubbornness, willfulness, and persistence.

Taureans are naturally affectionate, warm, and likeable. Just don't let that placid outer countenance fool you into thinking that you can mistreat them. They don't feel comfortable expressing their anger, but if pushed beyond their limit, they can respond with a violent temper. Coping with rivalry is difficult for them; in fact, they often pretend that whatever is out of their reach is not worthy of their consideration anyway!

Gemini

Gemini pals are quick to establish an affinity with others. They are mentally ambidextrous and delightfully creative, with a nonstop gift of gab. It seems to be their mission in life to communicate with others, share their ideas, and circulate information. In fact, sometimes they talk so much that others can hardly get a word in edgewise. You might think they simply love to hear themselves talk, when in truth, they have so many ideas flowing through their brain and such a strong desire to share them with others that they can't help themselves. In this manner, Geminis often use their friends as sounding boards. They'll talk to just about anyone, and they love recognition for their ideas, which are often quite ingenious.

Social activities are important to Geminis; they are pleasure-oriented with a light and airy approach to life. Friends recognize their fun-loving attitude, intellectual fluency, and lively, communicative style. You often learn a great deal from conversations with Geminis; they love to be in the know and on top of everything that is happening around them. Their brains are full of useful facts as well as useless trivia. If you want to get the word out about a party, tell a Gemini, and if you want to keep the party lively, invite several Geminis. Air signs know how to keep things circulating. However, don't be surprised if they arrive late, flirt with relish, and leave early; chances are they have another engagement that same evening.

Gemini is known to be a dual-natured sign, and Geminis have two distinct sides to their personality. They are very versatile and adaptable; in fact, they can be out-and-out quick-change artists.

Like a butterfly flitting from one flower to the next, they need to pollinate and circulate. If you expect to keep them as friends, you'll have to give them some room to move. Don't get upset if they are here one day and gone the next. By the time they get around to you again, they'll have all sorts of interesting new things to share with you.

Geminis are most comfortable in their local environment; home, family, neighborhood, and community are areas where they function best. Although interested in many different things, they focus mainly on matters that affect them daily and are within their realm of close, personal awareness. They are not as interested in the world at large or the big picture, which they have more trouble relating to. In fact, Geminis lose their sense of place when the crowd is too big; they prefer to develop their sense of self in a small, closer-knit community or group in which they can play a significant part. It is important for them to be up-to-date and well-informed.

The Gemini mind and body is constantly in motion. Geminis tend to move about at breakneck speeds; they think the faster they go, the more they can do in a day. If you ask them for directions, they'll give you the fastest route, not the scenic route. They excel at puzzles, word games, and brainteasers; in fact, they can outsmart most people. They grasp skills and ideas quickly, and their strong mental agility makes it easy for them to learn. However, the Gemini mind can be rather narrow in focus, skimming the surface instead of delving deep into a subject. At times Geminis need to cultivate the fine art of listening instead of jumping to conclusions and assuming what others mean. You may note that your Gemini friends have a tendency to be gossipy or a bit prankish; they are fond of pulling people's wires just for the fun of it. However, their pleasant, attractive personalities help them interact harmoniously with others by being flexible. If you are having a bad day, you can count on a conversation with a Gemini friend to lighten your mood, particularly their ability to offer a comedic twist to your dilemma.

Geminis enjoy expanding their viewpoints through one-on-one encounters with others and by sharing their knowledge and experience. They can be leaders among friends because of their zest for life and their ability to stir up excitement and get things going. It's unlikely, though, that they'll stick around long enough to see things through...chances are that something else will have grabbed their attention long before the finish line.

Cancer

Cancer chums desire loyalty from their friends and are usually very loyal in return. Above all, they need to be needed and are a bit reluctant to make the first move. They are tremendously understanding and highly sensitive, intuiting the moods and feelings of others around them. When they call to ask a favor, they can be a bit shy about speaking their mind and are rarely direct; they often beat around the bush before coming to the point. Fussy and finicky, they strive to be precise in their comments. They view society with a critical eye, and in their efforts to stay on top of things, they erroneously believe that if they are exacting, cooperative, and follow the rules perfectly, they can't be criticized.

Cancers are usually down to earth, with a naturally empathetic ear. They are attracted to people who share their interests, standards, and morals. You can call on them for practical advice, but after listening to your plight, they'll most likely leave the final decision up to you. Cancer friendships are enduring; in fact, it would take an awful lot to destroy a connection with one of them once it has been made. They prefer their friendships to be steady, and they cherish the memories of good times for their entire lives. They love to reminisce with old friends, and don't be surprised when they remember the names of your great aunt or your neighbor's dog. However, they can be quite unpredictable, often touchy and sensitive to the slightest thing, and you may notice that their moods change as often as they change their clothing.

Cancers are terrific organizers, and they enjoy helping out in practical ways at social gatherings. Their financial acumen and organizational talents make them a welcome asset to any fund-raising or administrative endeavor. They know how to organize a large dinner party and prepare it at a modest cost, usually with all the comforting touches of home cooking.

The Cancer's role in life is to show us how to operate purely from the senses. Cancers are quite spiritually minded and intuitive. They are sensitive to the plights of others and soft-hearted. They will go out of their way to lend aid to anyone in need and often are guilty of overreacting to the problems of those around them. Their behavior reflects like a mirror, often imitating the type of behavior they desperately want to receive from others. They must be cautious of their intense mothering urges. They are naturals at tending to others; that's why they make good parents, nurses, and teachers.

Cancers have a natural desire to establish emotional connections with other people, but they have a tendency to cling to situations or relationships that are not good for their well-being. Their motivation is a strong need for security and fear of the unknown. They will tolerate an adverse situation rather than take the chance of losing something or someone who is important to them. They are often drawn to those who are needy, which gives them a reason to nurture, a reason to be needed. They must learn to maintain high standards and a proper sense of self and not fall into the "give to get back" habit. They are often successful in associations with other females and prefer to meet others through friends or family members.

In fact, Cancers can be quite reclusive and secretive of their private enjoyments, preferring to go off alone or read a book rather than subject themselves to the demands of others. When in a negative state, they can be quite jealous of their friends, often looking sideways and wishing they possessed what others have. When your Cancer friends start looking sideways, remind them of their own resources and talents; they need constant encouragement to keep facing forward.

Cancers can be quite attached to their heritage and family. They view their home as a haven and find comfort in surrounding themselves with their special belongings. If you need to borrow something, remember that they don't lend their possessions easily and will be eager to have them returned in a timely manner.

If you leave conscientious Cancer friends in charge of watching your home while you are out of town, they will appreciate a list of instructions, which will be followed to the letter. Additionally, you can rest assured they will leave everything in its place; the plants will look healthier than they did when you left, and the mail will be organized on the kitchen counter next to a list of things they did while you were gone.

However, try to be mindful that your Cancer friends budget their time, so they may not be able to drop everything when you drop by unexpectedly. Don't get upset if your they are agreeable to everything at first, then back out at the last minute. This is a result of their desire to be agreeable and of their inability to say "no" and mean it, at least until they are backed into a corner. Cancers operate best doing things in their own way and in their own time.

Leo

Whether shy or flamboyant, "magnanimous of spirit" accurately describes the regal Leo personality. Leo pals are often popular and gregarious; in fact, when you are near them, their exuberance is downright contagious. People are drawn to them for their natural leadership ability, courage, and assertiveness. In turn, Leos are very aware of the world around them and are always poised for action.

Most Leos are easy to approach because of their friendly manner, and they are able to put other people at ease with their charming gift of gab. They care what other people think and say and are consciously aware that their ego gratification is dependent on cooperative efforts with others. Leos have a need to integrate their personal talents into the larger social realm, with a strong desire to be personally involved in something bigger than themselves that will also benefit or bring joy to others. To this end, they often form associations with others who have social influence.

Leo friends are incredibly fun to be around, for they know how to enjoy life. You'll know the party has begun when they walk into the room, and throughout the evening you will hear them telling their colorful tales. Life is like a playground in which to explore their creative talents, and they frequently gravitate toward a career in the entertainment fields or one that puts them in a position of social prominence. Leos can be demanding friends, expecting loyalty from their colleagues. They also expect you not to mind that they always grab the spotlight. Leos do best with a passel of adoring friends who are content to circle around them and bask in the rays of their shining light. They literally seem to thrive on attention. Yet when someone else grabs the spotlight, you'll notice that Leos leave the room in search of another audience of their own.

Friends often admire their Leo friends' confidence and self-assurance. It's rare that you see them in a bad mood, mostly because when they are feeling down they retreat to sort things out on their own and only come back around when the storm has passed and their sunny nature is once again illuminating every room they enter.

Although not as easy to spot, you'll find there are many quiet lions about. They are the kind who walk around with an upward tilt to the head; they are much too dignified to boast or make a scene. They wait for their well-deserved recognition in a proud, silent manner, like royal kings or queens. Of course, their egos are quite large, and they desperately need to be stroked and adored. Some Leos are too easily flattered. When things aren't going their way, they can be selfishly demanding, overbearing, and quite stubborn. Their pride often leads the way, so their worst punishment is to be humbled and humiliated.

Leos enjoy entertaining their friends in a lavish, expansive manner, sometimes beyond the bounds of good taste, although you can be sure their intent is to impress. Be prepared to offer flattering compliments as this often is all a Leo friend needs to feel successful. If you have a party, Leos won't come empty-handed. In fact, they usually bring the best gifts—yes, they appreciate your friendship enough to buy you copious gifts, but they also like the compliments they get for having such good taste! Unfortunately, the attention they give others is mostly meant to highlight their sense of generosity and often intended to bring applause or attention back to them.

Leos enjoy a variety of friends from all walks of life with whom they connect on an intellectual level. They have a strong need to communicate, often in a comedic and entertaining way. Easily bored by humdrum life, they are eloquent circulators who need to be where the action is. Because of this tendency, they can appear somewhat fickle in their friendships—whoever offers them the most is their best friend for the moment. Leos often ripen with age, like a fine wine. Once they have captured the audience in their own backyard, they need to grow toward a much larger audience. A Leo's light can shine brightest when it's for the benefit of all to bask in.

Virgo

Virgos are very attached to their friends; in fact, they treat their close friends like family. They are most at ease being part of small gatherings or close-knit groups. In larger circles, Virgos, who are typically shy and at times unsure of themselves, tend to blend into the background and visually size up the occupants of the room. It takes them quite a while before they begin to feel comfortable. Their thought processes are deep and analytical, as you will discover when you talk to them. They aren't much for small talk, unless you find a subject they happen to be very interested in. They can sense when others are uncomfortable and know this feeling intimately, so they are usually quite eager to put others at ease, possibly by offering to be of some sort of service. They appear very concerned about others, asking questions rather than offering personal commentary.

Your Virgo friends may deliver constructive comments that are meant to help, but at times their comments can make you feel as if you are under a microscope. They have an inherent need to be perfect in all details and turn their perfectionistic eye both on themselves and on those to whom they are close. Usually well-meaning, they may tuck your shirt label in if it is sticking out or point out that you have a stain on your collar. They are reluctant to offer an opinion, but occasionally they reveal their observations in a manner that is quite direct. Depending on the circumstances, this behavior can be helpful, or irritating and embarrassing. However, if you admonish a Virgo friend for making inappropriate statements, they will be shocked at your accusations. They never intend the wounds that periodically result from their remarks. Because of this tendency, they learn to keep their thoughts to themselves or choose their words very carefully.

Keep in mind that your Virgo friends are worriers. They take the smallest of disappointments to heart and can be easily discouraged by other people's negative reactions when their desire to please fails. The slightest adversity deflates their balloon. They are particular about method and prefer established routines in their life. Don't expect your Virgo friends to accept a wishy-washy answer or to be content with an appointment time of "two-ish"—they'll want a definite time, and you can be sure they will be slightly miffed if you are late, even if they don't show it. Remember, Virgos tend to take things personally, and their analytical minds begin reading into silent signals. However, they don't usually hide their feelings, and if they feel someone is being dishonest with them, they will say so in an effort to clear the air more than anything.

Virgos have the ability to zero in on any topic and are quite investigative. In conversation, they tend to be inquisitive, with a need to know. They process incoming sensory matter like they would scientific data. After they have had time to assimilate or sift through information, they will feel inclined to comment. However, they learn to contain their fact-finding revelations after they realize that others may not be as interested in all the little details as they are. They are terrific at secretarial and administrative work with their eye for order and organization. They also make fine writers, editors, and journalists as they try very hard to state the facts in a correct and concise manner. Many times you may hear your Virgo friends complain because the value of their work is not recognized. Often they find themselves lost in the ranks of a large company and, because of their modest posturing, don't always gain the recognition they desire and deserve.

If you go anywhere with your Virgo friends, make sure the food is good and the facilities are clean. They have distinct likes and dislikes when it comes to food, and fastidious Virgos are so keen on cleanliness that they can spot a germ a mile away!

Libra

Libra friends' most likeable qualities are their diplomacy and charming, affable nature. Friends are very important to them, and their purpose in life is to connect with others. They often gravitate toward people who are cultured and have achieved a position of intellectual or creative recognition. They have a friendly yet aloof intellectual quality and a broad-minded, worldly awareness. Optimistic and cheerful in their outlook on life, they are public personalities with an ability to sell themselves effectively through their wit and charm.

Libras can be thoughtful in their concern for others, but they are more likely to offer an intellectual solution to a problem rather than rolling up their sleeves and getting their hands dirty helping someone. Friendly and open-minded with their associates, they are charismatic, humorous, and politically correct. They are defenders of justice, and at times they can be quite forthright in their comments. They are eager to discuss their own philosophies and search for higher-minded qualities in others; yet they are intolerant of and equally quick to criticize those who are prejudiced or close-minded in any way. You can be sure they will deliver their comments with a bit of sugar coating, however. They won't utter an indignant word if it could ruin their image or reputation, or, heaven forbid, cause a brawl.

Libras have their sights set high, but they frequently go along with the crowd in lieu of carving their own path. They are drawn to those who exhibit strength and leadership in group activities. They enjoy teamwork and are graciously accepted as team leaders themselves because of their sense of justice, lack of self-absorption, and ability to make balanced assessments. You can count on your them to be fair-minded in their appraisal of situations; they want to consider both sides of an argument before reaching a conclusion and can be quite candid in their responses. If one of their friends is upset, Libras will suggest a walk together in the park or a stroll through the art museum—anything to gain distance and perspective. They are also quite content sharing moments of silence with their companions.

Libras often receive recognition when playing the gracious host or hostess. They know how to select just the right food and drink, and they know which people to join together. However, they can be quite changeable with their friends—not that they lack loyalty, they simply seek to spread their own wings socially. They may be reluctant to switch camps until they have secured themselves in another; after all, the worst thing for them would be to find themselves out in the cold. They will rarely do something that will offend their old friends. In fact, they will wholeheartedly deny any suggestion of abandonment. Easygoing Libras can be easily manipulated by emotional or controlling friends because of their desire to please. When confronted, they go into automatic denial and try very hard to appease the offended party. They abhor scenes or ugly behavior.

Don't expect your Libra friends to make decisions quickly. They weigh their options, evaluating the advantages and disadvantages, before they are willing to commit. Yet, when asked for their opinion, they may habitually say "whatever you want is fine with me," being reluctant to take a stand to get their own needs met. Since maintaining harmony is their top priority, they will often go along with the majority and hold their tongue in order to keep the peace. They have a frustrating tendency of saying what they believe others want to hear and then doing whatever they want, anyway. They don't see this as dishonest; their goal is to promote agreement and avoid confrontation, and they will sacrifice their own needs to achieve that end. In fact, it is rare that they will tell you exactly what they think. Wanting to be truthful, but more concerned with harmonious conditions, they tiptoe around, glossing over their words to make them as palatable as possible.

Libras can be quite concerned with their outer image, taking pride in what they wear, how they look, and with whom they spend time. They will be sure to notice your new hair color or how marvelous that shade of blue looks on you. They are drawn to beautiful people of elegance, class, and good taste, and they are impressed by those who have achieved a broad spectrum of accomplishments. They constantly seek to expand their own horizons through travel, education, and other forms of intellectual stimulation.

Just don't expect your Libra friends to be tolerant of your whining—no emotional tirades here, please! Get a grip!

Scorpio

People often admire their Scorpio friends' efficiency. Scorpios have the ability to take charge of any situation, and they wait for just the right moment to scoot in and do so.

Scorpio companions typically are true friends who give practical advice only when asked. They have a sense of propriety and appear highly in control of their own emotions, yet their facial expressions often reveal the sharp logical and methodical analysis that is constantly going on in their heads. They have an eye for success in any situation and are capable of making the most astute observations. They are excellent listeners and masters at giving advice—but don't waste any time offering yours. Their calculated minds already have everything figured out in more detail than most people even begin to concern themselves with.

Scorpios have their own exacting way of celebrating an occasion; in fact, things are so meticulously coordinated that your Scorpio hosts will be annoyed if you miss any part of their grand display. When they say dinner at eight, be there with bells on or you'll miss a lavishly prepared and precisely executed event, where the wine is just the right temperature and the puff pastry is exquisitely light and delicate. Scorpios are every bit as perfectionistic as Virgos, but much more willful.

Scorpios are highly complex individuals with penetrating gazes that give away their deep and keen minds. However, in private, they can be much gentler than they seem; in fact, they revel in a romantic dinner with soft music or a spiritual retreat where life's mysteries can be contemplated. They have true compassion for those they care about, but their tendency toward extremes often compels them either to be reluctant to offer assistance or, just the opposite, to completely take over. I'm afraid there is no halfway point with a Scorpio. Relationships can be just as consuming. Yes, they crave loyalty from friends and can be jealous at the slightest hint of a rival.

Nothing misses the eyes of your Scorpio friends. Their penetrating minds are not suited for whimsy, nor are they entertained by frivolous pastimes. (Don't even think about asking them to join in a game of Twister!) They do, however, become involved with great relish in anything in which they have a genuine interest. Your Scorpio friends are also quite perceptive and can easily detect dishonesty, so don't think any comment will easily slip by—you can't fool them for a second.

Scorpios come in several variations, but there are two distinct types: the Poker-Faced Strategists and the Un-Cover Agents. The Strategists always play their cards close to their chest. Friends may feel uncomfortable with their inability to discern where they stand with these Scorpio friends. It is quite obvious that there is much more going on beneath the surface with these people than is revealed. When they divulge information, they disclose only part of the whole story. The undercurrents that exist after a conversation with a Scorpio can leave you with a feeling that things are not totally on the up and up, and after discussions with others you may discover that the conversation was a bit distorted to extract your Scorpio friend's well-planned and desired result; and, yes, when they want their way, it is not beneath them to use underhanded methods.

The Un-Cover Agents have marvelous detective abilities, but also an annoying habit of incessant questioning. You'll recognize these more revealing Scorpios by their constant vocal scrutinization of every little thing. A steady diet of this, particularly the obvious questions, will drive the most sane individual crazy. This goes to show the amount of analysis that is constantly going on within their complex minds. The problem is that these people attempt to drag everybody else into their intellectual labyrinth, which leaves us with the question...do we really want to know what they are thinking, or would we all be better off if they kept it to themselves?

Sagittarius

Like their Leo fire sign counterparts, Sagittarians have a personality that is often larger than life. It isn't uncommon for them to have far-fetched, quixotic schemes and idealistic philosophies. What is interesting, though, is Sag's ability to convince others of their feasibility and validity. Anything is possible to your Sagittarius friends—just ask them.

These happy-go-lucky people have the proverbial gift of gab. They make friends wherever they go and are fun to be around. I haven't met a Sagittarius yet who didn't travel whenever he or she found the opportunity to and return with a passel of new acquaintances to boot. Friendly and adaptable, with a preference for impermanence, these freedom lovers seek to expand their horizons every chance they get. Well-meaning, optimistic Sagittarians often promise more than they could possibly deliver. These people are quite generous as well as being good sports with altruistic intentions, even thought they have a tendency to let others down on occasion.

Centaurs believe life is for the living, and they live it to the fullest. Physically fit Sagittarians are aggressive in sports and recreation and often do best with other pals who have the inclination to take risks and the enthusiasm to keep up with them. You'll find them in a hot air balloon, on a ski slope or tennis court, biking, or ascending the side of a mountain. Afterward, they will entertain you with stories of their adventures, which may be a bit exaggerated, but you'll be delighted by their colorful tales of their supposed conquests anyway. More diverse individuals are hard to find.

Of course, there is another side to the Sagittarius personality. If your friends are not the rugged, outdoor type, you will be equally amazed at their brain power. They are as intellectually vast as they are adventurous; Sagittarians are particularly enthralled with science and medicine, weather, space exploration, sales, and international business. In fact, they are such intellectual explorers that they often come up with their own theories and aren't afraid to challenge others.

Because Sagittarians are prone to move about, their friendships also need to be flexible. Sagittarians like to stay footloose, for they never know what new adventure might be just around the corner. A suitcase on wheels and e-mail are the perfect inventions for them.

However, Sagittarians feel rather uncomfortable in emotional situations and will usually try to jolt others out of a bad mood with a good joke or a humorous twist on their situation. Optimists to the extreme, you can count on your Sagittarius friends to help you see the bright side; they will most certainly be successful in helping to cheer you out of your doldrums. The truth is, Sagittarians can't face the down side of life; they always focus on the chance that in most situations there must be a light at the end of the tunnel and tease that hopefully it isn't an oncoming train! They are good listeners and have great depth of understanding, but you may have to take a number or catch them on the way to the airport if you hope to grab a few minutes of their time.

Sagittarians have big dreams and aspirations, but their success is dependent on how personally disciplined they are, and luck often plays a part as well. You can be sure your Sagittarius friends' homes contains trinkets from their many travels, service awards, and plaques of recognition, which are proudly displayed on the walls.

You can't help but admire your Sagittarius friends' positive attitude; their well of optimism is deep and their idealistic outlook often goes a long way in their favor. This attitude enables them to focus on the advantages of life's situations and capitalize on any opportunities that come their way. Most Sagittarians have won their share of uphill battles, and they'll be quick to help you tackle yours as well. They immediately zero in on the possibilities in any situation, but can have large blinders on when it comes to facing the cold, hard reality of most circumstances. Sagittarians don't know when to quit and often take big risks mostly due to their confidence that they will get a lucky break—and their friends often marvel at how often their Sagittarius friends land on their feet.

Capricorn

Capricorns are ambitious people, and heaven help anybody who gets in the way of them attaining their goals! Their objective in life is to attain a position of status, and they often appear dissatisfied, aspiring to surpass their latest accomplishment. Similar to Aries and Scorpio, Capricorns don't waste their energy. They participate in activities that specifically interest them, yet their focus is on getting ahead—what's in it for me. They won't waste their time on trivial matters. However, your Capricorn friends have very deep feelings that are not often revealed, and therefore they are not very easy to get to know. In fact, their outer persona can be quite cold and calculating, but this is only part of their true personality.

Capricorns are practical individuals who bring solid structure to any organization or group; they constantly have their eye on anything of importance. They take on responsibility as if no one else can do the task as well as they can. Frequently they appear to be caught up in their own thoughts (and worries); at times they have the ability to shut out the world, which doesn't help much in the way of cultivating friends. Actually, they are a bit shy, somewhat isolating, and far too serious for their own good. Be careful of criticizing your Capricorn friends, for they take things to heart. They are often very self-conscious and discontent with their own success, anyway.

Friendships are often made through their career, which is where Capricorns need to blend with others as they climb their own ladder to success. They can be steadfast friends and are attracted to those who share their sense of ambition, but they won't let a friendship get in the way of success, and they avoid superficial relationships like the plague! They value a comfortable and secure home life and can be quite lazy and contented when surrounded by their loved ones and the possessions they have worked so hard to acquire.

Capricorns focus on their responsibilities and career ambitions; they seem to spend more time in that realm of life than on home and leisure activities. However, they will work very hard to maintain a safe and sound domestic life, which is paramount to assure their outer success.

Capricorns are duty bound. They have a tendency to act rather parental at times toward those they care about. But they are highly dependable and loyal to those who return their devotion. Often Capricorns are born into an atmosphere that can either be quite chaotic or heavily disciplined, and they learn early on to accept responsibility. If you need sound, practical advice, a Capricorn friend is a godsend! Their sense of authority and practical solutions are comforting to those with less confidence, and their constancy is admirable as well as reassuring.

Always trying to define their accomplishments, Capricorns have a tendency to look sideways at other people's success and compare it to their own; they need some sort of concrete validation to prove how they are doing in life. Capricorns are rather selective about who they make friends with and are drawn to powerful, ambitious types. If they value your input and feel that your association is an advantageous one, you can be assured they will be there for the long haul; yet Capricorns can experience manipulation and power struggles where friends are concerned, particularly if their motives are to align themselves with others only to increase their own position.

Just don't expect your Capricorn friends to express their feelings easily. They will assume you know they care by their support and dedication. They show their affection by being of practical assistance. Capricorns appear self-sufficient and rarely ask for help; they try to do everything themselves. A basic insecurity causes them to conceal their feelings so others don't know they are needy in any way. The best compliment you can give your Capricorn friend is genuine heartfelt appreciation.

Aquarius

On the average, Aquarians are happy, optimistic people—but there is nothing really average about them. They assert their individuality in friendships; in fact, people often admire and envy Aquarians for their independent manner. They are the ones who can start new fads, say the unexpected, or add a jolt of eccentricity and excitement to a group to liven it up...when they choose to participate, that is.

Aquarius pals view things from a broad spectrum. They are often intellectually ahead of their peer group and may gravitate toward associations with mature individuals. They are social beings who seek to be involved in many different situations and with many types of people, and they prefer large social events to tight-knit friendships.

You can usually pick Aquarians out of a crowd; they are the tall, thin people who stand at the perimeter of the room, quietly observing everyone. Detached observation often precedes actual participation. The last thing Aquarians want is to be tied down by commitment or obligation. Freedom of movement is essential. Allowing them to contribute what they want and when they want to is often the best approach to maintaining their friendship. Although Aquarians are somewhat impersonal in their affection, they are not usually self-centered in any way.

Aquarians are quick to mentally size things up and are anxious to act. Their personal development throughout life is mainly through the intellect and the conscious mind. They are usually one step ahead of everyone else. Aquarians trust their own instincts and are highly intuitive. They jump to conclusions and believe that their assumptions are correct. They rarely consult others, having unflappable faith in their own judgments and analytical skills. People sense their self-containment; Aquarians are not too concerned about what other people think, and they are certainly not interested in getting involved in any emotional melodrama.

Friends may find Aquarians fun to be around, but they also never quite know what to expect from them. These rational-minded diplomats have much charisma when dealing with others, but they need their space and tend to distance themselves either physically or mentally when they feel the walls closing in. They desire to be around others who share their higher social principles and humanitarian philosophies. They happily participate in group activities and give freely of their time as long as their personal freedom isn't constrained. They make good friends because they offer others the same freedom that they demand. Just don't expect too much close and personal chumminess from them.

We could all learn a valuable lesson from Aquarians. They are terrific friends, and they know how to keep things on a nonemotional, easy level. However, don't look to them to be a shoulder to cry on; they'll feign good listening skills, but find an excuse to depart at the first sign of emotions. Just when you think you have them figured out, they do something completely unexpected and often a bit unsettling. Their goal in life is to be unpredictable.

Pisces

Gentle and peace loving, Pisceans are the most easygoing, compassionate, and empathetic friends you'll find. They seem to have an instinctual, intuitive understanding of other people's feelings. Yet sensitive Pisceans need to establish boundaries in their associations with others, for they are too easily sucked up into the emotional vortex of those around them. Often quite idealistic, you can count on your Pisces friends to be hopeful and optimistic. They try to see the best in others—just don't ask them to be realistic. Their strongest attributes include selfless compassion and visionary abilities.

Pisceans are highly social, but need to develop a more realistic awareness in their interactions and communication with others and in their everyday environment. They have an inherent belief that everyone is good. They appreciate the values of others and often enjoy being around people who have well-developed social skills and moral and spiritual values, as well as those who offer creative inspiration. It's not surprising that they have a tendency to glamorize or idolize those they encounter. They seek to align themselves with those who have social or monetary status.

You may have psychic links with your Pisces friends, who pick up the telephone to call you the same time you try to call them. Pisceans uses their sensory faculties to develop their minds and can be quite artistic and creative, specifically with regard to dance, music, poetry, or photography. They often have a melodious, soft, and soothing voice that is always thoughtful and never harsh.

Your Pisces friends will sacrifice their own needs for any worthy cause. They work with unending determination to help others and often find themselves in the position of empathetic listener of the plights of others. Because of self-doubt and guilt, they often take on responsibilities that are above and beyond the call of duty. You can count on your them to be there for you in a time of need, to listen for countless hours and provide soothing words of encouragement as you pour your heart out. Yet if your Pisces friends are in a quandary of their own, they may be incapable of responding to your crisis in an effective manner or offering any real assistance. They are not very good at facing the cruel realities of life when hit with them personally; yet they have great strength to deal with the plight of the downtrodden or those suffering from disease. This is why they make good nurses, crusaders, and social workers.

At times, it's tough to put a finger on your Pisces friends because they seem elusive and changeable. They may also be unintentionally dishonest, for they avoid saying anything that will make waves and usually take the easy way out of tight situations. Their indecisiveness can be frustrating at times, as well as their inability to be realistic. Pisceans are dreamers who find it hard to cope with the harshness of reality. Naive and gullible, their energies are fluid as they encounter their own life situations. Their optimistic idealism can lead them down many dead-end streets, leaving them disillusioned. They may begin to feel sorry for themselves and seek a friendly ear. They may be escape artists when it comes to the pressures of everyday living, yet when it comes to helping their friends they seem to know just what to do, letting practical service take over and not letting emotion get in the way.

Friendships with Pisceans can be very supportive and long lasting; however, at times Pisceans choose to avoid friendships if they seem too heavy or restrictive. Friends may notice that they are a bit insecure at times and often need a boost in the self-confidence department. Pisceans are drawn to those who are mature, successful, and even parental. They can be unaware of the impact of their creative imagination and visionary qualities, and they may look to friends for encouragement and help in structuring their goals.

What Gives You Joy?

The Sun: Bringer of All Things Bright and Beautiful

By Kim Rogers-Gallagher

You don't have to be an astrologer to understand how vital the Sun is. Just step outside on a warm, bright afternoon and feel the warmth of its touch on your skin. Look around and see how it sheds its golden light on all living things. The Sun is our very own star, the fiery orb who provides the Earth with the life force we depend on for our survival.

On a personal and astrological level, the Sun is equally important. It's the center of your individual universe, the core of your personality, and the most apt description of your life's quest you'll ever find. In fact, the strength of this star in your astrology chart simply can't be underestimated. Mercury allows you to communicate with others, exchange ideas, and navigate your way through a room, but he's working for your Sun, on a life-long fact-finding mission with the Sun's interests in mind. Life wouldn't be much fun without Venus, that lovely lady who shows who and what you love and how you love it—but she, too, takes her orders from the Sun. Even Saturn lays down his rules with the Sun's specific interests in mind.

In a nutshell, then, all of the planets in your chart have one very basic task: to help your Sun accumulate the experiences it needs so that you can eventually grow into the person you're "supposed" to be. In order to find that person, you've got to get to know yourself first; in other words, you've got to discover what it is that gives you joy, what it is that you automatically do best because you just love doing it. The Sun is your key to finding that joy, the planet that describes you at your creative best. It's your true self, pure You energy. It's you as you'd be if you never, ever had to do anything again that you didn't want to do. It's your ego, your pride, and your urge to shine and be recognized. Although that's the type of description of the Sun you'll find in just about every basic astrology text, there's one thing that's usually not mentioned about the Sun: the fact that its house position also tells an awful lot about who and what gives us joy—the pure joy of being alive. Needless to say, other folks are a very important part of our lives here on the Earth, since we've got an awful lot of company. But each and every person we encounter and everything we "do" has a message of some kind to share, and a reason to show up. The folks who are represented by the house the Sun occupies in our astrology chart are the ones who'll help us most with our journey, and the experiences described by that house show where to aim for maximum growth and maximum joy. Since the Sun shows your reason for being, its house position also describes who you might choose to emulate as you travel your path through life.

Let's take a look at each of the houses, then. We'll talk about the folks who "live" there, who occupy such an important position in our lives, and the experiences we should be looking towards for fun, life lessons, and joy. Keep in mind that each house in your astrology chart is very much like a "room" in a home, where a very particular "slice" of you lives. This side of you only comes out when that specific life situation presents itself—or when people who represent that side of life are in the neighborhood. We'll start our visit at the "front door" of the chart, the First House, where everything about our physical appearance and personal presentation is found.

Sun in the First House

Some folks say that first impressions are the most important ones, and that the initial impact we have on others is the one that lasts. Others say those first impressions are often misleading, that you've got to "get to know" someone to make a decision about what kind of person he or she is. Well, they're both right. It's very important to make a good impression on others by creating a front door they'll want to step through; otherwise, they might not take the time to get to know us at all. On the other hand, first impressions can be very inaccurate. After all, the front door of a house doesn't say much about who's inside. Still, this house describes what folks will remember about you, so any planet with permanent residence here contributes to that impression. It's as if we wear our First House planets like a t-shirt with huge letters on it. That word is the first thing folks spot, the first thing they "meet," and the first thing they'll associate with who they think we are.

With the Sun in this house, the Executive Director has an office right at the front of the building. When you enter that building, you're greeted by a bright, shiny creature, someone who can warm you up by the simple touch of their extended hand. If your Sun is in the first house, you're wearing a "welcome" sign. Every encounter will bring you joy, since it allows you to shine, to present yourself to another person. The Sun innately understands the beauty and potential that lies in each of us, the "specialness" we all hold. That potential is never clearer or fuller than during an introduction, when we encounter a brand-new bundle of energies for the very first time. There's no "baggage," no memories, nothing but what might be. In particular, then, your first meetings are the ones that will bring you joy and inspire you to be the very best that you can be. Put yourself in an occupation that allows you contact with new folks every day, and you'll be a very happy person.

On another level, the First House also describes your physical appearance. With the Sun here, pride in your body and the way you dress yourself are very important issues. Folks who help you to look and act your very best will bring you joy, too, then—whether it's an exercise instructor, a hair stylist or cosmetician, or a personality coach. Any way you shake it, the Sun in this house is looking for applause and recognition because of how it presents itself and how it looks to others. Taking special care with your appearance every day and dressing according to your mood is vital to your happiness.

Sun in the Second House

Although this house is traditionally described as the "money and possessions" house, in reality it shows what you hold dear, both with regard to what you own and those qualities you admire and respect in others. With the Sun in this house, your inner happiness will be on "high" when you're showing the world just how valuable you are. This could mean that you take great joy in your work, since it allows you to show off your own special talents. No matter what you actually "do" for money, be sure that you enjoy it, and that it's a true reflection of who you are. You'll need to feel as if you're being paid adequately for your time, too. On another level, you may be wonderfully adept at handling money and possessions, a regular whiz kid with stocks, financial deals, and money strategies that would leave most of us baffled. Tending to the care and order of your checkbook and your possessions will build your pride and self-confidence. It's probably also true that you'll need to have a rather sizable bank account set aside in order to feel secure. If that's the case, be careful not to become so wrapped up in money that you forget you're trading actual hours of your life to earn it. Remember, experiences are equally valuable to your growth as a person.

As with all the houses, there are people who "live" in this area of our lives. With the Sun here, folks who help you to hone your skills are the "residents" of this house, and those who will give you the most joy. Financial mentors or supervisors who teach you your trade will mean a great deal to you, then, as will those who help you make money. You'll also take great joy in folks whose personal qualities are described by your Sun sign. But there's much more to this house, on a much deeper level. Your real joy will come through those who show you their value, their worth in your life, by being faithful and steadfast. Spend your valuable time with tried and true friends, and you'll always be happy.

Sun in the Third House

The third house is a very busy place. It's owned and operated by Mercury, that fleet-footed messenger of the Gods—a guy who never did know how to sit still or be quiet. He was born with wings on his head and his feet, qualifications that made him the perfect "shuttle" between the gods and the mortals. This god always had people to see and things to do, so if you were born with the Sun residing in this house, you're probably very much like Mercury personified. Your greatest joy will come from taking care of mercurial tasks, then—errands, short trips, and quick communications. You may literally love to drive, and it may even be your occupation. If not, you may write, be a reporter, or speak for a living, and story-telling is probably one of your most amazing talents. Of all your skills, however, your ability to handle several tasks simultaneously is probably quite famous among your friends and family members. This wonderful skill means you're perfectly suited to work as a receptionist, switchboard operator, or grade school teacher.

Now, this house also pertains to that time when we learn all the routine functions we'll need to get by throughout life—childhood. As a result, siblings and schoolmates are very important to Third House Suns, as are the teachers who helped you learn the basics—your intellectual foundation. Since routine is such a pleasant part of your life, you'll probably also be quite involved with your neighbors and with those you see on a daily basis. You'll take great joy in greeting each and every familiar face in the post office, grocery store, and coffee shop, and in chatting with them, too. In fact, you're probably on a first name basis with everyone who works in the businesses you visit often.

In all, you're very much like a walking "hospitality committee," which means you're also very happy being involved in "chance encounters": with strangers, none of whom will stay strangers for long. Everyone around you will be warmed by the warmth of your presence and by your innate skill for carrying on at least three charming conversations at once. Be careful not to scatter your energies, however, or you'll suffer from stress. Take time to smell the roses, if for no other reason than that you'll be able to tell someone about them later.

Sun in the Fourth House

Born with the Sun in this house, you're a natural "family person." Whether your childhood was especially challenging or especially wonderful, it made quite an impact on the rest of your life—and you bring the tone of your emotional memories into every encounter. If your family unit was strong and supportive, you'll have an inner confidence and keen instinct that will carry you through even the most difficult situations beautifully. If your childhood was difficult, you may have matured with a very firm goal in mind: to undo the past and create a wonderful foundation for your own family. Either way, your parents and your own children will give you joy, if you lovingly accept them as they are.

You're probably a very private person, very fond of your home and all the articles in it. You may also have a special talent for crafts or hobbies that are home-oriented. The work that would bring you the most happiness on a daily basis, then, might be a job in interior design or real estate—or you may simply operate your business out of your home, perhaps doing daycare or working with others in their homes. Emotional security is primary for you, so no matter where you live or who you share your residence with, it will need to be a "nest" rather than a place to simply hang your hat. You're probably also very happy to putter around your home on weekends and not much of a traveler, unless it's in a motor home, the ideal solution for Fourth House Suns that long to see the world but can't bear the thought of not being "home." Your idea of the perfect "vacation," then, may be to simply stay home for the duration, tending to family matters and making each room warm and welcoming to all.

No matter what you do, remember that security and familiarity are the qualities that will bring you joy. Surround yourself with people you know you can trust, and don't ever ignore your instinct.

Sun in the Fifth House

The Sun naturally belongs to Leo, who's the proud and happy owner of this house. If you were born with the Sun here, then, you're probably a very contented individual—and you definitely know how to play. Your hobbies and leisure-time interests will be the activities that bring you joy, so if you haven't already, you should definitely find a way to incorporate what you love to do into your work. In fact, Fifth House Suns are often folks who make their living through mastering a hobby or making a part-time leisure interest into a full-time occupation. This includes athletes, collectors, and craftspersons, all of whom spend their time simply being themselves—and getting paid for it. Folks who are self-employed seem to be born quite often with the Sun in this house, especially if their chosen profession is a creative pursuit, such as art or poetry. This is a classic position for musicians, celebrities, and performers, too—"players," that is. In short, if you love it, make sure you do a lot of it, whatever it is. Remember, you're out to have fun here on planet Number Three. This is your lifetime for "recess" from that school we know as the Universe. You're on break, here for a little well-deserved R&R. Make sure you enjoy every moment to the fullest.

In particular, the people who'll bring you joy as you toddle happily through your life will be your playmates, and they'll come in all shapes and sizes. Anyone who makes you feel "like a kid again" will fit the bill just perfectly, and since this house has such a strong affinity with children, you'll be quite happy while you're in their company, too, regardless of whether or not they're yours. You may work with a preschool group, volunteer your time at your child's school to assist the teachers there, or have a day care center in your home. Although not traditionally associated with this house, I believe our pets are also mentioned here in the house of "lovers," since many of us treat our critters with the same TLC we reserve for only our dearest ones. This is the side of you who most loves being in love, by the way, the side of you who smiles charmingly across a candle-lit dinner table. To give your Sun joy, spend your time with those who inspire you to be more creative, romantic, and entertaining.

Sun in the Sixth House

The sixth house is associated with Virgo, one of the hardest-working signs in the zodiac. If your Sun is in this duty-oriented place, you're probably one of those rare individuals who get joy from giving, whether it's volunteering time at a homeless shelter, working with retired greyhounds, or sewing costumes for the kids' class play. You'll be at your happiest when you're busy, hard at work on a project of some kind that will serve a person, group, or cause you love. Watch out for a tendency to overload yourself, however, and be sure to rest between deadlines. Now, although some folks don't think of cleaning as "fun," you probably love it, and may even find that a good "binge clean" is a necessary first step toward any goal. In short, your Sun's house is one of the neatest, most organized places in the chart, so don't expect to function well in an environment that isn't in order. If you want to keep joy in your life, keep your surroundings meticulously clean, especially your work area.

And speaking of your work, whatever it is that you "do," you're probably very good at it. You simply wouldn't have it any other way. This Sun position is famous for its love of details and its ability to detect even the tiniest flaw. In fact, it's the perfect house for a master craftsperson or keen troubleshooter. Whether you work with fabric, wood, or paint, you're completely devoted to doing it right the first time, so your superiors and coworkers probably just adore you. In fact, you'll find that most of your close friends (and probably more than one long-term partnership) will spring out of your relationships with coworkers—and you'll probably treat them like a "second family." Since the people who surround you as you perform your daily duties are so important, then, be sure you're in a happy work environment, and give your Sun its daily dose of joy.

Sun in the Seventh House

This is the house that's traditionally given to one-to-one partnerships, and that makes sense. We tend to spend an awful lot of time alone with someone when we choose them for a partner, whether it's for romantic or business-oriented reasons. Since this is the house where we keep the side of us that comes out when we're in the company of just one other person, it stands to reason that those born with the Sun here definitely love to have company, no matter where they are or what they're doing. In fact, folks born with this Sun position don't like to spend time alone much. They find no greater joy than being involved in a committed relationship with a true "other half." If you're looking for true happiness, then, find yourself a solid partner and get comfortable.

Yes, with the Sun in this house, your spouse or significant other is probably at the center of your life, the person you consider before even yourself—but there's also more to it than that. Your ability to establish relationships is legendary. That goes for your friends, your primary partner, and anyone who's lucky enough to sit beside you on the bus. Being that good at relating with others makes you a master mediator, negotiator, and go-between, too. Just be careful not to exhaust yourself emotionally by taking on responsibility for the happiness of everyone around you. You owe it to your Sun—and yourself—to spend time in balanced, harmonious partnerships.

The folks that will bring you the most joy in your life will be those you can use the word "my" to describe: "my" best friend, "my" lover, "my" child, etc. You're an expert at wooing others, once you're got them alone, so give yourself a treat: spend a lot of time with just one other person, whether it's at work, at home, or at play.

Sun in the Eighth House

The eighth house is a very intense place for the Sun to be. This is the side of us that loves intimacy, depth, and mystery, the side that loves to "dig," whether it's for statistics, evidence, or gardening. Your joy comes from fascination with someone or something. Whether it's a person or a task, if there's a bit of intrigue involved, if it makes you shiver all over or spend days trying to figure it out, your Sun will be giddy with joy—and you don't ever have to tell a soul why you're smiling. In fact, you're probably quite fond of all kinds of mysteries, from novels to real-life melodramas. Be careful of a tendency to stir up a bit of turmoil when you're bored. Although you'll get a temporary "rush" from the intensity of the encounter, you may also stir up a power struggle, which isn't ever a joyful experience. Try to keep a careful distance between yourself and "dangerous" types who may get your adrenaline up on High, but for the wrong reasons. Turn your substantial energy towards establishing intimate relationships with quality friends, and you'll be a very happy person.

Now, intimacy comes in many forms. Physical intimacy, of course, is the first kind that comes to mind, and it's true that you're probably a very sensual creature. The Sun in this house wants to get very, very close to whom and what it's drawn towards, but you're also a very deep creature, unwilling to settle for light chatter or easy small talk, even in social situations. You want the blunt, bare facts—and the more urgent a conversation or encounter is, the more you'll love it. There's always something brewing just under the surface of You, and you'll truly appreciate any friend or acquaintance who sees it. You're on the lookout for soulmates of all shapes and sizes. Be sure you spend your time with others who aren't intimidated by your quiet power, with those who aren't afraid to let you get close—because that's what you live for.

Sun in the Ninth House

The planet Jupiter and his sign, Sagittarius, are the "landlords" of this house—and they're an easily bored pair. Jupiter just loves new experiences, whether it's a visit to a foreign shore, a meeting with someone who speaks with a delightful accent, or a class on a brand new subject. Sagittarius loves new things, too, so much, in fact, that it's not a sign who settles down easily, either with a partner or in a given location. With the Sun in this travel-hungry, experience-craving house, you'll be happiest when you're on the move, whether it's between locations or ideas. Travel, education, and learning life's lessons through "on the job training" will bring you your greatest joy. In fact, this is the house where teachers, students, and world travelers often have their Suns. If your work keeps you tied down, you're not spending your days happily. Find an occupation that's "different" every day, and you'll just love it. The travel industry and the teaching occupations are often just right for you, although many Ninth House Suns prefer to be life-long students, and constantly learning. Some Ninth House Suns can't stand to be inside for too long, needing the freedom of the land or the open road to feel comfortable. Just don't ever allow yourself to become bored—it's the worst thing in the world for you. Since this house is opposite to the Third House, where the side of us who loves routine lives, your Ninth House Sun will need to see, hear, and experience a variety of people, places, and things to stay happy. Don't expect to set your hat down anywhere for long, but rest assured, you can make your home anywhere.

Jupiter's influence on this Sun placement probably also means that you love to laugh, and that you're good at providing that service to others. No matter what you "do," then, make sure it's fun, and that you believe in it with your whole being, and you'll have a long, joyous life.

Sun in the Tenth House

The Tenth House is where we store the side of us who's the authority figure or the Honorary Principal. You have a knack for delegating authority, and you sense what's necessary for all major projects to be accomplished. As a result, you're probably very good at taking charge of situations, big and small. With the Sun in this spot, you were born an elder, and folks will recognize that quality in you. Just make sure you don't overburden yourself with responsibilities. You can only do so much, and you owe it to yourself to make your life a happy place to be. Put yourself in a position of authority in your own life before you take on anyone else's.

The people who'll bring you joy will be those who've earned their keep, anyone with a great deal of experience in a given area. This includes older folks, mentors, and long-term friends. In fact, many of your friends are probably older (or younger) than yourself, and your primary partner may be years apart from you, as well. The Sun in this house appreciates "wise ones," and strives to join their ranks. You love to give and receive respect, and you know how to earn it. You probably also have a very deep sense of loyalty, whether it's to a political party, a spouse, or a pet.

Now, we've already talked about how important your career is to you, and maintaining a career or professional name means keeping a spotless public image. If you were born with the Sun in the Tenth House, then, you're probably also very good at following orders and obeying the rules—and at making them. No matter what you do, be sure you can rise to the top. You'll be happiest if you're in charge.

Sun in the Eleventh House

There's strength in numbers, they say—and it's true. It's particularly true to you folks who were born with the Sun in this house, however. There's a very special feeling that comes from sharing a room with a group of kindred spirits, all of whom have gathered together with the same common denominator in mind. You're probably very group-oriented, then, and you probably love getting together with friends at a regular location. Being with "your people," in fact, at "your place," is one of the experiences that will give you your greatest joy in life. You should avoid associating with negative thinkers or pessimists since you easily absorb the opinions and views of "the tribe." Remember, if you were born with the Sun here, you're an individual in the truest sense of the word. Don't join up with just any group, then. Be particular. You can find "your people" and share your goals with them if you're not afraid to network. You're a real team player—make sure you're on the right team.

Now, since this house belongs to Aquarius, folks born with the Sun here also seem to like the more "unusual" types of groups. You may be an active member of an astrological organization, or the Society for Creative Anachronisms, or spend your vacations on rendezvous weekends with others who enjoy historical reenactment—or you may just be an avid member of Greenpeace. Whatever odd or "different" peer group you choose to nestle into, you'll be a staunch supporter, a wonderful helper, and a powerful ally. Since the Sun also tends to bring a spotlight of sorts with it wherever it goes, you'll probably also be put in charge of your group(s). At the very least, achieving some type of fame within your chosen circle of beings is part of your "job"—and part of what will make you the happiest you can be.

Sun in the Twelfth House

The Twelfth House is where we keep the side of ourselves who emerges when we're feeling completely safe—either because we're alone or in the company of those we trust with our deepest, darkest secrets. It s a very tender, very sensitive place for the Sun to live, since residence in this "room" turns any planet into a psychic "sponge." Having the Sun in this position makes the owner extremely intuitive; in fact, this is one of the most "psychic" houses of all. With no walls or boundaries to separate ourselves from what's out there in the world, it's easy to see how we might become quite tuned in to others, for better or worse. Avoid negative people at any cost to bring the maximum amount of joy into your life, then.

You're a bit more fragile than you think you are, and you need to be choosy about the energies you expose yourself to.

You'll probably be happiest when you're in complete and total quiet, or in dimly lit surroundings with very soft music playing. Many astrologers relate this house to the time we spent in our mothers' wombs. If you consider how safe, warm, and quiet that wonderful place was, you'll understand your Sun's need to keep that "safe" feeling intact throughout your life. Of course, we all need to share our private thoughts with others at times when we feel unable to share those thoughts with even our closest friends. If you need one, find a qualified counselor—someone to listen to those private thoughts and feelings. Getting to know yourself, and the side of you that's a secret even to yourself, is the most important thing you can do for you.

At times, with your Sun in this house, you'll find that you need to be completely alone, to draw back and regroup. That could mean you love steambaths, saunas, movie theaters, or places of worship, but remember—you can be alone anywhere if no one knows you. Find yourself a happy place to "escape" into for retreat, and avoid drugs, alcohol, or other addictive behaviors. Your truest joy will come from being in "sanctuary," and you'll probably need to indulge quite a bit. Give yourself quality time alone with You, and stay happy, healthy, and joyful.

The Millennial Showdown
Predictions for the Year 2000

By Leeda Alleyn Pacotti

The year 2000, Common Era or Anno Domino, etches itself indelibly on history. As Charles Dickens classed another turbulent set of days, "It was the best of times; it was the worst of times."

The year itself is a chronological and astronomical hallmark. A leap year underscoring a leap century, its events include one annular solar eclipse, four partial solar eclipses, and two total lunar eclipses. Even the cataclysmic prediction of Nostradamus, earmarked for early May, when the Sun, Moon, and five planets align in a Taurean stellium, brings tumult to an already impassioned transformation. Close on the heels of the stellium itself is a rare eclipse of the greater benefic Jupiter by the lesser benefic Venus, as seen from Earth. In August, the asteroid Mithra beckons toward Earth, in a close orbit of 4.6 million miles. This asteroid is a tantalizing portend, corruptedly named for Mithras, whose tradition so imperiled blossoming Christianity that his celebration date of December 25 was usurped. Who could have expected such an incidence during the designated year of the Second Coming?

Whether this year begins a new century or ends an old one, it is auspicious, the capstone of the twentieth century and the culmination of a 100-year explosion in knowledge, humanitarianism, art, and negotiation—and illiteracy, victimization, deprecation, and war. No country, person, or way of life escapes this benchmark. Alliances, power, and resources shift, inexorably laying the ground for a future we convinced ourselves not to expect. Echoing the lesson from Sinclair Lewis's novel *It Can't Happen Here*, we finally learn it can. By 2025, we look back at the year 2000 and say, "This is when it began."

Global Schism

Appearing as early as 1997, economic chaos erupted in the Orient after the return of Hong Kong to China, toppled the Japanese economy with a reverberating fall, and thrashed stock and commodity trades worldwide.

Bulwarks of power rocked from within. Gossip, backbiting, and death eclipsed the British monarchy. An indiscreet desire and a congressional obsession with bedroom twitter laid low the august presidency of the United States.

Despite what seemed an economic benevolence of the United States, Russia was left beleaguered and destitute, all too aware that it was ripe for siege and plunder. Held in check as a divided nation and newly reunified, Germany ached for national dignity. France, racked by inner political tensions since its overthrow of monarchial rule, sought reestablishment as a global power. Forced by Mao Tse-Tung to cast off the mantle of feudalism, China yearned to restore its empirical glory, surreptitiously and euphemistically referred to as "respect."

Roiling beneath events of thwarted power, economic bullying, and soiled prestige, resentment and unrequited desire for dominance have patiently forged dramatic and unthinkable alliances. What becomes apparent in the year 2000 makes the world war skirmishes and cold war maneuvering of the twentieth century seem like a child's dream. The game is afoot, started before we knew we were contenders. It is won not with armies and sophisticated weaponry, but with mind-numbing economic tactics, and is enforced with power-driven trade negotiations.

Two New Alliances

In the year 2000, we experience two major global alignments based on the disenfranchised and the established. Both share common principles of capability or need: directed knowledge, resources, and manpower. Inevitably they clash, because populations are voracious, with resources deciding the outcome. The alliance which attains the most brings the other low.

Expect a Eurasian Alliance among France, Germany, Russia, and China. France leads this quaternary, having usurped direction of the European Union. Beware France, which carries a vitriolic vengeance for global acquisition, more caustic than any resurrection of German conquest. Germany holds the technological cards of innovation, engineering, and planning. This reunified nation no longer preoccupies itself with projecting an image of power and grandeur, when their economic and corporate wealth give them the far-reaching and lasting ability to manipulate. Look no further for resources than Russia, a vast treasure of minerals, forests, and land. Its decimated scientific and labor communities welcome accession to this new alliance. Ultimately, China, the cardinal hinge, seals the pact with one-half the world's consumer force, all properly indoctrinated to work, earn, and spend.

Although not immediately obvious, the English-speaking countries are forced into the economic cold. Banning together, Great Britain, the United States, and Australia create a three-way alliance. Great Britain, like the other monarchial nations of the European community, delayed transition to the eurodollar, hedging its trading bets with the United States and Canada, where it maintains substantial holdings. The United States, falsely perceived as retaining power this year, has created unstable, lopsided domestic woes, due to being overly enamoured by the technological and managerial components of its economy. Without its formerly strong industrial base, the United States goes begging for resources and manufacturing, observing that more domestic monetary surpluses have been lured into offshore and cyberspace investments. The nation-continent of Australia, schooled in venture capitalism at the British knee, casts with this lot out of sheer self-preservation. Even the momentary events of hosting the 2000 Summer Olympics and its 100th anniversary cannot mask consumptive demands on its resources and labor.

A purely English-speaking triumvirate is a death knell in an age of globalism. Into this three-way partnership enters Japan. Operating under the constitution constructed by Gen. Douglas MacArthur,

Japan, like Germany, learned to enjoy economic growth under the United States' protection without resorting to nationalistic aggression. Since delivery of the hideous nuclear wallop to this nation of islands, Japan has remained a willing ally of the United States and an indulgent admirer of its social freedoms. Japan is an important addition to the alliance, finalizing a strategic triangle of power on the rims of the Pacific and providing a foothold in Asia; but it, like the other three nations, has become top-heavy with spending consumers and bottom-light in manufacturing and qualified labor.

What we find in the year 2000 is the advent of an economic battle for global dominance between these two groups: the intercontinental Eurasian Alliance of France, Germany, Russia, and China, and the Pan-Oceanic Alliance of Great Britain, the United States, Australia, and Japan.

The Eurasian Alliance controls a self-contained avenue for land trade across two populous, connected continents. It can sustain itself for a long time by quietly accumulating consumerism and trade throughout Southeast Asia and the Middle East. Certainly, overpopulated China and land-wealthy Russia have incentives for exchange.

The Pan-Oceanic Alliance controls the oceans, a major consideration in global trade. However, it lacks resources and manufacturing to sustain its own needs or create competition in other consumer markets. Ultimately, the need for resources and manufacturing must be fulfilled by other nations. Herein lies a failure.

During this year, the "First World," or wealthy, educated countries, make a dire misjudgment, producing a wildcard economic shift. Those who have followed the plump funding by the International Monetary Fund in the Orient throughout the 1990s are not surprised by this poor decision. Misdirection of thought and consequent misaction inadvertently fertilize the seed for global equality in the coming Aquarian Age. Because we are sore about relinquishing power or having it wrested away, this equality is not well-received.

"Third-World" Wildcard

Throughout the 1990s, economists have quietly discussed the misassessment of the so-called "Third World" countries as being "backward" philosophically and economically. Except for the countries of

North America, Western and Northern Europe, Russia, Japan, and Australia, all other countries have been mislabeled in this manner. This collective description no longer exists. This idea of backwardness is premised on Western philosophy, society, and economics: what is not Hellenic thought is backward; what is not Christian or Judaic is backward; what is not Caucasian is backward; what is not corporate, retail, or capitalized is backward.

While the Pan-Oceanic Alliance solidifies an exclusive manufacturing compact with Mexico and the remainder of Latin America, creating a convenient and necessary land route for the movement of goods, it finds itself in direct competition with the Eurasian Alliance for resources and consumer markets in other continents. Its hope for a migrating middle class of managers and technologists from India are hampered when renewed threats to that nation by Chinese invasion or obliteration manifest as oceanic and air blockades.

Dumping on the "Third World" nations, especially during the 1990s when trade loans were made specifically to elicit exclusive trade pacts, now produces a reverse isolationism. Africa, South America, and Southeast Asia are up for grabs, and they know it! Expect a backlash on the two alliances by countries on these continents. They have been watching the dominance game, determined not to be sucked in, used up, and left empty.

Here we have the unexpected come into full view. The greatest possibility for the year 2000 is a separate, distinct economic reality among these disenfranchised nations previously subjected to colonization and territorialization, and perceived merely as sources of resources and cheap labor. They are in a position to trade exclusively with each other, reserving their resources and manpower for goods that cater specifically to the needs of their trade partners. In an environment that relishes cultural, social, and political differences, they establish mutual respect for growth, wealth, and stability, turning up their noses at former economic tutors and plunderers.

The "Y2K" computer problem, or "Millennium Bug," helps this marketplace emerge. Reliant on computerization, "First World" countries have become narrow-minded about economic trends and sociopolitics. These countries are top-heavy with managers, professionals, and technologists. Rather than viewing the computer as a tool or adjunct to human talent, they have humanized it as a replacement for personnel and thought, forgetting it is reflective and unimaginative. Consequently, if the "Y2K" phenomenon severely hits utility, business, accounting, and governmental computers, nations with the greatest obstacles are those of the "First World." Their citizens have forgotten how to use a pencil to calculate or record transactions, payroll, and taxes. The chaos generated from private enterprise and governmental computerization spilling into personal pocketbooks is the marketing doorway for the underdeveloped nations.

Nations In Focus

Australia

Because of the 2000 Olympic Games, Australia gains the world's attention, and its new national status is a convenient platform for self-promotion. The nation is upgrading its seaports, communication lines, land travel, and health and education programs. Australia actively pursues land sales in an effort to extend its tax base, a hotly debated topic in its legislature. The Australians themselves are torn on this issue, as neighborhoods change face and land sales are overtaken by foreign owners. They are challenged by oppressive taxes on one hand and a loss of indigenous ownership on the other. During this year, construction, locally produced building materials, engineering, and recreational and environmental planning are the best investment markets. With a solar eclipse landing on the national Sun on July 1, expect a change in the Australian head of state.

China

China is definitely looking for new allies to secure resources for its population's changing needs, which drive the year. The stellium in Taurus indicates that national prestige is paramount. To preserve its public face and deter foreign observance of its human rights policies, China announces a new program of land ownership in order to give the appearance of individual autonomy of its citizens. Coupling this maneuver with the solar eclipse of July 1 on its national Ascendant, China reevaluates its domestic national image, focusing on education and health as avenues to develop a strengthened labor force.

However, the Communist Party is loath to extend personal freedoms inherent to a healthy, well-educated population. Overwhelmed with trying to control differences of thought, China gives primary construction ventures to Germany and shares its fiscal responsibilities with France. Investors from outside the Eurasian Alliance are discouraged or given stringent investment restrictions indicating low returns.

England

The British are asking more firmly for a hands-on, warm monarch who identifies with them; overall, the population is reshaping the national image. Generally, England enjoys an excellent economy, gearing for a new phase in journalism, literature, and recreation; the working masses are in position to enjoy the fruits of their labors. Because this is one of the technology-reliant nations, problems in banking and land transactions surface during the first three weeks of January and take up commercial attention after July. A solar eclipse on July 1 affects the queen; a debilitation begins or is publicly obvious. Although the queen is unlikely to abdicate, rumors surface that she will pass the scepter between 2005 and 2010. The solar eclipse on July 30 brings problems to Prince Charles, who suffers head and neural trauma during a recreational activity. The prince may take the opportunity to remove himself from succession to the throne.

France

A retrograde progressed Mars in France's Tenth House indicates a national attitude of denied international recognition. The progressed Ascendant in Leo shows the French are demanding world power. During this year, an opposition between the progressed Sun and progressed Mars antagonizes the current leadership, with the populace becoming increasingly nationalistic, owing to a sextile between the progressed Moon and progressed Jupiter. The transiting stellium in Taurus strides the progressed Midheaven, reinforcing resolve to be a leading global presence. During the first seven months of the year, France focuses on domestic concerns, with behind-the-scenes nationalistic propaganda fueled by secret religious sectarianism and mysticism. For the last five months of the year, turmoil in the universities and the general population provokes bickering between the Senate and National Assemblies, which try to fulfill domestic needs while wrangling with important Eurasian Alliance treaties. Throughout this time, the French president retreats from the fracas. Rumors of a nationwide illness surface due to mishandling of foods.

Germany

Major legislative changes are proposed which shortchange landowners. Most of the year is spent on internal matters, which gradually change Germany's self-image. Purposefully, the Germans are denying themselves national prestige; the true financial picture of the nation is being kept secret. After mid-May, the government begins a campaign to alter general thinking about its new alliances. Calls for war come from very liberal and very conservative groups, who are resistant to Germany accepting a position inferior to that of its allies. No war action occurs this year.

India

India continues with a strong economy and opens more communications with the rest of the world, displaying its new sense of confidence and adventure. During the first half of the year, it seeks foreign investments and alliances with its neighbors, sensing the threat of ambush from the Eurasian Alliance. To further stabilize its internal economy, India seeks more investment from its population at large. During the second half of the year, strife rises from domestic land sales. The change is upsetting to the populace, which fears that the demographics of the individual states will become unrecognizable. Although the Indians can accept wealth throughout the population, they cannot allow it to erase class distinctions.

Japan

This year, Japan experiences changes. The islands are rocked by the solar eclipse of February 5, which falls in the natal First House and opposes natal Pluto. This is the most likely time for an earthquake, which precedes a political shock when the stellium in Taurus coincides with the nation's Sun. Expect problems for the Japanese emperor and family. Foreign relations dominate the first four months of the year. An extreme amount of foreign money enters the Japanese market, weakening and eroding the population's self-confidence. To counteract a sense of foreign domination on home soil, the Japanese seek self-protection by escaping into strange beliefs about health cures, recreational healing, and spiritual quests. During the last eight months of the year, the national health comes into focus. Extravagant foods, which overheat the physical predisposition of the Japanese, cause chronic illnesses to degenerate swiftly. The domestic economy tightens further, and cash flow dries up. On July 16, the lunar eclipse conjuncts the natal Ascendant, forcing Japan to reevaluate its image at home and find answers for a directionless populace. During the second half of the year, foreign investment is severely constrained, although the nations of the Pan-Oceanic Alliance are consulted for remedies for Japan's social ills.

Mexico

Although Mexico presents a national image of conciliation toward other countries, internally a deep harshness is stewing: the people are in deep conflict with their authorities. Women with education and position disclose secrets about food and health, such as the lack of regulation of pesticides, which are causing mental turmoil among the general public. Throughout the first six months of the year, Mexico focuses on creating a self-sustaining economy, accepting foreign investments. However, problems arise over land ownership and use. During the last six months of the year, the population is enraged to find investments have really been sales. In secret discussions, civil war is touted as the best method to rid the nation of destructive technology. The solar eclipse of February 5 falls on Mexico's natal Sun, indicating a presidential change. On July 16, another solar eclipse on the natal Venus, opposing the natal Moon and Saturn, creates demands for universally applied basic education.

Russia

The Russian Federation is preparing for a leadership change, which occurs in October. The legislature is highly conflicted over a renewed program of foreign investments. The seeds for presidential change are sowed in January, when secret plans develop. However, new economic problems are in the foreground. From February through July, Russia focuses on national health and communications in an attempt to unify its hungry and disparate peoples. Nothing seems to work this year for Russia, which is easily seduced by its allies to ward off yet another economic collapse. The Taurean stellium falls on Saturn in the Second House of Russia's solar return and opposes Jupiter in the natal Second House. Delay and constriction characterize internal efforts to stabilize economic autonomy. After a long year of frustration and domestic strife, another possible leadership change could occur on Christmas Day.

United States

Throughout the campaign year, the people of the United States engage in a major grass-roots conflict, setting the stage for an elective rebellion. After a severe bout with the Millennium Bug during January and February, both Congress and the administration are put to blame. Transports, mail, satellite communications, documents, and public safety have been hampered, drawing many journalistic criticisms. The lunar eclipse on January 20, conjunct natal Uranus, deeply erodes foreign relations because of lost communications. This pinnacle loss of global prestige remains a secret within the administration. To redirect public attention, a threat of war is issued near March 1, although no war action is ultimately taken. By August 1, Congress and the president unite to resolve growing health and labor problems.

This year, the United States is forced back to earth. During January and February, the focus is on clean water, housing, and land, as the population reels from a lack of security and self-reliance. Legislation for cleanliness standards and non-ownership of water rights are opposed by health providers, who have a stake in the growing bottled water market, and by mining operators, who would have to develop new technology for cleanup. On the side of basic human need are the clergy, public administrators, and the media.

From March through July, the domestic economy dominates campaign rhetoric with ideas of "back to the land;" gardening and agriculture are bandied as fortifying recreations. The underlying truth is the nation cannot feed the increasing mass of the poor and hungry. The government gets the idea that no one is hungry who grows food. News organizations beat the drum for "One Person,

One Acre." The Taurean stellium on the natal Sixth House of the United States' Constitution ties national health problems to issues of the soil and land. After July, back-to-the-land legislation stalls in Congress, hindered by debate, filibuster, and states' rights to set land ownership.

The lost images of personal self-sustenance and national influence make for an angry electorate.

The president-elect is not a woman, a task for 2008. He has not previously held any federal position, whether elective, appointive, or civil. The new president is penetratingly Scorpionic in nature, exemplifying the United States' Constitutional Ascendant. He is genuinely sensitive to people, without charisma or feigned charm, demonstrating the Constitution's Piscean Sun. Although he met with personal success in business, he most likely has been schooled as a physician. Expect a man of self-made wealth, scarred by marital misfortune, exhibiting stance and determination.

Mundane Natalogy

Commonwealth of Australia, January 1, 1901,
12:00 a.m. GST, Canberra.

People's Republic of China, September 20, 1954,
12:00 a.m. CCT, Beijing.

Kingdom of Great Britain, December 25, 1066,
12:00 p.m. GMT, London (Julian Calendar).

Republic of France, October 4, 1958, 12:00 a.m. CET, Paris.

Federal Republic of Germany, May 23, 1949,
12:00 a.m. EET, Berlin.

Republic of India, January 26, 1950, 12:00 a.m. INT, New Delhi.

Japan (Nikkon Koku), May 3, 1947, 12:00 a.m. JST, Tokyo.

United States of Mexico, February 5, 1917,
12:00 a.m. CST, Mexico City.

Russian Federation, December 24, 1993, 12:00 a.m. BGT, Moscow.

United States of America, March 4, 1789,
12:13:12 a.m. LMT, New York City.

Your Sun Sign and Your Dharma

By Skye Alexander

I like to think of the Sun as the symbol of the "present you," the individual you are right now, in this lifetime. You could also view the Sun as representing your dharma, or your "role" in life. (Dharma is a Buddhist concept that means your divine duty.) Your Sun sign describes the essential and distinctly unique part of yourself that you aspire toward, the part you are striving to express and fulfill, the part for which you want to be recognized. It is your kernel of selfhood.

In fact, if someone were to ask you what you want to be (not do) in life or how you want others to view you, you might quickly describe yourself in terms of your Sun. An individual with the Sun in Leo, for example, might say she wants to be a leader, a figure who commands authority and respect. Someone with the Sun in Pisces might respond that he wants to be a compassionate, caring, creative person. The Sun also shows the part of yourself that you generally like and accept, flaws and all.

Aries

Your role in this lifetime is that of the pioneer, the explorer, the adventurer who forges ahead into uncharted territory. Perhaps you see yourself as a knight on a white horse or an astronaut speeding into space to discover the vast unknown. Like the military pilots depicted in Tom Wolfe's book *The Right Stuff*, you like to "push the envelope" and thrive on danger.

Easily bored, you constantly seek new challenges. You have great energy and enthusiasm, but lack persistence. Once something becomes routine, you lose interest and go off in search of new dragons to slay. As a result, you are much better at starting things than finishing them.

Aries is the most individualistic and independent sign, and those of you born under it are inherently self-oriented. Often you have difficulty relating to other people or understanding their side of things—as far as you're concerned, there is only one way to do something, and that's your way. You attempt to do everything yourself and are able to accomplish more than most people. When you run up against a problem you can't handle alone, however, you don't know where to turn for help.

Because your dharma is to break new ground, you must separate yourself from traditions, social conventions, and accepted norms. In doing so, you are likely to antagonize or upset people who are more orthodox than you. You'll probably end up butting heads with authority figures occasionally and may make as many enemies as friends. You cannot worry about what others think of you, though, or consider how your actions affect them, for doing so would inhibit your headlong charge down the road less traveled.

Taurus

Your role in life is to bring the dreams of others to fruition. You have the ability to put other people's plans into action and can bring the visionary's grand ideas down to earth. You are the builder who carries out the architect's designs. Patience and perseverance are your strong suits, and once you start something you rarely deviate from your path until you've reached your destination.

However, this single-minded determination can sometimes cause you to miss out on opportunities or become stuck in a rut, for you are reluctant to try something new even when it would benefit you to do so. As a result, you tend to accept conditions as they are rather than attempting to change them.

Good-natured and easygoing, it takes a lot to make you angry. You enjoy companionship and are at your best in social situations. To those you care about, you are loyal and generous to a fault. You also need other people to motivate you, for alone you are inclined to be rather lazy and plodding.

Taurus is the most sensual and materialistic sign of the zodiac, and those of you born under it have a great appreciation of physical pleasure. Your indulgence and love of beauty can lead you to overextend yourself financially, and you may put too much emphasis on money. Your self-worth may even be tied to your income.

Because your dharma is to create forms and make concepts manifest in the physical world, your focus is necessarily "earth-bound." Abstractions escape you. Your focus is on things that can be rendered materially, and your imagination is firmly rooted in the physical plane. If you can't wear it, eat it, sit on it, or smell it, what good is it?

Gemini

Your role in life is to gather and disseminate information. Thus, you are constantly in search of knowledge, facts, data, trivia, and gossip—everything is potential grist for your mental mill. You see friends, coworkers, and loved ones as sources for new information. Infinitely curious, you gather ideas like a child picking up seashells at the beach and store them away for some future time when they may come in handy. You might be an avid reader, a media junkie, or a lifelong student. One of your biggest problems, however, is distinguishing between the treasures and the trash.

Your mind requires constant stimulation and challenges. Nothing excites you more than learning something new. Curious and versatile, you can do a great many things at least passingly well, but your short attention span makes it challenging for you to stick with anything long enough to become proficient at it. You are truly a jack of all trades.

Your insatiable curiosity can lead you to attempt more than you can possibly accomplish. Afraid of missing out on something, you try to do too much and may either exhaust yourself or fail to complete what you begin. Many of you work two jobs simultaneously, not only to earn additional money, but because you can't decide between the two of them. Geminis are also quite capable of carrying on more than one love relationship at a time.

Your dharma is to collect and share information, much like a bee who gathers and spreads pollen, flying from flower to flower. In a positive sense, this desire to acquire knowledge and educate the world, as well as yourself, makes you a natural teacher; negatively, it manifests as gossiping and nosiness. Your role is to disseminate ideas, not to evaluate them.

Cancer

You have a compassionate, nurturing nature and are at your best when you can care for and shelter someone else. However, you must guard against being overly protective and controlling toward people in your care. You might be inclined to adopt a "benevolent dictator" attitude, believing that you know what's best for everyone, without allowing them any room for individuality.

Highly emotional and sensitive, you can be somewhat moody, and your moods may be linked to the phases of the Moon. You are also able to sense the emotions of others and might be easily influenced by people to whom you are close. As a result, you can't really separate yourself from the world around you, no matter how hard you try.

Security is all-important to you. Belonging to something larger than yourself gives you a sense of security, and you might define yourself through your family, community, workplace, ethnic or religious group, or country. Many of you also see money as security. Respectful of authority and hierarchy, you are loyal to family members, employers, and whoever is on "your side." However, different opinions or lifestyles can upset your sense of security. Consequently, you might surround yourself with people you find nonthreatening, who are just like yourself, and who are supportive of you.

Your dharma is to use your sensitivity to care for the needs of others and to build a safe, stable environment in which other people's children, as well as your own, can grow and thrive. But you must learn to give freely, to offer care and support to others without attaching strings to your gifts.

Leo

Like your ruler, the Sun, you see yourself as the center of your own personal universe. You imagine yourself showering those around you with life-giving warmth and expect them to turn toward you like flowers turning toward the sun. Your role is that of king, queen, or leader, and you assume this position as though it were your divine right, believing that others should naturally follow you. Often they do, simply because you project such confidence and enthusiasm.

You have difficulty seeing other people except in terms of their value to you. To those who are loyal and devoted to you, you are generous and affectionate, but anyone who questions your authority or expects you to prove yourself worthy will experience your self-righteous wrath.

It is essential for you to be creative, to express yourself in some special and distinctive way. You believe you have a gift to share with the world—and that gift is yourself. You love attention and are happiest when you can bask in the adoration of your "fans." Some of you will express yourself through the arts, leaving behind paintings, symphonies, books, or buildings as your legacy. Some of you consider your children to be an expression of your creativity.

Your dharma is to rule not only courageously, but also fairly, whether you are the head of state or the head of a business. Self-assurance and charisma, qualities we often associate with royalty, come easily to you. Fairness and equality, which are more often associated with your opposite sign, Aquarius, do not. In your haste to be Number One, remember that all rulers depend on their subjects, and all CEOs depend on their employees. One cannot exist without the other.

Virgo

The practical idealist, you want to put your concern for those less fortunate than yourself (including animals) into a pragmatic framework. Your role is to help them to help themselves. A "fixer," you'll try to fix anything from a broken garbage disposal to a broken leg. You enjoy being of service, knowing that you've done something worthwhile. Glory and money aren't particularly important to you, but you must feel useful and needed.

You are hard-working, meticulous, cautious, and analytical in all you do. Order and organization are important to you—you're the person who keeps things running smoothly. You want to know what's expected of you, and you like to have the rules of the game clearly stated so you can follow them to the letter. Diligent and conscientious, you always strive to do your best and can be depended on to get things done in a pinch.

A perfectionist, you want everything to be "just so" and are always trying to improve yourself and everyone else around you. You need to know when to quit, however, before you grind the diamond into dust!

Modest and unassuming, you dislike having attention focused on you and prefer to remain in the background. You are more comfortable following than leading and are well-suited to carrying out other people's grand plans. No matter how gifted or accomplished you may be, however, you are humble and want to be seen as just another ordinary person.

Your dharma might go something like the "Serenity Prayer": perfect what you can, accept what you can't improve, and learn to distinguish between the two.

Libra

Libra's symbol is the balance, and you are continually trying to maintain balance in all you do. Conflict and stress of any kind upset you, and you'll go to great lengths to avoid confrontation. You're a lover, not a fighter. You go along to get along, but may give in too quickly, sacrificing your principles or self-interest in the process. Your dharma is to be the peacemaker who weighs issues dispassionately, mediates disputes, and creates harmony out of chaos.

Known for your good manners and pleasant demeanor, you are at your best in social situations or positions that demand tact and savoir faire. You are neat and orderly in all you do, since appearances are important to you. Tactful, friendly, and even-tempered, you always make a good impression and can get along with just about anyone. Relationships are your main concern, and you function best as a member of a team or partnership.

Making decisions can be extremely difficult for you, partly because you always take other people's interests and opinions into consideration, and partly because you don't tend to develop strong emotions or attachments. As a result, you may vacillate rather than taking a stand.

You want everyone to like you and are easily influenced by other people's opinions. Often you take on the coloring of those around you. Afraid to stand out or be different, you are quite conventional and generally adapt to the status quo, rarely questioning what's expected of you. You are respectful of authority and traditions and don't buck the system.

Although you may be concerned with fairness, it's more important to you to play by the rules. Your challenge is to compromise and cooperate without sacrificing yourself or your principles in the process.

Scorpio

Life for you, Scorpio, is never simple, ordinary, or placid. Rather, it seems marked by intense, dramatic events and transformative situations that force you to rely on yourself from an early age.

An extremist, you don't do anything halfway. Stubborn and determined, you are not easily deterred from your goals and through sheer force of will you often accomplish them. You are a formidable adversary and a good person to have as an ally when the going gets tough. However, your tenacity can make you a difficult person to get along with.

Extremely sensitive and emotional, you hide your vulnerability behind an impenetrable wall. Because you fear being hurt, you may strike first and ask questions later. Under pressure, you appear contained and unflappable, and your acerbic wit can put opponents on the defensive.

You want to be in complete control at all times. Because you don't fully trust anyone else, you rarely share information with others. Privacy is important to you, and you'd like to classify your life "top secret." You want to know everything about everyone else, but reveal little about yourself.

Intuitive, you see into other people and understand their motives, though you often look on the dark side and expect the worst of people. Whether you are truly psychic or just perceptive, you are rarely duped. You probe beneath the surface to uncover what lies hidden from view, whether you're a detective investigating a crime or a psychotherapist probing a patient's unconscious.

You possess great personal magnetism and an aura of power that enables you to transform people, for better or worse. Though you may not seek the limelight, you can be a charismatic and forceful leader. Your dharma is to use your power toward constructive rather than destructive ends.

Sagittarius

Jovial, outgoing, and optimistic, you see life as a game and have a good time playing it. You expect to "win a few, lose a few," so you don't let failure get you down; instead, you move on to the next adventure, full of enthusiasm and confidence. Your self-confidence often helps you achieve your objectives. Even when you fail, people find it hard to blame you or stay mad at you for long.

Many of you possess a quick wit and a delightful sense of humor. Your smooth-talking style and engaging personality enable you to convince others to join your team or back you in your endeavors, no matter how outrageous. A big dreamer, you tend to overestimate your abilities and spread yourself too thin. As a result, your grandiose schemes—if they do come to fruition—are often late and overbudget. Always looking to the future, you quickly forget about the past and rarely learn from your mistakes. Although you never intend to hurt anyone, others may see you as unreliable.

Both physically and mentally active, you need plenty of room to move about, or you grow restless and bored. Frequent changes of scene are essential to you, and you balk at restrictions. You want to expand your horizons in every direction and are interested in anything foreign. Immensely curious, your desire to learn a little bit about everything, in this world as well as the next, could lead you to travel to foreign countries or explore spiritual realms of consciousness. Many of you have active fantasy lives that let you create your own magical worlds.

Your dharma is to use your vision and curiosity to explore the great beyond, without forgetting your responsibilities in the here and now.

Capricorn

You are pragmatic, determined, and cautious in your approach to life. Although you don't shy away from challenges, you always examine the pitfalls as well as the advantages of a situation before you go ahead. You take only carefully calculated risks. Consequently, you rarely make big mistakes, though you might miss out on opportunities because you are too cautious.

Conservative in your personal and professional pursuits, you prefer to stay with what you know rather than experimenting with the new or unusual. Things that have stood the test of time appeal to you. You respect tradition and are most comfortable in clearly defined hierarchical situations and relationships. Shy and sensitive, you aren't particularly good at socializing. Because you are uncomfortable with personal relationships, you may attempt to avoid them by throwing yourself into your work.

You possess managerial skills, common sense, financial acumen, and organizational ability. Not especially innovative, you have a knack for ironing out the kinks and for making things run efficiently. Your strengths are pragmatism, planning, and perseverance. You carefully prepare for the future and don't trust luck to see you through.

Your success will come through your own efforts, most likely. Rather than relying on others to help you, you must earn your own way and make progress slowly and steadily. This doesn't bother you, however—you aren't looking for a free ride and expect to encounter a few difficulties along the way.

Your dharma is to confront life's obstacles, learn from them, and overcome them, without letting them limit you. Work hard and accept your responsibilities, but don't sacrifice joy in the process.

Aquarius

Aquarians march to the beat of a different drummer, and you demand the freedom to think and act in your own way. You're never afraid to take an unpopular stand or try an unusual approach. You believe that if something has always been done a particular way, it's time for a change. Ever in pursuit of new experiences, you don't mind controversy or turmoil.

A rebel who points out "the system's" failings, you feel it is your responsibility to oppose the establishment. As a result, you often end up in trouble with the powers that be. Explosive and outspoken, you rarely hold your tongue and can be abrasive or tactless. You need to guard against tearing down old structures before you have a better alternative to offer in their place.

Fairness and equality are important to you, and you'd like to erase all barriers related to race, gender, age, or creed. You don't respect people for their money or position and treat the mailroom clerk and the company president identically. Gregarious, you enjoy sharing ideas with intelligent, forward-thinking people and function best when you can be part of a group, especially when that group is dedicated to a cause. You aren't particularly good in emotional situations, however, and can be rather impersonal in relationships.

Progressive and unconventional, you are usually ahead of your time and can awaken other people to new discoveries. Often you can be found on the cutting edge of technology or in the vanguard of social change.

Changeable, idiosyncratic, and idealistic, you may lack the patience and perseverance to bring your dreams to fruition. It's not enough for you to see the future—you must make it understandable and viable to the masses. Your dharma is to implement constructive changes that will benefit all, without rejecting the wisdom of the past in the process.

Pisces

Pisceans possess vivid imaginations and fantasy lives. Many of you are artistic or creative and seem to hear "the music of the spheres." You have a keen sensitivity to color and sound, and even if you aren't particularly talented you enjoy art, music, and beauty.

Dealing with the harsh realities of earthly life is extremely difficult for you. You are seeking a more spiritual and lofty existence and aren't at home in the physical world. Your concerns are of a higher nature, and you may overlook the mundane world around you. At your best, you are able to tune in to higher realms of consciousness to gain inspiration. At your worst, you are lost in a fog, more concerned with the hereafter than the here and now. Your dharma is to bring the wonders of the spiritual realm to earth.

In all you do, you expect yourself to be perfect. Overly idealistic, you become easily discouraged when things don't turn out as you'd hoped. Because you lack discipline and perseverance, you might not finish what you start. When things get rough, you might run away rather than working your problems through.

Very sensitive to other people's moods and feelings, you are able to empathize with the troubles of others—but you are also strongly influenced by them. Many of you possess some psychic ability. You have great sympathy for the helpless, the injured, and the unfortunate, human and animal alike. However, you must guard against sacrificing your own best interests. Trusting, compassionate, and extremely gullible, you sometimes allow others to take advantage of you. One of your challenges in this lifetime is to learn to give of yourself without giving yourself away.

You and Your Boss

By Alice DeVille

Bosses come in every model and management style. Male and female bosses are the usual suspects, but a few of you swear your bosses come from Mars (or you'd like to send them there). How well do you know your employer?

After all, you spend a lot of time in the company of this influential man or woman who pays your salary and offers you benefits that entice you to stay with the organization. Have you used this time productively? Do you know the recipe for carrying out your boss' wishes so that both of you win? Have proximity and insight given you the opportunity to jump ahead, or do you struggle to anticipate the best course of action for advancement?

Perhaps you are blessed with a creative, upbeat employer who relies on your expertise and gives you the space to work your magic. Who wouldn't want a boss who believes in autonomy and a participatory work environment? If your boss pads your palm with lucrative raises and well-deserved bonus money, wouldn't you find a way to stick around and look at the long-term options? What about your career ladder? Perhaps your boss is also a mentor and lets you know there is room to grow in the organization. Do you get the feeling that all you have to do is come up with a plan of action and your prestige will rise along with your salary?

Experts tell us that next to family, the person whose name comes up most frequently in conversation is that of one's boss. Is that true of you? If it is, what is the conversation like? Flattering or faltering?

Is your boss a "keeper," or are you a paycheck away from jumping ship? As you read this article, think of *one word* that best describes your boss. What do you think your boss would say about you?

Let's examine the boss-employee relationship. Ideally this duo connects in terms of ideas and execution. Solid teamwork results when each party shares responsibility for getting the job done. Receptivity to listening and clarifying expectations helps to promote a positive work climate. The desire for an environment that is mutually beneficial seems possible when communication is open and you know where you stand with each other.

What type of relationship do you have with your boss? Is your employer someone you talk about with admiration and respect, or do you work for an individual who gets marginal approval from you and who is the butt of all your work place jokes? Do you like your boss? How well do you think you get along?

Did you know that astrological insight can help you maintain a compatible relationship with your employer? Regardless of the current dynamics of your relationship with your boss, you may benefit from the information that follows. If you know your Sun sign and that of your boss, read the appropriate passages. You may recognize your boss by a description that does not match up with that person's Sun sign. In that case your boss may have a Moon or Ascendant or several planets in that particular sign. It's possible that the sign on either your Tenth (career) or Sixth (work environment) House cusp matches that of a prominent boss. If you have never had your astrology chart constructed, you may want to consult a career astrologer or order a natal chart from Llewellyn's Computerized Astrological Services (see coupon in the back of this book). Join me in reviewing the profiles in the Bosses Hall of Fame. As you turn the pages, note that for every ideal boss, there is a challenging alternate. How many have you encountered?

The Amiable Adventurer

Sun signs may include the fire signs, Aries, Leo, and Sagittarius; sometimes Gemini and Aquarius.

If you have the pleasure of working with an Amiable Adventurer, every day will feel like a new beginning. These bosses want to create concepts and maintain a smooth environment. They tend to live in the moment and forget about yesterday. As a matter of fact, Amiable Adventurers don't think too much about the future, either, because they hire staff to worry about the details. They need action to keep themselves happy and look for employees who are enthusiastic self-starters. Anyone who wants a "cookbook" approach to the work routine need not apply. Amiable Adventurers would rather tell you a joke than guide you through a volume of work guidelines, and they've been known to break a few rules to forge a new path in the world of progress. They don't have time to hold your hand while they're hatching ingenious ideas. Their trademark is spontaneity, so they're likely to make sudden, unplanned trips or ask you, at the last minute, to work overtime on a newly developed project. They may even ask you to join them on one of their trips to show you how entrepreneurs work, and they welcome your praise. Just don't hang on to "yesterday's news."

If the work place seems "stale," Amiable Adventurers find a way to infuse it with enthusiasm with a rousing pep talk. They may have a few choice words for slackers, but usually do not embarrass individuals in front of their peers. Believers in freestyle execution of work, these employers give you space to ignite your genius. Don't mistake their hiatus from your immediate work space for indifference to meeting deadlines, though. Amiable Adventurers want the two of you to have something to celebrate and have an innovative style when it comes to rewarding employees.

These action-oriented types can spot a passionate employee by the fun-loving sparkle in your eye. They may even forget about performance reviews unless you have messed up. If you are a hard charger who likes trekking through the "hot spots" of the world, this boss is for you. Every work day will be different, so enjoy the experience.

The Jovial Jerk

Sun signs include the fire signs, Aries, Leo, and Sagittarius; sometimes Gemini, Libra, and Aquarius.

The Jovial Jerk usually punctuates sentences, especially the endings, with a nervous laugh. Initially you may feel like you have landed in the Levity Zone. These bosses feed you a steady diet of flat jokes and puns. Somewhere inside this frivolity box lies a serious message, but you may need Houdini to pry it out. If you are new on the job, orientation is a real workout. You get the feeling you are supposed to laugh at everything, yet the essence of the humor is missing, and so is the gist of your work.

The Jovial Jerk's game takes a long time to learn. First you ask a question, and your boss answers with one. You ask another question, only to get a few fidgety chuckles. Then you are asked if you're confused. After the third round, you are sorry you bothered to ask any questions at all. Your boss "tests" you with the latest limericks, rhymes, and political quips, to which you are coaxed, wheedled, and cajoled to come up with the right answers.

Once you figure out that behind this "pleasant" demeanor lies a pained individual, you'll understand that joviality masks a poorly organized slave driver. You may find yourself short on information and time when work deadlines hit, not that you could have extricated the answers from your ever-evasive employer. Oh, yes, you are expected to perform in the Jerk's Three Ring Circus. This boss loves bonuses to prop up the team spirit...uh...wallet, but you'll have to make major contributions in a pinch to make sure the cash flows. Don't worry, when crunch time looms, your boss will keep you company with a steady barrage of one-liners and "jabs" about how fast you are putting out fires for the good of the organization.

If your employer is a Jovial Jokester, you may need to negotiate for uninterrupted time between one-liners. You may also have to locate the company experts and seek their counsel when you need information. Make a pitch for your sanity by pointing out your high productivity during uninterrupted work periods. Ask for the option of telecommuting when crunch time looms, and know that you are not alone.

The Connoisseur

Sun signs include the earth signs, Taurus, Virgo, and Capricorn; sometimes Cancer and Scorpio.

If you'd like a little class in the work place, watch the Connoisseur in action. In the office setting, these employers make an elegant personal statement. Furniture is carefully selected and well-placed to facilitate discussion or an efficient work station. Many Connoisseurs hire Feng Shui practitioners to create the right mood and stimulate positive energy for a thriving business. You may be treated to the harmony of an office water garden or a striking wall mural. Visitors may find themselves munching on seasonal fruit, chocolate-covered strawberries, or even homebaked tarts, washed down with imported lemon water.

Connoisseur employers don't expect staff members to fill the candy dish; in fact, some of them buy sweets for the whole office. A Taurus boss I know had a knack for remembering everyone's favorite candy and would replenish candy dishes with favorite treats after every business trip: gourmet jelly beans in one room, licorice in another, and fudge on the second floor. In fact, this Connoisseur went trick-or-treating at the office the day after Halloween using a reverse approach. Dressed in costume and toting a couple of bulging shopping bags, this Taurean stopped at each work space and offered employees as much candy as they could grab with both hands.

Every employed person deserves to have a Connoisseur boss at least once in a lifetime. If you're feeling like you want to be spoiled for a while, seek this boss out. The Connoisseur employer wants nothing but the best in the physical work place, including people, equipment, and amenities. Undoubtedly you wouldn't get the job if you didn't fit the first prerequisite, because the Connoisseur is a discriminating recruiter. Before you get the "thumbs up" from this prospective boss, you'll probably have to come back for more than one interview. Goodness! You'll have to fit—the image, the philosophy, and the pulse of the organization.

You'll never have to ask your Connoisseur boss for a new chair or draperies. Your thoughtful employer probably has part of the administrative budget earmarked for decorating and such necessities as back-saver chairs. The Connoisseur may ask about your favorite colors during the second interview and make a mental note to see what might be available to accommodate your preferences. The window view you'll enjoy has panes of sparkling glass that are regularly maintained by a contract cleaning service. Your office plants thrive under the loving attention of a trained horticulturist. Some Connoisseurs have a green thumb as well, and may bring you cuttings to start your own garden.

The Taurus Connoisseur invests in the best people and expects to pay an appropriate salary. This boss likes to keep you at arms length from head-hunting competitors. The Virgo wants to shop around for plum candidates who will accept mediocre starting salaries for the sake of working in a prestigious organization. Capricorn hires those who are looking for mentors on their climb to the top of the ladder. Cancer Connoisseurs focus on security needs like insurance benefits, 401k's, and vacations with pay. They wouldn't want to leave you at risk. The Scorpio boss is the one who closes the deal at a gourmet restaurant where the well-tipped maitre d' gives personal attention.

If you're already high on the perks of working for a Connoisseur, you won't be tempted to change jobs unless you're watching your waistline or turned on to bigger challenges. The Connoisseur usually guarantees you stability, generous benefits, and a pristine environment, but not necessarily an open door to go out on a limb.

The Private Eye

Sun signs include the earth signs, Taurus, Virgo, Capricorn; Scorpio; sometimes Leo and Aquarius.

The Private Eye's attention to detail seems meritorious initially. You get the impression you've landed a job with an unusually scrupulous employer. Private Eyes know exactly what everyone is doing and where the team is with meeting timelines. They have a hands-on approach to management and leave you satisfied that they have an interest in the people. (They don't tell you, though, about the number of people who have dropped off the employment rolls like flies.)

You ace the interview and like the idea that your prospective employer gives you an information packet to acquaint you with the organization. Later you notice the packet is long on policy and protocol and low on people benefits and success stories. Still, that starting salary is attractive and you find yourself accepting this tantalizing position. Then the fun begins. You enter a world where even your trips to the restroom are suspect...did you join the Secret Service? If you spend more than five minutes away from your work station, you get the penalty box in this company. Beware, your coworkers may be tapped for details. Get used to the idea that Private Eyes never call in advance before visiting your work space.

If you have had the experience of working with this type of boss, you probably know where I'm going. No one is above suspicion in the work environment ruled by a Private Eye. Their eyes are beamed on you when you least expect it. Your most innocent conversations undergo dissection. They play "Gotcha!", and the list of perceived infringements seems endless. Private Eyes have a style that is a bit confrontational, as though you might be bullied into giving away "secrets" if you are caught off guard. For what type of dirt are Private Eyes searching? They look for who is cheating on their travel expenditures, whether the figures you submitted for the printing estimate are "real" or "inflated," and if you know the name of the person your coworker sees for lunch—after all, that person could be an employee of a rival company.

The Taurus Private Eye wants to know who defaced the furniture and how many pairs of shoes you think your office mate owns. Don't worry, your peers get the same grilling. The Virgo Private Eye questions why you use more than two ball-point pens per month when they are good for 5,000 words. He also analyzes the crumbs you leave on your desk after lunch and may give you a citation for lack of a) neatness, b) nutrition, or c) rodent control. Capricorn thinks you make too many visits to the executive suite—what's on your mind? The Leo Private Eye thinks you're goofing off if she hears too many laughs coming from your cubicle. She's also making sure you're not ridiculing her decisions. The Aquarian Private Eye uses surveillance techniques to keep his pulse on your actions. Yep, he leaves the intercom open to listen in on your afterthoughts on how he handled the meeting you just left.

Count your blessings if you have never had to experience this type of employer. If a Private Eye does represent current reality for you, I hope you're looking for a new job. As an interim measure, consider installing mirrors in your workspace to catch a glimpse of your "skulker," hang a few bells on your door or slip a few into your boss' pockets so you have advance warning of surprise visits, or fake amnesia during an intense grilling session.

The Communicator

Sun signs include the air signs, Gemini, Libra, and Aquarius; sometimes Sagittarius and Leo.

Communicator employers needs little prompting to give a talk. Born with a microphone in their hands, they often deliver rousing pleas to the team for assistance on major projects. Their natural, friendly style easily motivates others to pitch in. Who can refuse when charisma reigns? Their style is so convincing that others want to jump on board and share in the vision.

If leadership is getting people to do what the leader wants, Communicators know the ropes. They make you aware of how vital you are to the effectiveness of the organization. Blessed with a glorious gift of gab, Communicators hold frequent staff meetings to update members on current affairs. They do their homework and seldom fail to acknowledge your accomplishments. They astutely convey a sensitivity to already pressing time demands.

Communicator believe in an all-channel network so everyone stays in the loop. Look for an abundance of interoffice memos and interim reports. Some Communicators hold frequent briefings, press conferences, or impromptu information-sharing sessions. Equipment sales in state-of-the-art technology are high among this boss group. You'll find the best TelePrompTers, cellular phones, recording devices, and media equipment in their offices. Communicators enjoy testing and purchasing the latest communication gadgetry. They thrive on getting the word out promptly.

With their endless charm and astute awareness of workload priorities, Communicators take an interest in keeping everyone informed and involved. If you work with a Communicator, your world revolves around frequent interpersonal exchanges. Count on daily e-mail messages, voice mail messages, and face-to-face visits with them. Be sure to read the messages you receive, though, because Communicators may give you a quiz to make sure you understood the gist of the message. Don't worry, their style will be friendly and encouraging. In fact, you'll receive routine orientation in all facets of the organization, often directly from your boss.

If you're high on career development, you couldn't ask for a better boss. Communicators invest in a well-educated work force.

You'll be encouraged to improve your skills and set your sights on mind improvement. If your public speaking skills are less than stellar, your Gemini boss may discreetly suggest that you join Toastmasters or enroll in a public-speaking course. The Libra Communicator is high on group dynamics and emphasizes cooperation and teambuilding. Mediation and negotiation are Libra's communication specialties. Your Aquarian boss advocates using the power of the word to deliver high-impact information in a variety of leading edge consulting fields. The Sagittarius Communicator throws you a bouquet of compliments in exchange for your willingness to pull out all the stops in a crunch. The Leo uses dramatic settings or verbiage to grab your attention. He usually wins based on his mastery of the art of persuasion.

The Communicator types are natural educators. Just about all of them write or speak prolifically, and many of them have published books, articles, or other materials like tapes and videos. Though their styles range from easy and breezy to formal and pontificating, they generally encourage feedback. If you would like an environment where communication flourishes, do some target networking to find the right fit.

The Gadabout

Sun signs include Gemini, Sagittarius, Aries; sometimes Aquarius and Libra.

Gadabout Bosses thrive on their reputation for being avid networkers. They join every organization remotely affiliated with their profession. Their goal is to gain high visibility for the company and, of course, themselves. Their daytimers read like a social calendar with grand openings, conventions, fund raisers, receptions, lunch dates, and galas. Somewhere in that maze are legitimate business meetings—they know everybody!

Typical Gadabouts have a collection of chicken a la king recipes from the hundreds of luncheons they couldn't turn down. They love photo ops and a whole lot of handshaking. Since they thrive on people-to-people contact, Gadabouts lobby for opportunities to be delegates or spokespersons for their group. With their tendency to overcommit, their spokesperson efforts often fall short. They run out of time to adequately prepare their comments. They summon their staff for last minute help, but even they can't bail them out in the performance arena. Not only that, but after their scheduled event ends, they make two or three stops before returning to their place of business. In the interim, they fail to notify staff of their whereabouts and leave them on hold when decisions are pressing.

Gadabout Bosses may not have a mean bone in their bodies, but they rake up the points as stress givers. Their exasperated staff has trouble locating them most of the time. Even when they are on-site, they have an annoying habit of wandering off. If their staff needs a decision made or their signature, Gadabouts are off on a lark "just visiting a colleague down the hall." These employers "forget" to mention the errands they are running or the meeting they're attending. Exasperated staff complain that their calendar is seldom current. Tracking Gadabouts when executive staff need their presence is a no-win situation. The Cover-Up Magicians who work for them go to bat coming up with excuses.

You probably figured it out, but productivity is low in this work group. The world does not turn in sync with the work demand under the leadership of Gadabouts. Although they are commonly mistaken for networking groupies, their skills are often the real issue. They abdicate rather than delegate authority, feeling that their staff will pick up the pieces. Oh, they do that all right, along with the letters of resignation they have written in a fit of exasperation and then shredded before the boss sees them. They're the Kings and Queens of Last Minute Management, and that includes decisions. When the product is ready to go to press, Gadabouts give it the once-over five minutes before quitting time, and their staff has to work late to make modifications.

This model has variations in stress-giving practices. Most Gadabouts shirk responsibility when a problem needs solving. They wait until it's too hot to handle and shell out money for a mediator. Gadabouts appear self-centered since they never seem to consider the impact their impromptu visiting has on their staff. When they are out of sight for long periods of time, employees make bets on their hiding places. Some of them are drinkers who slip away to bars. The Gemini Gadabout hides out in the lunch room and works on crossword puzzles; Sagittarius finds a vacant conference room to study travel brochures related to an exciting getaway; Libra works on relationships that need attention—sometimes that includes lunches, running home to walk the dog, or visiting a therapist. Aries shops for cars and electronics equipment on extended lunch hours. The Aquarius Gadabout grabs a sandwich and surfs the Internet, spending hours sending jokes and inside information to pals.

What's the environment like in your work place? Are you forever chasing a Gadabout? To survive you may need to schedule an appointment on her calendar to state your case. Let her know you have run out of excuses for explaining her whereabouts. Tell her what a lifesaver a pager might be and hand her the one you charged to her credit card. Then count to ten and think about kindred spirits out there who work for this type of employer.

The Relator

Sun signs include the water signs, Cancer, Pisces, and Scorpio; sometimes Libra and Aquarius.

The Relator group gets energy from people-to-people contact. They truly like people and love coaching others in problem solving. Relators feel that "problems" are merely life's little annoyances that need to be moved out of the way so the "hindered one" can move on with life. It gives Relators pleasure to see "lightbulbs" go off when an employee experiences relief and envisions a clear path of action. These bosses enjoy bouncing ideas off the wall that may bring to light a hidden course of action.

Relators get things done by putting people first. As bosses they spend considerable time recruiting employees with the right mix of skills for their team. They value differences in approach and personality. Most of them go out of their way to help team members understand each other. Relators are sensitive to the needs of staff and look for person-job congruence. They put your talents to good use, or they'll help you find another job. With their characteristic fluid communicating style, Relator employers praise your accomplishments. The message flows generously from the depth of their souls. They know how to say thank you.

Relators care more about developing employee potential than focusing on the organization. They believe that organizations need the human touch to reach their goals. They invest in testing instruments and motivational training to give employees both greater insight into their personalities and a new perspective for their work. Team building sessions appeal to them and are a favorite communications vehicle if they are held away from the interruptions of the work site.

Among bosses, Relators are the Personal Attention Wizards of the zodiac and make it their business to find out what makes employees tick. They learn the birthdays of staff members and often plan a small ceremony or lunch to celebrate it. Many of them hire astrologers on retainer to make sure they put a compatible team together. These sensitive bosses have a win-win philosophy and support overworked employees by enlisting help from others on the team. Since Relators are big on reward and recognition, they want approval from the organizational hierarchy in return for their outstanding staff contributions. A favorite Relator saying is "Let's make a difference"—and they do.

Observation skills come naturally to Relators. You won't have to worry about telling these employers that you are unhappy with your work; they read it in your body language. Have you got a problem with your work schedule? Relators may authorize telecommuting to keep production on target. Has it been a long time since you had a day off? Relators are likely to suggest you take a day off before you even figure out you need one. Relators have the mind-reading capability of making a suggestion before their employees even have the courage to broach the subject. Employees need not fear Relator bosses, who are normally very sympathetic toward them and sincerely concerned with their personal problems. In fact, the Achilles' heel of Relators is that they often put all others first and have no time to work on their own goals.

Cancer Relators have their pulse on the organizational climate and bring about change through their personal charisma and caring. Pisces Relators have patience and excel in complicated situations by weighing psychological factors before judging performance shortfalls. Scorpios see the phoenix rising in chaotic circumstances. They often turn liabilities into assets in dealing with people problems that arise during reorganizations or layoffs. Libras excel in public relations by selling subordinates on the benefits of working for an organization that values their contributions. The Aquarian Relators are universal optimists who convey a powerful message that the organization is a better place when employees care. If you work with a Relator, you probably know that understanding means a lot to your boss.

The Hermit

Sun signs include Capricorn, Cancer, Scorpio, and Pisces; sometimes Taurus and Virgo.

Employees who work with Hermit bosses have limited communication opportunities. Each day they play a game of hide and seek to gauge the boss' availability. Hermits prefer to work behind closed doors.

In the hiding mode, Hermits may surface only when nature calls. They are so private that many of them bring a bag lunch and eat it at their desks. Among them are shy types who lack good people skills. Interruptions and questions from others exhaust them. Some compare the human voice to noise pollution. You might say they are complete opposites of Relators, and, to some extent, Communicators. Most Hermits lobby for private offices instead of open space work environments.

Hermits often have no interest in rubbing elbows with hierarchy, much less subordinates. If asked, they state that they are paid to do their work, not to socialize, and they expect the same from their team. This attitude is especially apparent if they are at odds with the organization's philosophy or leaders. Some Hiding Hermits stoop to posting "Do Not Disturb" signs when they want privacy. A few order their secretaries to hold calls indefinitely, while others have set times when they are willing to receive calls and expect to have their wishes carried out.

In the "seek" phase, employees need answers and look desperately for signs the office door might open a crack. When the "thumbs up" signal flashes, employees line up, jockeying for position to see the boss. If they step out of line, they lose their turn. Most of them are unwilling to push their luck, although a few of them are tempted to yell "fire!"

When Hermits turn into "seekers," they emerge from their caves looking for warm bodies to carry out the work. These bosses create a stressful work place by keeping things close to the chest. Employees understand the drill, but secretly desire more ownership and involvement in the goals of the organization. Robotic types respond to the cookbook assignments much more easily than creative, enterprising types who usually get frustrated and leave. Capricorn Hermits have good decision-making skills, yet often appear aloof; Cancer Hermits get into the cocooning rut when they feel deadended in a job or get passed over for a promotion. Secretive Scorpios share information when they are sure they have solid approval for their products and don't want anyone else to get credit for what they have done. Pisces Hermits may be suffering from low self-esteem and feel safer in retreat. The Taurus Hermits hide out when they feel they lack appropriate skills to get the job done effectively. If they don't develop essential talents, they move on to more suitable structures that give them a chance to shine. Lack of mental stimulation drives Virgos to the Hermit Farm. Holed up, they become the nit-pickers of the zodiac because they secretly perceive their assignments as "busy work."

The Hermit's work environment is hardly going to win the Playground of the Year Award. It needs a boost of creative energy, a little levity and pizzazz. Employees need evidence that their bosses appreciate them and enjoy their company once in a while.

The Entertainer

Sun signs include Leo, Aries, and Aquarius; sometimes Pisces, Taurus, and Libra.

Entertainers believe in leading with flair. They are charming and at ease with employees, and their doors are always open to visitors. Entertainers' contacts enjoy their fascinating presence and seek their opinions, often to add levity to tense situations. Entertainers know when to execute a well-timed joke to break up a stormy discussion without seeming silly. They excel at quick verbal exchanges.

No two Entertainers express their style in quite the same way. The work place is a stage of sorts, and they play multiple roles. Colleagues describe them as scene stealers. They are high-spirited, warmly enthusiastic, and imaginative. Entertainers have an uncanny ability to relate to others and often take on their characteristics, emotions, and beliefs. When they want to illustrate a sensitive point, they often play the mime and exaggerate the behavior that needs modification. Of course their antics bring down the house, and that's what Entertainers desire.

These bosses greatly influence work-place dynamics. Their body language and other forms of nonverbal communication have an extraordinary impact on motivating employees. Entertainers are aware of the messages their presence carries and strive for authenticity in dealing with others. Like Relators, they feel energized by interactions with people. When they use masterful, dramatic statements, these employers expect bottom line results, and they usually get them. A meeting, conference, or event chaired by an Entertainer draws a crowd. It may have a humorous theme, yet attendees know the Entertainer influences the wheels of progress, and they came to get with the program.

Since they crave the spotlight, Entertainers enjoy making a big splash in the company. Most of them enjoy putting on a show. Their signature style gives sagging morale a boost. This group excels at highlighting major facets of the work and in showing appreciation to staff members for their significant contributions. Leo Entertainers dislike small, boring meeting rooms. They use theatrics, high-impact visual techniques, and unusual settings to inspire the team and convey important messages. Aries Entertainers opt for Outward Bound experiences or competitive events to promote bonding with the staff. Pisces Entertainers involve staff in community projects. They create imaginative campaign slogans and promotional materials to attract passion and interest in major undertakings. Taurus stimulates staff interaction by scheduling catered lunches or occasional potlucks. When it's time to say "thank you" for a job well done, the Taurus Entertainer says it with exquisite flowers and imported chocolates. Libra Entertainers give the staff the afternoon off and invite them to lunch in unique settings to encourage harmonious social exchanges. A relaxing dining option might include a show and a meal on a local cruise ship.

If you like the roar of an appreciative crowd, find employment with a free-spirited Entertainer. You'll have the inside track on learning poise and basking in the limelight.

The Smiling Executioner

Sun signs include Leo, Aquarius, Sagittarius; sometimes Scorpio, Gemini, and Aries.

If you are a typical employee, you want to know as much as you can about your boss so your relationship gets off to a good start. You'll probably first assess your employer based on outer appearance. Isn't what you see usually what you get? Just look at the packaging! A pleasant face, a twinkle in the eye, a charming smile, and a good conversationalist. How lucky can you get? Think you might have Good Boss Karma, or does it all sound too good to be true? If your boss is the Smiling Executioner, you had better look again!

Next time you terminate a conversation with your boss, turn around and look at the so-called friendly face to see if that grin has been replaced with a scowl. As for those twinkling eyes—they are looking mighty shifty. Notice how they keep darting around while your boss is nodding "yes" to something you propose? And what's with the disappearing act on the ear-to-ear smile? Was it merely pasted on? You exchanged considerable dialogue, but now you wonder if what you heard was really a lot of double talk. Is the strategy you discussed a "go" or a "no"?

Feeling confused by the next course of action? You should be. With the Smiling Executioner as your boss, you'll seldom know where you stand. Clueless is the operative word. This species of bosses is among the most dangerous. They'll seal a deal with a smile and maybe a handshake and reverse their position the moment you leave. You may be the last to know the winds of change are blowing cold air on your great ideas, and that's only for starters.

Smiling Executioners falsely give employees a sense of security about their status in the company, the quality of their work, and the state of their involvement in organizational goals. After an exchange, these treacherous bosses act in total disregard to the positive messages they just delivered. Executioners give themselves broad latitude to change their minds and let their venomous chips annihilate unsuspecting "victims." Sadly, employees don't understand they've been "had" in early exchanges with these bosses. When the ax falls, they realize they've been dealing with a viper.

Smiling Executioners are masters at setting people up for a fall. Their double-dealing antics cost talented employees their self-confidence and often their careers. When staff members sift through the destruction, they often make a beeline to the grievance officer to report the Smiling Executioners' underhanded tactics.

It's difficult to describe how you ought to read a Smiling Executioner. These employers have many faces, most of them covered up by that perpetual grin; if only it was genuine! The root of their manipulative behavior is usually low self-esteem.

Leo Executioners throw in a pat on the back and replace it with a knife when you exit the scene. Aquarius gets you all pumped up for action, then throws the manuscript you worked on for six months into the round file. Sagittarius discusses your flaws with the next person on the scene and sends your reputation to the shredder. Scorpio Executioners wait until you're going on vacation and then smilingly inform you that you have five minutes to pack up because it's your last day on the job. Gemini springs for lunch and glowingly critiques your performance. Over dessert, she tells you the company is reorganizing without you. The Smiling Aries Executioner looks at you with those lying eyes and tells you you're going places. At quitting time, he gives you a pink slip.

You can be sure of one thing when it comes to a Smiling Executioner: Behind that grin there's a hidden agenda. You may not get fired, but you will get tired of the amount of damage control required to work for the Smiling Executioner. If you are currently employed by one of these smiley bosses, anticipate that you will soon be job hunting.

The Producer

Sun signs include Virgo, Capricorn, and Cancer; sometimes Pisces, Taurus, and Libra.

One of the most action-oriented bosses is the Producer. These employers enjoy tackling piles of work or checklists with complex action items. If a staff member appears "stuck" or perplexed over how to handle the work load, Producers jump right in and tactfully help the employee make a decision. These bosses seldom get annoyed by questions from the staff; in fact, they are thoughtful problem solvers who prefer closure to loose ends. Producers put excellent tracking systems in place. Their mental filing systems are razor sharp, yet they post flow charts and use visual aids as well to keep employees aware of task status.

Producers feel it is their innate duty to make those "mountains" of problems disappear. It gives them a high to know they have accomplished something of value. These employers are masters at multiple tasking, and they enjoy the countdown to successful completion of the task at hand. They roll up their sleeves and pitch right in when deadlines loom. No task is beneath them, yet they usually know how to distribute the work load to maximize the skills of the team. Driven by a desire to get things done, these bosses combine excellent analytical skills with adept decision making. They are not necessarily the creative mission shapers of the organization, but you can count on them to take the ball and run with it. Their niche is to develop efficiency techniques that expedite work load completion and keep the goals on target. They tell you how to get where you want to go.

Producers know when you are not pulling your share of the weight. To make them happy, you need to be a bit of a clone because they want evidence of responsibility, ambition, and loyalty in getting the job done. While quantity is an important driver, these bosses believe that having a logical process in place helps cut through the red tape that slows down progress. Producers act on matters that need attention. To them, life's a breeze when they can shift hindsight into accelerated insight and get the wheels in gear again.

Virgo Producers understand that blocks to progress need attention before production resumes in full bloom. Like the Pisces example, they prefer to analyze conditions before creating their voluminous output. Capricorn leads with a passion and wants to beat previous accomplishment goals so the entire team gains recognition. Cancer works extra hours and misses a few meals to clear the decks of unfinished tasks rather than force employees to give up weekends or work late. Imaginative Pisces invents concepts that put a little fun into the production plans and help to motivate the team in the process. Taurus looks for ways to save money on production techniques that might be converted into better salaries for the employees. Libra's holistic approach to motivating the team involves balancing the work with the personal life for true effectiveness, and Libra sweetens the pot for all employees who contribute to the end results. Every version of the Producer anticipates praise for a job well done. Be sure to acknowledge your Producer employer's impeccable performance.

If you enjoy a busy environment where challenging work taps your talents, check out the Producer. This employer appreciates you for the quantity of work you complete and the quality of the product.

The Wimp

Sun signs include Virgo, Taurus, and Pisces; sometimes Capricorn; Libra and Cancer.

Among the most frustrating of bosses are individuals who have trouble making decisions. When it is clear to staff members that action is needed, Wimps become lethargic and seem incapable of acting on pressing issues. Employees talk about these bosses with a fair share of disdain. Why? Because they appear to have no concern about how their inactivity affects the work place. They just stick their heads in the sand and hope the problems—and you—will go away. Wimpy employers disappoint staff by letting important matters slide when they really need a decision. Consequently, employees seldom know the true status of their standing in the work place or the value of the work they produce.

The Wimp's style is opposite that of the highly organized Producer who thrives on analysis and action. These bosses get through their day by hiding out in meetings, taking extended lunch breaks, or chewing the fat on the telephone. They secretly hope no one finds them to tax their brains with pressing problems. The Wimp's real issue is a lack of confidence that what they decide will be acceptable to higher authorities. In other words, they are afraid of getting fired for making a mistake, only they'll never admit it to you. Instead, they manage the work environment in a fog. Almost nothing gets done by intention—default rules their world; or someone else with a better idea takes action and sets the wheels in motion. They find distractions to keep them from acting logically.

Never pass the baton to Wimp employers. They'll hide it under the desk and forget they have the power to make meaningful changes in the work place. Instead, Wimps practice Lame Excuse Management. They invariably keep others holding the bag while precious time is wasted waiting for answers, assistance, or closure. Don't look for Wimps to seal the deal! These bosses prefer stalling. When a problem arises between personnel, Wimps play both sides of the coin and earn the scorn of peers and subordinates.

You seldom know where Wimps stand on a given issue. When a decision is needed, they never show their hand as to how they might be leaning. The coward in them lies low until the last person votes on an option—then they pick the side with the most votes. Wimps often tell people what they want to hear, and then fall short of delivering the goods. When Wimps go limp on a promise, you probably won't trust their word in future encounters—and you shouldn't. They follow a slippery path, and you feel like you are holding on to a bowl of Jello.

Each of the wimpy types adds their own unique twist to decision dodging. Virgo Wimps often busy themselves in busywork projects to avoid confrontations with employees. Who is going to argue with a boss who says, "I'm too busy"? Taurus Wimps blame all their decision reversals on reduced budgets. That way they don't have to explain to disappointed employees why they failed to effectively showcase staff accomplishments. The Pisces Wimp reads urgent memos citing pressing issues and pretends to blow off steam. As soon as the messenger leaves, Pisces shreds the evidence. The Capricorn Wimp delegates authority for anything that sounds messy, especially personnel problems. Libra Wimps look for a legal loophole and pass the buck to a higher authority. Cancer Wimps act like they are going to do something to correct the problem at the next opportunity, and then they lose their memory.

Exploring the Eclipses of the Year 2000

By Dorothy Oja

An eclipse is a dramatic event. Eclipses have a long and mysterious history and have always held a special place in the consciousness of humanity. For instance, look at the old woodcuts found in art and history books. They often depict our ancestors looking askance at a sky darkened by this strange phenomenon of altered light and darkness during the day. Life and light are operating in a seemingly abnormal manner—but that's just it. Eclipses are entirely natural occurrences in the cycles of the Moon and Earth in relation to the Sun; however, something truly strange does happen. Animals feel the weirdness and respond to the extreme changes in the electromagnetic field and certainly to the darkening effect produced when a solar eclipse takes place.

Even at night, our big "night light," the Moon, seemingly disappears in the Earth's shadow. Scientists can measure the changes in the electromagnetic field during an eclipse, but we don't understand exactly how those changes affect us.

A natural psychological reaction to something strange is to become at least momentarily more alert. This hyperalertness will then induce us to respond in one of two ways: fight or flight. This, at least, has been the prevailing psychological theory. All theories are subject to review, and they change as time and experience teach us. Not fully understanding the way in which the electromagnetic forces affect us, we may have subtle responses that we can't identify. Partly because of this, I like to think of eclipses as magical and mysterious moments in the historical development of our lives and that of society and culture. Certainly our ancient ancestors revered and even feared eclipses. The traditional view is that they are portents, a foreshadowing or foretelling of things to come. They were seen as harbingers (mostly negative) of changes in the lives of rulers (the Sun) during solar eclipses and affecting the public (the Moon) during lunar eclipses. As we explore the wondrously detailed world of the eclipse, we shall see that even the same types of solar and lunar eclipses are not all alike in their basic nature nor in their manifestation in our lives.

The What and Why of an Eclipse

Eclipses take place when the centers of the Sun, Moon, and Earth are in a straight or nearly straight line. The Sun or Moon must be at or near one of the Moon's nodes at New or Full Moon. In addition, the Sun and Moon must be within 1° of the same degree of declination or parallel to each other for a solar eclipse, and contraparallel (one north and one south) in the case of a lunar eclipse. Declination is the position of a planet either north or south of the celestial equator. The New Moon must be within at least 18° 31' of the North or South Node to produce a partial solar eclipse. Between 0° and 9° 55' of a node, it becomes a total solar eclipse. The orbs for a lunar eclipse are similar but somewhat smaller. If the Full Moon occurs within 9° 30' to 12° 15' of either node, a partial eclipse can take place; between 3° 45' and 6° 00' of either node, the lunar eclipse can be either partial or total. If the Full Moon is within 0° to 3° 45' of either node, it must be a total lunar eclipse.

Eclipses occur with great regularity, and that is why ancient astrologer and astronomers were able to predict their occurrence with such great accuracy. In fact, solar eclipses take place about every 169.5 days. Solar and lunar eclipses usually occur in pairs, and when this happens, the lunar eclipse takes place either fourteen days before or after the solar eclipse. Occasionally, solar eclipses occur without an accompanying lunar eclipse, but there can never be a lunar eclipse without an accompanying solar eclipse. The greatest number of eclipses that are possible in one year is seven: five solar and two lunar, or four solar and three lunar. The least number of eclipses in one year is two, and they would both be solar, since the Sun crosses over the nodal axis twice a year, once over the North Node, then six months later, over the South Node.

We experience distortions of the Sun's energy field during a solar eclipse. We can gauge the inherent strength of transmission from an eclipse by the amount of distortion produced in the energy fields of the Sun, Moon, and Earth. Total eclipses create more disturbances than partial eclipses because they shadow more of the light of either the Sun or Moon when they take place.

The more we study eclipses, the more it becomes apparent what an organized cosmic pulsation is at work in eclipse patterns, and what a strong effect this regular rhythm has on our lives here on Earth. During a lunar eclipse, there is a cessation of infrared electromagnetic waves that are normally refracted by the Moon.

How Eclipses Affect our Lives

Because eclipses occur in the same sign pair numerous times and then move on to the next sign pair, they will activate a house polarity in your chart sometimes for as long as two years. This is highly significant and deserves careful study. The eclipse energy will be channeled through the planet in your chart closest in aspect to the eclipse degree. On a mundane or social level, the planet, planets, or fixed stars that are the closest in aspect to the eclipse degree describe, in part, the activity that will result from a particular eclipse! Those planets or fixed stars are then called the rulers of that particular eclipse.

We must remember that eclipses emphasize the intimate relationship between the Sun, Moon, and Earth. We as inhabitants of Earth are uniquely affected by this dynamic shifting in the typical relationship between these planets. We could postulate that our equilibrium is temporarily upset, and we need to adjust to that shift in some way. Changes in the electromagnetic energy must also affect us neurologically and, therefore, mentally. It is not too far-fetched to deduce that we experience some residual effect from these electromagnetic changes. Our bodies are magnetized or maybe even realigned in some mysterious way, perhaps to keep us centered or focused on our destiny or our purpose.

Like all cycles, eclipse cycles are developmental movements in our lives. Eclipses can shake us up, somewhat. Shock, they say, is good for the soul and a reminder of our humanness. Eclipses shock our system with their own particular brand of awareness and induce us to take notice of a specific area of our lives. The intensity of the eclipse jolts us free from our lethargy and wakes us up to what needs repair. This process can then enable us to review our lives and reevaluate our actions and intentions. We can say that an eclipse reminds us of how, with whom, and why we are connecting through the eclipse-activated house environment of our chart. The hidden quality (the darkening and distortion) inherent in eclipses can mean that they mark significant milestones in the life of an individual (or nation) that is not at first recognizable. The significance of a particular eclipse is vastly increased if the eclipse degree aspects a planet or point in the horoscope exactly. You can expect even more intense registration of the eclipse effect if a particular eclipse conjuncts or opposes either your natal Sun or Moon. Light is displaced, but only temporarily. Even temporarily, being separated from the light is truly frightening. Our light is blocked and with it the life-giving energy that we associate with it. We could say that eclipses ask us to consider death on some level, and at the very least, that a stage in our lives has ended and we must go on to the next one.

In this way, an eclipse is prominent in your chart by its intimate or exact connection to a planet, point, or angle in the natal or the progressed chart. An eclipse can stir the issues of a particular house but won't be strongly relevant unless it connects by aspects. If this is the case with the eclipses of 2000, you will want to take note of the ninteen-year eclipse cycles that are of great importance. Every nineteen years approximately, the Sun and Moon return almost exactly to the same position in relation to the nodes of the Moon, and eclipses occur close to the same degree plus 10°, each time. Take stock of your life and review what happened of importance nineteen years ago. You are now one spiral up from that time in your life, but you ought to be able to observe a similar theme or themes. Not every eclipse follows this nineteen-year cycle—some return earlier, some later, and there are some eclipses families (Saros series) that do not repeat at all in your lifetime. Still, the majority of eclipses you experience will reappear each nineteen years and are therefore significant in tracking the development of your life themes.

It is unclear how long the effects of an eclipse last. From the writings of others and my own experience, I would estimate that an eclipse certainly lasts until the next one of the same type comes along. Sometimes eclipse effects last for a year or years, particularly if there are important transits to the eclipse degree after it takes place. If you want to work with eclipses in your chart, I'd suggest keeping a log of major transiting planets and even lunations (Moon phases) to the eclipse degree, particularly if the eclipse was prominent by aspect to your natal chart. You may be surprised, as you keep your eclipse journal, how long the effects follow you into the future.

Working with Eclipses

First, analyze the eclipse in question by assessing the overall eclipse chart (timed for the start of darkening) for the eclipse ruler, the planet or fixed star most closely connected to the eclipse degree. Next, observe in which house the eclipse is taking place in your chart. Third, notice which planet or point in your chart makes the closest mathematical aspect to the eclipse degree. Conjunctions and oppositions seem to register the loudest and are certainly the most responsible for the crises that an eclipse can trigger in your life; and let me state here that I do not consider the word "crisis" to indicate a completely negative effect. I do feel it is a challenge to be met and usually one that is urgent and can't wait. The dictionary describes crisis as "a decisive or crucial time, stage, or event." Certainly, not all eclipses will affect you as strongly as others; however, even though you may not have a planet connected to the eclipse degree, the activities of the house polarity stimulated by the eclipse are likely to be somehow affected. Next, and very important, determine to which Saros Series a particular eclipse belongs, and discover its basic nature and whether it is essentially more positive or difficult.

The Saros Series

The Saros Series refers to eclipse families or groups first discovered by the ancient Babylonians. The word Saros means "repetition" or "to repeat." In the Saros cycle, eclipses begin at either the North or South Pole as partial eclipses. Approximately every eighteen years, another eclipse occurs a bit closer to the nodal axis. Eventually the partial eclipse becomes a total eclipse as it moves closer and closer to the nodal axis. After reaching a conjunction with the nodes and totality, the eclipse continues toward the opposite pole from where it began and moves further and further away from the nodal axis. Now it moves away from totality and becomes a partial eclipse again until it ends at the opposite pole. This is a very long process of approximately 1,300 years. The eclipse that began the particular series, which is then assigned a number in the Saros Series, describes the basic nature of that series. There are a number of Saros Series eclipses taking place in the same time span and all at different levels in their development. Determining the Saros Series number that an eclipse belongs to and whether it began at the North or South Pole gives amazing meaning to the type of effect that can be expected. Some of the Saros Series eclipses are very difficult indeed, while others are beneficent. As you can see, there are many things to take into consideration when analyzing eclipses and their potential effects.

The Prenatal Solar Eclipse

While on the subject of eclipses, we ought to at least mention the prenatal solar eclipse. This is the nearest solar eclipse occurring prior to birth. This eclipse highlights an area that is of major importance in your life and, more often than not, becomes a dominant theme in your life. The reason I mention this is that one of the year 2000 eclipses may be a prenatal eclipse return if you are aged 18, 36, 54, etc., (an approximate eighteen-year cycle). Or you could be receiving an opposition to your prenatal eclipse if you are 27, 45, 63, etc. If you are expecting a child, one of the solar eclipses of 2000 would become your child's prenatal solar eclipse. There is all kind of room here for study and research. I do hope you'll agree, however, that eclipses are full of vital clues to the reason and consequence of our lives on Earth.

Eclipse Paths

The path of a solar eclipse is the precise shadow cast by the Moon on the Earth for the duration of its occurrence. The parts of the Earth shadowed by the solar eclipse are more often than not sensitized in a particular way. However, the manner in which an eclipse connects with the actual chart of a country or person is most relevant, as is the basic character of the Saros Series it belongs to. The length of the effect of an eclipse varies, but the eclipse degree and the place that received the eclipse shadow can remain sensitive for years.

Eclipses of the Year 2000

I've relocated all the eclipse charts from Greenwich Mean Time to Washington, D.C., since that is the seat of government in the United States. Notice that there are three, count them, three eclipses in the month of July!

Eclipses have noticeable patterns. A lunar eclipse is said to partly support the themes defined in the solar eclipse closest to it. Sometimes lunar eclipses occur two weeks prior to the next solar eclipse. In this case, the two eclipses bracket the waning phase of the Moon cycle. In this sequence (lunar first, then solar), there is likely to be more reaction than action. The tone tends to be subjective and is concerned with unfulfilled needs and emotions. When a solar eclipse precedes a lunar eclipse, the two eclipses bracket the waxing Moon phase. In this sequence (solar first, then lunar), the energy is more objective and action-oriented. The need is to initiate action in the areas outlined by the lunar eclipse and to reinforce the issues stimulated by the solar eclipse in the sequence. In July of 2000, we have three eclipses in one month, a rare condition. The sequence solar, lunar, solar is also uncommon. The lunar eclipse sandwiched between two solar eclipses supports both solar eclipses. This lunar eclipse will point to an area of reaction or necessary development, and the two solar eclipses lend the energy and take the necessary action characterized by sign and eclipse ruler. Another fact of major importance is that the lunar eclipse of July 16, 2000 is the longest lunar eclipse of the century, lasting a full one hour and forty-seven minutes! The July series of eclipses promises to be of major importance in world affairs. Read on!

Solar Eclipses of 2000

A solar eclipse takes place only at the time of the New Moon. All the solar eclipses of 2000 are partial. A partial eclipse occurs when the Moon's disc does not fully cover the disc of the Sun. To the ancients, the fact that a fixed star was either conjunct the eclipse degree or on the eastern or western horizon had to be taken into consideration in interpreting the overall theme of the eclipse. The fixed star associated with the eclipse then became one of the rulers of the eclipse. Solar eclipses activate ego needs for recognition and self-awareness, as well as issues of vitality, love, and the drive for expression or prominence. During a solar eclipse, the Moon is positioned between the Sun and the Earth. The Moon is always the reflector of the Sun's light as well as its collector. Because of the exact or near-exact alignment of the three bodies (Sun, Moon, Earth), the Sun focuses the Moon's shadow on the Earth. It's a concentrated application, almost like a laser's ray in reverse. The hidden side of the Moon is bright with the Sun's illumination, while the visible side of the Moon (toward us) is dark. The darkest part or the complete shadow cast is called the umbra and the partial shadow area surrounding the umbra is called the penumbra.

Lunar Eclipses of 2000

Lunar eclipses take place only at a Full Moon. All the lunar eclipses of 2000 are total which makes them stronger and more intense in their effect as they displace more of the infrared electromagnetic waves naturally given off by the Moon. A total eclipse means that the Earth's shadow completely covers the surface of the Moon. Lunar eclipses are longer in duration than solar eclipses. Lunar eclipses stimulate the emotional and natural instincts and the collective needs of groups of people.

1. Total Lunar Eclipse, January 21, 2000 at 0° 26' Leo

This is a Saros Series 1 South eclipse. The basic nature of S.S. 1 South is the expression and discussion of ideas in a large public forum. The planetary picture shows Mercury conjunct South Node equals New Moon, Mars, and Jupiter. The eclipse characteristic is the broad and enthusiastic expression of new ideas with some impulsiveness mixed in and impatience to advance ideas, philosophies, and theories. We could expect continued shifts in the publishing world (already occurring) and advanced ways of communicating and reaching public awareness. It is essentially a positive combination and excellent for problem solving and pioneering solutions, primarily in any of the vast array of communication and educational fields.

This eclipse opposes the fixed star Albireo at 0° Aquarius and makes Albireo the ruler of the eclipse. Albireo (The Song of the Dying Swan) is said to give a handsome appearance, a lovable disposition, and beneficence in despair. The collective mood of the people embraces new and better ideas in a spirit of excited exploration. This indicates a surge of good will and hope for the new millennium and for a new American presidency. People gather and band together for mutual caring, sharing, and positive growth. There is a sense of community that expands to all those in need. People will respond to sincerity, necessity, and efficient resolution of issues. Great collective ideas will be born. Social Security issues may very well be resolved, or new and better systems put in place to stabilize the lives of older Americans. The eclipse takes place near the North Node of the Moon and has most to do with energy gathered together, reaching critical mass, and rushing toward progress and advancement.

2. Partial Solar Eclipse, February 5, 2000 at 16° 02' Aquarius

This eclipse also belongs to the Saros Series 1 South family, as explained above. We can expect scientific innovation and advances in sports and communications. Uranus at 16° Aquarius conjuncts the eclipse degree at 16° Aquarius. Uranus in focus reinforces innovation, invention, and scientific or technological discovery. In the Washington, D.C. location, the fixed star Fomalhaut is rising on the eastern horizon at 3° Pisces. Thus Uranus and Fomalhaut are both rulers of this eclipse. Uranus always brings about the unexpected, the surprise, the truth, and creative invention. Fomalhaut (the Fish's Mouth) is one of the four Royal Stars of ancient Persia. (The other Royal Stars are Regulus, Aldebaran, and Antares.) Fomalhaut was called the Watcher of the South and marked the Winter Solstice. Fame or infamy and conflict between matter and spirit characterize Fomalhaut. There could be controversial debate around some of these scientific advances and discoveries. A revolutionary spirit of discovery, innovation, and unexpectedly precipitous events prevails.

This solar eclipse is close to the Moon of the USA chart at 18° Aquarius and at the midpoint of the Moon and the 14° Aquarius Medium Coeli, in the 8° Sagittarius-rising chart. The basic nature of this eclipse is benign and deals with healthy though often heated discussion of some very controversial topics. However, with the Uranian influence, the people (the Moon) are electrified and excitable over the debate, possibly even polarized. Unforeseen, unexpected, abrupt events can upset the status quo. This eclipse portends some wild and unruly times although it contains a saving grace. Taking place at the South Node of the Moon, it connotes old, unfinished issues resurfacing and needing revision. The call is for greater clarity and a biting kind of truthfulness that will disturb some groups of people. The greatest shadow of this eclipse occurs around Antarctica and the South Pole. What new discoveries emerge from the ice?

3. Partial Solar Eclipse, July 1, 2000 at 10° 14' Cancer

This eclipse belongs to the Saros Series 2 Old North. New Moon conjunct Jupiter at the Mars/Uranus midpoint and Mercury at the Venus/Saturn midpoint characterize this Saros Series. This is traditionally a difficult eclipse series. The planetary patterns are inherently separative and abrupt and concern actions of severing friendships and personal relationships. Although there is a sudden severity to the combination, the message or truth of the situation will be quickly grasped and positive in outcome.

The planet Mars is conjunct the eclipse degree of 10° Cancer, adding to aggression and potential violent action. In Washington, D.C., the fixed star Spica is rising on the eastern horizon at 22° Libra. Thus Mars and Spica are rulers of this eclipse. Spica rising is noted for unexpected honors, fame, refinement, good fortune, social success, or advancement beyond one's hopes mixed with possible turbulence. The eclipse is close to the USA Sun at 12° Cancer, indicating a need to re-identify a course of direction or action. There is need for potential intervention in an international problem. A sudden uprising prompts severe action and can affect large groups of innocent people. The actions demanded by this eclipse need careful scrutiny and a larger vision. A unique and wise individual rises to the foreground of public awareness. This eclipse takes place near the North Node of the Moon and is ultimately progressive. The path of this partial solar eclipse is located around the very southern tip of South America. We can expect some activity in that area.

4. Total Lunar Eclipse, July 16, 2000 at 24° 19' Capricorn

This eclipse also belongs to the Saros Series 2 Old North, again indicating separative issues regarding friendships and relationships. The fixed star Regulus, one of the four Royal Stars, is rising on the eastern horizon at 28° Leo in Washington, D.C. at the time of this eclipse. According to the ancient Persians, Regulus was the Watcher of the North and marked the Summer Solstice. Regulus (a Little King) gives success, high and lofty ideals, and strength of spirit, and makes its natives magnanimous, grandly liberal, generous, ambitious, fond of power, high-spirited, and independent. If rising, Regulus gives great honor and power, but also trouble. The fixed star Procyon is opposite the eclipse degree at 25° Cancer. Procyon (Before the Dog) gives activity and makes its natives petulant, timid, unfortunate, easily angered, and violent. Regulus and Procyon share the rulership of this eclipse. This eclipse is close to the South Node of the Moon, indicating that issues need to be revisited and unresolved material dealt with.

This eclipse is of immense importance for a number of reasons. First it is a total lunar eclipse, and all total eclipses create the most interruption of electromagnetic energy including light and, therefore, they herald disruption and crisis in our lives as well. (Please note the definition of "crisis" earlier in this article.) This particular lunar eclipse holds the record for this century as being the longest in duration, one hour and forty-seven minutes. It is sandwiched between two solar eclipses, and all three take place within the month of July. There's more. The eclipse degree is exactly opposite the U.S. Mercury at 24° Cancer! Mercury rules the U.S. Mars in Gemini. There will be continued ideological debate and some fractious situations at the same time. Out of this disruptive climate, advanced ideas are formed, appropriate to the sophistication and vision of the millennial trend. With the royal star Regulus prominent, political matters of great consequence will emerge. The person running for U.S. President will be highlighted in some grand way. The country will be ideologically and philosophically divided. Whoever emerges as a presidential candidate will have his or her hands full in mending the political and social rifts of the country. Remember also that the solar eclipse of February 5 sits within a few degrees of the U.S. Moon and sets a tone for changes and potential disruption in the country. The solar eclipses in July are close (2°) to the U.S. Sun and U.S. North Node. The United States will play a major role in global skirmishes concerning financial markets, weapons of mass destruction, and continuing border problems.

5. Partial Solar Eclipse, July 31, 2000 at 8° 12' Leo

This eclipse belongs to the Saros Series 2 New North. This Saros family is quite difficult. The planetary picture is New Moon on the Mercury/Node midpoint, Uranus on the New Moon/Pluto midpoint, the Node is on the Jupiter/Pluto midpoint, and Saturn is on the Venus/Node midpoint. This is a combination of transformation and includes the dissolution or destruction of pre-existing patterns or lifestyles. There is the necessity to rebuild, and effects can be long-lasting. This eclipse conjuncts the fixed star South Asellus at 8° Leo. South Asellus (the Mare Ass), when joined to the Sun, is characterized by unfavorable dealings with the public and influential people, as well as trouble in business. When joined with the Moon, it is bad for business affairs and brings trouble through enemies. This eclipse is close to the North Node of the Moon, indicating the need to move ahead and strive for greater progress, particularly in the area of leadership.

Fomalhaut, one of the four Royal fixed stars, is again on the eastern horizon in Washington, D.C. at 2° Pisces at the moment of the eclipse. Fortune and power characterize Fomalhaut and, if rising, great and lasting honors. Taking everything into consideration, this means trouble in governmental institutions and likely the breaking up or certainly the restructuring of political and power groups. Also indicated is a strong reaction from the public. There seems to be a violation of sorts that incenses the populace and brings vigorous reaction. Systems tend to break down under this eclipse combination. Watch for crisis in the money markets and with large and powerful corporations. This eclipse essentially brings disruption and deflation to systems that have become abusive or out of control in some way. You can apply this on a personal level or on the collective, social level. This eclipse is close to the North Node of the U.S. chart and indicates a need to move forward, that drastic measures are required, and that our country's leadership will be tested. The path of this eclipse is across the northern portions of Russia, grazing the northernmost portion of China covering Alaska, Greenland, and the western United States. These areas are highlighted for possible problems.

6. Partial Solar Eclipse, December 25, 2000 at 4° 14' Capricorn
This eclipse belongs to the Saros Series 2 South. The node on the midpoint of Mercury/Jupiter and Jupiter on the Pluto/Node midpoint, Mercury on the New Moon/Venus midpoint, and Neptune on the Uranus/Pluto midpoint characterize this Christmas eclipse. There is a need to find solace in an inspirational or spiritual group movement, and a need and desire to advance philosophically and spiritually. The effects of such seeking can be profound and transforming to the individuals involved. New spiritual and religious groups and affiliations emerge from a collective need for meaningful rituals. The major religions go through overhaul, revival, and inevitable change to meet the needs of more sophisticated and critical times. Watch for amazing visual as well as technical advancement in the all of the arts, music, and film. Communication matters are in focus, and inspirational writing can be prolific. This eclipse pattern promises euphoric artistic expressions of all forms and a wonderful support of individuality. The eclipse is close to the South Node of the Moon, indicating that issues from the past need to be resolved and realigned. South Node eclipses ask us to let go of negative habit patterns.

The planet Mercury is conjunct the eclipse degree. This degree is opposite the fixed star Dirah at 4° Cancer. The characteristics of Dirah (Seed or Branch) are that it gives force, energy, power, and protection. The fixed star Alpheraz (the Horse's Navel) is rising on the eastern horizon in Washington, D.C. at the time of the eclipse. The nature of Alpheraz is independence, love, riches, honor, and a keen intellect. Associated with the Sun, it gives honor and favor from others. In relation to the Moon, it is energetic, persevering, and portends business success and many friends. The planet Mercury and the fixed stars Dirah and Alpharez are rulers of this eclipse. There are indications of a great and inspiring orator as the next leader of our country who will lead us fully into the new millennium. We do need a strong presence and someone with a clear mind, lots of vision, and a peacemaker to mediate and heal the mistrust that has erupted in American politics. This eclipse is opposite the U.S. Jupiter (by 1°) at 5° Cancer. Much will be asked of the United States in the coming years. The path of this eclipse moves across the United States, Canada, Central America, Mexico, and the Caribbean. The United States will have to deal with domestic issues and financial and trade negotiations with its closest neighbors.

Conclusion

Taken together, the eclipses of 2000 hold promise for a new wave and movement to rally us not around personal issues as much as the pressing global issues we are and will be facing. As the numerical beginning of the twenty-first century, the year 2000 contains eclipse sequences in the sign pairs Leo/Aquarius and Cancer/Capricorn. Leo/Aquarius signifies the need to express oneself both creatively and authentically and to embody fully the sum total of life in all its surprising idiosyncrasies. Leo/Aquarius also signifies the inherent struggle of the ego with the greater good of the whole, or ego and pride versus the perspective of the larger dimension. Cancer/Capricorn is the polarity of family, community, foundation, commerce, and the basic human needs of nurturance, security, and safe spaces for growth and development. The intrinsic struggle of Capricorn/Cancer is holding onto habit and history indiscriminately. This sign pair can be rigid and fearful of change, which can limit successful living. These combinations of eclipse/sign pairs tell the story of where we need to go at the advent of the twenty-first century. We are called to embrace the next level of understanding, true multicultural acceptance, and to become more humane.

Personality Types in Astrology and Psychology

By Mark Kenski

I am excited about the prospect of bridging the gap between the art of astrology and the science of psychology. I saw a psychology book in the library recently that may be of interest to other astrologers. It is called *Personality Self-Portrait: Why You Think, Love, and Act the Way You Do* by John M. Oldham, M.D. and Lois B. Morris.

Lois is a professional writer, and Dr. Oldham is Professor of Clinical Psychiatry at Columbia University College of Physicians and Surgeons, Acting Director of the New York State Psychiatric Institute, and Chief Medical Officer of the New York State Office of Mental Health. He also helped develop a new diagnostic system for personality disorders for the American Psychiatric Association.

In this book, you take a test that is based on the different personality disorders recognized in the psychiatric handbook called *DSM-III-R (Diagnostic and Statistical Manual of Mental Disorders-Third Edition-Revised)*. After you take the test, the book helps you interpret the results and tells you about the personality types you exhibit. The premise of the book is that there are healthy "types" that correspond to the unhealthy symptoms that are usually the basis for medical diagnosis with some psychological condition. For example, one can be conscientious to a fault, for example, (though Virgos may reject that idea as absurd!). When conscientiousness becomes a disabling condition, it is termed "obsessive-compulsive disorder" by the psychological community.

I liked this concept because it is so in tune with astrology's conception of each sign as having both positive (healthy) and negative (unhealthy) expressions.

As I read, I was a little surprised at the transparent way that astrology was reclothed in modern psychological terminology. The test recognizes thirteen personality types. Each one corresponds to a pretty standard astrological sign type, except the thirteenth, which is simply another aspect of the ever-inscrutable Pisces type. The book does not credit astrology as playing a role in its development, but it could, nevertheless, serve as an astrology primer.

Not only were the types a very close fit, but the section where the book interprets the different types is reminiscent of Linda Goodman's book *Sun Signs*. There are sections on such topics as "how to get along with your conscientious spouse," and "how to deal with your dramatic boss." Some of the suggestions are good, and the book is imaginative and a fun read.

Each one of the book's thirteen types is essentially the positive expression of an astrological sign. The associated personality disorder is basically the full negative expression of the same sign.

The types break down as follows (perhaps you can guess as you go along):

Psychological Type	DSM III Disorder	Astrological Sign
1. Conscientious	Obsessive-Compulsive	Virgo
2. Self-Confident	Narcissistic	Aries
3. Devoted	Dependent	Libra
4. Dramatic	Histrionic	Leo
5. Vigilant	Paranoid	Scorpio
6. Sensitive	Avoidant	Cancer
7. Leisurely	Passive-Aggressive	Taurus
8. Adventurous	Anti-Social	Sagittarius
9. Idiosyncratic	Schizotypal	Aquarius
10. Solitary	Schizoid	Pisces #1
11. Mercurial	Borderline	Gemini
12. Self-Sacrificing	Self-Defeating	Pisces #2
13. Aggressive	Sadistic	Capricorn

Anyone who has read a single book on astrology would be able to match the names of these types to signs with probably 80 percent success, although "aggressive" and "self-confident" are a little ambiguous, astrologically.

The addition of the thirteenth type is especially interesting to me. I wonder if it would have been too obvious if the test confirmed the existence of twelve basic personality types, so a thirteenth was added. Did the authors purposely try to obscure the fact that they had essentially validated astrology's 4,000 year-old typology? Sadly, I personally don't think they even realized it. I think the test was simply able to distinguish more than one type of Pisces, since there are certainly subtypes of each sign.

Well, I took the test. Astrologically, I am a Virgo with a Cancer Moon and Leo rising. The test indicated I am a combination of (in order of strength):

Psychological Type	Astrological Sign
1. Conscientious	Virgo
2. Sensitive	Cancer
3. Dramatic	Leo

I was impressed that the test did precisely correspond to the most basic level of examination of my natal chart: the signs of the Sun, Moon, and Ascendant, respectively.

Maybe it was just luck. If I had Uranus conjunct the Ascendant in the First House, I might have registered as an Idiosyncratic (Aquarius) type. So there is a difference—the test basically gives you a weighted average of the typologies as expressed in your chart at the time you took the test. I think astrology might well benefit from the incorporation of some of these testing methodologies as an aid in chart synthesis and rectification.

The fact remains that an astrologer can ascertain the same information, and much more, with just your birthplace, date, and time, without having to ask you 104 questions and play around with a score sheet. Moreover, the book does not tell you much about how these types combine within the personality to form a unified sense of self. They do not, for example, have a concept of different "elements" of personality (each with their own type of expression) that would correspond to the Sun, Moon, and Ascendant, let alone Mercury and so on. Astrology's techniques are so much richer and more refined than this test.

There were a few nuances that came out differently in the book's description of the types than would be expected by traditional astrologers. The authors feel that Gemini (oops, the "Mercurial type") is very emotional and expresses emotions freely. I guess it depends on what you call emotions. Geminis express everything freely!

My hunch is that the test allows some astrological "bleedover" where the symbolism of one sign merges with adjacent signs. In the above case, people with inner planets in Gemini might have Mercury in Cancer (which would certainly lead them to express emotions more easily). This may have created a distortion in their sample, and thus in the typologies based on those samples.

The Devoted style (Libra) contains a few elements of Conscientious (Virgo). The Dramatic (Leo) and the Mercurial (Gemini) each contain some references to characteristics that make more sense as being part of Sensitive (Cancer). In each of these cases, it is the adjacent signs that are getting confused with one another. This makes sense, since a cross section of people will show such mixtures being more common than the "pure" types, because, astrologically, you almost never see a "pure" type.

Astrologers can learn by watching the progress of psychology in the areas of typology and diagnostics, and I definitely feel that psychology can benefit from the incorporation of astrological philosophy, if not practice. I hope this book prepares the minds of some psychiatrists to allow themselves to actually pick up an astrology book and read it. They will discover that astrology has an incredibly rich and specific language for dealing with personality and personality disorders. If they insist on keeping the *DSM* terminology, fine, but maybe they can learn something from the 4,000 years of observation that has gone into astrology. For example, look at these five types:

Psychological Type	DSM III Disorder	Astrological Sign
1. Conscientious	Obsessive-Compulsive	Virgo
2. Adventurous	Anti-Social	Sagittarius
3. Solitary	Schizoid	Pisces #1
4. Mercurial	Borderline	Gemini
5. Self-Sacrificing	Self-Defeating	Pisces #2

These five types will find each other very stimulating, but their interaction with each other is likely to emphasize the disorder side of the personality type. The square and opposition (to use astrological terminology) between any two of them will energize and challenge both types, but it also weakens their style and creates a conflict, thus making them more likely to display characteristics of the associated personality disorder.

On the other hand, Conscientious (Virgo) will be supported and strengthened by Leisurely (Taurus), and also by Aggressive (Capricorn). Any combination of these three will tend to produce a more stable union, with each type less likely to display characteristics of personality disorders.

Drawing more deeply from astrology's tradition and its understanding of the cyclical nature of all things, including human beings, we find more helpful insights. For example, when Saturn is in Taurus, the culture will shift into a period where the "fixed sign" types have more difficulties:

Psychological Type	DSM III Disorder	Astrological Sign
1. Dramatic	Histrionic	Leo
2. Vigilant	Paranoid	Scorpio
3. Leisurely	Passive-Aggressive	Taurus
4. Idiosyncratic	Schizotypal	Aquarius

Another consideration is that in addition to "styles" that correspond to the signs and types we've been discussing, there are also "compartments" in one's life. You may be a Conscientious (Virgo) type when it comes to one area, your thinking or your home, let's say, and a Dramatic type when it comes to interacting with other people. Astrology already has a way to think and talk about this. The house placement of each planet allows for a precise determination of focal points of expression where one mode of functioning (typology) will dominate.

Furthermore, psychologists using the *DSM* typology may find it helpful to think of the personality types as pairs, where some of the characteristics of the opposite pole could be helpful in reducing disordered behavior. Vigilant/Scorpio for example, while being challenged by the polarity with a person with a Leisurely/Taurus nature, will find that they grow through the conscious adoption of some of those qualities. "Relax a little, take a slower, steadier approach instead of being so intense, and you'll get more things done in the long run," the Leisurely Taurus might advise the Vigilant Scorpio.

There are other psychological typologies, such as the sixteen Myers-Briggs types and the Berkeley Personality Profile, that are quite popular, and books on these subject are interesting and rewarding material for astrologers wishing to broaden their symbolic imagination. But in the end, all of these typological systems offer only the barest beginning of the refinement and sophistication of the systems used by astrological practitioners all over the world today.

Oh, and astrology can make predictions!

Economic Forecasts for the Year 2000

By Kaye Shinker

Since ancient times astrologers have looked at a select number of charts set for the capital of their country to determine the future. Financial astrologers look at the same charts, studying the position of the Sun, Jupiter, and Saturn, specifically. First they look at the position of these planets in the Solstice and Equinox charts (when the Sun reaches zero degrees of the cardinal signs Capricorn, Aries, Cancer, and Libra). Next they look at the solar eclipses: there will be three in the year 2000. Finally they look for any special aspects between the business planets Jupiter and Saturn, which will be conjunct in the year 2000. This is called the Great Mutation and happens every twenty years. Financial astrologers study all of these charts to determine market trends in the year ahead.

Jupiter in Aries, Taurus, Gemini

Jupiter returns to Aries on October 24, 1999, and remains there until February16, 2000, when it re-enters Taurus. It remains in Taurus until July 1, 2000, when it enters Gemini and remains there until the end of the year.

Things that are in abundant supply are marked down in price; items in short supply carry a premium price. Read the entries below and make your shopping list. For example, you might want to buy a car in August because there will be an abundant supply of them, since Jupiter indicates abundance and Gemini rules cars.

In the year 2000, when Jupiter is still in Taurus, it will seem like there is an abundant supply of everything, which is almost true. Jupiter is expanding in three directions. There will still be plenty of steel, building materials, machinery, and inventions. There will be an abundant supply of banks, currency, wood, beans, costume jewelry, and leather, as well as vehicles with wheels, newspapers, tires, and communications devices that plug into the wall. Do you want to make a million dollars? Then figure out what to do with bald tires!

Industries still suffering from oversupply during the early part of the year will be scrap metals, steel, hardware, durable goods, the military, hair care supplies, and diamonds. Merchants selling these items will be able to offer deep discount prices, in case you want to start a shopping list.

Industries experiencing shortages will be art, apparel, candy, fruit, and copper. These suppliers will be able to fetch a higher price.

People will seek adventure and search for intriguing opportunities to exercise their muscles and brains. Women will be the new adventurers. They want to be first. Their courage will be admired, and their self-confidence will increase as a result.

Issues of personal freedom and privacy will be discussed during the 1999-2000 holiday season. Impatience with authorities and excessive paperwork will be the subjects of many complaints. Oppression by governments, including our own, will make the headlines. People will reject any restrictions to their personal freedom. Laws meant to protect individuals from themselves will be ignored or repealed. Personal honesty will continue to be a topic of discussion, and public figures seeking office will reveal even the DNA of the dust bunnies in their attics.

In February, industries in abundant supply will be banks, financial services, lumber, agriculture, plant nurseries, real estate, and arts and crafts materials suppliers. Banks will compete vigorously for accounts. Folks with stable incomes or government checks will be their first targets. Real estate profits will be high now. If you need to sell property, this is the time to put it on the market. Builders will find material and supplies in abundance and take advantage of the opportunity to fill up vacant lots.

Industries with shortages will be container and packaging manufacturers, mortuaries, pipelines, insurance, surgical equipment, mining, and security systems. Recycling is expensive and labor-intensive. Packaging companies will have difficulty obtaining the materials required by Green laws.

Taurus is conservative and stubborn and insists on playing by the rules. This will be difficult for entrepreneurs seeking markets for their exciting ideas. Green parties and ecology groups will expand as flowers and trees get the undivided attention of the public. Presidential candidate Al Gore will promote their cause.

On July 1, Jupiter enters Gemini. The roads will fill up with vehicles of all sorts. Billboards will line the roads. Every truck will have www.___ painted on its door. Bumper stickers will become cutesy e-mail addresses. Your friends will live by their e-mail.

In short supply will be reservations out of town, passports, sporting goods, and university placements. Everyone suddenly will want to expand their learning options. Everyone will try new sports, and the sports equipment suppliers won't keep up with demand. Shipping to foreign countries will be difficult. There will be a shortage of boats, maritime labor, and airplanes. A sudden demand for books by popular authors will catch the publishing industry with empty shelves.

Gemini loves a party, and any excuse to throw one will be valid. By the time you're ready to usher in the twenty-first century, your party clothes will be threadbare and your dancing shoes full of holes.

Folks with stock in communications companies can expect good dividends. Travel-related industries will also do well. Good advertising will be in short supply. This is political campaign time, and once again the printing industry and the media will make a profit. Politicians will decide to run for office at the last possible minute, and the media will be surprised by the number of incumbents who are defeated.

Saturn in Taurus

Saturn made a preview transit of Taurus from June 10 to October 26 in 1998, and then returned to Aries. Saturn returned to transit Taurus on March 2, 1999, and will remain there until March 2001.

The flower children of the late sixties will return to become flower children in their sixties. Economically secure, with a pension and an IRA or Keogh account to draw on, they will live on the edge. The Volkswagen bus will be a little bigger, and they will be on the road to peace, love, and adventure.

These folks, however, will not retire from their favorite sport—shopping. Older and wiser, their key word will be value. Efficiency will be their mantra. Saturn in Taurus makes profit margins difficult to maintain. Luxury items will be new tires and a phone card.

The New York Stock Exchange has a Taurus Sun, and it will be headache time. The stock exchange's problems will be structures, procedures, and interaction with foreign markets, and its employees will be stretched to the limit. Too much money will change hands. Expect transaction delays throughout the year with the year 2000 or satellites taking most of the blame for system crashes. Congress will make changes in the tax laws in order to gain reelection.

October will be difficult, as usual. The year's end will find the Dow Jones Industrial Average past 14,000 points and the Standard and Poor's 500 will be trying for 2,000 points. During Saturn's transit of Taurus, shrewd buyers will look at price earnings ratios and search for bargains in the broader markets. Incidentally, 300-point swings in the Dow will become meaningless; therefore, reporters will begin to use percentage as the measurement.

The technology-heavy NASDAQ's problems will begin in May. They will be forced to rethink rules and procedures and tighten requirements for new issues. They will certainly have to tighten their requirements for initial public offerings. Their systems for 24-hour trading will be under stress and threatened with security breaches.

Saturn in Taurus is thrifty, and this will be difficult for big banks whose income depends on credit card interest rates. Competition for new card holders who maintain a balance will be fierce. The group they will target is known as the baby bust. The baby bust will have grown into net worth mode. Sometimes called the boomerang gang because of their extended visits with their parents, they will have returned home to stay until their bills are paid.

Hoping for greater volume and market share, big banks will continue to merge. Boutique banks catering to the older baby boomers will flourish. Midsized banks will be in a squeeze. The savings rate will climb slowly even though interest rates won't move.

Gambling and spectator sports will have money problems in the United States. Fewer customers will equal fewer revenues. The casinos will suggest building more establishments, and the sports teams will want more television coverage. The problem is their wealthiest audience, the baby boomers, will like to participate and will find interactive games more fun. Local governments will not be amused since not enough "sin" tax revenue will be collected.

The babyboomlet will be in grammar school, and their baby boom parents and grandparents will not be happy with the quality of education. Expect change. Home schools, charter schools, and online schools will be popular. More innovative, small educational publishing businesses will start to appear.

Uranus in Aquarius

The year 2000 is the year for the White Elephant Skyscraper Sale. Without big nonprofit institutions to occupy their corridors, these monsters of steel will either fall of their own accord or implode.

Voluntary associations will be unable to support staff due to low membership. People will meet online and will not need a central location to publish newsletters or membership lists. National volunteer and professional organizations will cut back staff since they will only need someone to maintain their web sites.

Computer recycling bins were introduced in 1999. Word processors and game players will be able to buy any machine they want for micro amounts of cash. Excellent used machines will be in good supply, and businesses will generously donate them to anyone willing to take them. The year 2000 will be the excuse; new operating systems will be the reason.

The birthday of the computer is February 1, 1946, so it stands to reason that these little machines should dominate the world while Uranus is in Aquarius. Many of you will look at the cheap new portable variety that phones, faxes, pages, and accesses the Internet while you're camping on Mount McKinley.

Manufacturers of cables, satellites, miscellaneous wires, and switches will have difficulty keeping up with demand. The installers of electrical services are usually contract laborers, and they will be able to command even higher wages.

Instant education will be the keyword. A labor shortage in technology will worsen, and anyone who promises to learn will be sent to high-tech classes. Retired shop teachers will be asked to hang up their fishing poles and return to the classroom. Signing bonuses will be offered nationwide to first-year teachers.

The old ways won't work, and that will include volunteer organizations. Networking will always be important, but potential young members will not want to take the time to gossip over lunch or dinner when they could be gossiping over the Internet. Individuals will change their goals, and professional organizations will need to change theirs. Groups organized to educate, protect, or discipline their members will suddenly disappear. New groups with unusual and specialized interests will form. Fraternal organizations with charities to support will have difficulty retaining members. Charities will give up. Trade unions will be antique.

We will demand more control over our own lives. Professionals will demand to be paid for their skills with a fair contract. Labor will work when they need the funds. Service workers will set their own hours. Grandma and grandpa will have jobs. The work ethic will definitely be different.

Neptune in Aquarius

Neptune made a brief visit to Aquarius from January 30 to August 24, 1998. Neptune reentered Aquarius on November 28, 1998, and will stay until 2012. Its last visit to Aquarius was in 1830, before it was discovered by astronomers with newfangled telescopes.

In Aquarius, Neptune expects us to learn new ways of doing business. Just as the steam engine changed communications in the 1830s, new operating systems with liquid crystals will dissolve further the geographic barriers between people. The old rules of marketing, demographics, and statistics won't work because it will be impossible to pigeonhole people.

The Neptune in Aquarius transit will help us release our dependence on various material possessions. Garbage will be the result.

Disposal will occupy creative city planners and politicians. It will be everyone's local issue.

This year, corporate boards will save a lot of money by letting their stockholders vote on the Internet. This is the paradigm shift in action. People will begin to learn that they need not feel voiceless. In the 1830s, European governments began to recognize the power of the individual. Now the individual will take that power seriously.

Success will begin to take on a new definition. Dress for success will go out of fashion, and communication skills will be emphasized. The ability to use written and spoken English will become a status symbol. *Pygmalion* or *My Fair Lady* will return as a popular myth.

Expect to see all sorts of new-style universities. The current institutions will be too rigid to accept the new style of learning and, for that matter, the new type of student. Ivy League educational institutions will go the way of the Gray Flannel Suit.

News organizations will report the theft of intellectual property. Artists will have to create new methods of cashing in on their talents.

You can expect that most creative work will continue to be computer generated until the year 2012. Film and videotape will become antique. Equities tied to the new mediums will thrive.

The lesson of this Neptune transit will be: "Throwing money at a problem solves nothing. It just extends the life of the problem." The real issue will be the greed of the problem solvers.

This is the year when we will see many new trends among institutions. The hospital concept will dissolve, and doctors will find their offices on wheels. There will be a population shift. Folks will find the countryside attractive and cities inconvenient. Professional folks will have to follow.

On December 31, 2000, most of us will just go to yet another outrageous party to celebrate the beginning of the twenty-first century.

Pluto in Sagittarius

Achieving an Economic Manifest Destiny

Pluto has been in Sagittarius since November 11, 1995. The first few degrees of the transit have found the law in need of transformation. Next will be higher education and philosophy. Anxious for headlines, reporters will probably begin reporting scandals concerning endowments and charitable trusts. The ease of distributing desktop-published material will also expose unpublished scientific breakthroughs that were of no economic benefit to industry and therefore left in the archives.

The power of the U.S. dollar and the necessity of competing with the eurodollar will determine corporate dividends. Both economies will be forced to keep interest rates low to prevent all-out economic war.

Pluto rules billions and trillions of dollars. Sagittarius rules the traveling person. Money will move abroad and into the second and third worlds. Multinational corporations will multiply and continue extending their reach. Managers of manufacturing enterprises in remote locations will become more powerful than the local governments there. The law of economics will rule. It will be in the best interest of commerce to maintain peace; allowing good employees to shoot it out will not be good business. Expect fewer revolutions and assume terrorism will wane.

The twenty-first century will start with a new kind of corporate tribalism emerging. Independent contractors will merge their small cadres of labor in order to develop products. Creative marketing groups will sell the products, and multinational corporations will keep the supply lines flowing. That is why the Dow Jones Industrial Average will top 12,000 points by year's end.

The Gray Flannel Suit will become extinct; sweats will rule.

Winter Solstice

Capricorn Ingress — December 22, 1999, 7:45 a.m. GMT.

The Capricorn ingress predicts the year ahead for government and business.

It will be a great celebration for all of us—the survivors of the tabloids, the Nostradamus eclipse, and the millennium Apocalypse prophets. Have fun. Send cool e-mails. Call all your old friends.

The preparation is for the new millennium of partners. This can take the form of buddies, marriage partners, or business partners.

The idea is sharing knowledge, responsibility, and talents. The feminine principle will begin its time of emphasis. Aggressive behavior will go unrewarded.

Let's talk about the important stuff—money. People will be on the move, and fresh air will be the excuse. This means companies that provide trucks, such as U-Haul and Ryder, will make money. Hardware stores, home centers, and furniture stores will do very well. Of course, real estate companies and builders will continue earning good money.

Folks will demand changes in local, state, and federal taxes. The elected officials of these taxing bodies will campaign on their ideas for reform. Listen carefully. The top local issue will be garbage.

Once again, foreign affairs will be an issue. The media will point out the ability of terrorists to sabotage our computer systems.

Labor will feel fairly compensated for their work. People will be healthy and won't have much interest in health care issues.

February Eclipse

February 5, 2000, 1:02 p.m. GMT, Washington D.C.

Yes, the market will be in for another correction. It may even dip down to the moving average. When the Dow stays even for several days in a row, it is time to buy. The New York exchanges will be the only game in the global village. The dollar will rule. Study hard and spend your cash on good companies with excellent price earnings ratios. They will exist.

There will be a huge crisis in government-supported institutions. Some of their directors will make headlines because they pocketed too much money they did not earn. Scandals involving charities, welfare, and hospitals will result in changes in the laws concerning them. It will be a media circus that is boring to most people.

Stress and long hours will finally catch up with workers. The millennium bug will give everyone the flu. Most folks will claim the two-week variety because what they really need is some time off.

Snowy winter weather will be another factor keeping wage earners at their home computers. While recovering, they will review their personal budgets and determine their priorities for spending in the year ahead. A lower Dow will bring out the bargain hunters, and the financial pages on the Internet will be busy.

That's it, folks. Oh I forgot, Americans will be overemployed. Finding census takers will be a monumental challenge since even retired folks will have full-time jobs. The post office might know where everyone lives, but they will be busy delivering online orders.

Aries Ingress

March 20, 2000, 7:35 a.m. GMT, Washington D.C.

This ingress will find farmers having problems getting into their fields. Financing new equipment during the winter months will have been a problem; now finding calm weather to plant the crops will be a challenge. Many will just throw up their hands and let the banks and the insurance companies deal with it. Backyard gardeners will be equally perplexed by erratic weather.

Agriculture will be a major problem throughout the year. We will be lucky to have a surplus to export. Weather will be the problem.

Commodities traders will send the prices on their contracts higher. Industries dependent on a supply of American grains will anticipate higher costs for their raw materials. The stockholders will be concerned about the earnings of these older New York Stock Exchange companies. This will keep the Dow trading in a narrow range of about 10,000-10,500 points for the next few months.

The real news will be the NASDAQ. They will enforce their newly tightened rules for electronic trades and curbs on international speculators. Confidence will be the key. A lot of patents previously bought by big energy corporations will expire. Clever entrepreneurs will scan the government's patent site on the Internet looking for great ideas to help Americans become energy self-sufficient. Automobile companies will sell bigger and faster vehicles.

The Great Mutation

May 28, 2000, 4:04 p.m. GMT.

Jupiter and Saturn will be conjunct at 22° Taurus for the United States in the Ninth House. It has been called Techumasa's Revenge, and that means that the president elected in 2000 will pass on to the next world unless modern medicine saves him, as was the case with Ronald Reagan.

Now that that's out of the way, let's get to the important stuff like what the conjunction will mean for business. Jupiter represents the sales of a corporation, and Saturn represents the finances. When they are in the same sign, they are in the same office and they get in each other's way. This, then, will be a very difficult time to start a company or to initiate an initial public offering. Wait a few months and let Jupiter move into Gemini. For investors that means let your money earn interest in a savings account.

The housing market in the United States will be at its peak. If you want to sell one of your real estate holdings, this will be the time. If you are purchasing real estate, be sure you absolutely love what you are buying. You will keep the property a long time, because there will be changes in tax incentives that encourage you to keep the property.

Management methods, advertising styles, communications equipment, international transport, and international law are in sharp focus. In other words, they will be a mess and changes will be absolutely necessary. This will mean a lot of adjustments in the labor market associated with these sections of industry. Head hunters and temporary agencies will profit. The labor shortage will continue with the focus on clerical skills of all kinds.

The Dow will slow its upward trend, and there will be fewer mergers and acquisitions to stimulate speculators. Price earnings ratios will improve, and people will begin to discuss dividends as a key factor in adding a stock or mutual fund to their portfolios.

Cancer Ingress

June 21, 2000, 1:48 a.m. GMT.

Banks and financial institutions will be in abundance. Everyone will want to borrow your money to lend to someone else. There will be a lot of money coming in from foreign sources. Commodities traders will be mystified by outrageous weather patterns. All this will add to the summer volatility of the markets.

Diplomacy will be successful, and trade negotiations with other nations will be easily accomplished. Rebuilding the systems for the electronic transfer of funds will dominate the financial news. Industries providing these machines and services will thrive.

Families will work together for the good of the family, pooling their resources and successfully negotiating to move the work place into their homes. Builders and building supply companies will continue to benefit from this trend. Office supply outfits will be busy filling orders and selling equipment. With so much work to do, families will forgo vacations.

Expect full employment. People with professional work will be well-compensated. The biggest problem will be that everyone is too busy.

Cancer Eclipse

July 1, 2000, 7:21 p.m. GMT.

In the United States, it will be a visible eclipse. The weather will remain like that on the day of the eclipse until the next eclipse on July 31.

The markets will be at a high. For the next six months they will be extremely volatile. If you have nerves of steel, stay invested. If you are the nervous type, turn off the electricity. This eclipse will cause the markets to dip and recover for about two weeks. They do that so folks can go bargain hunting.

Mergers and acquisitions will suddenly be everywhere. U.S. corporations who handle foreign competitors by buying them will be out stalking the globe looking for any likely candidates. Companies in South America will be the favored group. Travel, airlines, shipping, publishing, and sporting equipment will be the favored industries for acquisition. The U.S. dollar will be the currency of choice, but foreign funds will be best invested in the areas where they are earned. That means that New York Stock Exchange companies will be anxious to add to the value of their corporations with capital assets and not too anxious to please stockholders with dividends.

TV and movies will lose their appeal. People will prefer the radio and will start to buy new music styles and attend concerts.

Low prices for home computers will keep the office supply market busy. Indulgent grandparents will have found a new way to spoil their grandkids. Expect the software designers and Internet software dealers to benefit.

Leo Eclipse

July 31, 2000, 2:25 a.m. GMT.

Investors with a nervous stomach might as well go on a long trip where there is no electricity. The markets will take another dip. This time it will last longer because the day traders and hedge fund managers will be on vacation, also. They will come back about the first week in September, giving the bargain hunters plenty of time to study and find some great deals.

Foreign markets will show some improvement, and the risk takers will move in that direction. That means they will take their New York Stock Exchange profits and put them to work overseas.

Stockholders will be pretty upset with the lack of consideration by corporate America; they were hoping to reinvest dividends. Equities related to financial services, beauty supplies, apparel, and candy will look like good values.

No matter how you look at it, the market place will be very exciting. Forget baseball and politics—reading the ticker tape will become the national pastime. Online trading will become a personal game with the individual in control of his or her own savings.

The Olympics will be controversial because of corporate sponsorship. Improved equipment will be featured at the games, sending many new customers to the stores. Sporting equipment manufacturers will improve their bottom lines.

The reality is that people will enjoy playing sports. Many will be getting too old for their favorite games and will search for new ones.

Libra Ingress

September 22, 2000, 5:29 p.m. GMT.

This will be the most outrageous market since 1940 except that there won't be a world war supporting American industry in the background. Dow Jones Industrial averages won't make sense with the overall economy very strong. The NASDAQ averages will be strong, and emerging markets will interest the investing public.

The Sun of the New York Stock Exchange is in Taurus, and it's Midheaven is at 28° Taurus. Saturn will transit 28° Taurus on July 27, 2000. Jupiter crossed it's Midheaven on the way to Gemini in June. Saturn will retrograde to 29° Taurus on October 16, 2000, and will go direct sometime in February 2001.

The New York Stock Exchange and the Dow Jones Industrial averages love to fall in October. Even an election year will not put Humpty Dumpty back together again. The media will blame the Federal Reserve for raising interest rates. The Democrats will say the Republicans forced the Federal Reserve to raise interest rates. Is this a fearless prediction, or should I bet a dollar that the Dow will reach 9,000 points again? Mercury will be stationary retrograde that day, so if you still own some stocks just put them in your safe deposit box, study hard, and research some buying opportunities. Hang on to your cash until February 2001. You'll have the opportunity to go bargain shopping then.

This will be a tight labor market with a lot of training still being given to employees. The babyboomlet will be eligible to work, but studies will keep them out of their traditional part-time service jobs.

Folks will be extremely upset about privacy issues. Politicians won't know how to fix the problem. Incumbents will be in and out of favor. The media, looking to increase revenues, will proclaim every race a tossup, which will be true. Most people will be too busy working, decorating their homes, or studying to pay attention. The public will be apathetic because they know the job of president is losing its appeal. There will be a change in the administration; however, it is Congress and the Federal Reserve who will really be in charge.

Traveling Americans will be concerned about the dollar and its problems abroad with duplicating machines. The yen and the eurodollar will be strong and will therefore suffer the same challenge.

Capricorn Ingress

December 21, 2000, 1:37 p.m. GMT.

The elections will give Washington D.C. moving companies a lot of business. Women will command good salaries.

The years 2000 and 2001 will be the top of the market for land values. Farms will be the first to notice a fall in price per acre. Wise farmers will find ways to subdivide their acreage and thereby decrease any debt load acquired from thin harvests. They will be competing with land-rich insurance companies and mortgage banks for customers; therefore, clever marketing will be required.

The stock market will recover, heading toward 13,000 points on the Dow because international corporations will finally report good profits from their foreign operations. Bargain hunters will have made their selections, and some will take the plunge.

Garbage will remain a hot issue during the year ahead. Companies promising to deal with it will profit. Hot commodities will be iron, copper, wheat, and corn. Once again the Russians will have a lot of gold, oil, lumber, and labor. The prices for these commodities will remain in a narrow trading range until the Russians pay their debts. That won't be for a long time, folks.

Capricorn Eclipse

December 25, 2000, 5:22 p.m. GMT.

This eclipse will be visible in the United States. Everyone will be in a great mood, and the holiday will take on the flavor of an additional Thanksgiving. Americans will be very grateful for their bonuses and their pretty houses. Politicians will be exhausted, and the new administration will be busy sending out party invitations.

Fortunately, this will be a cardinal eclipse and a holiday, and its effect on the markets will be fleeting. Pension and profit sharing money will sit on the sidelines until February, but the market will be set to rise after the first of January. Americans will keep the shopkeepers busy and the profits high. Computer and electronics vendors will sell their wares faster than they can manufacture them.

Grandparents will be on the road laden with educational gifts for the kids. Make your reservations early. Airplane ticket prices will be at a premium.

Fuel prices will follow the weather. It promises to be a dry, chilly winter.

This will be the season for parties. Plan a few and make sure they are outrageous. Be thrifty, be careful, and go for it. Happy twenty-first century!

Down With Sun Signs?

By Derek and Julia Parker

The Birth of Sun Sign Astrology

So here you are, reading a book focusing entirely on Sun sign astrology.

You wouldn't have been doing that a hundred years ago. Until the 1930s, much less emphasis was placed on the Sun sign than has been the case for the past seventy years. Look at William Lilly's *Christian Astrology*, which came out in 1647 and was the first comprehensive astrological textbook published in English, and you will find relatively little space given over to the Sun signs. Moreover, if someone had asked you "What's your sign?" as recently as 1925, you would have replied with your rising sign—the sign rising over the eastern horizon at the moment of your birth.

In September 1930, a British astrologer, R. H. Naylor, was asked to write an article for the *London Sunday Express* about Princess Margaret, who had been born the previous month. There was a great deal of interest in his article (which incidentally said that "events of tremendous importance to the Royal Family and the nation will come about near her seventh year"—and her father became king a month before her seventh birthday!). The editor was pleased and asked Naylor for a second article about what was in store for readers born during September. Interest increased, and a third article was commissioned and appeared on October 5, 1930.

In it, Naylor wrote that British aircraft were likely to be in serious danger. On the very day his article appeared, the great British airship R-101 crashed in France, killing everyone on board.

Naturally, astrology now became a hot talking point, and the editor of the *Sunday Express* asked Naylor to write for the paper every month. The only way the astrologer thought he could involve every reader at a personal level was to attempt to make predictions on the basis of the Sun signs, since every reader knew when he or she was born. The readers were fascinated, and Naylor's column soon became weekly. Then he was also hired by the sister paper, the *Daily Express*, and daily horoscope columns were born. Other newspapers soon followed suit, and by the end of the 1930s, almost every newspaper and many magazines had their own astrologer. (Sun sign astrology had begun in the United States a couple of years earlier.) The uncertainty of life during the Second World War undoubtedly contributed to the popularity of these columns. A British government-sponsored survey by *Mass Observation* conducted in 1941 concluded that three out of every five people in the country read their daily horoscope, and four in ten placed more confidence in the astrologer than in their priest.

Fifteen years later, in 1968, an official poll reported that 77 percent of the population of Britain between the ages of twenty-one and twenty-four read their horoscopes, while 68 percent of the entire population (53 percent of all men, 77 percent of all women) read theirs. The statistics probably haven't changed much in the past thirty years, so from 1930 onwards, we have been reading the daily newspaper columns and picking up information about our Sun signs from mugs, greetings cards, t-shirts, and packaging of all kinds.

This seems to us to have seriously disturbed the balance between the Sun and rising signs. Classically, it was always believed that the Sun sign spoke of the secret you—the you that only your closest family member or perhaps your lover knew, while the rising sign represented the outward you—the you presented to workmates, casual acquaintances, and the world at large; but it seems highly likely that this situation has now been reversed. As soon as children are able to read, they are fed descriptions of how "an Arien" or "a Piscean" behaves. By the time they are adolescents, they have heard their Sun sign characteristics described so often that they begin to think of themselves in that way and to behave in the manner of their Sun sign. The rising sign now seems to tell us more about the secret self.

The Validity of Sun Sign Predictions

The fact remains that, on a daily basis, a large proportion of the population of the Western world reads their horoscope in a Sun sign column in a newspaper, or perhaps in a Sun sign book. They usually do so without pausing for a moment to consider whether it is rational to suppose that one can learn anything useful about oneself by being bracketed with one-twelfth of the population of the world.

Is this rational? Maybe not, in the strictest sense. But on the other hand, can anyone really deny that a great many Geminians tend to shoot their mouths off or that many Ariens tend to act rashly and be accident-prone? Even though we may wonder sometimes whether the whole Sun sign thing may be nonsense, we must also acknowledge that it is in the area of Sun sign astrology that some of the most persuasive statistical evidence in favor of astrology actually exists.

For instance, in 1979, the *News of the World* newspaper conducted a meticulously constructed blind test in which Julia took part. Four astrologers were faced with twelve people, each of a different Sun sign, and after asking them brief questions about anything but their birth date, had to guess the Sun sign for each. They identified eight correctly, a result far beyond the possibility of chance.

What that experiment confirmed is what we all suspect—that at the very least, some personality traits are shared by most people with a common Sun sign. Fine. But what about prediction? That's why most people read the Sun sign columns. On the whole, people aren't all that interested in being told that they are talkative or accident-prone. What they want to learn is how that date on Tuesday evening is going to go, if their promotion is going to come through, or whether they're going to get a raise sometime in the next six months. Are they wasting their time turning to the daily Sun sign columns for that kind of information?

Rationally, the answer must be yes. Go out one morning and collect half a dozen newspapers and a dozen magazines and read the columns. If they are all being properly prepared and written, there may be some vague similarities between the predictions. More than likely, there won't be. The reason for this is that for a Sun sign columnist, it's far more important to be a good journalist than a good astrologer. Editors aren't really interested in an astrologer being accurate; they're interested in an astrologer being "a good read."

The best example of this is the late Patric Walker, the British astrologer whose columns were syndicated all over the world, and who was the most successful (and highly paid) Sun sign journalist of his generation. He came to dinner at our house many years ago and was aghast at the work Julia did as a professional consultant. It turned out that he could barely set up a full birth chart, let alone interpret it.

This is not to put him down—he wrote his columns on a proper astrological basis, and they were widely admired. Time and time again, people would say, "Oh, yes, I always read Patrick Walker—he's so accurate." Was this because he was a good Sun sign astrologer (assuming there is such a creature), or because he was simply clever enough to write in such a way that what he said would apply to the largest number of readers? Probably a bit of both.

The actual writing of a Sun sign column is far more difficult than the astrological technique used. In one of our books, *The Future Now*, we actually teach lay readers with no previous knowledge of astrology how to be their own Sun sign astrologer. It's not difficult, but putting your findings into readable form is another matter. Moreover, writing a newspaper or magazine column is very different from writing a book. It's often necessary to cheat a little in search of a phrase that will capture the attention of your readers, so you may actually choose to mention an astrological indication that is not the most important one in the chart, but that is easier to write amusingly about than a stronger one.

If you're writing a monthly column, the problem is not so keen. Writing a daily column is much more difficult and, indeed, horrifically boring! If the writers of daily newspaper columns are paid what can seem an astonishing amount of money, they probably deserve it on the basis of sheer bludgeoning hard work. Yes, writing popular horoscope columns is a very particular and tricky craft, and not all astrologers can do it. (Incidentally, many stories are told about the newspaper whose astrologer failed to deliver and whose column was written by the editor. If they're true, we don't envy the editor: It's much easier to write a column properly, using the astrological technique, than to make it up!)

Returning to the question of what purpose the columns actually serve, it is true that most readers go to them to learn about the future. Here we tread upon shaky ground. Many astrologers would claim that prediction is indeed what astrology is about, though they often avoid the word, not least because it tends to annoy almost everyone outside of astrology. Church members claim that only God knows or can know what's going to happen in the future (Where, by the way, does that leave weather forecasters?), and rationalists simply believe that it's impossible to predict future events. At the very least, consultant astrologers at work with individual clients almost always venture part of the way into the marsh, even if it's only to suggest a time when some psychological pressure might be expected to ease, or to indicate a time when one should pay particular attention to one's health.

The problem for the serious astrologer working on a full birth chart is much the same as that of the Sun sign astrologer: what most people want to know is what is going to happen rather than the circumstances in which it is going to happen. One of the most thoughtful contemporary British astrologers, Dennis Elwell, wrote to us many years ago: "Suppose we see that a person is coming under a strong Mars configuration. We know that he will have some sort of fight on his hands, an opportunity to develop the self-assertive, incisive side of his nature. We also know that if it is a major configuration, that what he will acquire for himself at this point in life will remain his for the rest of his days. Surely it is of some interest to know that our destiny is organized in this purposeful way?"

In other words, what an astrologer can best describe is not an event itself, but what that event will mean, although that is not usually what clients want to know. They want to know not only that a fight of some kind is ahead, but whether they are going to win or lose the fight. If an astrologer cannot answer that question definitively based on a full birth chart, a Sun sign astrologer is even less likely to be able to do so.

Can a Sun sign column even be depended on to foretell a coming fight? Admirers of Patric Walker would probably claim that if he said they were going to feel "low" in the second half of February, then that would undoubtedly be the case. This probably isn't the place to ask whether his readers were more suggestible than perhaps they should have been.

Is Sun Sign Astrology Dangerous?

We could go off on a tangent here about "suggestibility" in general. It may be the case that most people who turn to astrologers for help tend to be more suggestible than those who are more likely to give themselves a stern talking to, sit down with a glass of iced water, and look at their problems coolly and rationally. People who are interested in and turn to what might loosely be called "alternative" means of dealing with problems can probably be put into a different category than those who are more likely to rely on their own strength of character, or ask their doctor for advice or prescribed drugs. No study that we know of tells us this; it's simply a hunch. But those who "believe in" or rely on Sun sign columns may well be less rational by nature than those who read them "for fun" and immediately forget or ignore what they say.

How dangerous is Sun sign astrology? Should each column carry a government health warning "Believing what this astrologer says may seriously derange your life"? Is addiction to astrology as dangerous as any other form of addiction?

For some people the answer has to be yes. In the 1970s when we first visited the United States on a promotion tour for our book *The Compleat Astrologer*, we were quickly astonished and depressed by the amount of dependency some people had on astrology and by their ignorance of what astrology could and could not do. We had not yet met many people whose inevitable first question was "What's your sign?", but on that trip we heard it continually—on aircraft, in restaurants, on street corners, and from people who seemed to have no idea that there was more to astrology than the fact that they happened to have been born between, say, April 21 and May 20. They read the newspaper columns as people of earlier centuries would have read the daily Collect in the *Book of Common Prayer*.

Those who knew more about astrology sometimes depressed us even more. Some who had the means (mostly, it must be said, from the West Coast) traveled with their own personal astrologers. One got the impression that they probably telephoned them at 3 A.M. to ask whether, since they were a little hot, the time was propitious for turning up the air conditioning.

The truth about most of these people was, of course, that they needed a prop of some sort to make decisions and used their astrologers as others might have used a psychologist or a priest. Things are now much better in this regard, though some clients are still in this category. It is the astrologer's duty to find a way of standing them on their own two legs and giving them a sense of balance sufficient to send them steadily off on their own independent journey through life.

Those who depend on the daily newspaper horoscope (and there really aren't many of them) are at once more and less of a problem. Many of them really do need their "fix," though very few indeed are so dependent on their horoscope that they would be seriously worried if they were deprived of it. Our impression is that most people are perfectly aware of the superficial nature of horoscope columns. The accusation that popular Sun sign astrologers do their readers serious damage is nonsense except in the case of a very few seriously unbalanced people who, again, would be equally likely to be endangered by reading a medical textbook and concluding that they had every disease they found mentioned in it.

In general, people take Sun sign astrology with the requisite grain of salt. Years ago, the *Daily Express* published a Sun sign column that included such entries as "Cancer: For you Dame Fortune's smile is always a cynical leer. This week she will be thumbing her nose at you. All your bad luck in the past will seem like paradise to what will hit you between now and next Sunday."

Almost ever reader quickly realized that the column had in fact been written by the newspaper's famous humorist Nat Gubbins. Readers don't need to be told not to take the daily forecasts too seriously, and they're right not to do so.

The "need" to read one's daily horoscope then is not usually serious in the sense that deprivation would be more than mildly irritating; but the evidence is that it would be at least that, and
probably more. From time to time newspaper and magazine editors
have decided that the space given over to the astrology columns
might be more profitably used on something else and have with-
drawn them, only to find that the effect upon circulation is so serious that they are forced to reinstate them immediately. It is not for
nothing that the advertisement rate charged for the page opposite
the horoscope in most women's magazines is higher than for any
other page; or that the leading serious British broadsheet newspapers have, within the past ten years, hired their own astrologers,
something that would have been thought inconceivable not too
long ago.

Are we sniggering at the readers who are devoted to the newspaper horoscope columns? Not at all. One of the things we have always stressed determinedly in books and interviews is that astrology
is not only a serious matter, but also something with which you can
and should have fun. Sun sign astrology is almost made for this—
for helping you to choose a holiday destination, the food to serve
your friends, a present for a relative stranger...all matters that aren't
going to bring the world to an end if you get them wrong.

On the other hand, approaching any kind of personal problem
through Sun signs can be dangerous. For instance, time and again
we have been asked on a television or radio show whether it's true
that a Cancerian shouldn't go out with a Leo ("They don't get
along, do they?"). That's the kind of statement that really should be
subject to a government health warning! A person of any sign potentially can have a splendid and fulfilling relationship with a person of any other sign. A look at the full birth chart may indicate
certain areas of potential difficulty, but that is all. To tell someone
of one Sun sign to avoid someone else of another Sun sign is im-
moral. Worse, it is stupid!

If the validity of daily forecasts is somewhat suspect, that of the
monthly columns is perhaps less so. Within any given month there
are significant changes in planetary positions and relationships, sufficient in many cases to make it possible to say something that may
be helpful. It is worth finding the column that speaks to you most

persuasively (which will usually mean that you like the style of the astrologer who writes it) and sticking with it, but it is still necessary to underline the fact that it would be extremely silly to make any important decisions on the basis of even the best and most "reliable" Sun sign forecast.

In addition, it is probably extremely silly to make any important decision on the basis of the best and most "reliable" full astrological advice! In their enthusiasm for astrology, people sometimes fail to remember that it is only one part of life—that genetic make-up, environment, financial considerations, personal relationships, and the myriad other constituents of life have their own important place in decision making. Astrology is here not to direct us, but to assist us.

The Importance of Sun Sign Astrology

Another thing to consider about Sun sign columns and books is if they actually damage "real astrology." Any writer of Sun sign astrology will have had complaints that this is so—that in writing a Sun sign book, what one is doing is helping to confirm in the minds of readers the fact that astrology only deals with the four-week slices of the year during which they were born. But on the whole, those who are under the delusion that the Sun signs are the be-all and end-all of the subject are those who are so uninterested, or so antagonistic, that they have not bothered to look into astrology at all. Is it worth doing away with what might be called the entertainment branch of astrology just because some people can't or won't be bothered to take a serious interest in the subject?

One positive result of the popularity of Sun sign astrology is that it has inspired a great number of people to study astrology seriously. Ask almost any professional astrologer how he or she got into the field, and you'll probably get the answer, "Well, in 1974 I picked up this Sun sign book, and..." A sprat to catch a mackerel.

Not all Sun sign books have anything to say about "real" astrology, of course, but some do. When asked to write Sun sign books over the past thirty years, we have only agreed to do so provided that the publishers allow us space for our own particular form of health warning: "This book is only for fun. The Sun sign is only a small part of your whole astrological chart, so don't make any important decisions on the basis of your Sun sign. If you have a problem, seek out a properly trained astrologer, and if you want to find out about real astrology..."

The irresistible Sun signs are a wonderful way of leading people into the subject—and a great number of them want to be led. Publishers have to be persuaded of this, as well as astrologers. In 1969, when we were asked to write "a really big book about astrology" by the new British publishing firm of Mitchell Beazley, they had a Sun sign book in mind that explored the signs with lavish illustrations. We suggested that it would be far more interesting to show people astrology in its wider form. No such popular book then existed. There were many Sun sign books and, at the other end of the spectrum, some teaching manuals that looked like teaching manuals and were bought only by people who had already convinced themselves that they wanted to study the subject seriously.

We had the greatest difficulty in persuading the publishers that our idea was a viable one. They turned pale with horror at the thought of producing a popular book that contained sixty-four pages of planetary positions, proportional logarithms, the Moon's nodes, sidereal times, and houses for northern latitudes! Who would buy such a book? In the end we convinced them, and the result was *The Compleat Astrologer*. In this book the Sun sign pages are as brightly illustrated as in any other book, and cartoons illustrate the properties of the twelve houses, but the book also contains sections that teach the readers as simply as possible how to calculate a chart and how to interpret it. (Derek was then entirely ignorant of the technical aspects of astrology, so Julia taught him how to do it, and every time he made a mistake, they said, "We must find a simpler way of explaining that.")

Without being unnecessarily immodest, it is fair to claim that that book brought an enormous number of people into astrology. Time and time again at the 1998 United Astrological Congress in Atlanta, people came up to us and said, "You know, yours was the very first book..." or "Do you know how I got into astrology...?" It was a very pleasant experience indeed, and it has happened all over the world—in Europe, India, Australia...

We have carried on with the work. *Parkers' Astrology*, which came out in 1991, is identical in conception to *The Compleat Astrologer*. It too has brightly and attractively designed Sun sign pages that hopefully capture the attention of anyone who idly picks the book up. It then goes on to teach astrology up to intermediate examination level, with the addition of many pages illustrating interpretations from Julia's thirty-year files of work with clients.

Ah, yes, clients. If we have benefited from our Sun sign books (and you can't sell over three million books without making a little profit), so have other people. It is difficult, if not impossible, for professional astrologers to charge fees on a level with other professionals. Few clients are prepared to pay more than perhaps $60 or $100 for advice. Serious astrologers frequently use the income earned from writing Sun sign books or columns to subsidize clients who need help and advice, but cannot afford it. Similarly, we make a point of never charging money for talking to astrological groups and passing on knowledge and experience. One must plough back what one has gained.

So...down with the Sun signs?

Not quite.

Activities Ruled by the Planets

To check aspects for the activity you have in mind, find the planet that rules it.

Sun: Advertising, buying, selling, speculating, short trips, meeting people, anything involving groups or showmanship, putting up exhibits, running fairs and raffles, growing crops, health matters.

Moon: Any small change in routine, asking favors, borrowing or lending money, household activities such as baking, canning, cooking, washing, ironing, cleaning, and taking care of small children.

Mercury: Bargaining, bookkeeping, dealing with literary agents, publishing, filing, hiring employees, learning languages, literary work, placing ads, preparing accounts, studying, telephoning, visiting friends.

Venus: Amusement, beauty care, courtship, dating, decorating homes, designing, getting together with friends, household improvements, planning parties, shopping.

Mars: Good for all business matters, mechanical affairs, buying or selling animals, dealing with contractors, hunting, studying.

Jupiter: Activities involving charity, education, or science, correspondence courses, self-improvement, reading, researching, studying.

Saturn: Anything involving family ties or legal matters such as wills and estates, taking care of debts, dealing with lawyers, financing, joint money matters, real estate, relations with older people.

Uranus: Air travel, all partnerships, changes and adjustment, civil rights, new contacts, new ideas, new rules, patenting inventions, progress, social action, starting journeys.

Neptune: Advertising, dealing with psychological upsets, health foods and resorts, large social affairs, nightclubs, psychic healing, travel by water, restaurants, visits, welfare, working with institutions.

Pluto: Anything dealing with energy and enthusiasm, skill and alertness, personal relationships, original thought.

Planetary Business Guide

Collections: Try to make collections on days when your Sun is well-aspected. Avoid days when Mars or Saturn are aspected. If possible, the Moon should be in a cardinal sign: Aries, Cancer, Libra, or Capricorn. It is more difficult to collect when the Moon is in Taurus or Scorpio.

Employment, Promotion: Choose a day when your Sun is favorably aspected or the Moon is in your Tenth House. Good aspects of Venus or Jupiter to your Tenth House are beneficial.

Loans: Moon in the first and second quarters favors the lender; Moon in the third and fourth quarters favors the borrower. Good aspects of Jupiter or Venus to the Moon are favorable to both, as is Moon in Leo, Sagittarius, Aquarius, or Pisces.

New Ventures: Things usually get off to a better start during the increase of the Moon. If there is impatience, anxiety, or deadlock, it can often be broken at the Full Moon. Agreements can be reached then.

Partnerships: Agreements and partnerships should be made on a day that is favorable to both parties. Mars, Neptune, Pluto, and Saturn should not be square or opposite the Moon. It is best to make an agreement or partnership when the Moon is in a mutable sign, especially Gemini or Virgo. The other signs are not favorable, with the possible exception of Leo or Capricorn. Begin partnerships when the Moon is increasing in light, as this is a favorable time for starting new ventures.

Public Relations: The Moon rules the public, so this must be well-aspected, particularly by the Sun, Mercury, Uranus, or Neptune.

Selling: In general, selling is favored by good aspects of Venus, Jupiter, or Mercury to the Moon. Afflictions of Saturn retard. If you know the planetary ruler of your product, try to get this well-aspected by Venus, Jupiter, or the Moon. Your product will be more highly valued then.

Signing Important Papers: Sign contracts or agreements when the Moon is increasing in a fruitful sign. Avoid days when Mars, Saturn, Neptune, or Pluto are afflicting the Moon. Don't sign anything if your Sun is badly afflicted.

Planetary Associations

Sun: Authority figures, favors, advancement, health, success, display, drama, promotion, fun, matters related to Leo and the Fifth House.

Moon: Short trips, women, children, the public, domestic concerns, emotions, fluids, matters related to Cancer and the Fourth House.

Mercury: Communications, correspondence, phone calls, computers, messages, education, students, travel, merchants, editing, writing, advertising, signing contracts, siblings, neighbors, kin, matters related to Gemini, Virgo, and the Third and Sixth Houses.

Venus: Affection, relationships, partnerships, alliances, grace, beauty, harmony, luxury, love, art, music, social activity, marriage, decorating, cosmetics, gifts, income, matters related to Taurus, Libra, and the Second and Seventh Houses.

Mars: Strife, aggression, sex, physical energy, muscular activity, guns, tools, metals, cutting, surgery, police, soldiers, combat, confrontation, matters related to Aries, Scorpio, and the First and Eighth Houses.

Jupiter: Publishing, college education, long-distance travel, foreign interests, religion, philosophy, forecasting, broadcasting, publicity, expansion, luck, growth, sports, horses, the law, matters related to Sagittarius, Pisces, and the Ninth and Twelfth Houses.

Saturn: Structure, reality, the laws of society, limits, obstacles, tests, hard work, endurance, real estate, dentists, bones, teeth, matters related to Capricorn, Aquarius, and the Tenth and Eleventh Houses.

Uranus: Astrology, the New Age, technology, computers, modern gadgets, lecturing, advising, counseling, inventions, reforms, electricity, new methods, originality, sudden events, matters related to Aquarius and the Eleventh House.

Neptune: Mysticism, music, creative imagination, dance, illusion, sacrifice, service oil, chemicals, paint, drugs, anesthesia, sleep, religious experience, matters related to Pisces and the Twelfth House.

Pluto: Probing, penetration, goods of the dead, investigation, insurance, taxes, other people's money, loans, the masses, the underworld, transformation, death, matters related to Scorpio and the Eighth House.

About the Authors

Skye Alexander is the author of *Planets in Signs* and the astrological mystery *Hidden Agenda*. An astrologer since the mid-1970s, she may be reached through Mojo Publishing, P.O. Box 7121, Gloucester, MA 01930. Her website is www.shore.net/~ mojo.

Alice DeVille has been a consulting astrologer, metaphysician, and writer for more than 25 years. Alice develops and conducts workshops, seminars, and lectures on a variety of subjects. You may reach Alice via e-mail at DeVilleAA@aol.com.

Sasha Fenton has been reading hands, cards, and horoscopes since childhood, and she eventually teamed her talents with her writing ability to become the author of 23 books and 5 years worth of annual horoscope guides (total sales of over 5 million copies worldwide)—with more in the pipeline!

Mark Kenski can be reached via e-mail at mark@rhythms.org, or you can find out more about him and read other articles at his web site called "Universal Rhythms" at www.rhythms.org.

Dorothy Oja is a career astrologer with 28 years of experience, offering full-spectrum astrological counseling through her practice MIND-WORKS. Her specialties include timing/electional work and composite/Davison relationship analysis. Contact her at 309 School St. Watertown, MA 02472 (617) 926-8841 or by e-mail at DOja96@aol.com.

Leeda Alleyn Pacotti embarked on metaphysical self-studies at the age of 14. Her career encompassed anti-trust law, international treaties, and governmental management. She now plies a gentle practice as a naturopathic physician, master herbalist, and certified nutritional counselor.

Derek and Julia Parker are the authors of *The Compleat Astrologer* (1971) and *Parkers' Astrology* (1991), and of about forty other books in between, including several on dream interpretation. You can visit their Internet site and write to them at www.parkeriters.com.

Kim Rogers-Gallagher edits the astrology magazine *Kosmos* and is the author of *Astrology for the Light Side of the Future* from ACS Publications. She contributes frequently to several astrology magazines, including *Dell Horoscope* and *Aspects*.

Kaye Shinker, C.A.-NCGR, teaches financial astrology at the Online College of Astrology, www.astrocollege.com. She serves on the NCGR Board of Examiners. A former teacher, she and her huband own race horses and travel around the United States in an RV.

Cathy L. Zornes is a professional astrologer, writer, national speaker, and astrological columnist for several Midwest publications. She offers personal insights, classes, and endeavors to enlighten the community with her website, www.chart-works.com. She publishes a newsletter called *StarWatch*.

Directory of Products and Services

Resources for the New Age

Astrological Readings and Counseling
Llewellyn Books, Calendars, and
Personal Services
Astrological Software
New Age Bookstores and
Gift Shops
Metaphysical Schools
Psychic Advice Lines

Harness the Power of the Moon

It's true—the cycles and energies of the Moon have a powerful impact on your day-to-day life. The *Moon Sign Book* explains how you can harness this power to work *with* the energies of the Moon—and give all your activities an extra boost of positive energy and success. Use our astro-almanac, Moon tables, lunar astrological forecasts, and a wealth of Moon-related articles to be more successful at home, in business, in your garden, and in all that you do.

- *Consult the astro almanac or Moon tables to find the most favorable dates for undertaking any activity—from buying a house, to entertaining, to stopping a bad habit.*

- *Get Moon-wise advice on finances, romance, gardening, cooking, travel, health, beauty, and more.*

- *Preview the Moon's effect on your emotional cycles every month with Gloria Star's lunar forecasts.*

- *Check U.S. weather and earthquake forecasts.*

- *Grow your knowledge with our gardening section: time planting for healthier and more vigorous flowers, fruits and vegetables.*

Llewellyn's 2000 Moon Sign Book

480 pp. • 5¼" x 8" • Order # K-953 • $6.95

To order call 1-877-NEW-WRLD

Or fill out the order form in back of book

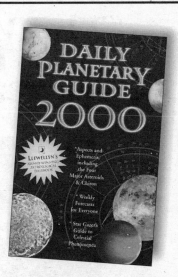

Save $$ on Llewellyn Annuals

Llewellyn has two ways for you to save money on our annuals. With a four-year subscription, you receive your books as soon as they are published—and your price stays the same every year, even if there's an increase in the cover price! Llewellyn pays postage and handling for subscriptions. Buy any 2 subscriptions and take $2 off; buy 3 and take $3 off; buy 4 subscriptions and take an additional $5 off the cost!

Please check boxes below and send this form along with the order form on the next page.

Subscriptions (4 years, 2001–2004):

☐ Astrological Calendar.................$51.80		☐ Astrological Pocket Planner......$27.80	
☐ Witches' Calendar......................$51.80		☐ Sun Sign Book..............................$27.80	
☐ Tarot Calendar............................$51.80		☐ Moon Sign Book.........................$27.80	
☐ Crop Circle Calendar................$51.80		☐ Herbal Almanac...........................$27.80	
☐ Daily Planetary Guide...............$39.80		☐ Magical Almanac.........................$27.80	
☐ Witches' Datebook...................$39.80			

Order a Dozen and Save 40%: Sell them to your friends or give them as gifts. Llewellyn pays all postage and handling when you order annuals by the dozen.

2000	2001		
☐	☐	Astrological Calendar...	$93.24
☐	☐	Witches' Calendar..	$93.24
☐	☐	Tarot Calendar...	$93.24
☐	☐	Crop Circle Calendar...	$93.24
☐	☐	Daily Planetary Guide...	$71.64
☐	☐	Witches' Datebook...	$71.64
☐	☐	Astrological Pocket Planner..	$50.04
☐	☐	Sun Sign Book..	$50.04
☐	☐	Moon Sign Book..	$50.04
☐	☐	Herbal Almanac...	$50.04
☐	☐	Magical Almanac...	$50.04

Individual Copies of Annuals: Include $4 postage for order $15 and under and $5 for orders over $15. Llewellyn pays postage for all orders over $100.

2000	2001		
☐	☐	Astrological Calendar...	$12.95
☐	☐	Witches' Calendar..	$12.95
☐	☐	Tarot Calendar...	$12.95
☐	☐	Crop Circle Calendar...	$12.95
☐	☐	Daily Planetary Guide...	$9.95
☐	☐	Witches' Datebook...	$9.95
☐	☐	Astrological Pocket Planner..	$6.95
☐	☐	Sun Sign Book..	$6.95
☐	☐	Moon Sign Book..	$6.95
☐	☐	Herbal Almanac...	$6.95
☐	☐	Magical Almanac...	$6.95

Llewellyn Order Form

Call 1-877-NEW-WRLD or use this form to order any of the
Llewellyn books or services listed in this publication.

SEND TO: **Llewellyn Publications, P.O. Box 64383,
Dept. K-954, St. Paul, MN 55164-0383**

Qty	Order #	Title/Author	Total Price

Postage/handling:		
ORDERS $15 AND UNDER: **$4.00**	Total price	
ORDERS OVER $15: **$5.00**	MN residents add 7% sales tax	
Subscription orders, dozen orders, or orders over $100: **FREE SHIPPING**		
2ND DAY AIR: **$8.00 for one book** (add $1 for each additional book)	Postage/handling (see left)	
We cannot deliver to P.O. Boxes; please supply a street address. Please allow 4-6 weeks for delivery.	**Total enclosed**	

☐ VISA   ☐ MasterCard   ☐ American Express
☐ Check or money order – U.S. funds, payable to Llewellyn Publications

Account # _____   Expiration Date _____

Cardholder Signature _____

Name _____   Phone (_____) _____

Address _____

City _____   State _____   Zip/PC _____

Questions? Call Customer Service at 1-877-NEW-WRLD

Llewellyn's Computerized Astrological Services

Llewellyn has been a leading authority in astrological chart readings for more than 30 years. We feature a wide variety of readings with the intent to satisfy the needs of any astrological enthusiast. Our goal is to give you the best possible service so that you can achieve your goals and live your life successfully. **Be sure to give accurate and complete birth data on the order form. This includes exact time (a.m. or p.m.), date, year, city, county, and country of birth. Note: Noon will be used as your birth time if you don't provide an exact time. Check your birth certificate for this information! Llewellyn cannot be responsible for mistakes made by you.** An order form follows these listings.

Services Available

Simple Natal Chart
This is your best choice if you want a detailed birth chart and prefer to do your own interpretations. It is loaded with information, including a chart wheel, aspects, declinations, nodes, major asteroids, and more. (Tropical zodiac/Placidus houses, unless specified otherwise.)
APS03-119 . . . . **$5.00**

Astro*Talk Advanced Natal Report
One of the best interpretations of your birth chart you'll ever read. These no-nonsense descriptions of the unique effects of the planets on your character will amaze and enlighten you.
APS03-525 . . . .**$30.00**

TimeLine Transit/Progression Forecast
Love, money, health—everybody wants to know what lies ahead, and this report will keep you one-up on your future. The TimeLine forecast is invaluable for seizing opportunities and timing your moves. Reports begin the first day of the month you choose. Specify current residence.
3-month TimeLine Forecast - APS03-526. . . . .**$12.00**
6-month TimeLine Forecast - APS03-527. . . . .**$20.00**
1-year TimeLine Forecast - APS03-528. . . . .**$30.00**

Friends and Lovers

Find out how you relate to others, and whether you are really compatible with your current or potential lover, spouse, friend, or business partner! This service includes planetary placements for both people, so send birth data for both and specify "friends" or "lovers."

APS03-529 . . . . **$20.00**

Child*Star

An astrological look at your child's inner world through a skillful interpretation of his or her unique birth chart. As relevant for teens as it is for newborns. Specify your child's sex.

APS03-530 . . . . **$20.00**

Woman to Woman

Finally, astrology from a feminine point of view! Gloria Star brings her special style and insight to this detailed look into the mind, soul, and spirit of contemporary women.

APS03-531 . . . . **$30.00**

Heaven Knows What

Discover who you are and where you're headed. This report contains a classic interpretation of your birth chart *and* a look at upcoming events, as presented by the time-honored master of the astrological arts, Grant Lewi.

APS03-532 . . . . **$30.00**

Biorhythm Report

Some days you have unlimited energy, then the next day you feel sluggish and awkward. These cycles are called biorhythms. This individual report accurately maps your daily biorhythms and thoroughly discusses each day. Now you can plan your days to the fullest!

APS03-515 – 3-month report **$12.00**
APS03-516 – 6-month report **$18.00**
APS03-517 – 1-year report **$25.00**

Tarot Reading

Find out what the cards have in store for you with this 12-page report that features a 10-card "Celtic Cross" spread shuffled and selected especially for you. For every card that turns up there is a detailed corresponding explanation of what each means for you. Order this tarot reading today! Indicate the number of shuffles you want.

APS03-120 . . . .**$10.00**

Lucky Lotto Report (State Lottery Report)

Do you play the state lotteries? This report will determine your luckiest sequence of numbers for each day based on specific planets, degrees, and other indicators in your own chart. Give your full birth data and middle name. Tell us how many numbers your state lottery requires in sequence, and the highest possible numeral. Indicate the month you want to start.

APS03-512 – 3-month report **$10.00**
APS03-513 – 6-month report **$15.00**
APS03-514 – 1-year report **$25.00**

Numerology Report

Find out which numbers are right for you with this insightful report. This report uses an ancient form of numerology invented by Pythagoras to determine the significant numbers in your life. Using both your name and date of birth, this report will calculate those numbers that stand out as yours. With these numbers, you can tell when the important periods of your life will occur. Please indicate your full birth name.

APS03-508 – 3-month report **$12.00**
APS03-509 – 6-month report **$18.00**
APS03-510 – 1-year report **$25.00**

Astrological Services Order Form

Report name & number_____

_____

Provide the following data on all persons receiving a report:

1st Person's Full Name, including current middle & last name(s)

_____

Birthplace (city, county, state, country) _____

_____

Birthtime _____ ❏ a.m. ❏ p.m. Month _____ Day _____ Year _____

2nd Person's Full Name (if ordering for more than one person)

_____

Birthplace (city, county, state, country) _____

_____

Birthtime _____ ❏ a.m. ❏ p.m. Month _____ Day _____ Year _____

Billing Information

Name_____

Address_____

_____

City _____ State _____ Zip _____

Country _____ Day phone:_____

Make check or money order payable to Llewellyn Publications, or charge it!

Check one: ❏ VISA ❏ MasterCard ❏ American Express

Acct. No. _____ Exp. Date _____

Cardholder Signature _____

❏ Yes! Send me my free copy of *New Worlds*!

Mail this form and payment to:

Llewellyn's Computerized Astrological Services
P.O. Box 64383, Dept. K-954 • St. Paul, MN 55164-0383

Allow 4-6 weeks for delivery.

Live the Craft Every Day ...

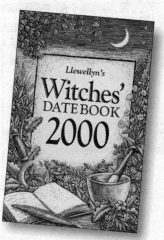

Carry this portable companion to the *Llewellyn Witches' Calendar* with you everywhere to aid your spiritual journey throughout the year. It's the perfect way to keep track of coven meetings, festivals, and daily appointments, of course. But you can also use it to whip up a tasty seasonal recipe every month; or celebrate the Full Moon with rituals written by Priestess Yasmine Galenorn; or to connect with the Divine with powerful Goddess meditations by Patricia Monaghan.

In addition to herb lore, daily color correspondences, historic Wiccan dates, planetary motion, *and* the Moon's sign and phase, you'll find pages devoted to the sabbats; the Celtic Moon signs; and how the movement of the Moon affects spellwork. Articles by astrologer Kim Rogers-Gallagher and Witches Silver RavenWolf, Edain McCoy, and Marguerite Elsbeth will enhance your practice. And handy features like a mini-calendar for 2001, and a telephone/address log make this datebook completely indispensable for the practicing Witch.

Llewellyn's 2000 Witches' Datebook
144 pp. • 5¼" x 8" • Order # K-952 • $9.95
To order call 1-877-NEW-WRLD
or use order form in back of book

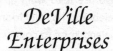

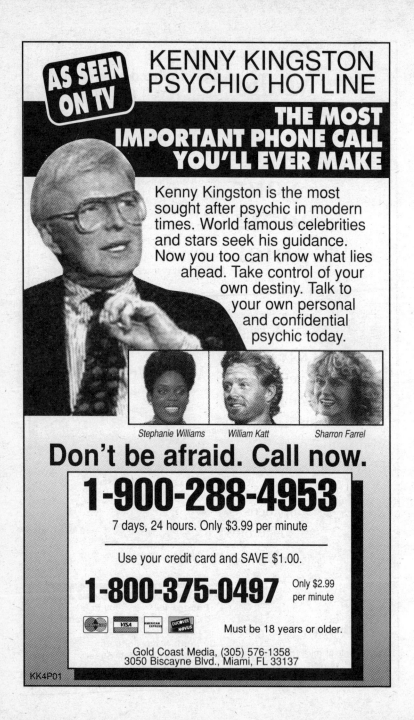